Health Inequities in India

T.K. Sundari Ravindran · Rakhal Gaitonde
Editors

Health Inequities in India

A Synthesis of Recent Evidence

With Forewords by Sharmila Mhatre and Lesley Doyal

Springer

Editors
T.K. Sundari Ravindran
Achutha Menon Centre for Health Science Studies
Sree Chitra Tirunal Institute for Medical Sciences and Technology
Trivandrum, Kerala
India

Rakhal Gaitonde
Centre for Technology and Policy (CTaP)
Indian Institute of Technology Madras
Chennai, Tamil Nadu
India

ISBN 978-981-10-5088-6 ISBN 978-981-10-5089-3 (eBook)
https://doi.org/10.1007/978-981-10-5089-3

Library of Congress Control Number: 2017941545

Printed on acid-free paper

This Springer imprint is published by Springer Nature
The registered company is Springer Nature Singapore Pte Ltd.
The registered company address is: 152 Beach Road, #21-01/04 Gateway East, Singapore 189721, Singapore

Foreword I

The inception of this book stems from a desire to understand and profile the theory and practice of redressing inequities in the Indian context and the admiration for Prof. Ravindran, who in our first meeting elegantly argued both the theory and politics of equity. At that time in 2012, I headed a health systems programme for the International Development Research Centre (IDRC), a Canadian crown corporation mandated to support research for development. The IDRC programme at that time wanted to build a critical mass of researchers who could unpack the theoretical layers of equity, innovate new frameworks and methods to contribute to healthier communities. This book shows only some of the fruits of labour by Prof. Ravindran and her colleagues. It does not reveal the innumerable consultations, the mobilisation of researchers, the training of emerging scholars, the forged collaborations among researchers and practitioners across India and outside the country in the "journey of ideas" articulated in this book.

The introductory chapter provides an overview of the chapters in this book with the last chapter asking researchers to join the political project of researchers, funders, practitioners and policymakers coming together to redress inequities. In 2017, this call for action strikes a chord—with the rise of nationalism and discrimination by those who threaten social order explicitly on the lines of race and religion. In the world we live in today, the urgency for this political project is even clearer. The concept of health equity as discussed by the authors continues to be a greater challenge and cannot be relegated to the boundaries of research. As a construct and analytical frame, health equity as a political project is one strategy to achieve fairness, and open and vibrant democratic societies.

Sharmila Mhatre, Ph.D.
Deputy Director
Public Health Program, Open Society Foundations
New York, USA

Foreword II

This book represents an important contribution to the global literature on inequities in health. Much has been written on this topic in recent years, but India has received relatively little attention. This is especially surprising since it has a particular relevance to current debates about the relationship between health and economic growth. Viewed from a geopolitical perspective, it is counted among the six countries referred to as BRICS (Brazil, Russia, India, China and South Africa). All have experienced rapid economic growth in recent years and all are advancing rapidly through both demographic and epidemiological transitions. However, the benefits of this growth remain unequally distributed in all BRICS but especially in India.

Data on the distribution of economic resources are relatively sparse, but there is clear evidence that inequalities within India increased over the past two decades. A major reason for this has been the failure of economic growth to generate enough formal employment with about half the workforce still engaged in low productivity agriculture. This in turn reflects the earlier shift in government policies from public spending as a stimulus to economic growth towards neo-liberal strategies involving deregulation and an emphasis on increasing the consumption of the rich and the growing middle class. As a result, India now has the highest poverty rate among the BRICS countries with more than 40% of the population living on less than USD 1.25 per day. We can begin to see from this very crude data that the resources available to meet the basic needs of the Indian population as a whole, are very limited when measured against comparable countries. Similarly, there are dramatic internal inequalities in access to resources. While some groups and individuals are becoming extremely rich, the vast majority remains poor and, as the book shows, this is reflected in patterns of morbidity and mortality.

In order to make sense of these variations, we need to look in much more detail at the nature of Indian society and the obstacles it presents to the optimisation of health. So far, there is little more than statistical data available to facilitate this analysis. However, this collection aims to go a step further. It will begin by outlining some of the new conceptual frameworks emerging in the health field to make sense of national and global diversity. This will be followed by case studies applying these new approaches to what is known about the complex and heterogeneous structures of Indian society.

Recent literature in the field of health has moved away from what has been called the "medical model" towards the recognition that an individual's health is shaped not just by biological factors, but by the "social determinants of health" as key factors in explaining variations in morbidity and mortality both between and within countries. The most obvious link is of course the one between socio-economic status and sickness or early death. But gender too has been identified as a key determinant along with other factors including race/ethnicity and age.

However, it is often forgotten that the form and significance of these influences will vary between settings as will their impact on health. Hence, a major section of this collection outlines the particular nature of these social processes as they are played out in India. At the same time researchers have increasingly recognised that these different influences do not operate in isolation but are in constant interaction with each other.

This has led to the increasing use of the paradigm of "intersectionality" which began in the US in the context of activism among black women. (The basic proposition was that it was inappropriate to simply add together "black" and "women" when the relationship was in fact multiplicative and mutually reinforcing.) This interactive framework is now being used more widely in the context of health, although most studies have been done in the global North. This collection attempts to apply these ideas in a specifically Indian context as we can illustrate here through examining the case of female gender.

South Asia in general and India, in particular, are frequently cited as extreme examples of male domination. One of the most widely used illustrations of this point is the data on sex ratio at birth. Between 1951 and 2011, a UN study found that the child sex ratio dropped from 976 girls per 1000 boys in 1961, to 927 girls in 2001 and to 918 girls in 2011. Viewed more broadly, recent research by the World Economic Forum showed that India came lowest among all the BRICS countries on the global gender gap index and ranked 108 in the world overall. This is not of course a biological phenomenon, but rather a cultural one based on "son preference" which in turn has economic origins.

Girl children are frequently viewed as a burden since they require a dowry in order to marry and are unlikely to be able to support their parents in old age. This low status and discrimination follows them through life. A foetus known to be female may be aborted before birth and a newborn girl abandoned while female children are often given less food and medical attention. In adulthood, most women have little power in the family especially in the context of sex and reproduction and are usually employed in low-paid informal work as well as having responsibility for subsistence work and domestic labour.

Not surprisingly, this can have serious effects on their health in a number of different ways. One of the most striking effects in recent years has been their increased vulnerability to HIV infection. This does have some biological basis since women are more vulnerable than men to infection from a single heterosexual encounter. But more importantly evidence shows that some 90% of monogamous married women who are positive have been infected by their husbands, showing their limited autonomy even in the most intimate parts of their lives. Closely linked to their situation in the family, Indian women exhibit high rates of depression with some studies showing them to be two or three times more likely than men to be affected in this way especially during their childbearing years.

Hence, we can see that any attempt to link the health of women to their gender must explore the links with other aspects of their social location. This is especially important when we come to issues of poverty and discrimination. Unlike many other countries socio-economic status in India cannot be read off in any simple way from the distribution of income and wealth. Instead the caste system defines a group at the very bottom of the social hierarchy. Previously defined as "untouchables" they are now referred to as Dalits (officially known as Scheduled Castes), and constitute one-sixth of the population. Within the Dalit group itself, women are usually the "poorest of the poor" with their position at the intersection of caste, class and gender, rendering them vulnerable to both direct and indirect violence. They have little access to basic services including health care with cultural norms of "natural" caste hierarchies and female subjugation combining to prevent them from realising their potential for health.

This brief example of the impact of female gender on health is developed further as this collection explores the heterogeneity of Indian society. The aim is not just to describe inequities in health as they emerge from official statistics, but rather to explore their origins in the constantly shifting dynamics not just within India but also between India and the rest of the world. This requires the use of a range of both quantitative and qualitative methodologies across a variety of settings. By this means, the book plays an important part in the creation of an effective evidence base for tackling the health inequalities that have so plagued India despite recent economic growth.

Lesley Doyal
Emeritus Professor
University of Bristol
Bristol, UK

Acknowledgements

The research on which this book is based, was undertaken as part of the project, *Closing the Gap: Health Equity Research Initiative in India* supported by IDRC, Canada, implemented by the Achutha Menon Centre for Health Science Studies, Sree Chitra Tirunal Institute for Medical Sciences and Technology, Thiruvananthapuram, India. This book was inspired by many people who have spent a life time working towards social justice and equity in health, and we owe much to all their work. The editors would like to express our gratitude to all those who offered comments at various stages of development of the chapters in this book, and to Dr. Sharmila Mhatre and Prof. Lesley Doyal who graciously agreed to write the Forewords to the book. Special thanks are due to the Institute and its administration for the support they have provided, and members of the *Closing the Gap* Project Team and students of the Achutha Menon Centre for Health Science Studies, who helped with editing and finalising the manuscript.

Contents

Editors and Contributors

About the Editors

T.K. Sundari Ravindran has a Ph.D. in applied economics from the Centre for Development Studies, Thiruvananthapuram, Kerala, India. She is currently Professor at the Achutha Menon Centre for Health Science Studies, Sree Chitra Tirunal Institute for Medical Sciences and Technology, Trivandrum, and Visiting Faculty at the School of Public Health at the University of Witwatersrand, Johannesburg, South Africa.

Rakhal Gaitonde completed his MBBS from Government Kilpauk Medical College and MD Community Medicine from Christian Medical College, Vellore, India. He has since worked with NGOs implementing projects on community-based accountability and governance of health systems, including at the state level in Tamil Nadu under the National Rural Health Mission. He is presently pursuing a Ph.D. with the University of Umeå, Sweden and is a Senior Scientist at the Centre for Technology and Policy (CTaP) at the Indian Institute of Technology Madras, Chennai, where he is working in the area of vaccine-related decision-making and the evaluation of medical technology from a system and social perspective. He also works on issues of environment and occupational health, and supports a number of pollution-impacted communities through research and advocacy. He is a member of the Patient Advisory Board and International Editorial Advisory Board of the *British Medical Journal*. He is a member of the Accredited Social Health Activist (ASHA) mentoring group of the Government of India and is a trustee of the Anusandhan Trust, which works towards removing socio-economic disparities related to health and related inequities in India. He is also a part of the People's Health Movement and the Medico Friend Circle.

Contributors

Priyadarshini Chidambaram is a public health specialist and medical college teacher in Bengaluru. She completed her postgraduation in community medicine from the Madras Medical College and was the university medallist in M.D. She has keen interest in the areas of social determinants of health, gender studies, and ethics in health.

Grace A. Chitra works as an Associate Professor in the Global Institute of Public Health in Thiruvananthapuram, Kerala. Her research interests include areas such as environmental health, health policy, epidemiology, health inequity, and sustainable development. She is currently involved in projects looking at the ecosystem impacts of developmental initiatives at Kuttanad in southern India, the impact of indoor air pollution on non-communicable diseases and social and health transformation to sustainability in low-income settings.

Prashanth Nuggehalli Srinivas is a Faculty at the Institute of Public Health, Bengaluru, India. His research interests are in health policy and systems research, especially theory-driven and realist inquiry. He is involved in research and evaluation studies on tribal health and heads the health equity and evaluation cluster at the Institute. He is a passionate birdwatcher and works closely with ecologists and conservationists on topics at the interface of health and environment.

Sudharshini Subramaniam holds an M.D. in community medicine from the Madras Medical College, Chennai, India. She is currently working as an Assistant Professor in the Institute of Community Medicine at the Madras Medical College, Chennai. She has a keen interest in social determinants of health and has worked in various areas of statistical and epidemiological applications in public health.

Abbreviations

ABAD	Apni Beti Apna Dhan (Your Daughter, Your Asset)
AIDS	Acquired Immuno Deficiency Syndrome
ANC	Ante Natal Care
ANM	Auxiliary Nursing Midwifery
AoA	Agreement on Agriculture
ARI	Acute Respiratory Infection
ART	Antiretroviral Treatment
ASHA	Accredited Social Health Activist
BMI	Body Mass Index
BPL	Below Poverty Line
CD	Communicable Diseases
CESM	Community Earth System Model
CI	Concentration Index
CMD	Common Mental Disorder
CSDH	Committee on Social Determinants of Health
DLHS	District-Level Household Survey
DPT	Diphtheria, Pertussis, and Tetanus
EAG	Empowered Action Group
FSW	Female Sex Worker
GATS	General Agreement on Trade in Services
GDP	Gross Domestic Product
HIV	Human Immunodeficiency Virus
HPA	Hypothalamo–Pituitary Axis
ICDS	Integrated Child Development Services
ICESCR	International Covenant on Economic, Social and Cultural Rights
ICMR	Indian Council of Medical Research
ICT	Information and Communication Technology
ICTC	Integrated Counselling and Testing Centre
IDRC	International Development Research Centre
IDU	Injecting Drug User

IIHDS	India Human Development Surveys
IMF	International Monetary Fund
IMNCI	Integrated Management of Neonatal and Childhood Illnesses
IMR	Infant Mortality Rate
IPV	Intimate Partner Violence
JSY	Janani Suraksha Yojana (Plan for Protection of Mothers)
KBK	Kalahandi Balangir Koraput
MAI	Multilateral Agreements on Investments
MAPEDIR	Maternal and Perinatal Death Inquiry and Response
MCH	Maternal and Child Health
MMR	Maternal Mortality Rate
MoHFW	Ministry of Health and Family Welfare
MSM	Men having Sex with Men
NCAER	National Council of Applied Economic Research
NCD	Non-communicable Diseases
NDP	Net Domestic Product
NFHS	National Family Health Survey
NGO	Non-governmental Organization
NHM	National Health Mission
NHS	National Health Service
NMR	Neonatal Mortality Rates
NSS	National Sample Survey
NSSO	National Sample Survey Organisation
OBC	Other Backward Classes
OOP	Out-of-Pocket
OPEC	Organization of Petroleum Exporting Countries
OPV	Oral Poliovirus Vaccines
PAPs	Proportion of Ailing Persons
PDS	Public Distribution System
PESA	Panchayats Extension to Scheduled Areas
PLHA	People Living with HIV and AIDS
QOL	Quality of Life
RHI	Reproductive Health Index
RMNCH+A	Reproductive, Maternal, Neonatal, Child and Adolescent Health
RSB	Risky Sexual Behaviour
RSBY	Rashtriya Swasthya Bima Yojna (National Health Insurance Scheme)
RTI	Reproductive Tract Infection
SC	Scheduled Caste
SDG	Sustainable Development Goal
SDH	Social Determinants of Health
SDP	State Domestic Product
SEP	Socio-Economic Position
SES	Socio-Economic Status
SHGs	Self-Help Group

SLI	Standard of Living Index
ST	Scheduled Tribe
STI	Sexually Transmitted Infections
TFR	Total Fertility Rate
TRIPS	Trade-Related Aspects of Intellectual Property Rights
U5MR	Under-5 Mortality Rate
UK	United Kingdom
UNICEF	United Nations International Children's Emergency Fund
UP	Uttar Pradesh
USA	United States of America
VPDs	Vaccine-Preventable Diseases
WHO	World Health Organization
WTO	World Trade Organization

List of Figures

List of Tables

List of Boxes

Chapter 1
Structural Drivers of Inequities in Health

T.K. Sundari Ravindran, Rakhal Gaitonde and Prashanth Nuggehalli Srinivas

Abstract This introductory chapter provides the backdrop against which the evidence on health inequities in India, synthesised in later chapters, may be understood. In this chapter, we argue that the extreme economic inequalities underlying significant inequities in health are fuelled by forces of neo-liberal globalisation. The chapter illustrates with facts and figures that the neo-liberal economic policies that were adopted in India since the mid-1980s have increased income and wealth inequalities. While economic growth has been significant, the benefits have not accrued to those in the lowest income and wealth categories. Growth has not generated adequate employment to absorb the surplus rural labour or the new entrants into the labour force. A large proportion of workers experience insecure livelihoods and poor living and working conditions. These adversities are experienced disproportionately by those already disadvantaged based *inter alia* on class, caste and gender, and may be expected to impact the pattern of inequities in health in India.

Keywords Health inequities · Neo-liberal globalisation · India
Neo-liberal economic policies

T.K.S. Ravindran (✉)
Achutha Menon Centre for Health Science Studies, Sree Chitra Tirunal
Institute for Medical Sciences and Technology, Trivandrum 695011, India
e-mail: ravindransundari@gmail.com

R. Gaitonde
Centre for Technology and Policy (CTaP) IIT-M, Chennai, India
e-mail: rakhal.gaitonde@gmail.com

P.N. Srinivas
Faculty at the Institute of Public Health, Bangalore, India
e-mail: prashanth.ns@gmail.com

T.K.S. Ravindran and R. Gaitonde (eds.), *Health Inequities in India*,
https://doi.org/10.1007/978-981-10-5089-3_1

1.1 Introduction

In this book, we present a critical synthesis of public health literature pertaining to health inequities in India published since 2000, as a means of taking stock of where we are. While focusing on the literature in the public health field, we draw upon insights from a range of disciplines to critically interrogate what we find. It is this engagement that forms the basis for charting what we believe is an agenda for future research on health inequities.

The evidence-base on health inequities in India is limited and narrow. Several dimensions remain unexplored and many others are scarcely understood. Many factors appear to have contributed to the limited and narrow evidence-base on health equity in India. The first is the fragmentation of health equity research and researchers by disciplinary and sectoral boundaries. Health equity work in India has come from economists and social scientists, public health researchers with a biomedical background and specialisation in community medicine, and a small minority of public health researchers with a multidisciplinary training including in health economics. Each subgroup has tended to examine issues from within their disciplinary perspectives, to share their results in conferences and meetings of their respective disciplines, and to publish their research in specialised journals. There is also a diverse group of civil society actors who have engaged in health equity research to inform action and advocacy, but interaction between academia and civil society actors to address health equity concerns has been limited. Complex phenomena like multiple and intersecting inequities could truly benefit from transdisciplinary and multidisciplinary research, which draws on the strengths of different disciplines and sectors to unravel the many-layered pathways through which social and economic deprivation interacts with other factors to result in or aggravate health inequities. One consequence of this fragmentation is the large research gaps on important issues. In the absence of a *community* of health equity researchers, there has thus far been no process of synthesising what is known, identifying research gaps and agreeing on priority areas for research to inform national policy. Thus, even if more research is undertaken, it may not help bridge the research gaps and add to a critical and crucially usable body of knowledge.

Health equity research would include *inter alia*

- Identifying disparities in health and health care across caste, economic status, gender and other relevant axes of social stratification.
- Enquiring into the proximate and distal factors and mechanisms across multiple levels contributing to health inequities.
- Examining the intersection of multiple axes of deprivation/oppression in creating and reinforcing inequities.
- Studying the outcomes of interventions aimed at reducing health inequities.

- Examining how the current trajectory of health governance impacts on accentuating or mitigating health inequities (e.g. position taken vis-à-vis promotion of privatisation in health) and on whether and how health equity features as a priority objective for health and health research (e.g. awareness and understanding of policy makers and programme managers on health inequities and their determinants).

In addition to the evidence-base on health equity being narrow, other factors have contributed to the relatively scarce research on health equity altogether. One important reason has been the relative dominance of biomedical and technological research in publishing or in grant-making. A related issue is that public health research itself (in India) has tended to depend on doctor-researchers from departments of community medicine or other fields of medicine. Finally, linguistic barriers in initiating and completing research processes in English could also account for limited involvement of a huge number of local universities in attempting health equity research.

Third, health equity issues have had a low visibility in media and policy circles due to a lack of well-planned, cohesive and sustained efforts by a well-organised group of relevant stakeholders. Despite being mentioned in the National Health Policies of 1983 and quite centrally in 2002, an examination of the Twelfth Five Year Plan (2012–2017) document and the subsequent draft Health Policy of 2015 reveal that health equity is mentioned more as an aspiration than as an objective to be achieved within a set time period through well-designed strategies. Policy and programme evaluation being a nascent discipline in India has also not helped the case. Systematic efforts at evaluating policies and programmes have not occurred both due to poor agenda-setting for commissioning such studies within Governments, as well as limitations in research capacity to conduct large-scale evaluation studies.

This edited volume aims to draw attention to the urgent need for academic, programmatic, and policy attention to health inequities in India. The volume is a result of a synthesis exercise carried out as part of a project entitled "*Closing the Gap: Health Equity Research Initiative in India*" implemented by the Achutha Menon Centre for Health Science Studies, the Public Health Wing of Sree Chitra Tirunal Institute for Medical Sciences and Technology, Trivandrum, Kerala, India. The 4-year project (2014–2018) is supported by the International Development Research Centre (IDRC), Canada.

The book is divided into three foundational chapters, five core chapters containing the syntheses of research evidence on health inequities in India and a concluding chapter. This chapter provides an overview of the global and national scenarios of economic inequalities, which underlie and fuel health inequities. In this chapter we describe the widening economic inequalities globally and within India and examine how this has impacted on inequalities by caste and gender and on other socially constructed vulnerabilities. The second chapter focuses on and traces the development of concepts and frameworks on the pathways to health inequities, including the concept of *intersectionality*, which drives home the need to go beyond a unitary axis of disadvantage and look at the social and health consequences of multiple disadvantages or vulnerability. This is followed by a chapter, which tells us the lay of the land on who has done what on health inequities in India and how.

Subsequently, the five core chapters follow. These are devoted to syntheses of research evidence on inequities in health by socio-economic position; caste/ethnicity; gender; other socially constructed vulnerabilities with a focus on people living with HIV and AIDS and migrants; and health system factors contributing to or mitigating inequities in health. Each core chapter not only summarises research findings but also engages critically with the perspectives reflected in the papers and proposes a framework for understanding the mechanisms through which health inequities result.

We have chosen socio-economic position, caste/ethnicity and gender as themes for synthesis of evidence for two reasons. One, the studies seemed to cluster around these categories, and two, these categories are among key axes of stratification of society manifested in unequal distribution of power and resources; and the stratification results in unequal exposure and vulnerability to health risks. The extent to which social stratification would precipitate health inequities depends on the effectiveness with which policies and programmes and especially the public health system mitigate or exacerbate existing inequalities and the extent of social action by affected communities. The focus on People Living with HIV and AIDS and migrants as other groups whose health vulnerabilities are socially constructed (and the exclusion of other, similarly placed groups such as people living with disabilities) was pragmatic, based on the relatively better evidence-base on these groups as compared to the others.

In the final chapter, we highlight the main conclusions from the syntheses of evidence on inequities in health in India; and reflect on the kind of conceptual and methodological tools needed for future research on health inequities in India that could meaningfully inform policy and social action.

1.2 Underlying Worldview, Concepts and Definitions

1.2.1 The Context: Widening Global Economic Inequalities

Opportunities and resources for good health are not distributed equally in our societies, causing inequities in health. Health inequities are perhaps the most pernicious of all inequalities, resulting in deaths and disability that need never have taken place, affecting not only the present but also future generations through their intergenerational effects, causing much human suffering and compromising the ability of individuals and nations to live life as they would choose to and attain their highest potential. As eloquently spelt out in the Report of the WHO Commission on Social Determinants of Health (2008), addressing health inequities calls for dealing with their root causes: unequal distribution of power, income and resources within and across countries of the world (CSDH, 2008).

To better understand and interpret the evidence on the patterns and extent of health inequities in India, and the pathways through which they are created and sustained, this introductory chapter presents an overview of the present day global and national political, economic and social context. The reasons for starting with the wider political, social and economic context are twofold. The first is the premise that health is socially determined, and inequities in health are therefore influenced by economic, political and social factors at the macro, meso and micro levels. The second reason is that in the present era of globalisation, the economies and polity of countries across the globe are so intertwined, that we would be left with an incomplete picture unless we made the linkages from the global to the national and local. The global context affects national policies and economies through trade, international norms, policies and social and cultural interactions. These in turn interact with pre-existent social hierarchies and inequalities across the national and local levels to shape the conditions in which people grow, learn, live, work and age, their vulnerability to ill health and the consequences of ill health.

The world today is marked by levels of economic inequality unprecedented in more than a century (Piketty, 2014). Global leaders and institutions as diverse as the Pope and the President of the Bank of England, Oxfam and the International Monetary Fund, have expressed concern about the vast and widening gap in income and wealth across and within countries. In recognition of the serious threat to human well-being posed by increasing economic and social inequalities, one of the Sustainable Development Goals (SDG Goal 10) to be achieved by 2030 is to "reduce inequality within and among countries" (UN, 2016, p. 8).

And yet, such widespread concern about economic inequality is somewhat recent. There has existed for more than a century the view that the unequal distribution of rewards and resources are essential for the efficient functioning of society; that the unequal share of resources enjoyed by a few are society's way of rewarding talent; and that a generous welfare state that supports the poor would encourage idleness and dampen the motivation to be industrious (Davis & Moore, 1945). In 1955, an influential paper by the economist Simon Kuznets became the basis for considering high economic inequality as an inevitable but transient phase in a country's economic development. As economic growth advanced, economic inequality would at first remain stable, and eventually taper off as the fruits of economic growth trickled down to low-income populations (Kuznets, 1955). As recently as in 2004, the Nobel laureate Robert Lucas argued forcibly that to focus on questions of distribution and on redistributive policies was "harmful to sound economics"… (and) "poisonous" (Lucas, 2004).

The widespread attention received by economic inequality within and across countries in the present times is often without an underpinning of social justice and human rights of all persons to have equal opportunities in life. Economists such as

Joseph Stiglitz and Raghuram Rajan have successfully put economic inequality on the global agenda. They have pointed out that high levels of economic inequality could undermine economic growth and efficiency (Stiglitz, 2012; Rajan, 2010). The concern with inequalities seems to have arisen not because inequalities are morally and ethically wrong, but because they have reached the point of undermining capitalist economic development.

The present book is concerned about economic and social inequalities and the resulting health inequities as an issue of justice and rights. The book echoes Braveman's view that "health equity means social justice in health (i.e. no one is denied the possibility to be healthy for belonging to a group that has historically been economically/socially disadvantaged)". The foundation for health equity is "the right of everyone to the enjoyment of the highest attainable standard of physical and mental health" enshrined in the International Covenant on Economic, Social and Cultural Rights (ICESCR), ratified by 160 States (UNHCHR, 1976, p. 4, Article 12). A human rights perspective frames social and economic equality and health equity as an entitlement of all people and an obligation of the state, rather than as acts of benevolence and charity (Braveman & Gruskin, 2003). As per the principle of social justice, equitable access to health care and to the resources necessary to remain healthy is a social responsibility, to be available to all irrespective of ability to pay. Action towards health equity is a political process that calls for the systematic redistribution of power and resources in favour of dispossessed and oppressed groups through deliberate policies (Solar & Irwin, 2010). Such a world view is fundamentally different from a *market justice* approach to the distribution of health care and to the determinants of health. The latter assumes that market forces would ensure the efficient distribution of health care and health resources in a free economy.

In this introductory chapter, we argue that the extreme economic inequalities underlying significant inequities in health are fuelled by forces of neo-liberal globalisation (see Sect. 1.2 below). The impact of the growing inequalities falls disproportionately on those already disadvantaged based on class, gender, caste/ethnicity/race and other differences. Recent evidence confirms that neo-liberal globalisation fuels health inequities through its impact on economic and social inequalities. In their famous work *The Spirit Level*, (Wilkinson & Pickett, 2009) show for 23 high-income countries including several in Europe, USA, Israel and Singapore, that as income gaps grow, diseases of poverty as well as those of affluence increase, compromising the quality of life of the people. In low-and middle-income countries, neo-liberal globalisation has resulted in insecure lives and livelihoods and worsening living and working conditions of the most marginalised, thereby increasing their risks of developing adverse health conditions. Indeed, a recent study by World Bank economist Wagstaff and colleagues reported that in developing countries, during 1990 and 2011 there was a decline in coverage by health services and a decline in the health status of the poorest 40% of the population (Wagstaff, Bredenkamp, & Buisman, 2014).

Periods of economic crises cause major setbacks in health: it is estimated that a 1% contraction in per capita GDP could result in an increase in infant mortality rate of between 0.18 and 0.44 per 1000 births. Between 1980 and 2004, a million more infants died because of economic setbacks suffered by countries (Chhibber, Ghosh, & Palanivel, 2009). Increases in food prices decrease the purchasing power of the population with the poorest groups bearing a disproportionate share of the burden. Lower purchasing power would compromise a household's ability to invest on essential resources for remaining healthy, e.g. preventive healthcare and nutritious food such as milk and fruits. The evidence on health consequences of social and economic inequalities are discussed in detail in later chapters.

This chapter is organised into three sections. Following this introduction, Sect. 1.2.2 lays out and defines equity-related concepts used throughout this book. Section 1.3 outlines the emergence and consolidation of forces of neo-liberal globalisation in the late twentieth and early twenty-first century and focuses on its consequences for economic and social inequalities and for health inequities globally. Section 1.4 describes the ways in which neo-liberal globalisation has impacted economic and social inequalities in India, resulting in health inequities significantly disadvantaging the less privileged.

1.2.2 Equality, Disparity and Equity in Health: Concepts and Definitions

Public health literature across different countries and regions has adopted different traditions in use of terminologies related to health gaps. We, therefore, lay out the definitions and concepts adopted in this book right at the outset. In the United Kingdom and in Europe, the term health inequalities refer to health differences that are *unfair* and *unjust* (Whitehead & Dahlgren, 2006). In the United States, the term *health disparity* has a comparable meaning, and refers to worse health among disadvantaged economic, racial and ethnic groups (Braveman, 2014).

In this book, we use the term health inequities that the World Health Organization has adopted, to denote "unjust differences in health between persons of different social groups, ...(which) can be linked to forms of disadvantage such as poverty, discrimination and lack of access to services or goods (WHO, 2013, p. 6)". Another term used interchangeably with health inequities is *social inequities in health* (Whitehead & Dahlgren, 2006).

We distinguish health inequities from *health inequalities*. Health inequalities include all differences in health across population groups including those arising from genetic, biological or random factors. Whitehead and Dahlgren (2006) identify the presence of *three distinguishing features* between health inequalities and health inequities. The first feature is that the differences are that health inequities are *systematic*, showing consistent patterns of advantage or disadvantage across specific population groups—for example, differences between rural and urban health. The second is that health inequities are the result of social processes rather than biological as in the case of higher mortality among low-income groups, a pattern observed across countries and over time. Since social processes underlie these health differences or gaps, we can expect that the gaps can be closed or significantly narrowed through suitable social policies. The third feature is that health inequities are differences that are created and sustained by *unjust social arrangements* resulting in unequal distribution of the resources essential for good health (Whitehead & Dahlgren, 2006). Health inequity is a normative concept that does not lend itself to measurement, and hence it is through monitoring health inequalities—observable differences between subgroups within a population—that health inequities are assessed (WHO, 2013).

If health inequities are about unfair and unjust health differences, what then is health equity? Equity in health is the situation where no one is denied the possibility of achieving their full health potential because of unfair social processes or arrangements. Health equity includes having equal opportunities to be healthy, as well as equitable access to health care and other social services to help address ill health and distress. Health equity is not about taking care of the most disadvantaged in society but about creating opportunities and removing barriers to achieving health potentials of all people (Whitehead & Dahlgren, 2006). Health equity may be achieved through an equitable redistribution of resources for health, *including the power and capabilities to demand and use these resources* (EQUINET, 2004).

Horizontal equity in health is about making available equal resources for equal need. This term refers to situations where there is equal health need, and therefore an equal need for resources. *Vertical equity* in health is about unequal resources for unequal need. This refers to situations when there are different needs and resources need to be adjusted to meet the different needs.

Inequities in health are the consequences not only of inequitable access to material resources, but also of social processes that deny equal opportunities for being healthy to all sections of the population. Some of these processes include stigma, prejudice, discrimination, social exclusion and marginalisation.[1] These are closely interlinked processes, and we introduce below definitions to these widely used terminologies.

Stigma is "an attribute that links a person to an undesirable stereotype, leading others to reduce the bearer from a whole and usual person to a tainted, discounted one (Goffman, 1963)". A closely related concept, *prejudice* is "an aversive or hostile attitude toward a person who belongs to a group, simply because she/he belongs to that group, and is therefore presumed to have the objectionable qualities ascribed to the group (Allport, 1958)". Both stigma and prejudice result in discrimination.

Discrimination is an "action or practice that excludes, disadvantages, or merely differentiates between individuals or groups of individuals based on some ascribed or perceived trait, although the *definition* itself is subject to substantial debate (Oxford Bibliographies, 2010)".

[1]It is our contention that these are the processes through which social inequality is enforced, and not the causes or drivers.

Conscious or unconscious discrimination brings about *social exclusion*, "a social process which involves denial of fair and equal opportunities to certain social groups in multiple spheres of society, resulting in the inability of individuals from excluded groups to participate in the basic political, economic and social spheres (Thorat & Sabharwal, 2010, p. 3)".

The result of discrimination and social exclusion is *marginalisation* of people or population subgroups that are rendered voiceless and invisible, and unable to make claims for resources to meet their legitimate needs, resulting in a vicious downward spiral of deprivation.

1.3 Neo-liberal Globalisation and Global Economic and Social Inequalities

This section provides an overview of the pathways through which neo-liberal globalisation has led to widening economic and social inequalities.

Neo (new) liberalism, also more recently christened as market fundamentalism is the successor of economic liberalism, the main tenets of which were outlined by Adam Smith in the eighteenth century. In the words of David Harvey, "neoliberalism is in the first instance a theory of political economic practices that proposes that human well-being can best be advanced by liberating individual entrepreneurial freedoms and skills within an institutional framework characterised by strong private property rights, free markets, and free trade. The role of the state is to create and preserve an institutional framework appropriate to such practices (Harvey, 2005, p. 2)". The re-emergence of neo-liberalism in the 1980s was preceded by a decade during which there were major global economic and political changes. These included the delinking in 1971 of the US Dollar from the Gold Exchange Standard; the spiralling of oil prices following the formation of the Organization of Petroleum Exporting Countries (OPEC); and the resultant debt-crisis in many low and middle-income countries of Asia, Africa and Latin America.

The ascent of neo-liberal economic policies during the Reagan–Thatcher Era of 1980s has been described by Harvey (2005) as a decisive move by the upper classes to ensure self-preservation in the face of collapse of economic growth and a plunge in the proportion of wealth controlled by the top 1% of the population, not only in countries such as the USA and the UK but also in Latin American countries such as Chile and Argentina.

A series of *structural adjustment policies* were coerced through global economic and political instruments over low- and middle-income countries reeling under debt crises when they approached the International Monetary Fund and the World Bank for loans. These policies, which came to be known as the Washington Consensus, included

- budget austerity and reduction in public spending by governments;
- trade and financial liberalisation;

- privatisation of state-run enterprises;
- deregulation or abolition of regulations such as tariffs and duties that impeded market entry; and
- facilitating foreign direct investments through various incentives including weakening regulations protecting labour rights (Juego & Schmidt, 2009).

The establishment in 1995 of the World Trade Organization or WTO created an institutional mechanism to support trade liberalisation. International Financial Institutions *encouraged* low-income countries into *full participation* in WTO-ruled trade agreements. These included agreements such as the Multilateral Agreements on Investments (MAI), which demanded a total liberation of all corporate activities; the General Agreement on Trade in Services (GATS), which required *open border* policies to allow private investment from abroad in the services sector, including health and education, water supply and sanitation; the Agreement on Trade-related Aspects of Intellectual Property Rights (TRIPS), which served to protect patent rights held mainly by transnational corporations; and the Agreement on Agriculture (AoA) that enforces *free trade* in agricultural products (Juego & Schmidt, 2009).

There are several pathways through which market fundamentalist economic policies have contributed to accentuating economic inequality. We outline below a few ways in which the *free markets* affected debt-ridden and relatively poorer countries in the South.

1.3.1 Economic Effects

As countries opened their markets to permit the free inflow of finance capital, countries faced the risk of economic destabilisation arising from speculative dealings in capital. The *open borders* policies of the WTO allowed foreign and domestic investors to buy national currency and any other financial instruments from any country and off-load them when they were no longer profitable. During the first decade of the new millennium, new financial instruments were created to attract finance capital in search of higher and higher returns, and paving the way for the global financial meltdown of 2008 (Kotz, 2015).

Financial liberalisation has in many countries also resulted in a shrinking of financial services available to small-scale producers and to low-income groups because public-sector banks, competing with international and national private banks, can no longer afford to offer subsidised credit. Cuts in agricultural subsidies and acquisition of land by real estate dealers and transnational corporations have impoverished farmers in many countries. Such effects on the banking and finance sector have immediate consequences for health, education and other social sectors, more so in countries (such as India) where health and education are not already guaranteed as a right.

Investment in capital-intensive and high-technology enterprises has dampened the growth of employment in some regions of the world. For example, in the Asia-Pacific region during the early 2000s, every 1% of GDP growth resulted in employment growth of only 0.4% (Chhibber et al., 2009). This created a large pool of unemployed, contributing to suppression of wages. Population groups that are already disadvantaged based on class, gender, caste/race/ethnicity and other differences have the least bargaining power in the labour market, and become cheap and compliant labour.

One of the key features of the growing within-country economic inequalities experienced by low- and middle-income as well as high-income countries is the dwindling returns to labour and increasing returns to capital. The growth of finance capital has privileged growth of income among owners of capital in the form of interest payments, dividends, retained profits and lower rate of taxation of top incomes (Oxfam International, 2016). Consequently, such macroeconomic trends tend to accentuate the inequalities that already exist. Recent estimates show that during 1990–2007, the wealthiest 20% of the world population enjoyed 70% of the total global income, while the poorest 20% received 2% (UNICEF, 2011).

1.3.2 Wealth Inequalities

If income inequalities are high, wealth inequalities are even higher. In almost all countries of the world the Gini coefficient of wealth distribution is almost double that of income distribution (Dabla-Norris, Kochhar, Suphaphiphat, Ricka & Tsounta, 2015). In July 2016, the World Economic Forum reported that the richest 1% now have more wealth than the remaining 99% of the world population. New wealth being produced accrues disproportionately to a miniscule group of hyper-elite. Since 2000, the bottom half of the world population received only 1% of the increase in global wealth, while the top 1% received 50% (WEF, 2016). The combined wealth of the top 10 Forbes' billionaires exceeds the total goods and services produced in a year by many of the world's nations. The global economic system is heavily skewed in favour of the top 1%, and this is not the result of economic forces alone. There has been elite capture of politics, and those with power and privilege have been able to influence those in government through lobbying, campaign funding and other means, the active collusion resulting in economic policies and ways of doing business that benefitted those at the top at the expense of all others (Stiglitz, 2012).

The consequences have been pervasive. Market fundamentalist economic policies on the one hand enforce the removal of tariffs, duties and taxes related to trade, leading to reduction in public revenue and on the other, also require cuts in public expenditure as part of fiscal discipline. When governments cut public spending on social protection measures, health and education, they add insult to injury for those with the least economic and social resources, by depriving them of access to public services that hold the key to an acceptable quality of life. In a democracy, the equality of all persons before the law is in stark contradiction with the huge inequalities in conditions of living (Marmot, 2015).

1.3.3 Meritocracy

The idea of *meritocracy* embedded in neo-liberalism, promotes the myth that the rich have made their way to the top through their merit, genius and/or hard work, while the poor have themselves to blame for their poverty (Davison & Shire, 2015). Meritocracy serves to justify social inequalities and the non-availability of subsidised public services for low-income groups and makes it appear that disparities in outcomes (in education, health, income) are natural and inevitable (Engel & Martin, 2015). This translates into victim-blaming and policies that infantilise the disadvantaged.

1.3.4 Exacerbation of Social Inequalities by Ethnicity

Rising economic inequalities exacerbate existing social inequalities. For example, expansion of global markets creates increasing demand on extraction of natural resources, the cost of which is disproportionately borne by indigenous populations. Low- and middle-income countries seeking to attract foreign investments have liberalised their laws, contributing to a tremendous growth in mining, oil and gas extraction, large infrastructural projects, logging and plantations, and commercial farming and fishing. In many parts of the world, indigenous populations have lost their land and livelihood and their traditional sources of food; suffered the negative fall-out of severe environmental degradation; been displaced from their traditional homes; experienced deterioration of their health; and seen the very fabric of their society destroyed (UN, 2009; Hershey, 2012; IFG, 2011; Altamirano-Jimenez, 2013).

1.3.5 Gendered Impact of Neo-liberalism

The gendered impact of market fundamentalist economic policies on women and men has been both positive and negative. New job opportunities opened up for women in "Export-promotion zones" in many low- and middle-income countries, in fully or partially foreign-owned enterprises. For example in Southeast Asia, Bangladesh and Sri Lanka, there were 2–5 female workers for every male worker in textiles, garments, and electronic sectors (Dejardin & Owens, 2009).

On the one hand, this meant the loosening of traditional patriarchal controls on women gave them access to cash incomes and afforded some degree of economic power within their households. On the other hand, to keep production costs low in the face of intense international competition, wages were kept low, working conditions were precarious and employment was insecure and unprotected by labour legislations. Moreover, despite the emerging job opportunities in export-oriented sectors, most women in low- and middle-income countries found employment in the informal sector or were self-employed. During times of crises, the probability of women being laid-off first was high because of the notion that men were bread-winners whose jobs deserved to be protected more: during the Asian economic crisis seven times as many women in South Korea were laid-off as men (Seguino, 2009).

The gendered impact of most other neo-liberal economic policies is unequivocal. Cuts in public expenditure in health and education and in basic needs and services, such as water supply and sanitation, public transport, and childcare services increases the time women have to spend on these domestic tasks, adding to women's workload (Balakrishnan, 2005). When education is commercialised, studies note that more girls drop out of school than boys. Recurring food crises resulting in food shortages and sharp increases in food prices affect women disproportionately because of their role in managing food procurement and availability within the household. Many women have to travel longer or work harder to access affordable food, and put in more hours processing it because of its lower quality. Women may also compromise on their own food intake to put food on the table for children and other members of the family (Uraguchi, 2010).

1.4 Neo-liberal Globalisation and Economic and Social Inequalities in India

Indian society has traditionally been characterised by entrenched hierarchies along the lines of class, caste, ethnicity, gender and other axes of power and privilege. In this section, we trace the rise of neo-liberal economic policies in India with the ascent of neo-liberal globalisation, resulting in the compounding of existing inequalities. In doing so, we draw on Wallerstein's (1974, 2000) World Systems Theory, according to which the nature of national economic development has to be understood in terms of how it fits into an overall global logic of capitalist accumulation; and the country's vulnerability to economic exploitation and political domination because of its specific economic, political and sociocultural characteristics.

Health inequities in India, described in later chapters, are the consequence of the interaction between global forces and specific national characteristics, and cannot be adequately understood or acted upon without a grasp of this larger macroeconomic and political context.

1.4.1 India's Transition from a Closed to Open Economy

After more than three decades of modest economic growth of about 3–4% of GDP per annum, India's GDP growth rate picked up in the early 1980s, and reached a high of 8.2% between 2003–04 and 2011–12. This period of accelerating economic growth registered a fall in proportion of population living below the poverty line, from 45.3% in 1993–94 to 29.8% in 2009–10 (Government of India, 2012).

The period after 1980 was marked by India's transition from a closed and controlled economy[2] focused on poverty eradication, to an open economy with economic growth as its primary goal. Starting 1991, the pace of economic reforms accelerated and a decisive break was achieved from previous policies. These changes were triggered both, by changes that were unfolding in the global economy discussed in the previous section, and a series of crises that the Indian government was faced with in 1991.

In 1991, the government did away with the production licensing in many industries in one stroke. Restrictions on monopoly firms for setting up new enterprises was progressively relaxed since the 1980s and finally repealed in 2009. Stock market rules were relaxed. The 40% upper ceiling on foreign investment was removed and many sectors were opened for foreign investment and collaboration. Import licensing was abolished and the 400% import duty levied on many products was removed permitting the import of all goods except harmful substances. Exchange controls that restricted the entry of foreign currency were relaxed, and the rupee was devalued, to make Indian exports competitive in the global market. India became a member of the World Trade Organization (WTO) in 1995, and has implemented its various treaties. This includes liberalisation of trade in banking and insurance as well as in educational and healthcare services (Kohli, 2006).

Neo-liberal economic reforms have supported privatisation of the health sector in India. Numerous policies have been implemented, which have encouraged and strengthened the private health sector. Since 2000, 100% foreign direct investment in the hospital sector is permitted, and long-term loans for investment in hospitals are provided at lower interest rates. Newly established hospitals with 100 beds or more located outside the eight urban agglomerations have been allowed 100% tax exemption for 5 years. Visa rules have been amended to promote medical tourism. India's membership in the WTO has led to its having to amend its Model Patent Act of 1970. This and the lifting of price controls on drugs and pharmaceuticals have

[2]Before the 1980s, national industry and agriculture were protected from competition from imported goods. The growth of monopolies was legally restricted. Small-scale and cottage industries were protected, incentives provided for setting up industries in economically less-developed regions; major public-sector enterprises were vested with responsibility for infrastructural development, mining and production of iron and steel. Subsidies for inputs in agriculture and low-interest credit for agricultural investment were provided. Price controls were in place in priority sectors including for drugs. Public investment in health and education made health services and education free or heavily subsidised at the point of delivery.

contributed to increases in drug prices. Privatisation of health care and the increasing costs of drugs, combined with cuts in the government's health budget year after year have substantially increased household financial burden for health care. Increased cost of medical care is the second most common cause of rural indebtedness in India (People's Health Movement—India, 2007).

1.4.2 *Economic Inequalities in India During the Period of Economic Liberalisation*

The period since 1990 during which the Indian economy grew substantially is also marked by a significant increase in economic inequalities in India, with a rise in the value of its net Gini index of inequality (based on income net of taxes and transfers) from 45.18 in 1990 to 51.36 in 2013. Only two countries in the Asia-Pacific: Papua New Guinea and China—are more unequal (Chakravarty, 2016) (Fig. 1.1).

In the late 1990s, the average income of the top 0.01% of India's population was 150–200 times the average of the rest of the population. The period starting 1980s was marked by a steep increase in the income share of the top 0.01 and 0.1% of the population, after having registered a steady decline between 1950s and 1980s. Income shares of the top 0.01 and 0.1% declined sharply from 1.5–2 to 12.13% respectively in 1950s to less than 0.5 and 4–5% respectively in the 1980s and then climbed back once again to 1.5–2.0 and 9–10% respectively in the late 1990s (Banerjee & Piketty, 2005).

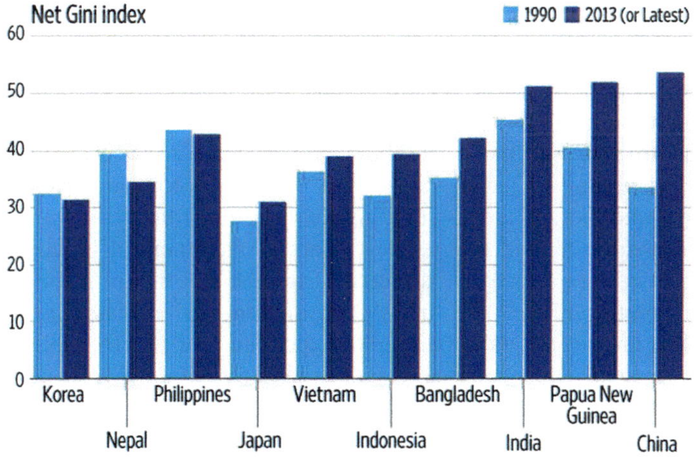

Fig. 1.1 Economic inequality in India and selected countries of Asia-Pacific: 1990 and 2013. Chakravarty (2016)

As is the case for the global economy, wealth inequality is much wider than income inequality. Credit Suisse's wealth data for 2015 shows that the top 1% owned 53% of the country's wealth, the top 10–76.3% while 90% owned less than a quarter of the country's wealth. Inequality had increased since 2000. The share of the richest 1% in national wealth was 36.80% in 2000 and that of the top 10% was 65.9% (Credit Suisse, 2015).

Inequalities in income and wealth are reflected also in inequalities in consumption expenditure, though to a slightly smaller extent. Several studies using the National Sample Survey data have shown, that consumption inequality in India rose significantly in the post-reform period starting in the early 1990s, and that this was more marked in urban as compared to rural areas. Even in the late 1980s, before the sharp increase in inequalities 1990s, it is estimated that the real consumption of the top 1% of Indian consumers was 25 times as much as the per person real consumption of the bottom 1% (Weisskopf, 2011; Ravallion, 2000; Sen & Himanshu, 2005; Sarkar & Mehta, 2010; Topalova, 2008).

There are also major inequalities in wage earnings in the post-reform period starting 1993–1994. Three factors are key—level of education, number of days of work and status of employment: regular or casual. Level of education contributed most to inequality in earnings. Number of days of work was affected by the fact that those in regular employment are paid for all days while casual workers are paid only for actual days worked. Third, daily wage rate is much lower for casual as compared to regular workers. Controlling for other confounding factors, the relative earnings of workers with graduate level education and above increased phenomenally between 1983 and 2004–05. There were also substantial wage differences within the group of graduate regular workers: during 1999–2000 to 2004–05, those working in the Information and Communication Technology (ICT) sector experienced an annual increase in daily wage of 4.75% as compared to only 0.91% for those working in non-ICT tertiary sector (Sarkar & Mehta, 2010).

Expressing concern over the increasing economic inequalities in India, the report of the 59th Parliamentary Standing Committee on Finance (2011–12) observed that "purchasing power is getting concentrated in the hands of a few, whereas the majority is struck below the expenditure curve". Rise in prices, growing unemployment and diminishing real wages have made the poor languish, even as the better off became more affluent, garnering the benefits of the economic growth our country had witnessed over the past few years (Government of India, 2012).

The extent of the gap may be discerned from the fact that in 2004–2005, more than three quarters (76.7%) of India's population—the *common people* of the country—had an average daily per capita expenditure of Rs. 16, while 4% of the high-income groups had a daily per capita expenditure of Rs. 93, close to six times that of the former (Sengupta, Kannan, & Raveendran, 2008).

India's fiscal policies have contributed to the limited ability of the government to address growing inequalities, as corroborated by a recent IMF report (IMF working paper). Progressive taxation with a higher level of taxation of corporate and personal incomes in top-income brackets, and higher levels of social spending on education, health and social protection is associated with low levels of economic inequality.

Governments can take from the rich and give to the poor to dampen the gaps in outcomes despite gaps in incomes and wealth. However, less than 3% of India's large population paid income tax (2008) and tax revenues stagnated at around 0.5% of GDP for several decades. In contrast, 20% of the population in China come under the income tax bracket and contributed to tax revenue of about 2.5% of GDP (2008), expected to rise to 5% by 2015. The ridiculously low proportion of formal sector employees and the increasing tax concessions to the top-income brackets has been one of the reasons for this (Piketty & Qian, 2009).

1.4.3 Geographical Inequalities

1.4.3.1 Rural–Urban

One of the major features of economic inequalities in India is spatial inequality. Rural–urban inequalities have widened since 1993–94, and so have inequalities within rural and within urban areas (Topalova, 2008; Vakulabharanam & Motiram, 2012). Economic liberalisation in India was accompanied by cuts in subsidies for agricultural inputs such as fertilisers and pesticides and cuts in low-interest agricultural credit. Farmers became dependent on merchant moneylenders who charged high interest rates. On the other hand, trade liberalisation subjected farmers to competition from imported agricultural products as well as competition from other countries in the export market for cash crops. Those working in agriculture faced a double squeeze and many had to seek work and income opportunities in the rural non-agricultural sector, including in Special Economic Zones located in rural areas and producing for an export market. Inequalities within this group increased dramatically (Vakulabharanam, 2010).

Urban growth has been concentrated in export-led, skill-intensive and overseas-demand-dependent sectors such as IT, biotechnology, finance, insurance and infrastructural development. Luxury consumption, non-agricultural investment and export-led sectors have grown. The urban elite, constituting 10–15% of the total population of India, has cornered almost all the gains from the GDP growth in India since the 1990s, while the rest of the economy has been left out. It is this skewed process that explains the growth of inequality since the 1990s (Vakulabharanam, 2010).

There are pockets of abject urban poverty in several states of India such as Bihar, Maharashtra, Madhya Pradesh and Chhattisgarh with one or more districts where more than 75% of its urban population lived below the poverty line in 2004–05. Gajapati district in Orissa was estimated to have more than 90% of its urban population living in poverty (Chaudhuri & Gupta, 2009). GDP growth has not been accompanied by increase in decent employment opportunities. Employment elasticity (increase in employment per percentage point increase in GDP) declined from 0.53 (mid-70s–mid-80s) to 0.40 (mid-80s–mid-90s), to 0.33 between 1994–95 and 2009–10 (Sood, 2016).

One of the direct consequences of agrarian distress and stagnation in the growth of employment opportunities is the increasing informality of the labour force. More than 80% of non-agricultural employment is informal, among the highest in Asia. This includes a substantial group of *circular* migrants who seek employment in urban informal sector and return to their villages when there is no work. They have no foothold in the urban economy and no sustainable livelihoods in agriculture, and remain poor. Others who migrate to urban areas form a massive pool of informal labour living in poorly equipped urban slums and eking out a living through providing services to the urban formal sector (Vakulabharanam, 2012). There has also been an increase in the proportion of informal workers working in the formal organised sector as contract labourers. Wage inequalities have widened between 1993–94 and 2009–10, with a worsening of the relative position of those at the bottom of the pile—informal casual wage labourers; and profit incomes have grown faster than total wage and mixed incomes (Vaidyanathan, 2014). Twenty-one percent of the poor in India are working poor, and 25% of them earn less than half the poverty-line income (Sood, 2016) (Fig. 1.2).

1.4.3.2 Inequalities Across and Within States

Inequality among states has also been increasing since the 1990s. Almost all the larger states of India registered more than double the SDP growth rate during 2001–09 (5.8%) as compared to 1993–2001 (2.8%) (The exceptions were Himachal Pradesh, Rajasthan and West Bengal, which had lower growth rates than the previous period). However, the richer states grew faster—if a state had a high per

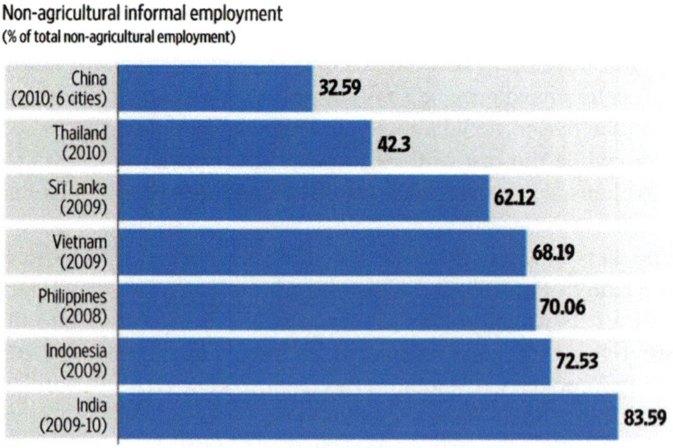

Fig. 1.2 Proportion of informal workers in non-agricultural employment: India and selected countries of Asia-Pacific. Chakravarty (2016)

capita income in 1993, it grew faster over the next 16 years, resulting in a divergence of SDP across states rather than convergence (Kumar & Subramanian, 2012).

A more recent study confirms this divergent trend. In 1960, the top three states were 1.7 times richer than the bottom three (per capita NDP); by 2014 this gap had almost doubled, to 3 times. The richest state in 1960 was twice as rich as the poorest state, but in 2014, the richest state was four times as rich as the poorest—Bihar being the poorest at both time points; (Chakravarty & Dehejia, 2016).

Inter-state inequalities may be high, but intra-state inequalities appear to be even higher. For example, a study using NSS data for 2004–05 to calculate poverty and inequality levels in 20 states of India reported that in Haryana, Chhattisgarh, Karnataka and Gujarat, the best districts had an average monthly per capita expenditure that was four times as high as the worst off districts within the same states, and in Madhya Pradesh, Maharashtra, Uttar Pradesh and Andhra Pradesh, the comparable figure was three times (Chaudhuri & Gupta, 2009). Further, within-state inequalities in educational opportunities by gender, caste and religion declined in Southern states which had better average educational attainments to begin with, and in the North-eastern and Eastern regions while in the educationally backward Central region, educational inequalities increased further (Asadullah & Yalonetzky, 2010).

1.4.4 Structural Inequalities

1.4.4.1 Inequalities by Dalit and Adivasi Status

A second major feature of inequalities in India is the existence of horizontal inequalities by caste and indigenity. The ex-untouchable Dalit groups who were historically positioned lowest in the caste hierarchy have for centuries, experienced social and economic marginalisation, while the indigenous or Adivasi populations of India are distinguished by their relative isolation from mainstream society.[3] The Constitution of independent India designated the ex-untouchable caste groups as Scheduled Castes (SCs), while a community was identified as a Scheduled Tribe (ST), if it had indications of primitive (sic!) traits; distinctive culture; geographical isolation; shyness of contact with mainstream society; and backwardness. The Indian Constitution guarantees SCs and STs political representation through reservations and lays down general principles of affirmative action for improving

[3]A note on terminologies is in order here. While we would prefer to use the terms Dalit and Adivasi, and have done so when we are referring to these population groups, where we cite data from published sources, we have maintained the terminologies used by the authors of the study. Thus in almost all places where studies are cited, the terms SC and ST, or as is often the case, SC/ST is used.

their educational and economic and social status. According to the census of 2011, the Scheduled Castes and Scheduled Tribes, respectively, constituted 16.6 and 8.6% of India's population (RGI, 2011). Although the historical sources and pathways of their marginalisation are very different, official surveys and data sources often club the data on SCs and STs together, contrasting their status with that of the rest of the population.

Half-a-century of affirmative action and the rapid economic growth witnessed by India since the 1990s have indeed resulted in upward mobility among some sections of the Dalit and Adivasi populations. However, Dalit/Adivasi population groups continue to occupy the bottom rungs in terms of social and economic status. For example, in 1999–2000 only around 3% of SC and ST persons aged 24–29 years were college graduates as compared to 11.7% among other Hindu castes and 4.4% among Muslims. In terms of occupation, while about 6% of SC and ST household heads were professionals, the figures were 15.4% for other Hindu castes and 11.5% for Muslims (Desai & Kulkarni, 2008). The same pattern of stratification by caste is found also in economic status, with between 40 and 50% of SC and ST populations concentrated in the bottom two quintiles of consumption expenditure classes in 2004–2005, and only about 3% in the *well-off* categories (Fig. 1.3).

While this is a snapshot view at a specific point in time, other studies examining changes during the period of high economic growth (1990–2004–05) present a mixed picture. Several studies report that Dalit/Adivasi populations had moved from their traditional occupations to other categories of work. Living conditions among Dalits/Adivasis improved vastly during 2001–2011 with improved housing conditions, access to electricity and possession of assets such as mobile phones, televisions and two- and four-wheelers. At the same time, the gap in income and affluence between non-Dalit/Adivasi and Dalit/Adivasi households had widened (Jayaraj & Subramanian, 2013; Thorat, 2007; Hnatkovska, Lahiri, & Paul, 2013; Bhagat, 2013). Across generations, while many belonging to Dalit/Adivasi groups had moved above from the bottom rungs, they were more likely to persist in low-income and low-status occupations as compared to non-Dalit/Adivasi groups, and also more likely to experience downward mobility (Motiram & Singh, 2012).

Gaps in average years of education between SC/ST and non-SC/ST groups narrowed from 2.57 years in 1983 to 1.74 years in 2004–05. This was the result of an expansion in SC/ST education at all levels, right from basic literacy to secondary and higher education. At the same time, large gaps in educational status persisted between 1980s and 2000s, with the average years of schooling for SC/STs in 2004–2005 (3.19 years) lower than that for non-SC/STs two decades earlier, in 1983 (3.62) (Hnatkovska et al., 2013). Another point to note is that education did not offer the same chances for upward mobility to all sections of the population. The disadvantaged initial conditions of SC/STs seemed to dampen their chances of upwards mobility, such that given the same level of education, a person who is SC/ST is more likely to be not well-off (with per capita expenditure levels below twice the poverty line) as compared to someone from the non-SC/ST population groups (Sengupta et al., 2008).

Fig. 1.3 Proportion of poor and well-off by caste status, India, 2004–05. Figure by the author based on data from Deshpande (2003) as quoted in Weisskopf (2011). *ST* Scheduled Tribes, *SC* Scheduled Castes, *H-OBC* Hindu Other Backward Caste, *H-FC* Hindu Forward Castes

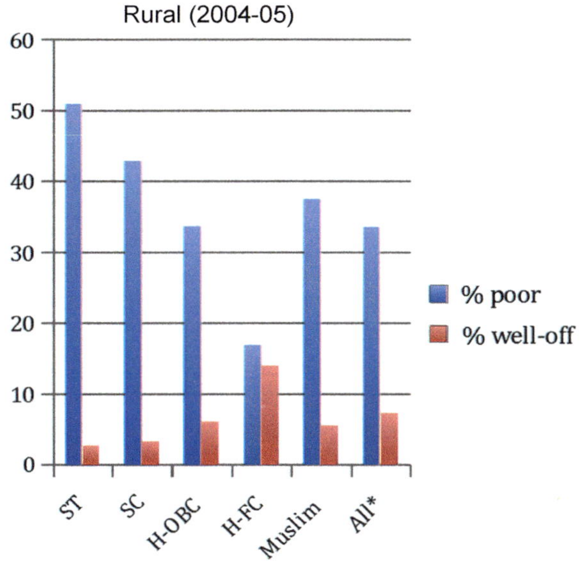

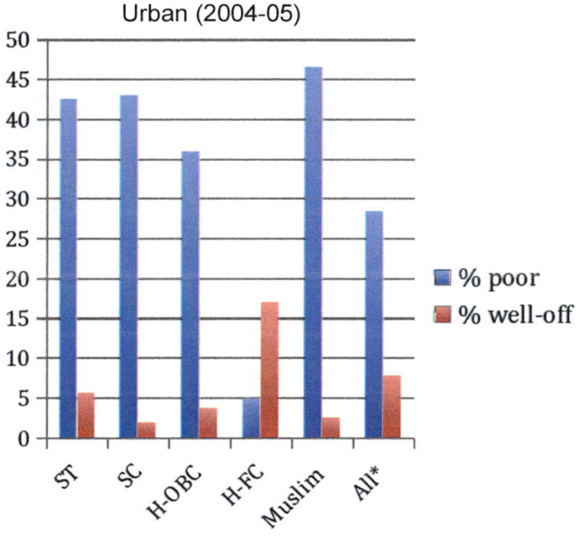

1.4.4.2 Scheduled Castes or Dalits

Micro-studies indicate a vast change in the relative status of Dalits in many rural settings that may not lend themselves to measurement through conventional indicators. In several states, Dalit groups have greater access to education than before, and have moved out of traditional and demeaning occupations and debt-bondage to non-farm activities in the rural areas and in the broader economy. Mobilisation of

Dalit groups has resulted in a loosening of practices of social subordination to upper caste groups and resulted in a greater sense of entitlement as equal citizens in an electoral democracy. However, there are many barriers and countervailing forces that limit their upward mobility to the middle rungs while the majority remained at the bottom of the pile. An emerging *creamy layer* among the Dalits is facing challenges in penetrating the upper caste bastions of political power within village governments, and in rising up the ladder as entrepreneurs and owners of large private enterprises (Djurfeldt et al., 2008; Deshpande & Palshikar, 2008; Martin, 2015; Singh, 2016; Kapur, Prasad, Pritchett, & Babu, 2010; Pikherit, 2015; Vijayabhaskar & Kalaiyarasan, 2014; Thorat & Sadana, 2009).

Gains made in educational and economic status and mobilisation to assert their rights not withstanding, one of the most striking things about caste is its persistence. The long-held assumption that caste in India would gradually disappear as the development process got underway in independent India and poverty and destitution were eliminated, has been belied (Kothari, 1997). As many authors have pointed out, despite extensive legal and constitutional safe guards and rights there only seems to be a never ending stream of explosive and outrageous atrocities against Dalits, which are probably the most prominent manifestations of a never ending, daily and continuous oppression and marginalisation that occurs. For example, as recently as 2010 a study in rural Gujarat showed the presence of 98 forms of discrimination being practised, with 90.8% not being allowed into temples, 98% respondents saying that they had separate utensils to serve Dalits in their homes and 98.1% of villages surveyed not allowing Dalits to rent a house in a non-Dalit neighbourhood (Teltumbde, 2010; Navsarjan Trust, 2010). Many commentators have noted that any attempt by Dalits to assert themselves is resisted with violence often *out of all proportion* to the event (Teltumbde, 2010; Mander, 2004; Guru, 2016). Further "…earlier caste violence was mostly committed by individuals in a fit of rage. Now it is carried out collectively, in a loosely planned manner, as a spectacle of demonstrative justice (Teltumbde, 2010, p. 17)".

1.4.4.3 Scheduled Tribes or Adivasis

Although they share the status of being at the bottom of the pile in terms of social and economic status, the trajectory of *development* (or lack of it) has been quite different for Adivasi populations as compared to their Dalit counterparts. Unlike Dalits, the Adivasi populations have been concentrated in a few states of India, with the majority located in the Central and in the North-Eastern regions.[4] Large sections of Adivasi populations lived in areas rich in forest, water and mineral resources, which saw the establishment of large-scale mining, industrial and infrastructure

[4]There is great diversity among those classified as "Scheduled Tribes" under the Constitution of India in terms of cultural traits, social organization and modes of living. They also vary with respect to their exposure to and integration into mainstream society.

projects including large dams for irrigation. A few from the Adivasi population found employment in the large factories established in their areas and many became low-paid workers with insecure and transient jobs. The designation of forest lands as Reserve Forests, Protected Forests and Wild Life sanctuaries deprived them of their traditional sources of livelihood and food and transformed them into encroachers in their own land, prior to the Forest Rights Act of 2006 (Government of India, 2014). It is estimated that one in ten of the tribal population has experienced involuntary displacement, a process that deprives them of their collective identity and cultural heritage. Economic liberalisation has resulted in the entry of private corporations into tribal areas, and has in many pockets been met with stiff resistance. Some of the most marginalised tribal areas in the country have become hotbeds of left-wing extremism, resulting in their further exclusion from state supported education, health and other social welfare services. In both situations, tribal communities find themselves often pitted against the State machinery (Raj, n. d.; Meher, 2009).

Health issues are also different for the Adivasi communities. Many of the Committees that have studied the health of the Adivasi communities have pointed out the lack of robust data on actual health outcomes. Given the isolated and clustered location of the Adivasi community, the numbers covered even in the large-scale national surveys, is very small and thus the robustness of the estimates of various health indicators is suspect. They also experience very different types of health issues because of their location. Not only are the Adivasi groups uniquely susceptible to various hemoglobinopathies like Thalassemia and sickle cell anaemia; injuries/bites/stings constitute a major proportion of their health issues due to their location in close contact with wildlife that is now being disturbed by the development activities of the mainstream Indian state. Equally importantly, the very world view of the Adivasi groups is radically different from the mainstream communities. The United Nation's State of the World's Indigenous People states that for indigenous peoples, "health is equivalent to the harmonious co-existence of human beings with nature, with themselves and with others, aimed at integral well-being, in spiritual, individual, and social wholeness and tranquillity (UN, 2009, p. 157)."

To summarise, the economic and educational status of the Dalit/Adivasi populations has improved over the past decades, but the gap between them and the rest of the populations has widened. There is evidence of upwards mobility over time and across generations among the Dalit, but the highest castes have further consolidated themselves in the top rungs of the economic hierarchy. Dalit access to political and economic power remains elusive. Comparable information on upward mobility of Adivasi populations is not available. What we know is that irrespective of the gains made in education and economic status, Adivasi populations have gone through a turbulent process of assimilation into the mainstream, best described in the following words of the Tribal Commission: "tribal communities face disregard for their values and culture, breach of protective legislations, serious material and social deprivation, and aggressive resource alienation (Government of India, 2014, p. 32)".

1.4.5 Gender-Based Inequalities

Indian society is marked by deep inequalities by gender; and persistent patriarchal norms despite rapid economic growth, increasing urbanisation and concomitant social changes. For example, India had higher female than male mortality in childhood (0–5 years) as recently as in 2013 indicative of discrimination against girl children (NITI Aayog, 2016). As per the Human Development Report 2016, India ranked 130th among 154 countries in terms of Gender Inequality Index (expressing gender gaps in education, economic status and life expectancy), and ranked below its neighbouring countries of Nepal (rank 108), Bangladesh (rank 111) and Pakistan (rank 121) (UNDP, 2016). Going by the Global Gender Gap Index for 2015, India ranked third-lowest in the Asian Region in terms of educational attainment, health and survival and economic participation and opportunity sub-indices (WEF, 2015).

Gender gaps in education have narrowed over time, but remain significant. As per the 2011 Census, about 34% of women were illiterate as compared to only 18% of men (RGI, 2011). Only about a third of adolescent girls enrolled in high school and the gender gaps in education remained wide at all points beyond the primary school level (Asian Development Bank, 2013).

Economic liberalisation has not been accompanied by increased employment opportunities for women of all classes. During 1993–94 to 2011–12, women's labour force participation rates and their share in the labour market declined. Overall, figures indicate that women are withdrawing from the labour force and engaging in other activities, and are also being edged out by their male counterparts. During the same period, their engagement in unpaid domestic activities has increased significantly (Abraham, 2013). Unlike other rapidly growing low-and middle-income countries such as China, India does not have a large reserve army of young, single women-migrant workers, and Rao (2014) attributes this to the remarkable resilience of the patriarchal family in India in which gender division of labour has been stubbornly resistant to change.

Women who are employed in the paid labour force appear to be predominantly in low-paid blue-collared jobs and in the informal sector. For example, NSSO data for 2004–05 reported that 40–50% of women workers from the lowest two Consumption Expenditure quintiles worked with private households, while less than 10% each worked in public sector and with the private corporate sector respectively (Unni & Raveendran, 2007).

The worsening of women's employment conditions with economic liberalisation is documented in the case of cashew-processing industry in Kerala, where disinvestments from public-sector cashew-processing units led to a transition from factory to cottage and commission-based processing. Women, the overwhelming majority of workers in the cashew industry had to work without job security for low wages under unsafe working conditions (Eapen, Jeyaranjan, Harilal, Swaminathan, & Kanji, 2003). Displacement of women from traditional employment because of commercialisation of fisheries and agrarian distress and indebtedness resulting from volatile global prices for cash crops have also caused women to seek jobs under duress as casual and marginalised workers (Mathew, 2012).

There are also significant gender disparities in wages. In 2004–05, the weekly average wages in rupees was three times higher for men as compared to women; women in the public sector earned less than half that of their male counterparts, while the gaps were narrower in the private formal and informal sectors (Das, 2012). For those in regular/ salaried employment, there were significant gender gaps in wage rates which persisted at every level of education throughout 1993–94 to 2009–10, and the gap widened in rural areas (Sengupta & Das, 2014).

Economic reforms since the 1990s have not brought about significant improvements in women's economic status. Reforms have been accompanied by cuts in social welfare expenditure in areas such as public distribution system, publicly financed childcare, education and health services making these services available only on out-of-pocket payment, squeezing women from both sides.

As observed by Rao (2014), patriarchal norms have persisted and in some instances, even strengthened. Increasing consumerism appears to have strengthened the dowry system, with groups who used to practice bride price till only a couple of decades ago switching to dowry payments. The low prevalence of dowry payments in Southern Indian states as observed by Dyson and Moore is no longer true (Rahman & Rao, 2004; Palriwala, 2005).

Rather than challenging gender inequalities, the policies of the new government seem to be promoting patrimony. One example of this is a fixed deposit scheme for financial inclusion of women announced in July 2015, wherein brothers could open fixed deposits in their sisters' names for Rs. 5000 which the government would top up with life and accident insurance, reinforcing the role of women as dependents and men as protectors (Purewal, 2016).

There are increasing news reports of public spaces as more unsafe for women, and violent crimes against women seem to be on the increase. One of the reasons may be increasing economic inequality and the resulting fracture of social cohesion. With increasing education and upward mobility of some sections of the Dalit/Adivasi populations and the ensuing opportunities for young women and men from diverse castes to interact in public spaces, honour killings to discourage marriages across caste and religion are a growing phenomenon (Rao, 2014).

And yet, a small but visible section of women have risen to positions of top leadership in diverse sectors and project an image of emancipated and empowered women. Political participation by women has also increased dramatically with the reservation of 50% of the seats for women in local government bodies.

In short, traditional gender-based inequalities in India have been mediated by forces of neo-liberal globalisation in complex and contradictory ways. Some have argued that the *gains* we see in terms of employment opportunities and greater individual freedom for women are in fact the handiwork of neo-liberal globalisation which has co-opted the feminist quest for greater autonomy for women; turned "a sow's ear into a silk purse by elaborating the narrative of female empowerment…" and has harnessed "the dream of women's emancipation to the engine of capitalist accumulation". Likewise, neo-liberalism has used feminist critique of the welfare state's paternalism for its infantilisation of the poor to justify the withdrawal of social sector services so essential for gender equality (Fraser, 2013). These arguments help us to make sense of the apparent contradictions between gains made by the more privileged groups of women as against the lack of improvement for the majority; as well as the individual freedoms gained by poorer women as against their collective losses as a class.

Following this introduction to the structural drivers of health inequities globally and in India, Chap. 2 examines various frameworks for conceptualising the pathways and mechanisms through which health inequities are generated and sustained.

References

Abraham, V. (2013). Missing labour or consistent de-feminisation. *Economic and Political Weekly, 48*(31), 99–108.

Allport, G. W. (1958). *The nature of prejudice*. New York: Garden City.

Altamirano-Jimenez, I. (2013). *Indigenous encounters with neoliberalism: Place, women and the environment in Canada and Mexico*. Vancouver: UBC Press.

Asadullah, M. N., & Yalonetzky, G. (2010). *Inequality of educational opportunity in India: Changes over time and across states*. Retrieved from http://ftp.iza.org/dp5146.pdf.

Asian Development Bank. (2013). *India: Gender equality diagnostic of selected sectors*. Manila: ADB. Retrieved from https://www.adb.org/sites/default/files/institutional-document/33970/files/india-gender-equality-diagnostic.pdf.

Balakrishnan, R. (2005). *Rural women and food security in Asia and the Pacific: Prospects and paradoxes*. Bangkok: Food and Agricultural Organisation, Regional Office for Asia and the Pacific.

Banerjee, A., & Piketty, T. (2005). Top Indian incomes 1922–2000. *The World Bank Economic Review, 19*(1), 1–20.

Bhagat, R. B. (2013). Conditions of SC/ST households: A story of unequal improvement. *Economic and Political Weekly, 48*(41), 62–66.

Braveman, P. (2014). What are health disparities and health equity? We need to be clear. *Public Health Reports, 129*(2), 5–8.

Braveman, P. & Gruskin, S. (2003). Defining equity in health. *Journal of Epidemiology and Community Health, 57*, 254–258.

Chakravarty, M. (2016). *Just how high is income inequality in India*. Retrieved from http://www.livemint.com/Opinion/JKZYjYjixRipa95tw2AOXK/Just-how-high-is-income-inequality-in-India.html.

Chakravarty, P., & Dehejia, V. (2016). *India's curious case of economic divergence*. Mumbai: IDFC Institute.

Chaudhuri, S., & Gupta, N. (2009). Levels of living and poverty patterns: A district-wise analysis for India. *Economic and Political Weekly, 44*(9), 94–110.

Chhibber, A., Ghosh, J., & Palanivel, T. (2009). *The global financial crisis and the Asia-Pacific region: A synthesis study incorporating evidence from country case studies*. UNDP Regional Centre for Asia and the Pacific, Colombo. Retrieved from www.indiaenvironmentporal.org.in/files/p116.pdf.

Commission on Social Determinants of Health. (2008). *Closing the gap in a generation: Health equity through action on the social determinants of health*. Geneva: World Health Organization.

Dabla-Norris, E., Kochhar, K., Suphaphiphat, N., Ricka, F., & Tsounta, E. (2015). *Causes and consequences of income inequality: A global perspective*. Washington, D.C.: IMF Staff Discussion Note.

Das, P. (2012). Wage inequality in India: Decomposition by sector, gender and activity status. *Economic and Political Weekly, 47*(50), 58–64.

Davis, K., & Moore, W. E. (1945). Some principles of stratification. *American Sociological Review, 10*(2), 242–249.

Davison, S., & Shire, G. (2015). *Race, migration and neoliberalism: How neoliberalism benefits from discourses of exclusion*. Retrieved from https://www.questia.com/magazine/1P3-3697090941/race-migration-and-neoliberalism.

Dejardin, A. K., & Owens, J. (2009). *Asia in the global economic crisis: Impacts and responses from a gender perspective*. Paper presented all ILO workshop on responding to the economic crisis-coherent policies for growth, employment and decent work in Asia and Pacific, Manila, Philippines.

Desai, S., & Kulkarni, V. (2008). Changing educational inequalities in India in the context of affirmative action. *Demography, 45*(2), 245–270.

Deshpande, R., & Palshikar, S. (2008). Occupational mobility: How much does caste matter? *Economic and Political Weekly, 43*(34), 61–70.

Deshpande, S. (2003). Caste inequalities in India today. In S. Deshpande (Ed.), *Contemporary India: A sociological view*. Penguin, New Delhi. Retrieved from http://cscs.res.in/dataarchive/textfiles/textfile.2009-08-19.3842312690/file.

Djurfeldt, G., Athreya, V., Jayakumar, N., Lindberg, S., Rajagopal, A., & Vidyasagar, R. (2008). Agrarian change and social mobility in Tamil Nadu. *Economic and Political Weekly, 43*(45), 50–61.

Eapen, M., Jeyaranjan, J., Harilal, N., Swaminathan, P., & Kanji, N. (2003). *Liberalisation, gender and livelihoods: The cashew nut case*. London: International Institute for Environment and Development.

Engel, S., & Martin, B. (2015). Challenging economic inequality: Tactics and stratgies. *Economic and Political Weekly, 50*(49), 42–48.

EQUINET Steering Committee. (2004). *Policy paper 15: Reclaiming the state: Advancing people's health, challenging injustice*. Harare: EQUINET.

Fraser, N. (2013). *How feminism became capitalism's handmaiden—And how to reclaim it*. Retrieved from https://www.theguardian.com/commentisfree/2013/oct/14/feminism-capitalist-handmaiden-neoliberal.

Goffman, E. (1963). *Stigma: Notes on the management of spoiled identity*. New York: Simon and Schuster In.

Government of India. (2012). *Report of the 59th standing committee on finance (2011–12), current economic situation and policy options*. New Delhi: Ministry of Finance.

Government of India. (2014). *Report of the high-level committee on the socio-economic, health and educational status of tribal communities in India*. New Delhi: Ministry of Tribal Affairs.

Guru, G. (2016). Shifting categories in the discourse on caste and class. *Economic and Political Weekly, 51*(47), 21–25.

Harvey, D. (2005). *History of neoliberalism*. New York: Oxford University Press.

Hershey, R. A. (2012). *Globalization and its special and significant impacts on indigenous communities*. Arizona Legal Studies Discussion Paper No 12–19, University of Arizona.

Hnatkovska, V., Lahiri, A., & Paul, S. B. (2013). Breaking the caste barrier: Intergenerational mobility in India. *Human Resources, 48*(2), 435–473.

International Forum on Globalization. (2011). *Globalization: Effects on indigenous people*. Retrieved from http://www.choike.org/nuevo_eng/informes/1755.html.

Jayaraj, D., & Subramanian, S. (2013). On the inter-group inclusiveness of India's consumption expenditure growth. *Economic and Political Weekly, 48*(10), 65–70.

Juego, B., & Schmidt, J. D. (2009). *The political economy of the global crisis: Neo-liberalism, financial crises, and emergent authoritarian liberalism in Asia*. Paper presented at the Fourth

Asian Political and International Studies Association [APISA] Congress—Asia in the Midst of Crises: Political, economic, and social Dimensions, Manila, Philippines.
Kapur, D., Prasad, C. B., Pritchett, L., & Babu, S. D. (2010). Rethinking inequality: Dalits in UP in the market reform era. *Economic and Political Weekly, 45*(35), 39–49.
Kersley, R., & Stierli, M. (2015). *Global wealth in 2015: Underlying trends remain positive, credit suisse*. Retrieved from https://www.credit-suisse.com/us/en/about-us/research/research-institute/news-and-videos/articles/news-and-expertise/2015/10/en/global-wealth-in-2015-underlying-trends-remain-positive.html.
Kohler-Hausmann, I. (2010). *Discrimination*. Oxford Bibliographies. Retrieved from http://www.oxfordbibliographies.com/view/document/obo-9780199756384/obo-9780199756384-0013.xml.
Kohli, A. (2006). Politics of economic growth in India, 1980–2005. Part II. The 1990s and beyond. *Economic and Political Weekly, 41*(14), 1361–1370.
Kothari, R. (1997). Rise of the Dalits and the renewed debate on caste. In C. Patha (Ed.), *State and politics in India*. New Delhi: Oxford University Press.
Kotz, D. M. (2015). *The rise and fall of neoliberal capitalism*. USA: Harvard University Press.
Kumar, U., & Subramanian, A. (2012). Growth in India's states in the first decade of the 21st century: Four facts. *Economic and Political Weekly, 47*(3), 48–57.
Kuznets, S. (1955). Economic growth and income inequality. *American Economic Review, 45*(1), 1–28.
Lucas, R. E. (2004). *The industrial revolution: Past and future*. Retrieved from https://minneapolisfed.org/publications/the-region/the-industrial-revolution-past-and-future.
Mander, H. (2004). *The ripped chest, public policy and the poor in India*. Bangalore: Books for Change.
Marmot, M. (2015). *The Health gap: The challenge of an unequal world*. London: Bloomsbury Publishing.
Martin, N. (2015). Rural elites and limits to SC assertiveness in rural Malwa, Punjab. *Economic and Political Weekly, 50*(52), 37–44.
Mathew, S. S. (2012). Distress-driven employment and feminisation of work in Kasargod district, Kerala. *Economic and Political Weekly, 47*(26&27), 65–73.
Meher, R. (2009). Globalization, displacement and the livelihood issues of tribal and agriculture dependent poor people: The case of mineral-based industries in India. *Journal of Developing Societies, 25*, 457–480. doi:10.1177/0169796X0902500403.
Motiram, S., & Singh, A. (2012). How close does the apple fall to the tree. Some evidence from India on intergenerational mobility. *Economic and Political Weekly, 47*(40), 56–65.
Navsarjan Trust and RFK Centre for Justice and Human Rights. (2010). *Understanding untouchability: A comprehensive study of practices and conditions in 1589 villages*. Surat and Washington, DC: Navsarjan Trust and RFK Centre for Justice and Human Rights. Retrieved from www.indianet.nl/pdf/UnderstandingUntouchability.pdf.
NITI Aayog. (2016). *Under five mortality in India*. Retrieved from http://niti.gov.in/content/under-5-mortality-rate-u-5mr-1000-live-births.
Oxfam International. (2016). *An economy for the 1%. How power and privilege in the economy drive extreme inequality and how this can be stopped*. 210 Oxfam Briefing Paper. Oxford, Oxfam International. Retrieved from https://www.oxfam.org/sites/www.oxfam.org/files/file_attachments/bp210-economy-one-percent-tax-havens-180116-en_0.pdf.
Palriwala, R. (2005). Dowry and globalised capitalism. In *Globalization and the women's movement in India. Delhi*. Retrieved from http://www.cwds.ac.in/wp-content/uploads/2016/09/GlobalisationReport.pdf.
People's Health Movement—India. (2007). *Indian women's health charter*. Retrieved from http://phm-india.org/index.php?option=com_content&view=category&layout=blog&id=12&Itemid=4.
Piketty, T. (2014). *Capital in the twenty-first century*. Cambridge, Massachusetts: The Belknap Press of Harvard University Press.
Piketty, T., & Qian, N. (2009). Income inequality and progressive income taxation in China and India, 1986–2015. *American Economic Journal: Applied Economics, 1*(2), 53–63.

Pikherit, D. (2015). Dalit mobilization and faction politics in rural Andhra Pradesh: Everyday life of a Dalit NGO and Agricultural Labour Union. *Economic and Political Weekly, 50*(52), 74–82.
Purewal, N. (2016). *Neoliberal patrimony in Modi's India*. Presentation at SSAI panel discussion: 'Assessing Modi's track record eighteen months on'. Retrieved from https://www.soas.ac.uk/south-asia-institute/events/file107717.pdf.
Rajan, R. G. (2010). *Fault lines, how hidden fractures still threaten the world economy*. New Jersey, USA: Princeton University Press.
Rahman, L., & Rao, V. (2004). The determinants of gender equity in India: Examining Dyson and Moore's thesis with new data. *Population and Development Review, 30*(2), 239–268.
Rao, S. (2014). *Women and the economy in India: Insights from the data on MIGRATION*. Massachusetts: Brenden University. Retrieved from https://www.aeaweb.org/conference/2015/retrieve.php?pdfid=1002.
Ravallion, M. (2000). Should poverty measures be anchored to national accounts? *Economic and Political Weekly, 35*(35/36), 3245–3252.
Registrar General of India. (2011). *Census of India, 2011*. New Delhi: Ministry of Home Affairs.
Sarkar, S., & Mehta, B. S. (2010). Income inequality in India: Pre- and post-reform periods. *Economic and Political Weekly, 45*(37), 45–55.
Seguino, S. (2009). *The global economic crisis, its gender implications and policy responses*. Paper prepared for gender perspectives on the financial crisis panel at the fifty-third session of the commission on the status of women, United Nations.
Sen, A., & Himanshu. (2005). *Poverty and inequality in India: Getting closer to the truth. Data and dogma: The great Indian poverty debate*. New Delhi: Macmillan. Retrieved from http://www.networkideas.org/featart/may2004/Poverty_WC.pdf.
Sengupta, A., & Das, P. (2014). Gender wage discrimination across social and religious groups in India: Estimates with unit level data. *Economic and Political Weekly, 49*(21), 71–76.
Sengupta, A., Kannan, K. P., & Raveendran, G. (2008). India's common people: Who are they, how many are they and how do they live? *Economic and Political Weekly, 43*(11), 49–64.
Singh, S. B. (2016). Living together separately: Dalits in an emergent collectivity in a Rajasthan Village. *Economic and Political Weekly, 51*(33), 65–72.
Stiglitz, J. E. (2012). *The price of inequality: How today's divided society endangers our future*. New York: Norton & Co. Retrieved from https://www.theguardian.com/business/2012/jun/05/price-of-inequality-united-states.
Solar, O., & Irwin, A. (2010). A conceptual framework for action on the social determinants of health. *Social Determinants of Health Discussion Paper 2 (Policy and Practice)*. Geneva: World Health Organization, p. 6.
Sood, A. (2016). Politics of growth-script and post script. *Economic and Political Weekly, 51*(29), 56–60.
Teltumbde, A. (2010). *The persistence of caste: The Khairlanji murders and India's hidden apartheid*. London: Zed.
Thorat, S. (2007). *Human poverty and socially disadvantaged groups in India*. New Delhi: UNDP. Retrieved from http://www.undp.org/content/dam/india/docs/human_poverty_socially_disadvantaged_groups_india.pdf.
Thorat, S., & Sabharwal, S. (2010). *Caste and social exclusion: Issues related to concept, indicators and measurement*. New Delhi: Indian Institute of Dalit Studies and UNICEF.
Thorat, S., & Sadana, N. (2009). Caste and ownership of private enterprises. *Economic and Political Weekly, 44*(23), 13–16.
Topalova, P. (2008). *India: Is the rising tide lifting all boats*. IMF working paper 08/54. Retrieved from http://www.imf.org/external/pubs/cat/longres.aspx?sk=21767.0.
United Nations. (2009). *State of the world's indigenous people 2009*. New York: United Nations, Department of Economic and Social Affairs.
United Nations. (2016). *The sustainable development goals report*. New York: United Nations. https://unstats.un.org/sdgs/report/2016/The%20Sustainable%20Development%20Goals%20Report%202016.pdf.

United Nations Children's Fund. (2011). *Global inequality: Beyond the bottom billion—A rapid review of income distribution in 141 countries*. New York: UNICEF.

United Nations Development Programme. (2016). *Human development report*. New York: UNDP.

United Nations High Commissioner for Human Rights. (1976). *International covenant on economic, social and cultural rights*. Geneva: UNHCHR. Retrieved from: http://www2.ohchr.org/english/law/cescr.htm.

Unni, J., & Raveendran, G. (2007). Growth of employment (1993-94 to 2004-05): Illusion of inclusiveness. *Economic and Political Weekly, 42*(3), 196–199.

Uraguchi, Z. B. (2010). Food price hikes, food security, and gender equality: Assessing the roles and vulnerability of women in households of Bangladesh and Ethiopia. *Gender and Development, 18*(3), 491–501.

Vaidyanathan, A. (2014). Some notes in the Indian economy in crisis. *Economic and Political Weekly, 49*(24), 108–117.

Vakulabharanam, V. (2010). Does class matter? Class structure and worsening inequality in India. *Economic and Political Weekly, 45*(29), 67–76.

Vakulabharanam, V., & Motiram, S. (2012). Understanding poverty and inequality in urban India since reforms. *Economic and Political Weekly, 47*(47&48), 44–52.

Vijayabhaskar, M., & Kalaiyarasan, A. (2014). Caste as social capital: The Tiruppurstory. *Economic and Political Weekly, 49*(10), 34–38.

Wagstaff, A., Bredenkamp, C., & Buisman, L. R. (2014). Progress on global health goals: Are the poor being left behind? *World Bank Research Observer, 29,* 137–162.

Wallerstein, I. (1974). *The modern world system: Capitalist agriculture and the origins of the European world-economy in the sixteenth century*. New York: Academic Press.

Wallerstein, I. (2000). *The essential Wallerstein*. New York: The New Press.

Weisskopf, T. E. (2011). Why worry about inequality in the booming Indian economy? *Economic and Political Weekly, 46*(47), 41–51.

Whitehead, M., & Dahlgren, G. (2006). *Concepts and principles for tackling social inequities in health: Levelling up Part 1*. Copenhagen: World Health Organization, Regional Office for Europe.

Wilkinson, R., & Pickett, K. (2009). *The spirit level: Why greater equality makes societies stronger*. New York: Bloomsbury Press.

World Economic Forum. (2015). *The global gender gap 2015*. Geneva: WEF.

World Economic Forum. (2016). *It's time to demolish the myth of trickle-down economics*. Retrieved from https://www.weforum.org/agenda/2016/07/it-s-time-to-demolish-the-myth-of-trickle-down-economics/.

World Health Organization. (2013). *Handbook on health inequality monitoring with a focus on low and middle income countries*. Geneva: WHO.

Chapter 2
Conceptual Approaches to Examining Health Inequities

Rakhal Gaitonde

Abstract This chapter maps key conceptual frameworks in the study of health inequities. Using the dominant approach in the public health literature termed the *risk factor* approach as a reference point; the chapter highlights the key critiques of this approach. These key critiques include the differentiation between the *causes of disease* and the *causes of causes*, the demand to move from demonstrating associations to exploring and defining mechanisms and a critical interrogation of the labels being used. Through a mapping of various frameworks drawn from diverse fields, the chapter presents conceptual approaches which contribute to the filling of these critical gaps in the mainstream public health literature. The chapter ends by identifying the recently articulated frameworks like the ecosocial theory and the intersectionality lens as having attempted to engage with health inequities in a more nuanced fashion and with more depth, and as representing the best conceptual theories we have presently to research this area. We ask in the review and critique that forms the core chapters of the book, how this literature and these frameworks have informed the research being reviewed? We also ask how these insights can help make newer sense by reading across the research in an attempt to delineate what the present literature implies about possible mechanisms as well as gaps in research.

Keywords Conceptual framework · Risk factor approaches
Ecosocial theory · Intersectionality · Social determinants of health

2.1 Introduction

Inequity in health by class, race/ethnicity, gender and other axes of power is well established. Inequity has been shown to be present not only in health outcomes, but also in terms of access to health services including in the design of healthcare

R. Gaitonde (✉)
Centre for Technology and Policy (CTaP) IIT-M, Chennai, India
e-mail: rakhal.gaitonde@gmail.com

T.K.S. Ravindran and R. Gaitonde (eds.), *Health Inequities in India*,
https://doi.org/10.1007/978-981-10-5089-3_2

programmes, the availability of health services, the quality of the services provided as well as the investments in and governance of health systems. Thus data today is characterised by increasing divergences along a number of axes (Baru, 2010; Balarajan, Selvaraj, & Subramanian, 2011). Studies have also explored the consequences of societal inequity and health along various axes and of various dimensions upon individuals, groups and of society as a whole (Whitehead, 2000).

The literature provides a large number of approaches to the research on health inequity. These include studies from the perspective of epidemiology and public health; the newly emergent field of social epidemiology; and from various social sciences approaches. In this chapter, I bring together some key conceptual approaches that have engaged with health inequity. The chapter thus also provides the basis to reflect on the theoretical underpinnings of the literature reviewed.

2.1.1 Research on the Causes of Inequity: A Brief Overview

The recognition of health inequity and its roots in social hierarchies and power differentials is well documented historically. Engels and Rudolph Virchow in the nineteenth century were early precursors (Birn, 2009). Both documented the poor health outcomes among the working class and among the poor living in rural areas, and traced these differentials to their living and working conditions. These early studies done during the pre-germ theory era focused on the larger macro-level observable determinants, and set the tone for subsequent work on health inequities. Subsequent research, however, took a more individualistic turn, probably due to the dominance of the germ theory and the emergent bio-medical view of health and disease.

In India, prior to independence and especially during the discussions on the nature of health systems to be set up in post-independent India, there was recognition of poor health *achievement* among the poor. The British attributed *backwardness* and *traditions* for the very high maternal mortality among Indians. Nationalist leaders on the other hand attributed these poor outcomes to the British rule. These debates continued during the planning of the health systems in newly independent India. The presence of inequity among the population at the time of independence made the reduction of inequity—especially the adverse health outcomes of the marginalised groups a major expressed priority of the government (Amrith, 2007).

Post World War II, the setting up of welfare states in Europe and the Americas paralleled a significant reduction in health inequities by socio-economic classes. However, the need for using multiple approaches to studying inequities in health became apparent by the findings that showed graded health outcomes in the United Kingdom despite universal health care provided through NHS (Blane, 1985). Across the Atlantic in the USA, yearly reviews of statistics on race and class played a similar role to highlight inequity (Krieger, 2012).

In the field of economics there is emerging consensus that the mere presence of or access to an equal set of resources is not sufficient to reduce inequity. Recent theories, particularly Sen's (1999) capability approach interrogate the capacity of individuals and the community to convert these resources or access to resources into actual benefit. According to the capability approach people are able to translate various personal endowments into welfare only if they possess so-called *conversion factors*. Based on this, it is suggested that, "people are only able to turn the financial compensation and other incentives provided by the welfare state into health benefits if they have the right resources (private household or public welfare) at their disposal to do so" (Beckfield et al., 2015, p. 234).

Another major strand is the re-conceptualisation of health equity by linking it with justice. Thus, Whitehead considers health inequity as something unnecessary, avoidable and unjust (Whitehead, 2000). Other scholars link inequity to human rights and social justice (Braveman & Gruskin, 2003), or alternatively to the distribution of power in society (Farmer, 2004). The deepening and sharpening of inequities are also linked to globalisation and particularly the neo-liberal paradigm as described in the first chapter (Kim, Millen, Irwin, & Gershman, 2000; Keshavjee, 2014).

2.1.2 Overview of the Chapter

In my reading of the literature, I perceive a dominant *risk factor approach* which draws largely on the definition of individual risk factors which, "has been concerned with associations—and ultimately causal connections and biologic pathways —between individual-level data and (1) social position (especially in relation to social class, race/ethnicity, and gender) and (2) health status (Beckfield & Krieger, 2009, p. 153)." The *risk factor* approach establishes associations between health outcomes and individual characteristics and stops there. Such an approach is reflected in the research conducted after the Black report and summarised in the book *Health Inequality* by Bartley (2004). While the approach has been critiqued extensively, there are three broad strands of the literature which seem to engage with the aspects neglected by the risk factor approach.

One of the key gaps in the *risk factor* approach has been the absence of adequate engagement with the multi-level problem. It was Geoffery Rose who pointed out the difference between *causes of diseases* and the *causes of causes* (Rose, 2001). The second major gap of the risk factor approach was the failure to engage with the concept of *mechanisms* (Bunge, 2004), as distinct from association. These two broad critiques underlined that it was important not only to have some idea about larger macro-level determinants but equally important to theorise about the actual processes or mechanisms that impact health outcomes. Theorising was essential to understand and act upon the phenomenon of health inequity in different settings. Very few approaches engage simultaneously with issues of macro-level determinants as well as mechanisms (at all levels).

The third key critique was with reference to the way labels such as *race* were used in health research. The critique pointed out that it was crucial to understand what a particular label such as race represented in the research study, whether the label was static over time and space (Beckfield & Krieger, 2009; Guru, 2016) and whether it represented a category, a process or a system of production of oppression such as racism (Dhamoon, 2011).

This chapter presents the main body of research that represents the dominant *risk factor* approach in public health (and its various attempts to engage with the critiques) as well as the key conceptual approaches that in my mind have addressed or attempted to address the key critiques noted above. Thus this chapter does not attempt to provide a comprehensive review of the conceptual and theoretical landscape, and is not a chronological journey. It is more a mapping of key ideas put forth by those who engaged with the question of health inequity from the perspective of this author.

2.2 The Public Health Approach

2.2.1 The Black Report and After

Globally the systematic study of disparities in health within nations came to the fore with the Black Report produced by the United Kingdom in 1980. The Black Report led to tremendous debate for its demonstration of a graded inequality throughout British society. One reason for the reaction was the fact that the remarkable institution NHS which provided free services of high quality to all who accessed it for nearly 20 years did not seem to have made an impact on inequity (Bartley, 2004). In the report the authors described the existing inequities and discussed various possible mechanisms that contributed to the inequities (Blane, 1985). The authors of the Black Report had their own opinions on the causes of health inequities but their discussion set off a long and continuing debate on the mechanisms underlying the creation of health inequities. However, this debate has been fuelled by research that was conducted largely in the traditional epidemiological and public health frameworks and relied mostly on the ability to demonstrate associations using regression analysis.

The Black Report and initial explanations suggested by the report led to the establishment of at least five distinct bodies of research on health inequity as described in a book authored by Bartley. In this section, I will describe the main perspectives of each of these explanations. A detailed critique of each of these is beyond the scope of this chapter and for those interested a very good starting point is the monograph by Mel Bartley referred to earlier (Bartley, 2004).

These are

- the materialist explanations.
- the cultural-behavioural explanations.

- the psychosocial explanations.
- the life cycle based explanations.
- the neo-materialist explanations.

2.2.2 The Materialist Explanations[1]

The materialist explanations simply link various forms of deprivation and inequality in material assets to having an impact on the health of the individual. These were referred to in the Black Report as the, "diffuse consequences of the class structure" which lists various forms of deprivation like "poverty, work conditions and at home" (Black, Morris, & Townsend, 1982). While the material explanations are almost intuitive, what is a challenge to this set of explanations is the almost monotonous and even fine gradation in the health outcomes, when disaggregated along measures of socio-economic status like income quintiles or consumption expenditure. Some authors have come up with explanations based on what they term *organisational resources*, which refer to the differences in power and the consequent differences in exposure to multiple hazards and events in the work place (Wright, 1985).

Scientists have also questioned whether *purely material* advantages will result in such finely graded yet prominent health differences. Some authors talk about the context in which this money is spent as a crucial factor. Money can buy different amounts of things in different contexts (Coburn, 2000). Thus it may well be that such material gaps result not from the fact that there is not enough money per se, but because money spent on goods needed for social acceptability may compete with the amounts available for spending on basic biological needs (Bartley, 2004).

2.2.3 The Cultural–Behavioural Explanations

While this was one of the explanations suggested in the original Black Report, most research does not seem to have convincingly presented why there may be systematic differences in behaviour between social classes (Bartley, 2004). Concepts such as the locus of control (Bosma, Mheen, & Mackenbach, 1999), Bourdieu's concept of *habitus* have been invoked to explain the way in which systematic differences in behaviour may occur in different groups of people, which in turn may affect their health (Williams, 1995). A key idea that emerges from this body of work is what has been called the achievement of the *central social role* as defined by a

---

[1]We draw on Mel Bartley's Book Health Inequality for descriptions of these five approaches.

particular society (Siegrist, 2000). In this case, it is postulated that all efforts are made to *achieve* or *perform* this role to feel a part of society. Thus, instances where this is not possible such as unemployment for men (whose social role is that of the bread winner), are supposed to lead to negative or even self-destructive behaviours.

These sets of explanations also encompass the notion of shared lifestyles, with community-level adoption of certain behaviours based on the norms evolved in a particular setting, which may vary systematically between groups.

2.2.4 The Psychosocial Explanation

The key psychosocial risk factors that have been suggested and researched include—social support, control and autonomy, and balance between efforts and rewards both at home and at work.

The psychosocial explanation links these *stressors* sometimes even called the *allostatic load*, with allostasis referring to the processes of the body to keep itself in a stable state (McEwen, 1998), especially through the activation of the hypothalamo–pituitary axis, leading to an increase in the secretion of glucocorticoids. This persistent or over-stimulation of the HPA is suggested as a cause for an increase in a range of disorders based on an activation of the inflammatory process (Brunner, 1997).

2.2.5 The Life Cycle Approach

The life cycle approach identifies particularly vulnerable points during the life cycle when exposure to hazards will produce particularly long-lasting effects. Deprivations and exposure to hazards during these periods are purported to accumulate over the life time and produce harmful effects even after the situation for the individual changed for the better. This explanation sets out to include the historically accumulated negative events and their effect on the overall health of the individual (Bartley, 2004).

2.2.6 Neo-materialist Explanations

This set of explanations look at the context within which processes causing inequities in health take place, and suggest that countries that provide more public funding for basic welfare than others, may have less inequity. In other words, while within countries materialist explanations concentrate on the relationship of income and what it can buy to health of individuals, neo-materialist explanations concentrate on the relationship of public provision such as schools and transport to health of everyone in a country.

A response to the above theories noted that

> The materialist, cultural-behavioural and psychosocial approaches can help to understand why some people have better or worse health than others when compared within societies. However, without considering these individual- or house- hold-level causes in institutional context, they are of limited utility in explaining why some of these individual-level determinants should vary in their frequency or in their effects across institutional contexts. That is, given a distribution of the social determinants of health and a set of class relations, materialist, cultural-behavioural and psychosocial approaches identify processes that translate these distributions into health outcomes, but these theoretical approaches tend not to problematise the distribution itself. They are also less well equipped to explain how the same individual or household-level causes vary in their effects across institutional settings (Beckfield et al., 2015, p. 230).

2.3 The Key Critiques

2.3.1 Geoffery Rose—The Causes of the Causes

Rose noted that the causes of the occurrence of the disease in an individual (the individual-level risk factors currently studied in epidemiology) were quite different from the determinants of the distribution of the disease at a societal level (Rose, 2001). We needed to consider multi-level factors to understand the issue of health inequity. This insight also underlined many theories that went beyond the individualistic approach to focus on the way macro-level issues impacted on the distribution of factors leading to the observed patterns of inequity. While socio-economic position, wealth, education, etc. could be associated with health inequities, theories of the *public health approach* did not yet answer the questions of why differences in wealth, education or status arose in the first place.

Association of the individual-level risk factor to the presence of the disease depended crucially on the population-level distribution of the risk factor itself. For example, if hypothetically everyone in a population had a high school education, *high school education* would never emerge as a risk factor even if it were a mechanism of individual risk. Rose further argued the importance of clearly differentiating what he termed as, "causes of disease" from the "causes of causes" (Rose, 2001). While the causes of the disease referred to the individual-level risk factors, the causes of causes he suggested should refer to the determinants of the distribution of these risk factors. These would not be discernible by studies at the individual level, and perforce required studies to look at higher levels. This was the first time the idea of thinking about levels (individual to multi-level) was applied to epidemiological theory and public health issues.

2.3.2 Mechanisms—The Causes of the Causes of the Causes

Even as there was a move from individual-level thinking to multi-level thinking there was a strong move to explore the actual processes involved in the translation of these statistical associations into the lived reality of societal-level inequity. Towards this Mario Bunge's contribution is significant. By formulating the concept of *systemism* and *mechanism*, he made a huge theoretical leap in the philosophy underlying the journey for the study of health inequity (Bunge, 2004).

Mario Bunge defines a system as something that consists of the following components (the CESM model). The environmental parts that act upon the system or are acted upon by the system; the structure or set of relationships that tie the various components of the system together; and the mechanisms or "characteristic processes" of a given system (Bunge, 2004). What is crucial for the conceptual progress in thinking of health inequity is the tying together of the concept of mechanism and a system. By mechanism he meant, "a process (or sequence of states, or pathway) in a concrete system, natural or social" (p. 186). He further notes that most mechanisms are concealed and thus they cannot be easily observed and measured and have in most cases, to be conjectured. It is this tying together of mechanism and a system that he terms *systemism* (Bunge, 2004).

Bunge's definition of mechanism in social sciences is best elaborated in his own words

> Note that our definition pre-supposes a distinction between system and mechanism: the latter is a process in a system. This distinction is familiar in natural science, where one is not expected to mistake, say, the cardiovascular system for the circulation of the blood or the brain with mental processes. But it is unusual in the social studies.... Mechanism is to system as motion is to body, combination (or dissociation) to chemical compound, and thinking to brain. [In the systemic view], agency is both constrained and motivated by structure, and in turn the latter is maintained or altered by individual action. In other words, social mechanisms reside neither in persons nor in their environment - they are part of the processes that unfold in or among social systems.... All mechanisms are system specific, there is no such thing as a universal or substrate-neutral mechanism (Pickel, 2004, p. 176).

To me the concept of mechanism of Bunge has a lot of parallel to the concept of embodiment of Krieger that we discuss later on. His concept of systems and systemism in many ways is parallel to the challenge put forth in the research using the intersectionality framework when they ask us to differentiate between using the label as a category, referring to a process or representing a whole system of oppression (and reproduction of that oppression). Both these are discussed in detail in subsequent sections.

2.3.3 Destabilising Labels

One of the key developments of the research approaches to inequity has been the invocation of the concept of intersectionality. As mentioned above not only did this development destabilise labels as such—with the demonstration of heterogeneity in what were earlier considered homogenous entities/groups. Another key issue with regard to these labels is the question on whether their meaning is stable over time and place? This line of questioning is very critical to the study socially constructed and at the same time socially challenged labels like caste in India (Guru, 2016). As Guru argues

> First, in times of globalisation, categories such as caste and class are undergoing radical change both in terms of their essence and existence. Second, …., at the methodological level these categories have lost their conceptual coherence because they have acquired new, perhaps more amorphous, descriptions. [The] third hypothetical claim is that the change in existence is the result of the corresponding change in the essence of these categories (Guru, 2016, p. 21).

With reference to the label of class for example, it has been noted that health researchers have tended to conceptualise social class as "social groups arising from interdependent economic relationships among people set of attributes and material conditions of life of individuals" (Krieger, Williams, & Moss, 1997, p. 345). The empiricist tradition of class as an individual attribute equates class to, "an *observation*, precluding the investigation of unobservable social mechanisms underlying its creation" (Muntaner et al., 2013). A consequence of this view of social class is that it cannot be, "conceptualised, measured or intervened upon at the meso- or macro-levels. Thus, population health disciplines marginalise rich traditions in Marxist theory, whereby *class* is understood as a *hidden* social mechanism such as *exploitation*" (Muntaner et al., 2013).

In the next sections, I will present key theoretical frameworks that to me reflect this philosophical/conceptual journey charted above.

2.3.4 In Response—Moving to Multi-level Models

In response to the models that focussed on the individual level, a host of frameworks that emphasised the social production of disease emerged in the 70s and 80s. These including the *Political economy of health* approach had as their core postulate that

> any given society's patterning of health disease - including its social inequalities in health - is produced by the structure, values, and priorities of its political and economic systems, in conjunction with those of the political and economic systems of the other societies with which it interacts, and also the ensemble of available technologies (Krieger, 2011a, p. 167).

This broad strand of thinking drawing its inspiration from the earlier work of those such as Virchow and Engels led to a number of influential theories. These include, theories and approaches such as social production of disease/political economy of health; social determinants of health; fundamental cause; political epidemiology; Latin American social medicine; and health and human rights, which Kreiger (2011a) classifies together as socio-political frameworks/approaches.

2.3.4.1 The Political Economy of Health Model

This theory states that in the research on the production of health inequity our focus needs to be on the larger context which imposes many restrictions on choices made by individuals, for example, on lifestyles. Doyal, who gave one of the clearest statements on the theory and wrote a land mark book in 1979 goes on to say that

> It is the detailed examination of how the power of capital structures the context in which personal choices are made that must lie at the heart of a Marxist epidemiology. Only in this way can we make sense of the impact of living and working conditions, and pattern of social and economic relationships, on the health of individuals and groups, while at the same time creating the possibility of collective action to transform those conditions (Doyal, 1979, p. 296).

2.3.4.2 The Hopkins Model

The Hopkins Model was developed by Vincent Navarro and colleagues who attempted to develop a theory-driven strategy to study the occurrence of health inequities. This model was used to define and study various variables at different levels in an attempt to research inequity in Europe. As shown in the diagram, in essence the model hypothesises four different levels of study. The ultimate outcome studied was mortality (an individual-level variable). The systematic differences in mortality among groups was hypothesised as occurring through the action of social inequalities like income inequalities, wage policies and women's participation in the labour force. This was balanced by a range of factors that attempted to capture the functioning of the welfare state to overcome systematic disadvantage of groups. This set of factors included such variables as percentage educated, public provision of health, public housing, public versus private education, etc. At the next level, it was suggested that this balance between social inequalities and an effectively functioning welfare state depended on the society level solidarity and civic behaviour. This was measured by trust in government, corruption and cynicism. Finally this in turn was attempted to be explained by a range of factors that defined overall power relations in a society—these included electoral behaviour, the activity of trade unions, the type of bargaining agreements, etc. And also governance by different hues of political parties defined as liberal, liberal-Christian, communitarian, etc. (Navarro & Muntaner, 2004).

The Hopkins model not only brought in a multi-level approach, but also attempted to flesh out possible mechanisms based on Marxist theory. The other important contribution of this theory is its delineation of the contribution of politics to health inequity (Fig. 2.1).

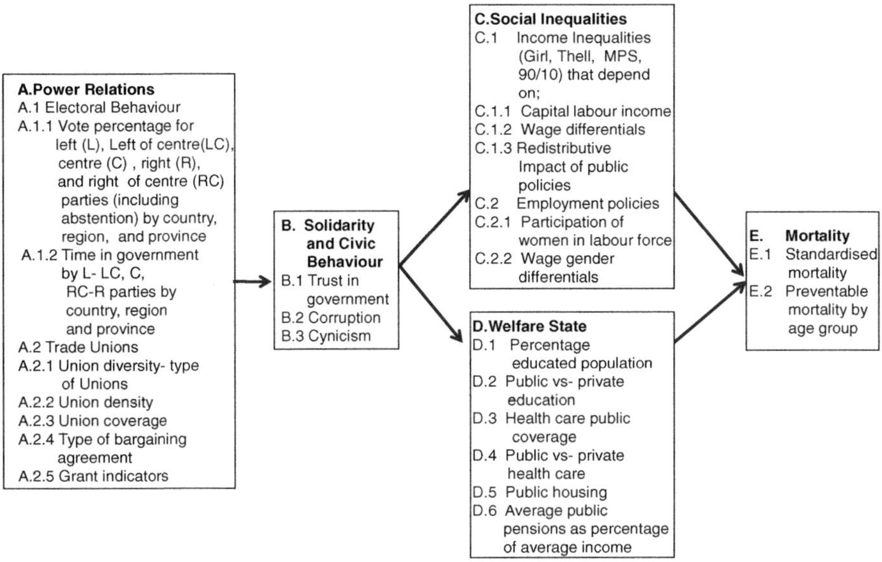

Fig. 2.1 The Hopkins model. Navarro (2004)

2.3.4.3 The Diederichsen Framework

An earlier framework from which the Committee on Social Determinants of Health (CSDH) framework draws on is that proposed by Diderichsen and others (Diderichsen, Evans, & Whitehead, 2001). It basically talks about the need for three levels of study.

- Individual risk factors associated with disease. These include age, sex, nutrition, consumption of alcohol, etc.
- These individual-level factors are seen to be clustered around *social position*.
- The distribution of *positions to occupy*; the entry into these *positions*; as well as the modifications of the impacts of occupying these positions are based on the *social context* in which individuals live and the research is being conducted.

The framework defines four mechanisms for the creation of health inequities, and thus four policy entry points for addressing these (Diderichsen et al., 2001).

The four mechanisms suggested are

- "Social stratification (I)
- Differential exposure (II)
- Differential vulnerability (III)
- Differential consequences (IV)"

And the four policy entry points being

- "Influencing social stratification (A)
- Decreasing exposures and vulnerability (B & C)
- Preventing unequal consequences of ill health (D)"

It may be noticed that entry points B, C and D are all functions of the health system, while A is concerned with advocacy that the health system needs to do, in the way of Health in ALL policies (for example).

2.3.4.4 The Framework of the Commission on the Social Determinants of Health

By far the most extensively discussed framework in the literature is the framework suggested by the Commission on Social Determinants of Health (CSDH). The CSDH framework is shown in Fig. 2.2.

There are three elements in the framework. The first element of the framework at the far left end—the structural determinants of health—consists of the macro, national level factors including governance, macroeconomic policies, social and public policies and cultural and societal values. The second element of the framework is social position, determined by social class, race/ethnicity, gender and factors determining socio-economic position such as education, occupation and income. The first element contributes to the second element and is in turn, influenced by it. The first and second elements are constituted of what we may call the *structural determinants* of health and health inequities.

The third element of the framework is constituted of the *intermediary determinants* of health and health inequities. These are factors such as material conditions within which individuals live and work, behavioural and biological factors,

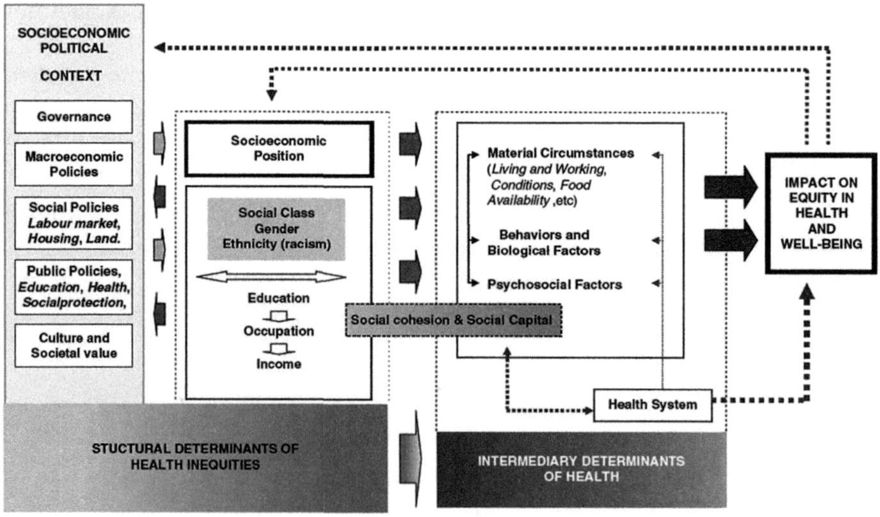

Fig. 2.2 The CSDH framework. Solar and Irwin (2010)

and social cohesion. Social position and its influence on access to resources and capabilities such as education and income influence these intermediary factors. The interaction results in differential exposure to risks of illness and differential vulnerability to health.

The health system is an important intermediary determinant of health. The affordability, access, acceptability and quality of the services delivered through the health system determine the distribution of health and well-being within a population (Sanneving, Trygg, Saxena, Mavalankar, & Thomsen, 2013).

While the CSDH report *Closing the gap in a generation* did indeed bring to prominence the critical role of the social determinants of health, the link to larger macro-level features of a system and the role of the health system as a crucial determinant, it has been criticised for not taking the theorisation far enough. Critics points out that while the report points out that inequality kills, in fact, "it is not inequalities that kill, but those who benefit from [and perpetuate] the inequalities that kill (Navarro, 2009, p. 15)." Similarly it was pointed out that there was no attempt in the report to examine why the policies that were advocated in the Alma-Ata declaration and were again reiterated in the CSDH report failed in the first place, and why nearly 30 years after Alma-Ata heath inequities were getting worse (Obregón, 2008; Irwin & Scali, 2005 as quoted Birn, 2009). Most importantly the critics point out that, "If the report echoes Virchow's understanding of the critical factors shaping health and disease—and does a magisterial job of documenting the existence and consequences of health inequity—it is unlike Virchow, profoundly apolitical (Navarro, 2009, p. 15)." The report did not say anything on what created inequity in the first place. In sum, while the CSDH framework did a lot to bring to fore the multi-level and the social determinants of health inequities, it did not do enough foreground an understanding of systems and root mechanisms that lead to health inequity in a society.

2.3.5 Link and Phelans' Fundamental Cause Theory

In contrast to the CSDH framework, Link and Phelans' fundamental cause theory talks specifically about the macro-factors and defines explicit social mechanisms.

> The theory suggests that the fundamental cause influences multiple disease outcomes, meaning that it is not limited to only one or a few diseases or health problems. Second, it affects these disease outcomes through multiple risk factors. Third, fundamental social causes involve access to resources that can be used to avoid risks or to minimise the consequences of disease once it occurs. Finally, the association between a fundamental cause and health is reproduced over time via the replacement of intervening mechanisms. It is their persistent effect on overall health in the face of dramatic changes in mechanisms that led us to call them *fundamental* (Phelan & Link, 2013, p. 106).

Deeming specific risk factors to be in the category of superficial causes, it instead emphasises, as fundamental causes, *flexible resources* including money, knowledge, power, prestige, and social support and social networks (Link & Phelan, 1996;

Phelan, Link, & Tehranifar, 2010). These key resources can be used no matter what the risk and protective factors are, in a given context. Because these resources can be used in different ways in different situations, they are referred to as flexible resources. According to the theory of fundamental causes, the reason that socio-economic position is related to multiple disease outcomes through multiple pathways that change over time is that individuals and groups deploy different sets of resources to avoid risks and adopt protective strategies, in different situations and contexts.

In a further addition to the Fundamental Cause theory, Freese suggests a set of four meta-mechanisms that help to further explicate the social mechanisms involved (Freese & Lutfey, 2011). These include the following—"the first metamechanism, *means,* overlaps most strongly with Link and Phelan's concept of resources. In this metamechanism, an individual purposefully uses his or her socio-economic resources, or means, to improve his or her health... *Spillovers* (the second metamechanism), described previously as contextual resources, occur when other people in an individual's social network purposefully use their resources to benefit their own health, and these efforts produce health benefits for the individual without any purposeful action on the individual's part... Freese and Lutfey's third metamechanism is *habitus*, whose role in health inequities was developed by Cockerham (2005). The fourth metamechanism lies in the actions of *institutions*. Lutfey and Freese refer here not to individuals' utilisation of or access to health-related institutions but to the agentic, dynamic action of institutions that treats people differentially according to their socio-economic positions in ways that affect health inequities" (Phelan & Link, 2013, p. 108).

2.3.6 Theories from Political Sociology

While the awareness of the role of political systems in health inequities is not new, the incorporation of this insight into research methods is relatively recent. The Hopkins Model suggested by Navarro and others is one good example of this approach. There are other theories in the broad field of political sociology that attempt to do this. This field has a different orientation as pointed out by Krieger who noted that "its orientation is in contrast to the more conventional epidemiologic approach of treating these categories and social relations as static *risk factors* construed as properties of an individual (Beckfield & Krieger, 2009, p. 153)." In this range of theories we find allusion to *welfare regimes*, *power constellations*, *varieties of capitalism* and *political-institutionalism of inequality* (Beckfield & Krieger, 2009). In this approach the welfare regimes refer to the three worlds of welfare capitalism—liberal, social-democratic and conservative (Esping-Andersen, 1990). Power constellations refer to the political parties in a central way (Moller, Huber, Stephens, Bradley, & Nielsen, 2003), varieties of capitalism refers to the "varied roles of employers and employees in welfare politics and policy within the context of international market competition" and the political institutional approach considers how, policy domains usually considered outside the realm of welfare economics, such as the penal system and the education system, also have implications for inequality (Beckfield & Krieger, 2009).

Social inequalities in health are persistent, but also vary, across time and geography. Building on research that documents this, recent research has focussed on the welfare state as a possible explanatory factor in the search for causes of health inequity. Such research posits an institutional theory that conceptualises the welfare state as an institutional arrangement—a set of *rules of the game*—that distributes health. "Drawing on this institutional approach in stratification scholarship, four mechanisms are hypothesised as connecting the welfare state to health inequalities by producing and modifying the effects of the social determinants of health. These mechanisms are: redistribution, compression, mediation and imbrication (or overlap)" (Beckfield et al., 2015).

This institutional theory, still undergoing development, suggests that inequality in some variable Y can be explained in part by institutional factors that (i) shift Y from people who have more Y to people who have less Y (or vice versa, through regressive taxation), (ii) limit how low or high Y can go for different population groups or (iii) affect other variables such as X that themselves affect Y and its *distribution* (Beckfield et al., 2015). These theories thus not only attempt to link the political context to the production of patterns of health-related inequity, but also attempt to tease out particular mechanisms as they identify specific aspects of this context to study.

2.3.6.1 In Summary—From Causes of Causes to Causes of Causes of Causes!

In his critique of the purely individual and risk factor based theorising, Geoffery Rose pointed out pithily the difference between the causes of the disease (risk factors at the individual level) and what he termed as "causes of causes" or the determinants of the distribution of disease in a given society. What is broadly referred to the social determinants approach (and includes the CSDH framework as its most recent iteration) viewed the social determinants of health as arising from a, *social environment*, "structured by government policies and status hierarchies, with social inequalities in health resulting from diverse groups being differently exposed to factors that influence health (Krieger, 2011a, p. 185)." Thus SDH represent the causes of causes of Rose.

As noted, the "social distribution of causes of causes is a function of institutional arrangements that vary systematically across societies. For example, collective bargaining institutions profoundly affect working conditions and unemployment, and welfare states structure access to goods, services, housing, health care and education by defining some and not others as among the social rights of citizenship... Thus, institutional arrangements explain not only the distribution of the social determinants of health, but also account for how and why the social determinants vary in their effects across institutional settings" (Beckfield et al., 2015, p. 235).

While the political economy approach was *political* in recognising political systems and power differentials, it was relatively silent on the biological pathways that linked these to patterns of inequity including the individual level. On the other hand, the CSDH framework and the Fundamental cause theory, talked explicitly about the biological (CSDH) and social mechanisms (fundamental cause theory), but crucially did not engage in political and economic analysis as to whose interested were being served by the inequities; nor did they draw attention to the pressure exerted by the status quo to reinforce existing inequities (Krieger, 2011a).

To counter the increasing tendency to focus solely on individual resources to the neglect of societal-level conflictual political-structural determinants of health inequities, some epidemiologists have begun to use the more expansive term, "societal determinants of health". Societal determinants of health are

> political-economic systems, whereby health inequities result from the promotion of the political and economic interests of those with power and privilege (within and across countries) against the rest, and whose wealth and better health is gained at the expense of those whom they subject to adverse living and working conditions; societal determinants of health thus become the causes of causes of causes (Kreiger et al., 2010, p. 748).

One theory that has attempted to take all of these criticisms into account is discussed next.

2.3.7 The Ecosocial Theory of Nancy Krieger

This is an epidemiological theory that attempts to systematise the inquiry into the societal distributions of health and determinants of health (Fig. 2.3).

> (The ecosocial theory) postulates that people literally incorporate the reality they live in, in their bodies. This occurs through various mechanisms that are determined by the distribution of power in the particular society. It exhorts us to ask "who or what drives the current and changing patterns of social inequities in health?" and speaks of both the accountability and agency of various actors (including the health system). The theory also stresses the fact that those who have knowledge and power to make decisions need to be held accountable for their stands or the lack of them (as the case may be) (Kreiger, 2011b, p. 215).

The core constructs of the theory refer to processes conditional upon extant political economy and political ecology. These include *embodiment* which refers to how we literally incorporate, biologically, in societal and ecological context, the material and social world we live in; *pathways of embodiment* which include a range of pathways including economic deprivation, exogenous hazards, degradation of ecosystems, targeted marketing of harmful substances, etc.; *cumulative interplay of exposure, susceptibility, and resistance across the life course* and *accountability and agency*, which refers to the responsibility of the researchers and those in power to make change to explain these inequities and make the necessary changes the players are empowered to (Krieger, 2011a).

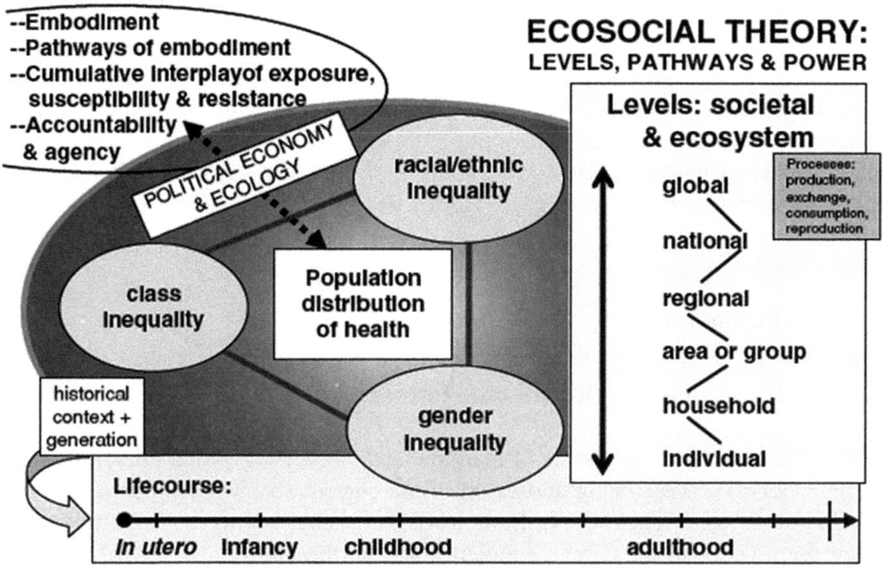

Fig. 2.3 The ecosocial theory framework. Krieger (2011b)

Apart from the core tenets referred to above the other tenets of the theory are (Krieger, 2011a)

- Determinants of current and changing social patterns of disease distribution, including health inequities are: (1) exogenous to people's bodies; (2) manifest at different levels and involve different spatiotemporal scales.
- Explanations of disease cannot be reduced solely to explanations of disease mechanisms, as the latter do not account for why rates and patterns change in complex ways over time and place.
- There needs to be a more reflexive epidemiology which situates the investigations motivating theories, hypothesis, analytical methods and interpretations of the investigator in the broader social context.

The ecosocial theory explicitly starts by striving to identify the drivers of the *causes of causes* by asking who or what drives the present distribution. Further by invoking the concept of embodiment it focuses on the mechanisms by which the social arrangements are imprinted on biology. There has been some interesting research that explicitly uses this theory, and such research is beginning to provide some insights into the way structures impact on biology. Thus in a recent study on immigrant's oral health the authors note, "Taking a critical medical anthropological approach, we argue that studies of embodiment must take into account the ways that socio-economic circumstances and public policies—not just culture—are physically embodied (Horton & Barker, 2010, p. 200)." In their study of oral health disparities among Mexican-American farm-worker children, Horton & Barker observe that the children's social vulnerability was physically embodied in the form of malformed arches and crooked teeth. An underfunded public health system and non-coverage of oral health by public insurance schemes cement the enduring effects of their social disadvantage, by creating a group whose bad teeth made them stand out as belonging to an underinsured class, finding their upward social mobility hindered by their distinctive bodily markings (Horton & Barker, 2010).

2.3.8 *Intersectionality*

2.3.8.1 Theoretical Considerations—Intersectionality

Born from the lived experiences of marginalised women who found that only parts of their identities were being addressed in the current social movements, intersectionality emerged as a key lens or framework that is challenging the mainstream *risk factor* approaches to the study of inequity and its theorisation.

Hankivsky notes that

> Intersectionality is concerned with bringing about a conceptual shift in how researchers, civil society, public health professionals and policy actors understand social categories, their relationships and interactions. It requires a consideration of the complex relationship between mutually constituting factors of social location and structural disadvantage so as to more accurately map and conceptualise determinants of equity and inequity in and beyond health (Hankivsky & Christoffersen, 2008, p. 18).

Researchers and activists who were intimately involved in women's struggles for basic livelihood, survival and dignity like those involved in the anti-race movement in US (Crenshaw, 1991; Purkayastha, Subramanian, Desai, & Bose, 2003) and in the various struggle for access to social resources in India in the 90 s argued against treating women as a homogenous entity and emphasised that it was crucial to grasp interactions of class, gender, caste, religion and regional specificities in order to understand the conditions of women and men (Purkayastha et al., 2003).

The key theoretical contributions of the concept of intersection of multiple axes are

> First, it changes the relationship between the categories of investigation from one that is determined a priori to one of empirical investigation … Second, intersectionality posits an interactive, mutually constitutive relationship among these categories and the way in which race (or ethnicity) and gender (or other relevant categories) play a role in the shaping of political institutions, political actors, the relationships between institutions and actors, and the relevant categories themselves (Hancock, 2007, p. 67).

Moreover, Hancock specifies that intersectionality is based on the idea that it was important to analyse more than one category; that individuals even within the same category were different; what no one category may be a priori considered as more important than the other; that the relationship between the different axes was to be understood through empirical investigation within a specific spatial and temporal location; that there existed a dynamic interaction between individual and institutional factors, because of which the analysis of one should be integrated with the analysis of the other (Hancock, 2007).

Both the race and *dalit* critiques of the universalising nature/aspects of feminism have questioned the erasure of lived experience from what is considered the universal norm, usually derived from a dominant groups or frameworks like *white women* or *brahminical institutions*. Both have demanded that such categories be kept open and based on empirical investigation rather than defined a priori (Rege, 2013; Chakravarthi, 2006).

Some approaches like those of Dhamoon have emphasised the process of formation of the identities and have invoked Foucault. Thus, they point out that in Foucauldian terms, the focus of analysis is not strictly on an individual, a category, a group or an institution (although these are not absent either) but on the techniques of power (Dhamoon, 2011). The "matrix of meaning-making" is a framework that draws on the Foucauldian approach, "It aims to foreground an expanded Foucauldian understanding of power so as to capture the ways in which processes of differentiation and systems of domination interrelate. The focus of analysis is thus not only domination but the very interactive processes and structures in which meanings of privilege and penalty are produced, reproduced and resisted in contingent and relational ways" (Dhamoon, 2011, p. 238).

Another sociologist/philosopher whose approach has been used in the study of inequity and intersectionality is Pierre Bourdieu, especially in his use of the concept of *habitus* and *field* (Anne, Callahan, & Kang, n.d.; McNay, 1999). A praxeological approach has been suggested for the study of intersectionality based on Bourdieu's work, which suggests that everyday life of people be the starting point of empirical analysis, even as we keep in sight the interrelationships between caste, gender, class and so on (Winker & Degele, 2011). While the simplistic and first stage of methodological development will be the study of the interaction of these various axes, used as individual-level labels, the intersectional approach challenges us to go beyond this interactionist approach to invoke a more complex and dialectical approach that challenges and re-names (Hancock, 2016).

2.4 Conclusions

Birn highlights the fact that "(1) evidence of the association between poverty and ill health is long standing; (2) social inequality in health data are interpreted according to diverse theoretical and ideological frameworks; and (3) the ways data are interpreted shape the kinds of action (or inaction) undertaken (Birn, 2009)." Thus the way in which an issue was problematised and theorised impacted on how the data was interpreted and acted upon. This underlines the importance of the conceptual framing of research on health inequity.

This chapter has attempted to map the conceptual terrain of thinking on health inequities. It does this by first presenting the dominant public health epidemiological paradigm and then using the other theories that have been developed to develop a critique of the mainstream. In doing so, three main points were highlighted. One was the need to elaborate on the *causes of the causes of the causes*, the second was to try and decipher mechanisms and the third point was the critique of the labels and variables used in the research process. Despite the presence of these theories in published mainstream literature there seems to be little in terms of these theories shaping methodologies and research agendas.

The almost monotonic increase in inequity along many dimensions of life calls for a serious questioning of the various approaches to the study of health inequities. An editorial to a recent special issue of a journal pointed out the emerging critique of the tendency within research on health inequities to focus on individual categories; the dependence on large data sets for analysing inequities in health, which in turn limited the analysis to categories and variables available within those data sets, and to cross-sectional rather than longitudinal and time-sensitive analysis (Kapilashrami, Hill, & Meer, 2015; Muntaner, Ng, Chung, & Prins, 2015; Scambler & Scambler, 2015). Indeed the editorial sought to, "highlight the need for theoretical frameworks that draw attention to historical processes so that we better understand not just how particular policies impact on health inequalities, but how and why those policies arise (Smith & Schrecker, 2015, p. 222)."

Today the largest proportion of literature is still descriptive, there being relatively little theoretically driven work. Not only are there relatively fewer studies which adopt theoretical approaches, but the few studies that do, apply it to explain existing findings rather than to help find ways of tackling the inequities (Smith & Schrecker, 2015).

In her article using the ecosocial theory to outline a study of discrimination, Krieger points out that

> Rigorous methods for the scientific study of discrimination and health require (1) conceptual clarity about the exploitative and oppressive realities of .... forms of discrimination; (2) careful attention to domains, pathways, level and spatiotemporal scale, in historical context; (3) structural - level measures; (4) individual-level measures, albeit without relying solely on self-reported data or reducing discrimination to solely a pyschosocial exposure; and (5) an embodied analytic approach (Krieger, 2012, p. 942).

While there are many common aspects of the theories discussed, each contributes something new to the overall discussion. In many ways the ecosocial theory is the most complete articulation of the collective knowledge built over the years.

It is clear that inequities in health arise from a combination of factors acting at multiple levels and result in particular patterns at particular times in history. The factors are a combination of personal genetic material interacting with external factors, the determinants of which depend on social structures. These structures may be institutional—like the public distribution system, the public health system or the educational system—or social—like the hierarchical relations of caste and gender. In our understanding it is these social and institutional structures that combine to form a *system* that results in health inequities. The interactions of factors happen at different levels. Individual behaviour is embedded in the family, in neighbourhood, in town, in region and so on, and each level, an individual may belong to multiple groups simultaneously. These arrangements are not static but dynamic with historical processes of struggle and negotiation leading to current states of equilibrium which are in reality mere transitions to other states in the trajectory.

We use this understanding of health inequity to guide our reading and critique of the literature pertaining to India. We examine the review from the perspective of whether the rich body of theoretical knowledge has informed health inequities-research being done about India. We also ask in the critical synthesis how these insights can help make newer sense by reading across the research in an attempt to delineate what the present literature says about possible mechanisms as well as the gaps in research.

References

Amrith, S. (2007). Political culture of health in India: A historical perspective. *Economic and Political Weekly, 42,* 114–121.

Anne, M., Callahan, J., & Kang, H. (n.d.). *Gender and caste intersectionality in the Indian context.* Retrieved from http://www.ufhrd.co.uk/wordpress/wp-content/uploads/2013/09/Mrudula-Callahan-Kang-full-paper.pdf.

Balarajan, Y., Selvaraj, S., & Subramanian, S. V. (2011). Health care and equity in India. *The Lancet, 377,* 505–515. Retrieved from http://dx.doi.org/10.1016/S0140-6736(10)61894-6.

Bartley, M. (2004). *Health inequality: An introduction to theories, concepts and methods* (1st ed.). Cambridge: Polity Press.

Baru, R. V. (2010). *Health service inequities as challenge to health security.* Oxfam India working papers series. Retrieved from https://www.oxfamindia.org/sites/default/files/IV.%20Health%20Service%20Inequities%20as%20Challenge%20to%20Health%20Security.pdf.

Beckfield, J., & Krieger, N. (2009). Epi + demos + cracy: Linking political systems and priorities to the magnitude of health inequities—Evidence, gaps, and a research agenda. *Epidemiologic Reviews, 31,* 152–177. doi:10.1093/epirev/mxp002.

Beckfield, J., Bambra, C., Eikemo, T. A., Huijts, T., McNamara, C., & Wendt, C. (2015). An institutional theory of welfare state effects on the distribution of population health. *Social Theory & Health, 13,* 227–244. Retrieved from http://www.palgrave-journals.com/sth/journal/vaop/ncurrent/full/sth201519a.html; http://www.palgrave-journals.com/sth/journal/v13/n3-4/full/sth201519a.html.

Birn, A. E. (2009). Making it politic (al): Closing the gap in a generation: Health equity through action on the social determinants of health. *Social Medicine, 4*(3), 166–182.

Black, D., Morris, J. N., & Townsend, P. (1982). Inequalities in health: The black report. In P. Townsend & N. Davidsn (Eds.), *The black report and the health divide* (pp. 39–233). Harmondsworth: Penguin.

Blane, D. (1985). An assessment of the black report's explanations of health inequalities. *Sociology of Health & Illness, 7*(3), 423–446.

Bosma, H., Van De Mheen, H. D., & Mackenbach, J. P. (1999). Social class in childhood and general health in adulthood: Questionnaire study of contribution of psychological attributes. *British Medical Journal, 318,* 18–22.

Braveman, P., & Gruskin, (2003). Defining equity in health. *Journal of Epidemiology and Community Health, 57,* 254–258.

Brunner, E. (1997). Socioeconomic determinants of health: Stress and the biology of inequality impact of early experience stressors in the hierarchy. *British Medical Journal, 314*(7092), 1472–1476.

Bunge, M. (2004). How does it work? The search for explanatory mechanisms. *Philosophy of the Social Sciences, 34*(2), 182–210. Retrieved from http://pos.sagepub.com/cgi/doi/10.1177/0048393103262550.

Chakravarthi, U. (2006). *Gendering caste: Through a feminist lens*. Kolkata: Stree.

Coburn, D. (2000). Income inequality, social cohesion and the health status of populations: The role of neo-liberalism. *Social Science and Medicine, 51*(1), 135–146.

Cockerham, W. C. (2005). Health lifestyle theory and the convergence of agency and structure. *Journal of Health and Social Behavior, 46*, 51–67.

Crenshaw, K. (1991). Mapping the margins: Intersectionality, identity politics, and violence against women of color. *Stanford Law Review, 43*(6), 1241–1299.

Dhamoon, R. K. (2011). Considerations on mainstreaming intersectionality. *Political Research Quarterly, 64*(1), 230–243.

Diderichsen, F., Evans, T., & Whitehead, M. (2001). The social basis of disparities in health. In T. Evans, M. Whitehead, & F. Diderichsen (Eds.), *Challenging inequities in health: From ethics to action*. Oxford, New York: Oxford University Press.

Doyal, L. (1979). *The political economy of health*. London: Pluto Press.

Esping-Andersen, G. (1990). *The three worlds of welfare capitalism*. Princeton, New Jersey: Princeton University Press. Retrieved from http://isites.harvard.edu/fs/docs/icb.topic1134169.files/Readings%20on%20Social%20Democracy/Esping%20Anderson%20%20THe%20Three%20Worlds%20of%20Welfare%20Capitalism.pdf.

Farmer, P. (2004). *Pathologies of power: Health, human rights, and the new war on the poor*. Berkeley and Los Angeles: University of California Press.

Freese, J., & Lutfey, K. (2011). Fundamental causality: Challenges of an animating concept for medical sociology. In B. A. Pescosolido et al. (Eds.), *Handbook of the sociology of health, illness, and healing: A blueprint for the 21st century* (pp. 67–81). New York: Springer.

Guru, G. (2016). Shifting categories in the discourse on caste and class. *Economic and Political Weekly, 51*(47), 21–25.

Hancock, A.-M. (2007). When multiplication doesn't equal quick addition: Examining intersectionality as a research paradigm. *Perspectives on Politics, 5*(1), 63–79. Retrieved from http://www.journals.cambridge.org/abstract_S1537592707070065.

Hancock, A.-M. (2016). *Intersectionality: An intellectual history*. New York: Oxford University Press.

Hankivsky, O., & Christoffersen, A. (2008). Intersectionality and the determinants of health: A Canadian perspective. *Critical Public Health, 18*(3), 271–283. http://www.tandfonline.com/doi/abs/10.1080/09581590802294296.

Hankivsky, O., Grace, D., Hunting, G., & Ferlatte, O. (2012). Introduction: Why intersectionality matters for health equity and policy analysis. In O. Hankivsky (Ed.), *An intersectionality based policy analysis framework* (p. 18). Vancouver, BC: Institute for Intersectionality Research and Policy, Simon Fraser University.

Horton, S., & Barker, J. C. (2010). Stigmatised biologies: Examining the cumulative effects of oral health disparities for Mexican American farm worker children. *Medical Anthropology Quarterly, 24*(2), 199–219.

Irwin, A., & Scali, E. (2005). Action on the social determinants of health: Learning from previous experiences. A background paper prepared for the commission on social determinants of health. Geneva: WHO, Secretariat of the Commission on Social Determinants of Health.

Kapilashrami, A., Hill, S., & Meer, N. (2015). What can health inequalities researchers learn from an intersectionality perspective? Understanding social dynamics with an inter-categorical approach? *Social Theory & Health, 13*(3–4), 288–307. Retrieved from http://www.palgrave-journals.com/doifinder/10.1057/sth.2015.16.

Keshavjee, S. (2014). *Blind spot: How neoliberalism infiltrated global health* (1st ed.). Berkeley and Los Angeles: University of California Press.

Kim, J. Y., Millen. J. V., Irwin, A., & Gershman, J. (2000). *Dying for growth: Global inequality and the health of the poor* (J. Y. Kim et al., Editors). Monroe, Maine: Common Courage Press.
Krieger, N. (2011a). Social epidemiologic alternatives: Socio-political and psycholosocial frameworks. In N. Krieger (Ed.), *Epidemiology and the people's health: Theory and context* (pp. 163–201). New York: Oxford University Press.
Krieger, N. (2011b). Ecosocial theory of disease distribution: Embodying societal and ecological context. In N. Krieger (Ed.), *Epidemiology and the people's health: Theory and context* (p. 215). New York: Oxford University Press.
Krieger, N. (2012). Methods for the scientific study of discrimination and health: An ecosocial approach. *American Journal of Public Health, 102*(5), 936–945.
Krieger, N., Alegrìa, M., Almeida-Filho, N., da Silva, J. B., Barreto, M. L., Beckfield, J., … Walters, K. L. (2010). Who, and what, causes health inequities? Reflections on emerging debates from an exploratory Latin American/North American workshop. *Journal of Epidemiology and Community Health, 64*(9), 747–749.
Krieger, N., Williams, D. R., & Moss, N. E. (1997). Measuring social class in us public health research: Concepts, methodologies, and guidelines. *Annual Review of Public Health, 18,* 341–378.
Link, B. G., & Phelan, J. C. (1996). Understanding sociodemographic differences in health—The role of fundamental social causes. *American Journal of Public Health, 86*(4), 471–473.
McEwen, B. S. (1998). Protective and damaging effects of stress mediators. *New England Journal of Medicine, 338*(3), 171–179.
McNay, L. (1999). Gender, Habitus and the field: Pierre Bourdieu and the limits of reflexivity. *Theory Culture Society, 16*(1), 95–117.
Moller, S., Huber, E., Stephens, J. D., Bradley, D., & Nielsen, F. (2003). Determinants of relative poverty in advanced capitalist democracies. *American Sociological Review, 68*(1), 22–51.
Muntaner, C., Ng, E., Chung, H., & Prins, S. J. (2015). Two decades of Neo-Marxist class analysis and health inequalities: A critical reconstruction. *Social Theory & Health, 13*(3–4), 267–287. Retrieved from http://www.ncbi.nlm.nih.gov/pubmed/26345311.
Muntaner, C., Ng, E., Vanroelen, C., Christ, S., & Eaton, W. W. (2013). Social stratification, social closure and social class as determinants of mental health disparities. In C. S. Aneshensel, J. C. Phelan, & A. Bierman (Eds.), *Handbook of the sociology of mental health* (pp. 205–227). Dordrecht, Netherlands: Springer.
Navarro, V. (2004). Introduction: Objectives and purposes of the study. In V. Navarro (Ed.), *The political and social contexts of health* (p. 8). Amityville, NY: Baywood Publishing Company.
Navarro, V. (2009). What we mean by social determinants of health. *Global Health Promotion, 16*(1), 5–16.
Navarro, V., & Muntaner, C. (2004). *Political and economic determinants of population health and well being: Controversies and developments.* Amityville, NY: Baywood Publishing Company.
Obregón, D. (2008). We are under no illusions: Closing the gap in a generation, the report of the WHO Commission on Social Determinants of Health. Paper presented at The World Health Organization and the Social Determinants of Health: Assessing theory, policy and practice. London, UK: Wellcome Trust Centre for the History of Medicine at UCL. November 26–28, 2008.
Phelan, J. C., & Link, B. G. (2013). Fundamental cause theory. In W. C. Cockerham (Ed.), *Medical sociology on the move: New directions in theory* (pp. 105–126, 1st ed.). Dordrecht: Springer.
Phelan, J. C., Link, B. G., & Tehranifar, P. (2010). Social conditions as fundamental causes of health inequalities: Theory, evidence and policy implications. *Journal of Health and Social Behavior, 51,* S28–S40.
Pickel, A. (2004). Systems and mechanisms a symposium on Mario Bunge's philosophy of social science. *Philosophy of the Social Sciences, 34*(2), 169–181.

Purkayastha, B., Subramanian, M., Desai, M., & Bose, S. (2003). The study of gender in India: A partial review. *Gender & Society, 17*(4), 503–524. Retrieved from http://gas.sagepub.com/cgi/doi/10.1177/0891243203253793.

Rege, S. (2013). *Against the madness of Manu: B R Ambedkars's writings on brahmanical patriarchy*. New Delhi: Navayana.

Rose, G. (2001). Sick individuals and sick populations. *International Journal of Epidemiology, 30* (1), 427–432.

Sanneving, L., Trygg, N., Saxena, D., Mavalankar, D., & Thomsen, S. (2013). Inequity in India: The case of maternal and reproductive health. *Global Health Action, 6,* 19145.

Scambler, G., & Scambler, S. (2015). Theorising health inequalities: The untapped potential of dialectical critical realism. *Social Theory & Health, 13*(3–4), 340–354. Retrieved from http://www.palgrave-journals.com/doifinder/10.1057/sth.2015.14.

Sen, A. (1999). *Inequality re-examined* (Seventh im.). New Delhi: Oxford University Press.

Siegrist, J. (2000). Place, social exchange and health: Proposed sociological framework. *Social Science and Medicine, 51,* 1283–1293.

Smith, K. E., & Schrecker, T. (2015). Theorising health inequalities: Introduction to a double special issue. *Social Theory & Health, 13*(3–4), 219–226.

Solar, O., & Irwin, A. (2010). A conceptual framework for action on the social determinants of health. Social determinants of health discussion paper 2 (policy and practice) (p. 6). Geneva: World Health Organization.

Whitehead, M. (2000). *The concepts and principles of equity in health.* Copenhagen: World Health Organisation, Regional Office for Europe. Retrieved from http://salud.ciee.flacso.org.ar/flacso/optativas/equity_and_health.pdf.

Williams, S. J. (1995). Theorising class, health and lifestyles: Can Bourdieu help us? *Sociology of Health & Illness, 17*(5), 577–604.

Winker, G., & Degele, N. (2011). Intersectionality as multi-level analysis: Dealing with social inequality. *European Journal of Women's Studies, 18*(1), 51–66.

Wright, E. O. (1985). *Classes* (pp. 37–42). London: Verso.

Chapter 3
Research on Inequities and Inequalities in Health in India: A Mapping of the Field

Rakhal Gaitonde

Abstract This chapter provides a summary of the methodology used for the synthesis of evidence presented in the core chapters (Chaps. 4–8) of the book. The chapter starts with presenting an overview of the search strategy used, the number of papers included in the synthesis exercise, and the axes of inequalities and the areas of health covered by the papers. It also provides a mapping of authors and institutions that produced this literature, their locations and disciplinary backgrounds. Overall we reviewed 224 individual papers with many of them being used in more than one chapter. The mapping of the individuals and institutions that actually did the research showed a preponderance of foreign institutions, a dominance of the econometric, demographic approaches, with very little of social and political sciences informing the literature. The methodology adopted for the synthesis included in individual chapters consisted of two steps. Each chapter first summarised the key findings from the papers. It then attempted to critique the methodological and conceptual approaches represented in the body of evidence, drawing on the perspective developed in Chap. 2. Further, the individual chapters, by reading papers and looking at patterns and trends within and across papers, attempted to identify key mechanisms contributing to health inequities implicit in the literature.

Keywords Synthesis · Mechanisms · Mapping · Health equity researchers · India

3.1 Introduction

The objective of this chapter is twofold. The first is to describe the methodology used in the core chapters, for synthesising the evidence from the papers on health inequities by socio-economic position; Dalit and Adivasi status; gender; other social vulnerabilities with a focus on People Living with HIV and AIDS and Internal

R. Gaitonde (✉)
Centre for Technology and Policy (CTaP) IIT-M, Chennai, India
e-mail: rakhal.gaitonde@gmail.com

T.K.S. Ravindran and R. Gaitonde (eds.), *Health Inequities in India*,
https://doi.org/10.1007/978-981-10-5089-3_3

Migrants; and on the role of the health system. The second is to present an overview of the areas of research and approaches used in the body of research on health equity in India during 2000–2014, and the location and disciplinary backgrounds of the researchers who have been engaged in this research. Such an overview of the lay of the land would be helpful to some extent in understanding why we know so much about some issues and so little about others, and in making sense of the research questions that have sought to be answered.

Section 3.1 presents the search strategy as well as the processes used for the inclusion of papers and the variables chosen for mapping these. Section 3.2 presents the main findings of the mapping exercise. Section 3.3 describes the methodology used for the synthesis of the evidence from the papers. Section 3.4 presents the conclusion.

3.1.1 Objectives of the Synthesis Exercise and Methodology for Identifying and Mapping the Studies

3.1.1.1 Objectives

The broad objectives of the synthesis exercise were to answer the following questions about evidence on inequities in health in India:

(a) What do we know about the existence and extent of inequities in various dimensions of health (in developing a health problem; obtaining appropriate and adequate health care; resolution or exacerbation of the health problem (including death); facing negative social and/or economic consequences because of the health problem)
(b) What do we know about the mechanisms and pathways contributing to the observed inequities? And what are possible frameworks that emerge from these to guide future research?
(c) What do we know about the success of interventions implemented to address the inequities?
(d) What are the methodological tools used for the study of a, b and c above?

3.1.1.2 Search Strategy and Inclusion Criteria

The papers included in the evidence synthesis were identified in several iterations. The attempt was more to be confident of including all the important and influential work as well as cover the range of research done, rather than include every single paper (like in a systematic review). This was especially since what we were attempting was an assessment of the overall state and direction of the field of health equity research in India rather than a meta-analysis.

An initial series of searches were carried out during December 2014–August 2015. We searched in PubMed, Google Scholar and Web of Science and Scopus for papers in English largely in public health literature published between 2000 and 2014. The keywords used were inequity; inequality; health; determinant of health; India; in combination with economic status; socio-economic status; caste; tribe; gender; discrimination; and vulnerability; intersectionality. Apart from the web-based search we wrote to 12 prominent researchers who had done or were currently engaged in research on health inequity, with a request to share key documents. Among other inputs the search was especially enhanced by the resources provided by the Social Determinants of Health group at the Public Health Foundation of India in Delhi.

We separated the papers based on the specific axes inequity that they studied. The initial mapping using this set of papers was presented in a seminar in August 2015; these papers were reviewed by individual experts as well as the collective group and opinion and suggestions were further sought to include any papers left out. We received suggestions for further sources and areas to follow-up. We included many new papers after this round of iteration, especially on sex differentials and gender-based inequities in health and on People Living with HIV and AIDS and internal migrants. At each stage references from papers being reviewed were perused for any additional papers we missed.

In these iterations and as the review process continued we did include a few papers from before 2000 as well as more recent papers to keep the review relevant. After a number of processes and iterations we are confident of including an elaborate representation of the research on health inequity in India, in the public health field.

For assessment of the quality of the paper, the following criteria suggested by Dixon-Woods et al. (2006) were used:

- Are the aims and objectives of the research clearly stated?
- Is the research design clearly specified and appropriate for the aims and objectives of the research?
- Do the researchers provide a clear account of the process by which their findings were produced?
- Do the researchers display enough data to support their interpretations and conclusions?
- Is the method of analysis appropriate and adequately explicated?

(Dixon-Woods et al., 2006, p. 4 of 13).

Each paper was graded by these criteria, but we chose to reject only a few papers that did not meet three or more of the above criteria. The reason for being more inclusive was that our purpose was not to arrive at a generalisable numerical estimate from various studies but to pull together answers to the main questions we started with. In all, 224 studies were used in the evidence synthesis. The next section describes the categories according to which we have mapped these studies.

3.1.1.3 Framework for the Mapping

The mapping of studies has been done to find answers to two different sets of questions:

- What are the key content areas covered by the studies, and what aspects of health inequities have they studied (in relation to the objectives of the synthesis)
- Who is doing/has done research (individuals and institutions) on health—inequity issues in India during 2000–2014? What are their locations and disciplinary backgrounds?

In order to answer the first of these questions, we carried out a three-way classification. The first classification was according to the five key themes adopted for the evidence synthesis in the core chapters, namely

- Socio-economic position
- Caste/tribal status
- Gender
- HIV status, migrant status
- Health system related.

The axes along which the chapters in the book engaged with the literature are based on the axes that were predominantly used in the literature. While we were uncomfortable with the usage of some labels like "SC/ST" which we believe to be more administrative labels rather than reflections of lived reality, others axes like gender, which invariably was referring only to biological sex, were clearly inadequate. However, we stuck to the usage of the authors in the original papers to accurately reflect what was in the literature. Similarly, we do not believe that these axes act separately or are even distinct in real life and strongly feel that there is an urgent need of the intersectional lens. However, again despite our reservations, we stuck to the way the literature has used these labels, though we highlighted the rare study that did attempt to engage with intersectionality. A more elaborate critique of the way the labels are used is to be found in Chap. 2 as well as in each of the chapters where relevant points are discussed.

We further mapped the studies by the nature of the enquiry into inequities in the papers, into those that

- Document the extent of the problem and/or examine various social, demographic or economic correlates of a health problem or outcome
- Explore the mechanisms or processes underlying/causing/sustaining inequities in health
- Assess the outcomes or impact of interventions to address or mitigate inequities in health or inequities in the determinants of health.

Papers on socio-economic position, caste/tribal status and gender were further classified by the nature of health problems (e.g. maternal health, child health, non-communicable and communicable diseases) examined.

Table 3.1 Classification of included papers along the five main themes of the synthesis

Axes	Number	Proportion (%)
1. Socio-economic position (e.g. income or expenditure class, wealth status, standard of living index, educational level)	47	18.88
2. Dalit/Adivasi status	40	16.1
3. Sex/Gender	75	30.12
4. Other socially constructed vulnerabilities (people living with HIV and AIDS, internal migrants)	55	22.1
5. Health system related	32[a] (65)	12.8
Total	N = (224)[b]	100

[a]If we include here the large number of papers that look at inequities in access, utilisation and quality by, socio-economic position and gender, and PLHA and migrant status, the total increases to 65
[b]Row numbers do not add up to total because some papers are repeated in more than one row because they deal with socio-economic position and caste and/or gender

Answers to the second question were sought by mapping the papers by a number of authors, sex, location of the lead author, disciplinary backgrounds of all authors and the nature of data used in the study (Table 3.1).

3.2 Results of the Mapping of Studies on Inequities and Inequalities in Health

3.2.1 Distribution of Papers by Main Themes, Health Problems Examined and Nature of the Enquiry into Health Inequities

Overall, the least number of papers on health inequities addressed caste and tribal status, and most of those which did identified caste and tribal status as correlates explaining differentials in specific health outcomes. Table 3.2 reveals two broad issues. One is the predominance of studies on maternal health and to an extent child health over studies on communicable diseases and non-communicable diseases, mental health and injuries. Within maternal and child health, the focus has been on utilisation of health care, especially preventive health care such as immunisation, antenatal, delivery and postpartum care and contraception. Inequities in well-being, mortality and morbidity, quality of life and so on are poorly represented. Entire population groups, such as children above 5 years of age, women beyond the reproductive age group, single women and men of all ages, have been largely excluded from research. This is probably both a reflection on the nature of data available from large data sets such as the NFHS and DLHS and of health system focus on MCH. Given the rising numbers of non-MCH-related conditions that people in India are facing, there is urgent need to expand beyond this narrow range of topics.

Table 3.2 Classification of papers discussing socio-economic position, caste or tribal status, or gender along areas of health and by type of study

Type of studies	Maternal health	Child health	NCDs and CDs	Others	Total
Socio-economic position					
Extent of inequity and associated factors	26	20	0	2	48
Pathways	1	0	0	0	1
Interventions	0	1	0	1	2
Other	0	0	0	2	2
Total	27	21	0	5	$N = 47$[a]
Dalit/Adivasi status					
Extent of inequity and associated factors	15	9	1	4	29
Pathways				3	3
Interventions			1	4	5
Review papers	1	1	1		3
Others					
Total	16	10	3	11	$N = 40$
Sex/gender					
Extent of inequity and associated factors	25	24	2	13	64
Pathways	6	1	4		11
Interventions	2	2			4
Review papers					
Others					
Total	33	27	6	13	$N = 77$[b]
In all categories	76	58	9	29[c]	

[a]Six papers were classified in more than one category
[b]Two papers were classified in more than one category
[c]Papers in this category included those on adult mortality and morbidity by age and sex; and papers giving a background on economic, social or gender inequalities

The second issue is with the predominantly descriptive nature of the studies, with most merely noting the presence of inequity along various axes. Where data sets are available there are attempts to explore various correlations through multiple regressions, but there is a paucity of studies with regards to the actual pathways through which these axes actually contribute to inequity in health. Table 3.3 confirms this overall pattern, but also shows that relatively more studies on PLHA have examined the pathways and mechanisms through which health inequities are created for PLHA.

Table 3.3 Classification of papers discussing other socially constructed vulnerabilities and health systems by nature of the study

	Other socially constructed vulnerabilities		Health systems
	PLHA (including migrants)[a]	Internal migrants	
Extent of inequity and associated factors	18	17	18
Pathways	11	4	6
Interventions	2	0	1
Review papers	2	0	1
Other	1	2	6 (policy analysis, commentaries)
Total	34	$N = 21^b$	32

[a]Six papers were about migrant PLHA
[b]Two papers were classified into two categories

3.2.2 Distribution of the Papers by Author Characteristics and Data Sources

Some interesting findings emerge from the mapping of papers by author characteristics and nature of data used (Table 3.4). A third of the papers were by four or more authors, most of which were collaborative projects across multiple institutions. Studies on PLHA/internal migrants had a higher proportion of papers (49%) with four or more authors. About 56% of the authors were men and 44% were women; the proportion of women authoring papers on gender and on PLHA and internal migration was just a little over 50%, and women authors were less represented in studies on socio-economic position and on health systems. Over forty percent (41.8%) of the lead authors were located in institutions outside India. Of the 60% of lead authors located in Indian institutions, most were affiliated to institutions in the Northern states, and were from Delhi and Chandigarh for the most part. Only 10% of the lead authors were from Institutions in the eastern states of India. Across the country, lead authors tended to be from autonomous institutions of medical research, public health and population sciences, and very few from university settings (not shown in the table). A third of the authors were public health professionals, mainly epidemiologists, while economists and demographers accounted for another third. About 15% were medical researchers and a slightly lower proportion (about 13%) was social scientists. Other disciplines represented included biostatistics, psychology, management and so on.

One of the most important findings to emerge from this mapping is that only 40% of the studies used any primary data, and 75% of studies using primary data were those related to PLHA and internal migrants, and to a lesser extent, gender. Studies on socio-economic position, Dalit and Adivasi populations (SC/ST) and health systems predominantly used secondary data from large-scale national

Table 3.4 Distribution of studies synthesised by author characteristics and nature of data

	SEP[a]	Caste/Tribal status	Sex/Gender	PLHA and internal migrants	Health system	Total
No. of authors						
1	5	12	17	9	10	53
2	13	9	20	9	7	58
3	11	7	18	10	9	55
4	11	7	8	12	2	40
5 or more	7	5	12	15	4	43
Sex of authors						
Male	100	65	110	93	53	421
Female	49	45	113	97	26	330
Location of lead author						
India	28	24	38	35	20	145
East[b]	3	3	6	1	2	15
West	13	7	5	9	4	38
North	10	13	16	13	9	61
South	2	1	11	12	5	31
Outside India	19	16	37	20	12	104
Disciplinary background of authors						
Economics	25	26	38	2	33	124
Demography	25	14	45	23	2	109
Public health	55	39	71	44	13	229
Medicine	11	17	36	42	11	117
Social sciences	19	7	19	52	3	100
Others	14	7	14	27	17	79
Nature of data used						
Primary	8	10	30	39	5	92
Secondary	34	18	30	8	15	105
NSSO[c]	2	5	5	0	8	20
NFHS	24	9	25	7	7	72
Census	3	1	0	0	0	4
DLHS	5	3	0	1	0	9
Primary and secondary	0	5	2	0	0	7
Other	5	7	13	8	12	45

[a]*SEP* Socio-economic position

[b]East includes the seven North-Eastern states, Sikkim, Bihar, Jharkhand, West Bengal and Odisha; West: Rajasthan, Gujarat, Maharashtra and Goa; North: Jammu and Kashmir, Punjab, Haryana, Delhi, Chandigarh, Uttar Pradesh, Uttarakhand, Madhya Pradesh and Chhattisgarh. South includes Kerala, Karnataka, Tamil Nadu, Andhra Pradesh and Telangana

[c] *NSSO* National Sample Survey Organisation; *NFHS* National Family Health Survey; *DLHS* District level household survey

surveys such as the National Sample Surveys conducted periodically (NSS), the National Family Health Surveys, and less frequently, the Census of India and the District Level Health Surveys. About 20% of the papers did not use survey data but were in the nature of reviews, commentaries or policy analyses.

Another observation was that the only two papers that explored at length the mechanisms underlying health disadvantages experienced by Dalit populations were produced by the Indian Institute of Dalit studies. All other studies merely noted SC/ST status as a correlate explaining disparities in health outcomes.

3.3 Methodology Adopted for the Synthesis of the Evidence

The synthesis of evidence has been carried out in two steps. In each chapter, after an introduction to the key concepts and terminologies, the authors summarise the findings from the studies so that an overall picture emerges of what is known about inequities in health by socio-economic position, caste and so on. The structuring of the summary has to some extent been shaped by the nature of the evidence. Given the preponderance of studies on inequities in healthcare utilisation and health outcome of mothers and children (less than five years of age), we have subsections on healthcare utilisation for preventive and curative care for mothers, children and others; and health outcomes such as mortality, morbidity and nutrition for children and for adults. Key findings have been summarised after each major subsection.

Following the summary section, the authors critique the methodological and conceptual approaches represented in the body of evidence, drawing on the perspective developed in Chap. 2. Subsequently, the authors read papers and look at patterns and trends within and across papers; and, going beyond the boundaries of the papers, locate the emerging themes against the larger macroeconomic and sociopolitical backdrop. The aim is to identify key mechanisms contributing to health inequities. For this, we draw inspiration from Dixon-Woods et al. critical interpretive synthesis methodology. The methodology involves both induction and interpretation, and integrates evidence from across the studies in the review so that "several disparate aspects of a phenomenon … (are) … unified in a more useful and explanatory way (Dixon-Woods et al., 2006, p. 5 of 13)".

Like the search process, the synthesis too went through many iterations. Following the initial search individual working papers were prepared which underwent peer review as well as were presented at a national seminar. All comments received were incorporated and the process of synthesis underwent further iteration to finalise the working paper. These papers formed the core material for the individual chapters, which were modified appropriately for the format of the present book.

The concluding chapter (Chap. 9) weaves together the key mechanisms identified in the core chapters into a coherent theoretical framework that provides more insightful, formalised and generalizable ways of understanding inequities in health so that entry points for action to mitigate it becomes clearer (Dixon-Woods et al., 2006, p. 5 of 13).

3.4 Conclusions

A few clear conclusions emerge from this mapping exercise.

Preponderance of Quantitative and Descriptive Approaches to the Study of Inequity in Health

There are very few qualitative studies that explore the mechanisms of the emergence of inequity in different settings and very few studies of initiatives aimed at the reduction of inequities or suggested to have inequity reducing effects.

Limitations of the Available Data Sets for the Study of Health Inequities Across all Population Groups and Health Issues

Descriptive studies on inequities in health and their trends require large data sets with the relevant identifiers/markers. The data sets so far used in India like NSSO and NFHS either only focus on markers of economic position or geography (NSSO) or mainly focus on MCH-related data (NFHS). There are no large data sets with information outcomes for many health issues by regarding caste and tribal status, and on health systems related issues. This is especially important with recent discussions on the future of the NFHS surveys.

Need to Move Beyond MCH

Most of the studies focus on MCH issues. This may be natural given both the systemic and the community-based needs and priorities; however, more research on communicable diseases and the seemingly fast increasing non-communicable diseases—especially issues like Mental Health and cancers—apart from Diabetes and Hypertension needs to be initiated.

Need to Move Beyond Looking Only at Outcomes and Correlates to Looking at Pathways

While there seems to be a lot of information on descriptive studies and those looking at the various correlations of the axes of inequity, there seems a paucity of studies looking at the underlying mechanisms. This is a crucial gap especially given the need for such studies to inform policy which till now seems to be quite ineffectual.

Identification and Research on Other Vulnerable Groups—Going Beyond Class/Caste/Gender Alone

While there is some research along the dominant axes of class and gender and to a lesser extent on caste, there are very few and preliminary studies on other axes of inequity (which may be emerging and gaining prominence) such as migrants, people with mental health issues, the elderly, etc.

The next five chapters synthesise the evidence on inequities in health in India from the papers mapped and using the synthesis methodology outlined in this chapter.

Reference

Dixon-Woods, M., Cavers, D., Agarwal, S., Annandale, E., Arthur, A., Harvey, J., … Sutton, A. J. (2006). Conducting a critical interpretive synthesis of the literature on access to healthcare by vulnerable groups. *BMC Medical Research Methodology*, *6*(35).

Chapter 4
Health Inequities in India by Socio-economic Position

Prashanth Nuggehalli Srinivas

Abstract Health inequities in India along socio-economic axis are relatively more studied among the different axes of health inequities. In this chapter, we present a synthesis of literature on India on inequities in health by socio-economic position. We begin with a discussion on the historical origins of research on socio-economic inequity in industrialised settings. These initial revelations on social patterning of illnesses (illness profiles) spurred efforts to categorise and describe these population differences on one hand as well as theorise and explain (or predict) why these differences are pervasive in societies on the other. We then summarise current knowledge on socio-economic inequities in health drawing from a synthesis of published literature. In the final section, we discuss how current research on socio-economic inequities can help us understand the possible pathways and mechanisms through which such inequities are mitigated, maintained or aggravated. There are clear patterns of socio-economic disadvantage with respect to healthcare seeking and access across the country albeit showing differences within and across states. This general pattern is seen across populations, services (maternal and child health, immunisation, nutrition, anaemia and various other health problems) and geographies, and mirrors a global disadvantage faced by the poor. However, the possible mechanisms through which these are brought about and/or sustained are based on an interaction between and within various other axes of inequity including caste, gender and other social disadvantages. The Commission on Social Determinants of Health framework is useful to organise explanations for recurring themes that emerge across the research on socio-economic inequity in India. Some of the explanatory mechanisms that emerge from the themes discussed in papers on socio-economic inequity are described.

Keywords Socio-economic health inequity · Socio-economic status
Socio-economic position

P.N. Srinivas (✉)
Health Equity and Evaluation Studies Cluster, Institute of Public Health, 250 2 C Main, 2 C Cross, Girinagar I Phase, Bengaluru 560085, Karnataka, India
e-mail: prashanthns@iphindia.org

T.K.S. Ravindran and R. Gaitonde (eds.), *Health Inequities in India*,
https://doi.org/10.1007/978-981-10-5089-3_4

4.1 Introduction

Among the inequities in health, those related to socio-economic status are most frequently reported in research studies. This could be in part due to the availability of large population-level datasets from periodic nationwide surveys. Nationwide and periodic surveys such as the National Family Health Survey (NFHS) and District-level Household Survey (DLHS), or the health expenditure data from National Sample Survey enables independent statistical analysis, testing of hypotheses and assessment of trends. Overall, published literature echoes the well-studied global pattern of poorer health status and healthcare access among the poor (Balarajan, Selvaraj, & Subramanian, 2011). However, socio-economic status (SES) cannot be comprehensively understood without unpacking the social and economic component and understanding status in SES vis-à-vis a related term, socio-economic position (SEP). SES (or SEP) is often conflated with other related socio-economic categories such as income categories, social class, and categories based on poverty assessment (income and/or wealth), statutorily identified economic categories such as people who possess a below poverty line card (BPL cardholders). This confusion stems from conceptual confusion on social and economic identities of individuals, and how these individual identities interact with social structures and in turn influence people's access to healthcare and their health status.

This chapter is organised in three sections.

In the first section, we present a summary of current understanding of SES with respect to its historical origins in industrialised settings where social stratification was associated with varying health and development attainment among the population. These initial revelations on social patterning of illnesses (illness profiles) spurred efforts to categorise and describe these population differences on one hand as well as theorise and explain (or predict) why these differences are pervasive in societies on the other.

In the second section, we summarise current knowledge on socio-economic inequities in health in India drawing from a synthesis of published literature (see Chaps. 2 and 3 for details of the mapping and the methodology for constructing the synthesis).

In the final section, we discuss how current research on socio-economic inequities can help us understand the possible pathways and mechanisms through which such inequities are mitigated, maintained or aggravated.

4.1.1 Understanding the Social and the Economic in Socio-economic

Socio-economic inequality is often treated as synonymous with economic inequality due to the relative ease of accessing data on economic attributes and the relative ease of measuring income or wealth. On the other hand, social status (or position) is complex, dynamic and history (or path) dependent. Social status could be due to factors that people are born with (*ascribed characteristics* of social status) or those factors that enable people to move from a particular social position to another. Such social mobility is much more dependent on *acquired characteristics* such as education, income or wealth and other social markers of status that are dependent on several factors including, but not limited to economic ones. The interactions between acquired characteristics of social status such as education or neighbourhood and the ascribed ones such as caste or gender, and other social factors, including which part of the country they live in, and for how many generations (cf. migrations driven by macroeconomic shifts or droughts) have differential effects within and across households and populations. For instance, over time or across generations, access to education or simply literacy may enable households to overcome difficulties due to poor income or wealth. However, it will have different effects on household members (cf. maternal education as an important determinant of child health). Seen in this sense, it appears straightforward that education may be a necessary condition for family's health, but may not be sufficient and may not have uniform effects either within or across households. These effects operate often through a path-dependent or historical accumulation of power or privilege either through structured pathways like caste or gender, or through micro- or meso-contextual phenomena such as locally powerful families or local majority groups, or else due to state neglect of certain areas/groups due to poor governance. Population datasets, however, seek to quantify such attributes at a specific point in time, thus missing out the dynamic nature of SES.

Hence, the assessment of how socio-economic status and health interact requires grounding in social structures that shape social norms or processes and hence bring about unequal (and often unfair) accumulation of power or privilege within socio-economic groups. There is also a need to acknowledge that these are context and history-dependent as well as continuously interacting with other drivers of inequity such as caste or gender. In this sense, economic inequity is a type of social inequity that results in the unfair accumulation of health (or healthcare or health outcomes) in the poor or less wealthy through social norms that either impose social barriers or systematically prevent the poor or less wealthy from enabling themselves to receive health or healthcare. Since social status includes an income and wealth component as well, in addition to other dimensions, it is often treated together as socio-economic status.

4.1.2 Origins of Research on Health Inequities by Socio-economic Position

Income and wealth may contribute to social status, but the broader idea of status is socially determined and varies from one society to another. Even within neighbourhoods or communities, the local social and cultural norms influence the distribution of resources or access to power structures. The norms could affect access to health, education, livelihoods differently. For example, in some homogenous tribal communities, the chief (often familial or by culturally determined normative processes) may enjoy a higher status only with respect to community rituals but may in fact have comparable or only slightly higher privilege in terms of access to natural resources or forest wealth. While such differential access may enable his family to overcome sociocultural or political barriers that fellow tribal households may still reel under, it may not be the same as being a *Gram Panchayat* President of a heterogeneous village with a more complex social structure.

Early research on health inequity focused on identifying differences in health status among population groups. There are several theoretical explanations advanced in literature for why socio-economic inequalities (widening income and wealth gaps) increased in industrialising societies. The one with compelling evidence-base is that the income and wealth generated by industrialising western Europe in eighteenth and nineteenth centuries interacted with a rigidly class-stratified society to result in an elite-captured unequal society where private wealth dwarfed national income (Piketty, 2014).

In a society (or a time period) where being born into a family implied privileged access to some social structures (the upper class in eighteenth-century western Europe, but crudely comparable to other social categories elsewhere in the world including caste in contemporary south Asian settings), income or wealth generation opportunities presented by rapid industrialisation accumulated within particular social categories based on their SES (or SEP). In such societies, a simple assessment of population-level differences by social category shows glaring differences. The most obvious difference seen in industrialised societies in the eighteenth and nineteenth century was the concentration of ill-health and poor health outcomes among the poor (Bartley, 2004). In the United Kingdom, studies on inequalities clearly identified the living conditions of the working class to be linked to "excessive mortality, an unbroken series of epidemics and a progressive deterioration in the physique of the working population" (Engels & McLellan, 1993, p. 109). Income, housing, poor access to material possessions (clothing, shelter, etc.), diet, working conditions and accumulation of stress and unhealthy behaviours among the poor were identified as correlates and causes for this. However, the fact that the working class did not have the power to change some of this *despite an awareness and/or an ability*, or that they did not have control over resources needed to bring about a change in their living or working conditions, was identified as the underlying driver of this unfair accumulation of ill-health.

Much later in 1980, the Black report published by the UK Department of Health and Social Security acknowledged the clear patterning of health across social classes. The report was prepared by an expert committee on health inequality chaired by Sir Douglas Black, then the President of the Royal College of Physicians. The report discussed the extent of unequal distribution of ill-health in the UK, and suggested that these inequalities were widening rather than diminishing since the establishment of the National Health Service (NHS) in 1948. However, their analyis suggested that this widening of inequalities was due to social inequalities such as income, education, housing, diet, employment and conditions of work influencing health rather than a failure of the NHS itself (Gray, 1982).

4.1.3 Socio-economic Status Versus Position

In some countries such as the UK, there has been a tradition of defining a social class based on occupation of the head of household. However, social class considers predominantly economic relationships among people, or groups of people, or at least their position within the social structures created by market or economic forces (Krieger, 2001a). The idea of social class is much more rooted in social structures created by the relationship between social groups characterised by their control over material resources and their underlying power relations with respect to other groups within the social hierarchy. Seen in this sense, social class draws conceptually from the theories on class struggle originating in the work of Karl Marx. The interaction between the social classes, according to this view, is characterised by the inherent conflict between exploited classes (e.g. the labour or working class) and the exploiting ones (e.g. the owners) who control the *means of production*. In this view, inequality is an inescapable consequence of the nature of the social structure itself.

In comparison to the overarching emphasis on the social hierarchy around means of production as an *explanandum* to all inequity, many European scholars have rather preferred a multidimensional origin of social stratification (rather than adopting an entirely class-based origin) (Galobardes, Lynch, & Smith, 2007). In this view, originating in theories of social stratification of Max Weber, the *agency* of individuals/societies in overcoming barriers posed by their relative *position* in society is introduced, through extending the drivers of social stratification beyond social class, to include status and access to power/resources to exercise political action (the three P's: property, prestige and power). In this sense, attributes other than those related to economic class acquire importance, such as for example, education, skills and other abilities that individuals/communities could harness to *negotiate* their relative position within the social hierarchy. In this view, the relative social position or status acquires an importance and allows for a more dynamic understanding of social mobility either within a given generation or across. It also broadens the scope of inquiry into inequity beyond those produced by economic class alone and integrates the concept of social position or status in society. Thus, the social, political and cultural norms at a given time, place and for a given person interact with their social class to result in a relative social position or status. The latter Weberian view is preferred by several European scholars as well as by many social epidemiologists—see for example the work of Nancy Krieger or recent books on measuring health inequalities by Mel Bartley—understanding the patterning of health along socio-economic status or position is a more dynamic and comprehensive indicator of inequity than class alone.

The other widely cited theory originating from research in French society by the sociologist Pierre Bordieu also integrates the dynamic nature of interaction between individual's agency and social structure by emphasising on the non-financial attributes such as education or adoption of ways and mannerisms that promote social mobility to upper classes, through the interactions between an individual's *habitus* (capital) with various spaces (fields) in society that result in a relative position in society (Swartz, 1997).

A distinction has been made in literature between social status and a more precise and better understood term, social position. Measures of status (as opposed to social position) give an impression of measuring an individual/household's standing within a given community or society. Such a standing often varies within and across households, neighbourhoods and societies and is difficult to capture and compare across populations. Conceptually speaking, social position, is more modest, and conventionally applied attributes such as education, occupation and income are likely to indicate social position than social (or economic or socio-economic) status (Shavers, 2007).

Given the lack of clear agreement on social class-based categorisation of population in many countries (including India), measurement of SEP or SES has been the starting point for understanding socio-economic inequity. Irrespective of whether we choose social position or social status, there is a need to acknowledge that societies are stratified into population categories that reflect underlying differences in control or access over material resources and power structures. The differential accumulation of risk of illness/disease at different stages of life course because of belonging to a particular population category is the typical starting point for socio-economic inequity research in health. In the case of Indian society, the existence of caste and gender hierarchies cut across social class orders and hence, social status (or position) is determined by multiple identities apart from education, occupation and income. Hence, assessing a composite SES of households based on a list of household attributes tends to oversimplify the concept of SES.

In fact, SES as a concept has been criticised for its admixture of two abstract constructs: relative position in social structure (social position) and the honour and prestige given to them by their community and culture (social status) (Krieger, 2001b; Shavers, 2007). Based on this critique many scholars have preferred SEP as a more modest and precise indicator of socio-economic inequity than SES. However, due to the wider prevalence and use of SES in literature in Indian studies, we have largely used SES in the current chapter, while being conscious that in most studies where SES is reported, SEP is being measured. In fact, there is no clear methodological guidance on determining social status (as opposed to social position), more so in Indian settings where the intersections between caste and class are poorly explored and tend to vary across time, person and place within districts and states, and there is likely to be widespread variations on their effects across states.

4.1.4 Socio-economic Drivers of Health

Health and healthcare differences by economic categories of population remain the most visible form of population health differences. In general, economists describe three distinct types of economic inequalities that apply to health as well: Income, wealth and consumption inequalities, across which most societies worldwide show varying degrees of differences. Globally, income has been shown to correlate highly with health outcomes across various countries (Peters et al., 2008). The WHO global burden of disease uses income along with education and time (largely as a proxy of technology) as a distal driver of health. For several years, the dominant thought among economists has been the use of standard of living (measured as GDP per capita) as an important determinant of health. This line of thought has been attributed to the "seductively simplistic and consistent association between historical decreases in mortality and improved living standards of people". This growth-oriented approach first emerged with the work of Thomas McKeown, English physician and epidemiologist who analysed historical data from England and Wales for the period between 1837 and 1990. As a result of his analysis, McKeown attributed 50% of the reductions in mortality during this period (much of it preceding the advent of specific medical technologies associated with health improvements) to improved living standards (Hughes, Kuhn, Peterson, Rothman, & Solorzano, 2011). Several subsequent studies also sought to understand reasons underlying health improvements over time and concluded with strong inferences in international reports and in literature about how people's living standard may account for their health, thus making health a consequence of economic development with wealth and income being ways of *buying into* health.

Income and wealth related differences affect various individual, familial and societal entitlements and aspirations with respect to health, education and livelihoods. This is more so in a country like India where healthcare is financed through Out-Of-Pocket (OOP) payments at the time of service delivery. In a health system that does not protect people from the devastating effects of unpredictable healthcare expenditure, it has been argued that SES and healthcare entangle themselves in a vicious cycle, one worsening the other (Dodd & Munck, 2005; Guerrero et al., 1998). In India, healthcare imposes economic burden on households due to absence of any risk protection mechanism; the entire healthcare expenditure burden, often unforeseen and unplanned, is absorbed by the individuals and households (Kanjilal, Mazumdar, Mukherjee, & Rahman, 2010). According to the 2004–5 National Health Accounts, households finance 71% of healthcare through OOP payments at the time and point of healthcare use. By allowing the financing of people's healthcare through OOP payments, our health system makes it more difficult for the poor to access health services. In fact, several studies have shown that healthcare payments could lead to significant impoverishment among those who use the services (Bhojani et al., 2012; Bonu, Bhushan, Rani, & Anderson, 2009). In fact in 2004 (and later confirmed by improved estimates in 2010) approximately 6.2% of Indians fell below the poverty line due to OOP payments for healthcare (Berman, Ahuja, & Bhandari, 2010).

However, several decades of subsequent work by economists and social scientists has established that a direct, one-way causal link between being poor and hence not being able to *afford* good standard of living does not entirely account for poor health. The WHO's Commission on Social Determinants of Health (CSDH) emphasised the social origins of disease in its assertion that the reason for the "poor health of the poor, the social gradients of health within countries, and the marked health inequities between (and within) countries" is due to unequal distribution of power, income, goods and services, globally and nationally, that in turn manifests as inequalities we see in access to healthcare (Commisson on Social Determinants of Health [CSDH], 2008). Seen from the viewpoint of social determinants of health, equity cannot be achieved merely by finding gaps in delivery of health services or through research on technical matters of health services delivery, but through a systematic social and political effort in correcting structural/societal factors that enable, aggravate or are indifferent to existing inequalities in people's ability to realise their individual and familial needs and aspirations.

Inequality with respect to SEP underlies, and is often associated with many of the other social determinants such as gender, caste, literacy and other social vulnerabilities. Among the social determinants, lower SEP alone could contribute to ill-health and worse off outcomes. Hence societies, communities and states, which are indifferent to socio-economic inequalities, tend to contribute to the accumulation of poor health among those who are poor, illiterate and otherwise socio-economically worse off.

4.2 Summary of Literature on Health Inequities by Socio-economic Position in India

In this section, we summarise the current understanding on health inequities by socio-economic position in India based on the published research that we reviewed. We begin with a brief overview of how socio-economic inequities in health have been assessed in the studies we reviewed. Following this, we summarise the patterns reported in the papers starting with patterns related to healthcare seeking and access to services and then covering access to and utilisation of maternal and child health services, and finally patterns related to health outcomes including nutrition.

4.2.1 Assessing Health Inequities by Socio-economic Position

Assessments of socio-economic inequity in society have generally relied on measuring income and wealth differences. Consequently, socio-economic inequities in health too have leaned heavily on econometric approaches. Due to the disciplinary focus of economics on the nature of distribution of income, wealth or consumption in societies, economists have classically worked on socio-economic inequities in health, beginning typically with accurate measurement of differences at a population-level through comparing indicators of health status (or health outcomes, healthcare utilisation or financing) across social groups. This requires quantitative econometric approaches applied on population-level datasets and examining the differences across socio-demographic categories. The association of poor health and development indicators with these categories is the usual starting point for studies, and depending on the method, may also proceed to inquire if and to what extent these differences (inequalities) are unfair (inequity). The use of the term *difference* and *variation* in these approaches is meant in the statistical sense. Since econometric methods seek to measure the extent and impact of socio-economic inequalities, and rely heavily on statistical approaches, they choose metrics of inequalities and inequities such as the range, range ratio, Gini coefficient, concentration index, asset index, *t*-statistic, McLoone's index, etc. The econometric approaches to inequity have their advantages in providing a verifiable and objective measurement of the nature and extent of the differences (inequality) across socio-demographic groups, and depending on the method used also indicate the disproportionate accumulation of these differences in social groups (inequity).

The underlying principle of the econometric approach (as well as the related approaches within public health, especially epidemiology), however, is large-scale population data gathered through household or individual surveys, typically one of the periodic nationwide surveys with standardised survey tools or in some instances data collected from a given area through survey tools.

Using survey data to investigate the relationship between social variables and differences in health, illness or mortality has a long history. In modern academic literature, the idea of collecting data from households and analysing differentials across particular regions and social groups has been traced back to 1840s when Edwin Chadwick, a journalist and a social reformer prepared a report (the Chadwick Report of 1842) which was one of the first to indicate a correlation between poor sanitation and higher disease prevalence, mortality and lower life expectancy in certain neighbourhoods in UK (Golding, 2006). The report contributed to sanitary reforms in the UK (the 1848 Public Health Act) and was used to support some of the central assertions in the 1845 treatise on the Condition of the Working Class in England by the German philosopher Friedrich Engels—one of the first systematic study of the industrial working class in Victorian England—showing the ill-effects of the industrial revolution on workers' health and living conditions (Engels & McLellan, 1993). Over the years, measurement of population-level differences across social groups has become more sophisticated through cross-fertilisation between epidemiology and economics, leading to a general global pattern showing that relative income distribution even in affluent societies is associated with negative health outcomes (Forbes & Wainwright, 2001; Peters et al., 2008).

Among Indian literature on socio-economic inequities in health, the econometric approaches were the most frequently used approach. In terms of data too, most papers were based on large nationwide survey data, which carried income and/or asset information of respondents. They then stratified respondents based on aggregate indices that allowed for comparison between these strata in terms of various health outcomes.

One of the indices used is the wealth index that more than half of the papers used. The wealth index is created based on ownership of one or more of 33 household assets or housing characteristics collected by the National Family Health Survey (NFHS). These studies computed the wealth index based on this ownership data, as a proxy for income and ranked households based on scores of assets ownership (see for example Saxena, Vangani, Mavalankar, & Thomsen, 2013; Singh, Rai, & Kumar, 2013).

A smaller proportion of papers used the concentration index as a measure of inequality. The concentration index (CI) approaches inequality by estimating the degree to which adverse health outcomes are found in a population group, given that the proportion of the outcome in the group ought not to be more than the proportion of that group in the population. Any *more than expected otherwise* accumulation of adverse health outcome in that population is taken as an indicator of inequity (unfair accumulation of inequality within socio-demographic population category). CI has been computed for various health outcomes (immunisation coverage, child mortality, undernutrition) as well as regional inequalities by state (comparing CI across state populations to understand if inequality is greater in one state with respect to another) (see for example Arokiasamy & Pradhan, 2011; Chalasani, 2012). Several studies further decomposed the measures of inequality such as the CI by trying to isolate the important drivers of poor CI, i.e. they tried to understand why there is a concentration of inequalities in particular groups. Using regression models or decomposition analysis, these authors isolated the extent to which income, literacy or other assumed variables could explain the majority of the inequality observed (Joe, Mishra, & Navaneetham, 2009; Pradhan & Arokiasamy, 2010). Most studies assessed inequalities with respect to specific health problems or health outcomes. Inequity in health outcomes especially maternal and child health outcomes (antenatal and postnatal care, immunisation coverage, low birth weight), and childhood malnutrition are the most researched, possibly because a large part of the NFHS focuses on this.

4.2.2 Healthcare Seeking and Access: Focus on Maternal and Child Health Services

In this section we summarise the evidence on utilisation of preventive health care such as child immunisation and antenatal, delivery, postnatal and contraceptive services. Inequities in access to inpatient and outpatient health care across socio-economic position, caste and gender have been discussed in the health systems chapter.

In terms of access to maternal and child health services, unequal access across the socio-economic spectrum is a nearly nationwide phenomenon. This is despite a decade of technical and financial investment in reproductive and child health especially through innovative approaches in the National Health Mission (Das, Rao, & Hagopian, 2011). Data from 2007–08 showed that across 28 states and union territories, the ratio of the mean coverage between the wealthiest and the poorest wealth quintile was 2 (coverage being two times better among the wealthiest quintile than the poorest) in almost 20 states. Coverage was measured using a composite index that included four intervention areas: family planning, maternal and neonatal health, immunisation and treatment of sick children (Singh et al., 2013).

4.2.2.1 Child Immunisation

All studies reported high degree of inequality in immunisation between children from poor and rich households persisting across time points (Pande & Yazeback, 2003; Arokiasamy, Jain, Goli, & Pradhan, 2013; Arokiasamy & Pradhan, 2011; Kanjilal et al., 2007; Joe, Mishra, & Navaneetham, 2008) while one study reported significant differences between children from slum and non-slum communities (Gupta, Thakur, & Kumar, 2008). In 1992–93 (NFHS-1) the most striking inequality was among urban children with no immunisation: 10 times as many of the poorest compared to the richest children were without any immunisation in urban areas. In rural India as well, children from poorer households were less likely to be fully immunised and more likely to have no immunisation than were those from the richest households. In states with high levels of immunisation, urban children were more likely to be fully immunised and less likely to have no vaccines than were rural children in the same state (Pande & Yazbeck, 2003). More than a decade later, the same pattern of unequal rates of immunisation between children from poor and rich household was found to persist (Arokiasamy et al., 2013).

States with seemingly similar performance may have very different patterns of inequalities by socio-economic status. One such difference is highlighted by Arokiasamy and Pradhan (2011) by taking the example of Jammu and Kashmir and Punjab in a study using NFHS-3 data. While children from economically better off households did similarly in both states, the poorest children were less likely to be fully immunised in Jammu than in Punjab. In the case of no immunisation, while Maharashtra, Kerala and Himachal Pradesh all had a similar low proportion of rural children who were completely not immunised, and thus on average were equally good performers; the poorest children were more likely to be completely not immunised in Maharashtra and Himachal Pradesh than was the case in Kerala.

Studies indicate that wealth-based inequalities may be widening overtime in relatively well-performing states with high average levels of immunisation prevalence. For example, in 1992–93 it was found that southern states with high average levels of immunisation had lower wealth-based inequalities in immunisation (Pande & Yazbeck, 2003). In 2005–06, wealth inequalities in child immunisation were more pronounced in the Southern states than in the EAG states with lower average child immunisation prevalence (Arokiasamy et al., 2013). In fact, another study reported that the decline in immunisation coverage in the economically better off state of Maharashtra was most noticeable among the poorest and poor wealth quintiles (Mohanty & Pathak, 2009).

4.2.2.2 Maternal Health Care Services

Studies based on data spanning 10–15 years consistently found that wealth was one of the strongest determinants of antenatal care (ANC) and skilled birth attendant use, with the poor being at a disadvantage, in urban as well as in rural areas (Saxena et al., 2013; Hazarika, 2009, 2011; Kumar & Mohanty, 2011; Kesterton, Cleland, Sloggett, & Ronsmans, 2010; Pathak, Singh, & Subramanian, 2010; Kanjilal et al., 2007; Salam & Siddiqui, 2006). In urban areas, there were significant gaps in utilisation of ANC services between women living in slum and non-slum communities (Hazarika, 2009). Pregnant women from poor and uneducated backgrounds with at least one child were the least likely to receive antenatal check-ups and services in the four large north Indian states of Bihar, Madhya Pradesh, Rajasthan and Uttar Pradesh (Pallikadavath, Foss, & Stones, 2004).

Poverty or economic constraint was an important factor behind exercising choice in terms of where to deliver. Kanjilal, Mukherjee, Singh, Mondal, Barman, and Mandal (2007) found that 62% of all pregnant mothers in the poorest quintile but only 19% of them in the richest quintile delivered at home clearly implying that barriers get easier as one progresses from poorest to richest quintile. This study in West Bengal identified three important barriers, geographical, financial and an additional barrier of poverty which reinforced the effects of the other two. Among the least privileged households in a district in West Bengal (with poorest access, wealth and education) only 10–15% of births were in a medical facility (Tuddenham, Rahman, Singh, Barman, & Kanjilal, 2010).

There were significant differences in the use of skilled delivery care among the urban and rural populations in India. Women in urban areas were more likely to use skilled attendants. Better educated, economically well-off and urban women availed the delivery care services to the maximum (Gupta et al., 2008; Hazarika, 2011). Poor women were the worse off in terms of access to services (Pallikadavath et al., 2004; Salam & Siddiqui, 2006). The empowered action group (EAG) states fared poorly with respect to several inequality indicators than the non-EAG states (Arokiasamy et al., 2013).

Of the maternal health services, postnatal care was reported to be particularly unequal, compared to antenatal and childbirth services, with the probability of mothers from rich households using postnatal services being three times more compared with those from poor households. The rich-poor ratio in case of babies receiving two or more check-ups within the first 10 days after birth, however, was only 1.8 (Singh, Pallikadavath, Ram, & Ogollah, 2012b).

Contraceptive services have been a major priority for the Reproductive and Child Health (currently Reproductive, Maternal, Neonatal, Child and Adolescent

Health RMNCH+A) Programme of the government. Even so, there is a rich–poor gap in coverage by contraceptive services. A study across six cities of Uttar Pradesh found that women in slum areas had a lower contraceptive prevalence than women from non-slum areas and poorer women were more likely to have an unmet need for contraception as compared to richer women (Speizer, Nanda, Achyut, Pillai, & Guilkey, 2012). However, the wealth-gap in contraceptive prevalence was smaller than for other maternal health services (Saxena et al., 2013), and there was evidence of the gap narrowing overtime. During 1992–93 to 2005–06, contraceptive prevalence among the urban poor increased by 45%, as compared to 21% among urban non-poor, narrowing the non-poor/poor ratio from 1.40 to 1.17 during that period (Kumar & Mohanty, 2011).

Two studies point to a disturbing trend of increasing wealth-based inequities in maternal health care. In a study of inequality among women in Uttar Pradesh, Maharashtra and Tamil Nadu using data for three time points from 1992–93 to 2005–06, the authors reported that increments in utilisation of antenatal care and institutional delivery were mainly noted among the non-poor mothers, and the poor mothers benefited least from the government sponsored maternal health care services over the past 15 years (Pathak et al., 2010). They also reported that the most advantageous position was held by non-poor mothers from Tamil Nadu or Maharashtra, living in urban areas, with above primary education and literate husband, with low parity and some exposure to mass media indicating the role of these with positive outcomes. Another study, which focused on changes over time in urban areas also found that between 1992–1993 and 2005–2006, service coverage for antenatal care and institutional delivery had increased in urban areas of the country. The gap in utilisation of antenatal care persisted but marginally declined during this period, but the gap in utilisation of skilled attendance at delivery marginally increased. In 1992–93, the urban non-poor to urban poor ratio in skilled delivery care was 1.73, and in 2005–06, it was 1.75 (Kumar & Mohanty, 2011).

Even in the process of providing maternal healthcare, there were inequities. In terms of quality and content of advice received, healthcare advice concentrated disproportionately among the rich (Pallikadavath et al., 2004; Singh et al., 2012b). In a study of four North Indian states (Bihar, Madhya Pradesh, Rajasthan and Uttar Pradesh), health workers were observed to visit better off rather than poorer households. Higher social and economic status was associated with increased chances of receiving specific components including blood pressure measurement, a blood test and urine testing (Pallikadavath et al., 2004). In a 2012 study, which examined the rich–poor gaps in seven types of advice given to pregnant and newly delivered women, it was found that the rich–poor ratios were consistently above one, thus indicating that the rich were more likely than the poor to receive advice. At the same time, the rich–poor ratios were higher in the lower level public facilities compared to the higher level public facilities, indicating that inequalities were more pronounced among women who availed themselves of antenatal care in the lower level facilities (Singh et al., 2012a). In terms of quality of health services for economically disadvantaged, the south Indian states were reported to be marginally better off (Rani, Bonu, & Harvey, 2008).

4.2.2.3 Use of Public Versus Private Health Care

Many studies have established the difference in healthcare seeking at government versus private facilities by socio-economic groups, with the rich more likely to use private health care. In a study among Mumbai slum-dwellers, government health services for institutional delivery were reported to be used more by people from lower wealth quintiles, suggesting that they were an inferior good, while demand for institutional deliveries and private services increased with wealth and as such were normal goods (Skordis-Worrall et al., 2011). Seeking healthcare for neonates was also socio-economically patterned (Skordis-Worrall et al., 2011; Singh et al., 2012c). In terms of point of care, there were regional variations, but in general, babies belonging to the richer households were more likely to be examined in a private facility compared to the poor who were more likely to be examined in the government facilities (Singh et al., 2012c).

However, these patterns varied for type of health service and for different parts of India. For example, in a study analysing post-partum care-seeking data from a rural poor neighbourhood in West Bengal, authors reported that women from lower socio-economic groups were less likely to seek post-partum care from formal providers (Tuddenham et al., 2010). However, in West Bengal itself this phenomenon is not shared across all services. A larger study across three districts purposively selected to represent both well-performing and poorly performing districts in terms of socio-economic and development indicators, found that the utilisation of unqualified practitioners of modern medicine in rural areas for general health problems was almost uniformly spread across various income groups. This implies that lower cost of treatment was not the only factor or the most important one to explain people's dependence on particular category of practitioners (Kanjilal et al., 2007). The same study reported that for hospitalisation, the rich almost equally used public hospitals as the poor. In Maharashtra, an analysis of NFHS data on women's choice of place of delivery found an increasing pattern of use of private sector by lower/middle income group (Thind, Mohani, Banerjee, & Hagigi, 2008). This may progressively increase their likelihood of impoverishment due to healthcare costs in these groups as opposed to the rich.

In spite of differing patterns across various SES with respect to healthcare access, generally speaking, wherever availability improves with ongoing reforms without an accompanying improvement in financial access (either through supply side reforms such as prepayment mechanisms or through better ability to pay due to poverty alleviation or cash transfers), utilisation of health services will be determined by ability to pay and hence favouring the upper SES (Speizer et al., 2012).

4.2.2.4 Regressive Healthcare Financing

Healthcare expenditure has been reported to be regressive by all papers. Indirect health expenditure was found to be (weakly) regressive as the poorest were more likely to use wage income to meet health expenses, while the less poor were more likely to use savings (Skordis-Worrall et al., 2011). In case of inpatient care, the West Bengal study found that the impact of OOP payment was relatively more severe on higher income groups indicating a progressive OOP financing system. The poorest households were likely to send fewer members, and spend proportionately much less on inpatient care (Kanjilal et al., 2007). However, delaying care-seeking and settling for less costly options are often a matter of lack of choice and/or access for people in lower socio-economic groups and the distribution of OOP across SES needs to be interpreted keeping the inequitable nature of access to services both across SES and within households (across gender). While some studies reported higher incidence of catastrophic healthcare payments for some services (e.g. inpatient care) among the economically well-off, others found no significant difference in the incidence of catastrophic spending across wealth quintiles (Skordis-Worrall et al., 2011; Speizer et al., 2012). In fact, some studies reported that total health expenditure was significantly higher in the highest quintile and therefore it cannot be concluded that health care financing was regressive (Skordis-Worrall et al., 2011).

4.2.3 Health Outcomes

4.2.3.1 Child Survival

There is evidence to show that wealth as well as literacy are predictors of better child survival (Rajan, Kennedy, & King, 2013; Pradhan & Arokiasamy, 2010). At state-level, only literacy remained a significant and negative predictor of infant and under-five mortality. At the less aggregated district level, both poverty and literacy predicted child survival, but literacy had a stronger effect than poverty (Rajan et al., 2013). Decomposition analysis by Pradhan and Arokiasamy (2010) showed that household economic status (46%), mother's illiteracy (35%) and rural residence (15%) contributed to 96% of socio-economic inequalities in under-2 mortality at the national level.

Many studies have found regional differences with respect to socio-economic inequalities in child survival across several states (Arokiasamy et al., 2013; Arokiasamy & Pradhan, 2011; De & Dhar, 2013). In many instances, the poor in the economically better off states faced higher inequality. For example, Maharashtra, Madhya Pradesh, Gujarat, Tamil Nadu and Punjab experienced greater income-related inequalities in under-five mortality as against Uttar Pradesh, Rajasthan and Bihar, which showed much lower levels of inequalities (De & Dhar, 2013; Joe et al., 2009). Another study reported that poverty contributed more in some states than in others to health inequalities. In Sikkim, Manipur, Meghalaya, Assam, Madhya Pradesh, Karnataka and Goa; it contributed to more than 70% of the inequalities in child survival (Pradhan & Arokiasamy, 2010).

4.2.3.2 Maternal Mortality and Morbidity

The pace of fall of maternal mortality too is unequal. One study from Rajasthan reported that the risk of death was nearly five times higher among women who belong to poor households (Gupta, Khanna, Gupta, Sharma, & Sharma, 2010). The *Janani Suraksha Yojana* introduced in 2005 under the National Rural Health Mission was intended to bring about reduction in MMR by providing cash incentives for institutional delivery. A study covering nine "low-performing" states (Assam, Bihar, Chhattisgarh, Jharkhand, Madhya Pradesh, Odisha, Rajasthan, Uttarakhand and Uttar Pradesh) found that between 2005 and 2010 the MMR declined four-times faster in the richest divisions of the nine states as compared to the poorest divisions, resulting in increased inequalities in maternal health outcomes (Randive, San Sebastian, De Costa, & Lindholm, 2014).

4.2.3.3 Other Morbidities

Save for one paper that questioned the apparent aggregation of cardiovascular mortality among the poor in India, all other studies generally reported worse off mortality and morbidity for the poor with respect to various health problems including dental caries and Tuberculosis. Even the one paper questioning the reported trend of aggregated cardiovascular risk among the poor, conceded that mortality due to these is likely to be higher among the poor (Gupta, 2006; Subramanian, Corsi, Subramanyan, & Smith, 2013).

4.2.3.4 Nutrition

In the case of childhood undernutrition, lower levels of household wealth and maternal education are consistently identified by studies as being important drivers (Arokiasamy & Pradhan, 2011). There was a clear gradient in the association between wealth quintiles and the probability of being undernourished. Poorer regions of central and eastern India displayed higher underweight population proportions.

In terms of trends over time (1992–93 to 2005–06), social disparities in child undernutrition either widened or were static, but never narrowed, against a background of national economic growth (Subramanian, Kawachi, & Smith, 2007; Subramanyam, Kawachi, Berman, & Subramanian, 2010). In fact, one study showed that children from better off families experienced a greater decline in undernutrition between 1992 and 2005 compared to children from households in the lowest wealth quintile, and these disparities widened over time. State-level income inequality was strongly associated with poor nutritional outcomes even after controlling for various individual and household characteristics, indicating policy and systemic contributors to this problem (Subramanian et al., 2007). In summary, many papers find that the trend of economic development tends to benefit the better off groups (Houweling et al., 2013; Kanjilal et al., 2010; Pathak et al., 2010).

Prevalence of anaemia in women also registered an increase during 1998–99 and 2005–06, from 51 to 56% at the national level, and only 5 of 25 states registered a decline. Prevalence of anaemia was patterned along social disadvantages, with a higher probability of prevalence among those from lower wealth quintiles, lower levels of education and belonging to the Scheduled Caste and Scheduled Tribe communities (Balarajan, Fawzi, & Subramanian, 2013).

- Inequities in health by socio-economic position is pervasive, and was found to exist in child survival, maternal mortality and morbidity, child nutrition and anaemia in women, as well as in utilisation of maternal and child health services (antenatal and postnatal care, skilled birth attendance and child immunisation). In addition to inequitable coverage, there were inequities in the quality of services provided. Health inequities within urban settings are found not only between the poor and non-poor but also between slum and non-slum populations.
- Inequities in health by socio-economic position have persisted during a period (1992–93 to 2010) of rapid economic growth of the country and the introduction of numerous schemes specifically to improve maternal and child survival.
- In many states and for many health indicators, the gap between rural and urban areas and that between the poor and non-poor have widened since 1992–93. States with higher average survival and coverage indicators have shown a trend of widening inequalities. It appears that non-poor, urban households have benefitted disproportionately from economic progress as well as health interventions meant for the poor and marginalised households.

From the papers on health inequities by SEP synthesised in the previous section, less than one-third discussed the possible mechanisms and/or pathways through which the inequities come about. The most obvious pathway reported is the open and unregulated market mechanism for seeking healthcare. In a health system where healthcare must be purchased from the open market, those who cannot afford it are likely to be disadvantaged with respect to health outcomes. Joe and colleagues reported that the degree of health inequalities escalated when the rising average income levels of the population were accompanied by rising income inequalities (Joe et al., 2009). The counterfactual for this is found in one of the child health studies; crucial inputs to neonatal and child healthcare often must be purchased and are hence likely to be financially inaccessible to the poor. However, according to Chalasani (2012) there has been a weakening of association between neonatal health and income in urban settings despite increasing economic inequalities. The authors believe that the potential effects of economic inequalities may have been influenced by the universally subsidising effect of public programmes aimed at reducing mortality among children, especially the various national programmes focusing on child health.

4.3 Mechanisms of Health Inequities by Socio-economic Position in India

The present section is based on a critical interpretive synthesis of the literature on socio-economic inequities in India (see Chap. 3 for methodology). We begin with a critique of the dominant methodological approaches to study socio-economic inequity in health. We then summarise the main themes emerging from the evidence synthesised in Sect. 4.2, organised along the factors and intermediate steps identified by the CSDH framework.

4.3.1 Bringing the Social into Socio-economic Inequity Research

Research on socio-economic inequity in India has generally focused on examining income and wealth distribution patterns in society vis-a-vis disease, health/healthcare and mortality in social groups. These studies, while confirming the widely prevalent global pattern that, in relatively unequal societies (such as the one in India) those at the bottom of the social order are more likely to experience ill-health or even behave in certain ways with respect to seeking (or not!) healthcare, they explain little about why or how this happens nor do they improve our understanding of the mechanisms through which these inequities come about in (Indian) society (Forbes & Wainwright, 2001). The main critique of survey-based epidemiological analysis of population datasets is that they simplify and isolate social and political processes that are inevitably dynamic, interacting and inter-dependent, context-specific and history-dependent to simple unidimensional explanations based on risk factors. They are unable to consider the individual and social circumstances that drive behaviour and neglect the complex interaction between social structures and individual or collective human agency to overcome the effect of, or align or influence these structures. This critique predominantly comes from disciplines in the social sciences which have approached socio-economic inequity from other perspectives (other than income, wealth or consumption). Other critiques have challenged the apparent objectivity of such analyses and have shown how value-laden inequity measures such as the Concentration Index can—especially in unequal societies where the value of increasing the weighting of health can produce marked differences in country or region rankings—challenge the notion of objectivity of such analyses (Wagstaff, 2002).

The econometric approaches to inequality have their advantages in providing a verifiable and objective measurement of the nature and extent of inequalities across socio-demographic groups. However, other approaches to studying inequalities including anthropological and critical ethnographic inquiry, psychological approaches and the newer inter-disciplinary approaches drawing upon the intersecting nature of inequalities seek to answer how or why questions related to inequity. One of the ways in which these approaches improve our understanding of health inequity is by seeking to build upon, refine or refute prevailing scientific or lay explanations for these inequities. The contribution of social science inquiry to our understanding of the social mechanisms is discussed later. However, the need to draw upon larger theories on how and why inequity is produced and framing context-based research studies within these larger theories is largely lacking.

By building upon current knowledge, these approaches uphold the emancipatory role of knowledge production through social inquiry and try to improve our understanding of social phenomena (such as inequity) at a mechanismic or explanatory level. They tend to supplement purported empiricist approaches driven by the aim to arrive at empirical generalisations with comparably lesser emphasis on conjecturing the underlying mechanisms positing that social phenomena that we see are embedded within history-dependent social structures that are constantly interacting with human agency, various theories in sociology, anthropology and political science offer useful anchors within which to begin inquiry into inequities (Bunge, 1997). For example, theories of macroeconomic reforms *trickling down* into improved income and wealth among the poor is an important structural reform in a given society which may have consequences within households, communities and health services, but may altogether be neglected from an empirical data collection and analysis exercise, unless the exercise was a priori guided by such a starting point.

4.3.2 Social Determinants View of Socio-economic Inequity in Health

According to the CSDH framework, various circumstances of daily life of people including their material circumstances, degree of social cohesion, psychosocial factors, behaviours and biological factors interface with the health system and together determine the distribution of well-being. However, it is not only these circumstances of daily life, but various wider societal factors (what the CSDH calls *structural drivers*) including macro-policy, socio-economic and political context on one hand as well as deep-rooted power imbalances, rules and norms in society, social position, gender, ethnicity, occupation, income, etc. which interact with the circumstances of daily life in producing the (mal) distribution of health and well-being that we see as patterns in our research.

The CSDH framework is useful to organise explanations for recurring themes that emerge across the research on socio-economic inequity in India. We describe below some of the explanatory mechanisms that emerge from the themes discussed in papers on socio-economic inequity. Within the CSDH framework, we see that themes related to socio-economic and political context (health financing and governance and macro-policy drivers), social position and other correlates and finally the material circumstances and social cohesion are relatively better discussed in the research. However, there is a total absence of research on, or discussion of psychosocial factors, or behaviour and biological factors. These are important drivers of social exclusion and hence important mechanisms through which social determinants act on people's health.

4.3.3 *Mechanisms Driving Inequity*

4.3.3.1 Socio-economic and Political Context

Several authors discussed themes related to the wider socio-economic and political context as a driver of inequities in health. The papers discussed factors related to governance, policy, cultural and societal norms and values.

4.3.3.2 Governance and Macro-policy Drivers

There is some reflection in the papers on important governance patterns that could explain the comparably worse socio-economic inequalities in health in some states, most prominently system leakages, poor adaptation to target group and regressive financing mechanisms. Non-poor could use public systems designed to provide shelter, water, sanitation and sewerage, health care and food grains for the poor in poorly targeted or poorly governed systems leading to an elite capture of government schemes and services. Integrated Child Development Services (ICDS) is given as an example by Subramanian et al. (2007) and Joe, Mishra, and Navaneetham (2010) of regressive policy. ICDS coverage is highest in states with the lowest levels of undernutrition and in states with high economic growth. In the poorer states, government budgetary allocations for the ICDS programme per undernourished child are lower. Indeed, poorer states also tend to spend only 65–75% of their allocation, suggesting poor governance. Some papers have applied theories of distributional justice to approach this question (Subramanian et al., 2007). Agenda setting with respect to equitable development is an important barrier identified. The worst performing states with respect to childhood malnutrition, such as Bihar and Uttar Pradesh do not spend available funds for the ICDS activities. On the contrary, highly unequal states are characterised by the simultaneous existence of overconsumption by privileged groups and food insecurity among the poor (Subramanian et al., 2007).

A mix of demand and supply failures has been advanced as an explanation by Pande and Yazbeck in 2003 for how governance failure is especially a feature of worse off states. This is based on their finding that there is low wealth inequalities at both ends of the spectrum of overall immunisation levels—the *worst* end where there is total system failure and thus high levels of no immunisation, and the *best* end where the system works very well and there are high levels of full immunisation. Wherever there is abysmal system failure (high no immunisation), inequalities are low because all are deprived. Their finding of system failure could be due to demand failure, particularly as regards information, such that the rural poor may not demand or may not use available immunisation services. Weak immunisation performance in poor, rural areas may also be indicative of supply issues or system failure in reaching underprivileged populations in that immunisation services may be inadequate or ineffective in such areas. That there is a systems failure that disproportionately affects the poor is borne out by other studies too where the economically better off utilised targeted schemes and services more than the worse off (Pande & Yazbeck, 2003).

The question of political will comes quite often as an important driver of inequalities (Saxena et al., 2013; Thorat & Sadana, 2009). Political will manifesting as more inclusive policymaking and implementation is put forward as likely to be ameliorative of inequalities. The role of socio-economic class in influencing political decision-making, which in turn influences policies that affect education, healthcare and employment, is of interest. Poorer political agenda setting on issues related to poverty has been identified as an important underlying cause for the policy malaise with respect to socio-economic inequalities (Saxena et al., 2013) While many papers report that reduction in economic disparities might lead to a great reduction in social disparities (see for example Subramanyam et al., 2010), some authors urge caution in the manner in which economic growth at the national level is affecting the economic status of various groups in the population, implying the need to critically unpack national or state-level growth and understand how the averages and means may be concealing worsening off or status-quo in some social groups (Kanjilal et al., 2010; Kumari, 2013; Subramanian et al., 2007). After adjusting for several individual and state-level development covariates, the finding that living in an unequal state itself was disadvantageous for the economically deprived shows the extent of state failure in terms of redistribution and equitable growth (Subramanian et al., 2007). Their initial hypothesis sums up their finding succinctly "Given the same level of income or socio-economic position, an individual might be better off in a more egalitarian area, in terms of having a reduced risk both of being undernourished and of being over nourished (p. 802)". Their study confirms this hypothesis with respect to nutrition, but the various reasons they find for this reveal larger governance and redistribution issues beyond ICDS programme or nutrition-related interventions.

4.3.3.3 Geographical Inequities Abound Across Districts and Sub-districts

Governance at district and sub-district level could impose adversities in addressing regional inequalities. For example, a recent analysis found that there are as many as 27 districts with sub-districts both in the top and bottom 10% with respect to performance on social and development indicators in the country. Furthermore, there are 92 districts with sub-districts from both the top and bottom 20% sub-districts. And finally, the top and bottom 30% of sub-districts coexist in as many as 166 districts of the 640 districts of India (Bakshi, Chawla, & Shah, 2015). The problems associated with systematic poverty and disadvantage would have stronger effects in districts where local capacity is already the weakest (Nguyen, Jimenez-Soto, Dayal, & Hodge, 2013).

4.3.3.4 Discrimination as a Driver of Inequality

The study of social discrimination as drivers of inequities emerged in very few papers. Although discrimination has been inferred as a possible driver of socio-economic inequities, methodological difficulties in designing and implementing studies to understand the nature of discrimination impose challenges.

Discrimination with respect to caste and/or class appears in many studies. Thorat and Sadana (2009) report significant differences in health status between social groups—in their analysis this caste differential operated in spite of class differences. The poor were more likely to make informal payments than the better off (Skordis-Worrall et al., 2011). In Gujarat, for example, one study reported that poor women belonging to a scheduled tribe (ST) were over five times less likely to use antenatal services than the non-poor advantaged groups. The same study reports that women in the poor scheduled caste (SC[1]) category were five times less likely to utilise antenatal services than the non-poor others (Saxena et al., 2013). Bribes, demeaning and discriminatory treatment also compromise access for the poor and marginalised (Jeffery & Jeffery, 2010).

In fact, few papers began with the question of trying to understand the mechanisms or drivers of inequality. One such paper was by Joe et al. (2009), who found that discrimination faced by some groups may be the underlying reason for socio-economic inequalities; they report that these groups are "discriminated against while accessing publicly provided entitlements such as subsidised food grain through the public distribution system (PDS), meal for children at schools (Mid-Day Meal Programme) and nutritional supplements at mother and child care centres". They further reflect on how—these caste identities being inherited—social welfare and redressal of socio-economic inequalities must look beyond targeting of the poor and ought to aim for the underlying social mechanisms of this poverty, an important one being caste. A few other papers also strongly posited caste as an important underlying driver of persistent socio-economic inequalities (Thorat & Sadana, 2009). SCs suffer from unequal access to public services, presumably because of caste and untouchability related discrimination and exclusion. One mechanismic explanation is the relatively high discrimination and selective disrespectful behaviour by public service personnel more than in private sector; they

[1]A note on terminologies is in order here. While we would prefer to use the terms Dalit and Adivasi, and have done so when we are referring to these population groups, where we cite data from published sources, we have maintained the terminologies used by the authors of the study. Thus in almost all places where studies are cited, the terms SC and ST, or as is often the case, SC/ST is used.

receive less frequent and less detailed awareness material and information on camps/schemes. Public health workers could play a role in perpetuating inequalities by being selective in providing treatment and advice. They tend to be biased in favour of the richer sections of the society. Caste and class discrimination is possibly worse off for the poorer classes or Dalit/Adivasi communities. The most poverty-stricken and powerless members of Indian society experience deep-seated class, caste and urban prejudices against them in many contexts and health seeking is no exception to this social phenomenon. In rural north India, one study found discrimination to be severe enough to lead to adverse health outcomes (Jeffery & Jeffery, 2010).

In one study, socio-economic inequalities in the utilisation of postnatal care among facility births could not be explained simply by access and cost factors only; the capacity of the public health care system in providing equitable care to its clients is called into question (Singh et al., 2012a, b; Thorat & Sadana, 2009). However, Rani et al. (2008) suggest that it is difficult to ascertain if the socio-economic differentials within each region are due to active discrimination by the providers or due to greater empowerment of the better off women to demand higher quality services from the providers. In some instances, hesitation to visit poorer households may also drive poor services coverage and quality. It is possible that health workers are more reluctant to visit the homes of poor women in some settings; conversely, some better off women may prefer not to invite health workers into their homes perhaps for reasons of caste or status (Pallikadavath et al., 2004). The only positive scenario, where such discrimination seems to have been apparently overcome, is with respect to SC/ST women who were more likely than other women to access surgical methods of family planning (Thorat & Sadana, 2009). However, this apparently positive finding has to be critically examined within a reproductive rights framework.

4.3.3.5 Social Cohesion

Subramanian et al. (2007) posit that poor social cohesion in unequal societies may underlie some of adverse health outcome patterns among the poor, the only theoretical explanation advanced for this perverse pattern seen across most papers. They report that income inequality may be a marker of a less generous, or inefficient PDS. It is likely that the existing PDS are vulnerable to manipulation by vested interests, a characteristic more likely to be present in states with high levels of income inequality and low social cohesion. Improvements in social cohesion are very likely to improve inequalities; an experimental study showed that socio-economic inequalities in neonatal mortality could be reduced through community-based participatory intervention (Houweling et al., 2013). The strategy of the implementing non-governmental organisation sums up many of the approaches that several research papers suggest: Use regional targeting (selecting underserved areas in poor districts in poor states) combined with a universal strategy at the community level (ensuring that no person is omitted and that social cohesion is not disrupted by overt-targeting or by inclusion or exclusion criteria), while ensuring that the messages and activities of the intervention are understandable for and refer to those who need them most.

Poor social networks among the poor has also been posited as an explanation for poor awareness and utilisation; more so in states or societies where vested interests control local governance, access to social networks could determine who obtains benefit from which scheme and who does not. For example, poor immigrants in large cities (driven in turn by inter-state macroeconomic differences) lack social networks and are rarely aware of their entitlements and the availability of free or affordable health services in urban centres (Mathur, Tsakos, Millett, Arora, & Watt, 2014; Nguyen et al., 2013).

4.3.3.6 Material Circumstances of Everyday Living

As described by Kanjilal et al. (2010), the two important (economic) pathways tying together socio-economic inequalities and health is the loss in productivity due to health problem and/or the financial burden of treatment. The degree of impact on the household would depend not only on the frequency and gravity of the healthcare expenditure, but also on the preexisting vulnerability of the affected household to health poverty. In a family that is also battling real life challenges of trying to educate their children and organise daily needs, such unforeseen healthcare shocks can be devastating. For families that are not at the extremes of income deprivation, the effects may manifest in the way of choosing lesser or inferior goods; this is the explanation provided for a significantly higher proportion of catastrophic spending occurred in the highest quintile among Mumbai slum-dwellers, possibly because women in the lowest quintile were forced to control spending by opting for inferior services (such as public providers and home deliveries) or by foregoing care altogether, a phenomenon also observed in several other studies (Bhanderi & Kannan, 2010; Skordis-Worrall et al., 2011).

4.3.3.7 Other Correlates

It has also been suggested that the influence of income and education would diminish as geographical access improves, thus one could expect that nationwide reforms such as the National Rural Health Mission would eventually improve equitable access, but interactions between distance and all other factors as tested in the case of institutional deliveries did not find this (Kesterton et al., 2010). Another assessment of the *Janani Suraksha Yojana* programme of the national rural health mission found that the decline in maternal mortality is slower in the poorest areas (Randive et al., 2014). Expansion of services may therefore not be sufficient to promote equitable utilisation. Even if there is latent demand for services (as is the case among the poor), poor quality of government services and high cost in the case of the private services, it can inhibit utilisation.

Many papers attribute a lot of socio-economic inequalities to poor literacy (especially maternal literacy), awareness of schemes, caste and other factors related to well-being. Many papers also caution against framing inequality exclusively around income, as this may be misleading. They argue that non-income goods like literacy may make an important contribution to public health and that policy should be based on a broader understanding of societal well-being and the factors that promote it rather than focusing exclusively on income. In the case of women empowerment for example (Kumar, 2007), it is the combination of caste and class at the individual and household level that drives inequality, more so among women. According to Rajan et al. (2013), "although wealthier is healthier, wealth cannot be understood simply in terms of average income". The effect of average income levels on health is indirect according to them: Higher average incomes may improve public health but only through reduced poverty and improved literacy. The influence of female literacy has been mentioned by several papers (Arokiasamy et al., 2013). It becomes more significant when a developing country experiences a first major spurt in the growth rate of the economy and the associated changes in society. The increased availability of health and other public infrastructures supporting child survival that comes with rapid economic development helps women to improve the survival chances of their children, and the literate women are better able to take advantage of these opportunities (Bhattacharya, 2012). In many other papers, although this linkage with maternal education is reported, the analysis is insufficient to demonstrate clear links on whether these merely co-occur. A related construct, maternal autonomy (a complex construct to measure that includes literacy among others) has been posited as being central to overcoming the adversities imposed by economic inequalities (Pallikadavath et al., 2004). That said many of the constituents of maternal autonomy are better attained in relatively high income households.

4.4 Conclusion

There are clearly large gaps in our understanding of how health inequities by socio-economic position are brought about, aggravated or maintained in our society. That said, existing research has unearthed several underlying mechanisms that are resulting in the inequity patterns that we see. As seen above, some of them are better researched than others, while a few plausible mechanisms (like those at the individual level or those related to social exclusion) are poorly investigated. A fundamental reason, however, for the insufficient *mechanismic* understanding of the drivers of health inequities by socio-economic position in India, is because several research studies stop at providing lucid descriptions of inequality and reflect only in their discussion section on the possible reasons or drivers. Often, the mechanisms are brought in the discussion section of papers and they tend to be speculative (because the drivers were rarely a priori the subject of the study) or important mechanisms operating at the macro-policy or governance level get left out because they were too far away from the given geographical scope of the study. Hence, the framing of research questions on socio-economic inequity needs to begin with the prevailing understanding on the topic. Currently, few research studies begin with *how* and *why* questions, possibly due to methodological limitations, but also possibly due to the disciplinary capture of socio-economic inequity research by econometric approaches.

References

Arokiasamy, P., Jain, K., Goli, S., & Pradhan, J. (2013). Health inequalities among urban children in India: A comparative assessment of empowered action group (EAG) and south Indian states. *Journal of Biosocial Science, 45*(2), 167–185. doi:10.1017/S0021932012000211.

Arokiasamy, P., & Pradhan, J. (2011). Measuring wealth-based health inequality among Indian children: The importance of equity vs efficiency. *Health Policy and Planning, 26*(5), 429–440. doi:10.1093/heapol/czq075.

Bakshi, S., Chawla, A., & Shah, M. (2015). Regional disparities in India: A moving frontier. *Economic & Political Weekly, 50*(1), 44–52.

Balarajan, Y. S., Fawzi, W. W., & Subramanian, S. V. (2013). Changing patterns of social inequalities in anaemia among women in India: Cross-sectional study using nationally representative data. *British Medical Journal Open, 3*(3), e002233–e002233. doi:10.1136/bmjopen-2012-002233.

Balarajan, Y. S., Selvaraj, S., & Subramanian, S. (2011). Health care and equity in India. *The Lancet, 377*(9764), 505–515. doi:10.1016/S0140-6736(10)61894-6.

Bartley, M. (2004). *Health inequality: An introduction to theories, concepts, and methods*. Cambridge, UK: Polity Press.

Berman, P. A., Ahuja, R. C., & Bhandari, L. (2010). The impoverishing effect of healthcare payments. *Economic & Political Weekly, 45*(16), 65–71.

Bhanderi, M. N., & Kannan, S. (2010). Untreated reproductive morbidities among ever married women of slums of Rajkot City, Gujarat: The role of class, distance, provider attitudes, and perceived quality of care. *Journal of Urban Health, 87*(2), 254–263. doi:10.1007/s11524-009-9423-y.

Bhattacharya, P. C. (2012). *Inequalities in child mortality in India: A district-level analysis*. Retrieved from http://repo.sire.ac.uk/handle/10943/402.

Bhojani, U., Triveni, B. S., Devadasan, R., Munegowda, C., Devadasan, N., Kolsteren, P., & Criel, B. (2012). Out-of-pocket healthcare payments on chronic conditions impoverish urban poor in Bangalore, India. *BMC Public Health, 12*(1), 990. doi:10.1186/1471-2458-12-990.

Bonu, S., Bhushan, I., Rani, M., & Anderson, I. (2009). Incidence and correlates of "catastrophic" maternal health care expenditure in India. *Health Policy and Planning, 24*(6), 445–456. doi:10.1093/heapol/czp032.

Bunge, M. (1997). Mechanism and explanation. *Philosophy of the Social Sciences, 27*(4), 410–465.

Chalasani, S. (2012). Understanding wealth-based inequalities in child health in India: A decomposition approach. *Social Science and Medicine, 75*(12), 2160–2169. doi:10.1016/j.socscimed.2012.08.012.

Commisson on Social Determinants of Health. (2008). *Closing the gap in a generation: Health equity through action on the social determinants of health*. Geneva: World Health Organization. Retrieved from http://whqlibdoc.who.int/publications/2008/9789241563703_eng.pdf.

Das, A., Rao, D., & Hagopian, A. (2011). India's Janani Suraksha Yojana: Further review needed. *Lancet, 377*(9762), 295–296–297. doi:10.1016/S0140-6736(11)60085-8.
De, P., & Dhar, A. (2013). Inequality in child mortality across different states of India: A comparative study. *Journal of Child Health Care, 17*(4), 397–409. doi:10.1177/1367493512468359.
Dodd, R., & Munck, L. (2005). *Dying for change: Poor people's experience of health and ill-health*. Retrieved from http://documents.worldbank.org/curated/en/123521468332446432/Dying-for-change-Poor-peoples-experience-of-health-and-ill-health.
Engels, F., & McLellan, D. (1993). *The condition of the working class in England*. Oxford: Oxford University Press.
Forbes, A., & Wainwright, S. P. (2001). On the methodological, theoretical and philosophical context of health inequalities research: Acritique. *Social Science and Medicine, 53*, 801–816.
Galobardes, B., Lynch, J., & Smith, G. D. (2007). Measuring socioeconomic position in health research. *British Medical Bulletin, 81–82*(1), 21–37. doi:10.1093/bmb/ldm001.
Golding, A. M. B. (2006). Sir Edwin Chadwick and inequalities. *Public Health, 120*(5), 474–476. doi:10.1016/j.puhe.2005.11.002.
Gray, A. M. (1982). Inequalities in health. The black report: A summary and comment. *International Journal of Health Services: Planning, Administration, Evaluation, 12*(3), 349–380. doi:10.2190/XXMM-JMQU-2A7Y-HX1E.
Guerrero, R., Jancloes, M., Martin, J. D., Haines, A., Kaseje, D., & Wasserman, M. P. (1998). How the cycle of poverty and ill health can be broken. *British Medical Journal, 316*(7142), 1456. doi:10.1136/bmj.316.7142.1456.
Gupta, R. (2006). Smoking, educational status & health inequity in India. *Indian Journal of Medical Research, 124*(1), 15–22.
Gupta, S. D., Khanna, A., Gupta, R., Sharma, N. K., & Sharma, N. D. (2010). Maternal mortality ratio and predictors of maternal deaths in selected desert districts in Rajasthan. *Women's Health Issues, 20*(1), 80–85. doi:10.1016/j.whi.2009.10.003.
Gupta, M., Thakur, J. S., & Kumar, R. (2008). Reproductive and child health inequities in Chandigarh union territory of India. *Journal of Urban Health, 85*(2), 291–299. doi:10.1007/s11524-007-9250-y.
Hazarika, I. (2009). Women's reproductive health in slum populations in India: Evidence from NFHS-3. *Journal of Urban Health: Bulletin of the New York Academy of Medicine, 87*(2). doi:10.1007/s11524-009-9421-0.
Hazarika, I. (2011). Factors that determine the use of skilled care during delivery in India: Implications for achievement of MDG-5 targets. *Maternal and Child Health Journal, 15*(8), 1381–1388. doi:10.1007/s10995-010-0687-3.
Houweling, T. A., Tripathy, P., Nair, N., Rath, S., Rath, S., Gope, R., … Prost, A. (2013). The equity impact of participatory women's groups to reduce neonatal mortality in India: Secondary analysis of a cluster-randomised trial. *International Journal of Epidemiology, 42*(2), 520–532. doi:10.1093/ije/dyt012.
Hughes, B. B., Kuhn, R., Peterson, C. M., Rothman, D. S., & Solorzano, J. R. (2011). *Improving global health: Patterns of potential human progress* (Vol. 3). New Dehli: Paradigm Publishers.
Jeffery, P., & Jeffery, R. (2010). Only when the boat has started sinking: A maternal death in rural north India. *Social Science and Medicine, 71*(10), 1711–1718. doi:10.1016/j.socscimed.2010.05.002.
Joe, W., Mishra, U. S., & Navaneetham, K. (2008). Health inequality in India: Evidence from NFHS-3. *Economic & Political Weekly*. Retrieved from http://citeseerx.ist.psu.edu/viewdoc/download?doi=10.1.1.575.1976&rep=rep1&type=pdf.
Joe, W., Mishra, U. S., & Navaneetham, K. (2009). Inequalities in childhood malnutrition in India: Some evidence on group disparities. *Journal of Human Development and Capabilities, 10*(3), 417–439. doi:10.1080/19452820903048886.
Joe, W., Mishra, U. S., & Navaneetham, K. (2010). Socio-economic inequalities in child health: Recent evidence from India. *An International Journal for Research, Policy and Practice, 5*(5), 493–508.

Kanjilal, B., Mazumdar, P. G., Mukherjee, M., & Rahman, M. H. (2010). Nutritional status of children in India: Household socio-economic condition as the contextual determinant. *International Journal for Equity in Health, 9*(1), 19. doi:10.1186/1475-9276-9-19.

Kanjilal, B., Mukherjee, M., Singh, S., Mondal, S., Barman, D., & Mandal, A. (2007). *Health, equity and poverty exploring the links in West Bengal, India.* Future Health Systems Innovations for Equity, Research Monograph, Indian Series. Retrieved from https://www.researchgate.net/publication/237479493_Health_Equity_and_Poverty_Exploring_the_Links_in_West_Bengal_India.

Kesterton, A. J., Cleland, J., Sloggett, A., & Ronsmans, C. (2010). Institutional delivery in rural India: The relative importance of accessibility and economic status. *BMC Pregnancy and Childbirth, 10*(1), 30. doi:10.1186/1471-2393-10-30.

Krieger, N. (2001a). A glossary for social epidemiology. *Journal of Epidemiology and Community Health, 55*(10), 693 LP-700. Retrieved from http://jech.bmj.com/content/55/10/693.abstract.

Krieger, N. (2001b). Theories for social epidemiology in the 21st century: An ecosocial perspective. *International Journal of Epidemiology, 30*(4), 668–677. doi:10.1093/ije/30.4.668.

Kumar, A. (2007). Health inequity and women's self-help groups in India: The role of caste and class. *Health Sociology Review, 16*(2), 160–168. doi:10.5172/hesr.2007.16.2.160.

Kumar, A., & Mohanty, S. K. (2011). Intra-urban differentials in the utilization of reproductive healthcare in India, 1992–2006. *Journal of Urban Health, 88*(2), 311–328. doi:10.1007/s11524-010-9532-7.

Kumari, D. (2013). Is socio-economic inequality in childhood undernutrition increasing in urban India? In *XXVII IUSSP Conference, Busan, South Korea, 2013*. Busan.

Mathur, M. R., Tsakos, G., Millett, C., Arora, M., & Watt, R. (2014). Socioeconomic inequalities in dental caries and their determinants in adolescents in New Delhi, India. *BMJ Open, 4*(12), e006391–e006391. doi:10.1136/bmjopen-2014-006391.

Mohanty, S. K., & Pathak, P. K. (2009). Rich-poor gap in utilization of reproductive and child health services in India, 1992–2005. *Journal of Biosocial Science, 41*(3), 381. doi:10.1017/S002193200800309X.

Nguyen, K., Jimenez-Soto, E., Dayal, P., & Hodge, A. (2013). Disparities in child mortality trends: What is the evidence from disadvantaged states in India? The case of Orissa and Madhya Pradesh. *International Journal for Equity in Health, 12*(1), 45. doi:10.1186/1475-9276-12-45.

Pallikadavath, S., Foss, M., & Stones, R. W. (2004). Antenatal care: Provision and inequality in rural north India. *Social Science and Medicine, 59*(6), 1147–1158. doi:10.1016/j.socscimed.2003.11.045.

Pande, R. P., & Yazbeck, A. S. (2003). What's in a country average? Wealth, gender, and regional inequalities in immunisation in India. *Social Science and Medicine, 57*(11), 2075–2088. doi:10.1016/S0277-9536(03)00085-6.

Pathak, P. K., Singh, A., & Subramanian, S. V. (2010). Economic inequalities in maternal health care: Prenatal care and skilled birth attendance in India, 1992–2006. *PLoS ONE, 5*(10), e13593. doi:10.1371/journal.pone.0013593.

Peters, D. H., Garg, A., Bloom, G., Walker, D. G., Brieger, W. R., & Rahman, M. H. (2008). Poverty and access to health care in developing countries. *Annals of the New York Academy of Sciences, 1136*(1), 161–171. doi:10.1196/annals.1425.011.

Piketty, T. (2014). Technical appendix. In *Capital in the 21st century* (p. 696). Harvard University Press. Retrieved from http://piketty.pse.ens.fr/files/Piketty2014Capital21c.pdf.

Pradhan, J., & Arokiasamy, P. (2010). Socio-economic inequalities in child survival in India: A decomposition analysis. *Health Policy, 98*(2–3), 114–120. doi:10.1016/j.healthpol.2010.05.010.

Rajan, K., Kennedy, J., & King, L. (2013). Is wealthier always healthier in poor countries? The health implications of income, inequality, poverty, and literacy in India. *Social Science and Medicine, 88,* 98–107. doi:10.1016/j.socscimed.2013.04.004.

Randive, B., San Sebastian, M., De Costa, A., & Lindholm, L. (2014). Inequalities in institutional delivery uptake and maternal mortality reduction in the context of cash incentive program, Janani Suraksha Yojana: Results from nine states in India. *Social Science and Medicine, 123,* 1–6. doi:10.1016/j.socscimed.2014.10.042.

Rani, M., Bonu, S., & Harvey, S. (2008). Differentials in the quality of antenatal care in India. *International Journal for Quality in Health Care, 20*(1), 62–71.

Salam, A., & Siddiqui, S. A. (2006). Socioeconomic inequalities in use of delivery care services in India. *The Journal of Obstetrics and Gynecology of India, 56*(2), 123–127.

Saxena, D., Vangani, R., Mavalankar, D. V., & Thomsen, S. (2013). Inequity in maternal health care service utilization in Gujarat: Analyses of district-level health survey data. *Global Health Action, 6*(1), 1–9. doi:10.3402/gha.v6i0.19652.

Shavers, V. L. (2007). Measurement of socioeconomic status in health disparities research. *Journal of the National Medical Association, 99*(9), 1013–1023. Retrieved from http://www.ncbi.nlm.nih.gov/pubmed/17913111.

Singh, A., Padmadas, S. S., Mishra, U. S., Pallikadavath, S., Johnson, F. A., & Matthews, Z. (2012a). Socio-economic inequalities in the use of postnatal care in India. *PLoS ONE, 7*(5). doi:10.1371/journal.pone.0037037.

Singh, A., Pallikadavath, S., Ram, F., & Ogollah, R. (2012b). Inequalities in advice provided by public health workers to women during antenatal sessions in rural India. *PLoS ONE, 7*(9). doi:10.1371/journal.pone.0044931.

Singh, P. K., Rai, R. K., Alagarajan, M., & Singh, L. (2012c). Determinants of maternity care services utilization among married adolescents in rural India. *PLoS ONE, 7*(2). doi:10.1371/journal.pone.0031666.

Singh, P. K., Rai, R. K., & Kumar, C. (2013). Equity in maternal, newborn, and child health care coverage in India. *Global Health Action, 6,* 1–6. doi:10.3402/gha.v6i0.22217.

Skordis-Worrall, J., Pace, N., Bapat, U., Das, S., More, N. S., Joshi, W., Pulkki-Brannstrom, A. M., & Osrin, D. (2011). Maternal and neonatal health expenditure in Mumbai slums (India): A cross sectional study. *BMC Public Health, 11*(1), 150. doi:10.1186/1471-2458-11-150.

Speizer, I. S., Nanda, P., Achyut, P., Pillai, G., & Guilkey, D. K. (2012). Family planning use among urban poor women from six cities of Uttar Pradesh, India. *Journal of Urban Health, 89* (4), 639–658. doi:10.1007/s11524-011-9667-1.

Subramanian, S. V., Corsi, D. J., Subramanyam, M. A., & Davey Smith, G. (2013). Jumping the gun: The problematic discourse on socioeconomic status and cardiovascular health in India. *International Journal of Epidemiology, 42*(5), 1410–1426. doi:10.1093/ije/dyt017.

Subramanian, S. V., Kawachi, I., & Smith, G. D. (2007). Income inequality and the double burden of under- and overnutrition in India. *Journal of Epidemiology and Community Health, 61*(9), 802–809. doi:10.1136/jech.2006.053801.

Subramanyam, M. A., Kawachi, I., Berkman, L. F., & Subramanian, S. V. (2010). Socioeconomic inequalities in childhood undernutrition in India: Analyzing trends between 1992 and 2005. *PLoS ONE, 5*(6), e11392. doi:10.1371/journal.pone.0011392.

Swartz, D. (1997). *Culture and power: The sociology of Pierre Bourdieu*. University of Chicago Press.

Thind, A., Mohani, A., Banerjee, K., & Hagigi, F. (2008). Where to deliver? Analysis of choice of delivery location from a national survey in India. *BMC Public Health, 8*(1), 29. doi:10.1186/1471-2458-8-29.

Thorat, S., & Sadana, N. (2009). Discrimination and children's nutritional status in India. *IDS Bulletin, 40*(4), 25–29.

Tuddenham, S. A., Rahman, M. H., Singh, S., Barman, D., & Kanjilal, B. (2010). Care seeking for postpartum morbidities in Murshidabad, rural India. *International Journal of Gynecology & Obstetrics, 109*(3), 245–246. doi:10.1016/j.ijgo.2010.01.016.

Wagstaff, A. (2002). Inequality aversion, health inequalities and health achievement. *Journal of Health Economics, 21*(4), 627–641. Retrieved from http://www.ncbi.nlm.nih.gov/pubmed/12146594.

Chapter 5
Inequities in Health in India and Dalit and Adivasi Populations

Sudharshini Subramaniam

Abstract Caste in modern India is no longer just a social phenomenon but an indivisible part of the political process. This chapter summarises the recent literature on health inequities in India by Dalit or Scheduled Caste (SC) and Adivasi or Scheduled Tribe (ST) status. Through a synthesis across the various papers, the chapter also attempts to discern the possible mechanisms and processes underlying the observed health inequities, and changes in these over time. All studies consistently reported that the Scheduled Tribe and Scheduled Caste populations had worse health as compared to other sections of the population. The poor health of this disadvantaged group is evident in the higher levels of morbidity and undernutrition, higher rates of mortality and early onset of death. They also have relatively lower utilisation of both preventive and curative services, and receive poor quality of services when they do access services. In many instances, Dalit and Adivasi status-based health inequities are found even after adjusting for education and income. These health inequities have persisted over the time period under review (2000–2014). A reading across the studies suggests that three possible sets of mechanisms may underlie Dalit/Adivasi status-based inequities in health. The first set consists of disadvantages experienced by members of these population groups because of their historical social exclusion or isolation and their marginalisation. The second includes intermediary factors such as education, occupation and income, access to which is limited or constrained by the social location of SC and ST populations; and the third mechanism consists of differences in the way the institutions such as health and education and social welfare systems behave towards them. From the synthesis, it is evident that the current body of evidence affords only a superficial understanding on how Dalit and Adivasi status leads to health inequities. We need to ask the *why* and *how* questions, and explore the hypotheses emerging about possible mechanisms if we are to make meaningful contribution to policy and social action.

S. Subramaniam (✉)
Institute of Community Medicine, Madras Medical College, Chennai, India
e-mail: sudharshini.subramaniam90@gmail.com

T.K.S. Ravindran and R. Gaitonde (eds.), *Health Inequities in India*,
https://doi.org/10.1007/978-981-10-5089-3_5

Keywords India · Health inequities · Scheduled Caste · Scheduled Tribe
Dalit · Adivasi

5.1 Background

This chapter deals with health inequities among those who form the Dalit and Adivasi (or Scheduled Caste and Scheduled Tribe, i.e. SC/ST) categories in Indian administrative parlance. This label refers to two lists or schedules in the Constitution of India in which are enlisted the names of social groups who are identified as the most oppressed/marginalised groups historically. Although the two labels are often clubbed together as one category, i.e. SC/ST, the label refers to two very distinct social groups. While Scheduled Castes refers to those social groups who were treated historically as *untouchables*, and were the lowest and most oppressed in the caste hierarchy, Scheduled Tribes refers to ethnic groups who do not believe in or espouse the caste hierarchy, who historically lived in relative isolation from caste society, mainly in thickly forested and mountainous areas. The Dalit and Adivasi populations are in themselves far from homogenous and constituted of many different and distinct subgroups. The bringing of these groups administratively under these labels is more of an acknowledgment of the Indian State's commitment to provide special provisions and concessions (in other words affirmative action) to SC/ST groups who are acknowledged to have been oppressed and exploited historically (National Commission to Review the Working of the Constitution [NCRWC], 2002).[1]

The groups listed as SCs suffered due to the hierarchy and power differentials inherent in the caste system, whereas the groups listed as STs were affected mainly as the State (in pre-independence and later in post-independence times) and more recently private capital have severed their intimate links with natural resources in the name of development. This systematic cutting of the Scheduled Tribe population's links to forests and the natural resources like minerals and water has led to great alteration in the alteration of life styles, livelihoods and massive displacement and migration (Ministry of Tribal Affairs, 2009).

Both these processes of oppression have not gone without resistance. There has been a movement questioning caste over the centuries in different forms. Buddhism and Jainism, and the *bhakti* movement within the Hindu religion, were all challenges to the caste system within the dominant Hindu religion (Verma, 2011). In the late nineteenth and early to mid-twentieth centuries, lower caste resistance took more organised forms under the leaders such as Phule, Periyar and Ambedkar. The

---

[1]A note on terminologies is in order here. While we would prefer to use the terms Dalit and Adivasi, and have done so when we are referring to these population groups, where we cite data from published sources, we have maintained the terminologies used by the authors of the study. Thus in almost all places where studies are cited, the terms SC and ST, or as is often the case, SC/ST is used.

groups then referred to as *Harijans* by Gandhi refused that name as patronising and instead chose to call themselves *Dalits*. On the other hand, groups included in the ST list have been waging a prolonged struggle for more rights over their land. These groups usually refer to themselves as *Adivasis*.[2] Thus, what unite the two groups are historical oppression and a commitment by the post-independence Indian State to right the historical wrongs through a series of legal and administrative arrangements. After more than six decades since this commitment was made, and following nearly two decades of neo-liberal reform, we have a complex situation of improvement in the average levels of education, income and health of the SC and ST populations alongside widening gaps between them and the rest of the population.

In the next two sub-sections we trace briefly the location of Dalit and Adivasi populations in present-day Indian society, which would give a glimpse of the underlying factors that are likely to have an impact on their health and wellbeing.

5.1.1 The Caste System and the Dalit

It is suggested that caste in Indian society *exists* in at least two ways. "One in the fragmented unarticulated normally unconscious rules of behaviour embodied in the social relations characteristic of caste societies, and the second in the articulated and elaborated ideologies which are used by those seeking to maintain or contest hegemony within the society or to challenge the society in a basic way" (Omvedt, 1994, p. 13).

A survey of the literature today reveals that there are four very different things that are referred to when different people refer to caste and thus it is crucial to clarify this in research on the impact of caste on health. These four are:

- The reference to the four *Varnas* or social classes of Hindus, sanctioned by the scriptures, which by all accounts is more historic than a reflection of reality.
- The *jati* as empirical reality of hierarchical group formation—the essence seemingly the profession-production-duty determined by birth complex rather than anything else.
- Caste as a system of exploitation and surplus extraction with its own peculiar set of material and ideological legitimisation.
- Caste as an administrative reality *created* as it were by the State, through the decennial Censuses of the colonial powers and the SC/ST lists of the post-independence Indian State.

What is of interest to us when examining the role of caste in the creation and sustenance of health inequities, is its role as an ideology that provides for surplus

[2]ST groups such as the Bodo in the North-East of India prefer to refer to themselves as "Tribal" because the term *Adivasi* is used to refer to migrant STs from other states.

extraction, accumulation and consumption by non-producers who are higher up in the caste hierarchy. Caste may thus be seen as one of many multidimensional modes of surplus extraction (alongside economic class and gender, for example) that interact with each other. It is within this system of exploitation that we need to recognise the positions of Dalits as the most marginalised groups. Traditionally without any land, and refused access to education or to artisanal skills, Dalits were tied to production processes though oppressive arrangements like slavery and later, bonded labour. They were relegated by tradition as responsible for carrying out menial and ritually *polluting* tasks such as scavenging, skinning dead animals, and attending to cremation and burial of the dead (Human Rights Watch Report, 1999).

While the expectation of the modern state was that these relationships would be dissolved with development and the additional legal and administrative concessions given to these groups, the reality has belied this expectation. Dalits continue to be underrepresented in various levels and types of employment and in terms of land ownership, prompting commentators to observe that, "Throughout India's post-Independence history, we see the state weaving an intricate web of protective and developmental policies in favour of the marginalised but not touching the economic base of the village system" (Teltumbde, 2010, p. 49).

This line of thinking is also echoed by Chatterjee when he talks about community development in which,

> the benefits of the plan projects meant for the countryside were supposed to be shared collectively by the whole community. That the concrete structures of existent communities were by no means homogeneous or egalitarian were in fact not so much ignored or forgotten as tacitly acknowledged, for these were precisely the structures through which the "modernizing" state secured legitimation for itself in the representative process of elections (Chatterjee, 2010, p. 258).

Apart from administrative unresponsiveness, the Dalit*s* continue to face discrimination in many ways as part of their everyday life (vide Chap. 1).

5.1.2 Scheduled Tribes or Adivasis

The Scheduled list of tribal groups identified under Article 342 provides for increased allocation of resources for these populations and recognises the need for their special protection. However in the same way as the preference by communities listed under the SC list to refer to themselves as *Dalits*, the communities included in the ST lists have preferred to refer to themselves as *Adivasis.*[3]

Some characteristics set the Adivasi groups apart from the Dalit groups. Unlike Dalits, Adivasis have lived in isolation from mainstream society. There are two

[3]Some such as Bodo in the North-Eastern states of India, however, prefer to be known as tribals, to distinguish themselves from the 'Adivasis', a term used in the North-Eastern states to refer to migrant tribal communities from neighbouring states.

distinct contiguous areas with particularly high proportion of Adivasi groups which include the areas of VIth schedule which includes the North-East states, and the areas of the Vth schedule which includes the areas of various states along a band in central and eastern India. Characteristically the Adivasi groups live in areas which are extremely rich in natural resources. While in the Dalit groups the historical development trajectory has been one of increasing political mobilisation, and attempted integration within mainstream society, for the Adivasis who were relatively independent up to the coming of the British, subsequent integration with mainstream society and especially the development paradigm adopted by the post-Independent state (which was largely in continuity with the colonial state as far as Adivasis are concerned) has actually meant further disenfranchisement. Despite living in areas with the largest concentration of natural resources, Adivasi groups have among the highest poverty rate of any group, and constitute almost 80% of all bonded labour (for example), showing that integration with the mainstream Indian state has in fact made them marginalised and vulnerable.

There are many gaps in what we know about the experience of the Adivasis with the various development attempts of the Indian State. For example, there is a Ministry of Tribal Affairs dedicated to the improvement of ST populations. Sustained struggles by Adivasi communities for a greater role in local governance led to the passing of PESA (Panchayats—Extension to Scheduled Areas) Act of 1996, and to the Scheduled Tribes and Other Traditional Forest Dwellers (Recognition of Forest Rights) Act, 2006 to safeguard the rights of ST populations to forest products. The continued marginalised status of ST populations despite these measures has called to question the India State's strategy for tribal development adopted thus far. As in the case of the SCs, these measures do not adequately address some of the critical problems of STs such as loss of close connection to the forest and its resources and displacement for the sake of development projects, and with it, alienation from their traditional ways of living.

Many of the points mentioned above have a direct bearing on research on these groups of people and especially the inequity in relation to their health outcomes.

- First and foremost the label *SC/ST* emerges as a purely administrative label. While it may have been coined with the good intention of identifying groups in need of special treatment, it is important to realise that the label hides a huge amount of diversity among the various groups that constitute the label. Dalits and Adivasis have had very different trajectories of marginalisation and further within each group there is wide diversity. This means that there are likely different mechanisms working at the micro as well as the macro-level in the production of health inequities in these groups.
- Second, what exactly the label stands for varies widely over time and place. This has a crucial bearing on public health research which uses the label merely as a category with little understanding of its differing meaning for different groups and settings.

- Linked to this is the diversity in the comparison group being used. Obviously, like the SC and ST label even the groups constituting the *Other Backward Classes* or *Backward Classes* are also complementarily diverse and subject to very different historical processes. This raises the question of how to meaningfully interpret the comparisons between SC/ST and OBC or *General Castes* in health status.

It would be useful to bear in mind these key points when trying to make sense of the evidence on health inequities by Scheduled Caste and Scheduled Tribe status in India, laid out in the next section.

5.2 Evidence on Health Inequities Based on Dalit and Adivasi Status

In general, one finds that the disaggregation in the literature is only to the level of "SC" or "ST" with no further disaggregation within these categories. Moreover, these groups are invariably compared either with the average or with all other groups lumped together as "Non-SC/ST".

This section starts with a description of what is known about health inequities in utilisation of preventive and curative healthcare services. It then documents the evidence on inequities in health status, and in the delivery and financing of healthcare services.

5.2.1 Utilisation of Healthcare Services

5.2.1.1 Preventive Health Care

Child Immunisation

Although there has been a consistent increase in immunisation coverage of children below 2 years of age between 1992–1993 and 2005–2006, the period covered by the three National Health Surveys, ST children have the least proportion fully immunised and the highest proportion not immunised across all three time points (Figs. 5.1 and 5.2). There was a narrowing of gaps between SC and ST children, but the gap between each of these groups and other castes did not narrow over time (Baru, Acharya, Acharya, Kumar, & Nagaraj, 2010; Shrivastwa, Gillespie, Kolenic, Lepkowski, & Boulton, 2015; UNICEF, 2009).

Among SC/ST populations, those who face additional economic and social disadvantages did especially badly in terms of immunisation coverage. In the slums of Bhubaneswar, Odisha, among the largely migrant SC/ST populations, only 59% of children had received BCG vaccine at birth, one fourth of the children did not

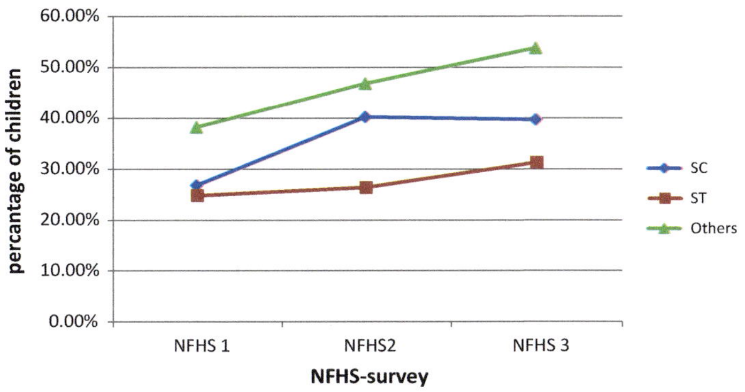

Fig. 5.1 Full vaccination coverage among children aged 12–23 months by caste group

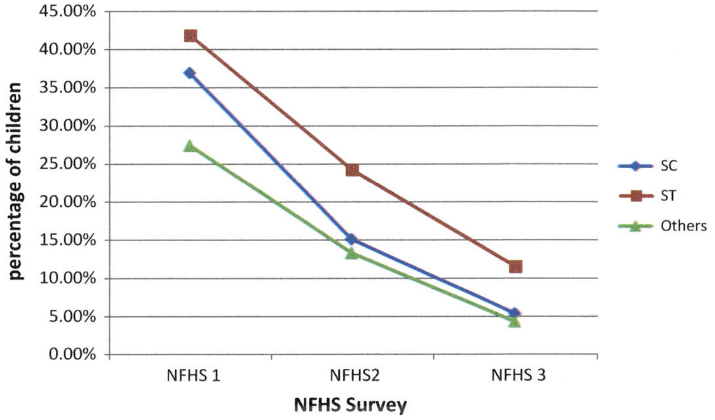

Fig. 5.2 No vaccination among children aged 12–23 months by caste

receive a single vaccine and no child was fully vaccinated, despite 90% of the mothers being aware of vaccination. Only 56% children possessed vaccination cards. As migrant families were new to the urban health system, the vaccination coverage of their children was not up to the desired level (Swain & Mishra, 2006). A systematic review reported that among SCs in rural India, almost 56% percent of children belonging to households with low standard of living index did not receive any vaccination, as compared to less than 3% of children belonging to households with a high standard of living index (Sadana, 2009).

In one of the few intervention studies we came across, a cluster randomised trial was conducted in villages of Uttar Pradesh, to study the impact of informing resource poor rural populations about their entitled services on delivery of health and social services. The study found that the vaccination rates by caste were similar in the control group population at baseline as well as after the 1-year trial. Though there was a significant increase in the vaccination rate among the intervention group, the lower caste groups did not seem to benefit as much as the middle or high caste groups in the intervention cluster, thus pointing out that education interventions are not enough on their own to overcome the caste disadvantages. Moreover, the intervention was not able to bring an improvement in the number of visits made by the midwives (Pandey, Sehgal, Riboud, Levine, & Goyal, 2007).

Vitamin A Supplementation

Vitamin A supplementation is one of the most cost effective interventions in reducing childhood mortality (Imdad, Herzer, Mayo-Wilson, Yakoob, & Bhutta, 2010). The average coverage by Vitamin A supplementation services in India is only 18.3% of children aged 6–59 months. As in the case of immunisation, data for 2005–06 show that here too ST children had the lowest rates of coverage (14.6%) as compared to SC children (18%) and children from other castes (20.9%) (International Institute for Population Sciences and ORC Macro International, 2007). Caste-based difference varied by state with states like Maharashtra, Andhra Pradesh and Orissa having a wide gap of more than 15% points (Baraik & Kulkarni, 2006).

Integrated Child Development Scheme (ICDS)[4] *Services*

ICDS services are aimed at improving the nutritional status of children under 6 years of age while also providing early childhood education stimulating their intellectual development. NFHS-3 data for 2005–06 found that only a third of the children aged 0–71 months received any service from ICDS centres. However unlike other services, ICDS service utilisation was highest among ST children (nearly 50%) followed by 36.1% of SC children, and 28.3% of other caste children (International Institute for Population Sciences and Macro International, 2007). This finding is confirmed by a survey of 5000 households and 200 ICDS centres conducted in rural Uttar Pradesh, Madhya Pradesh and Karnataka. This primary survey revealed further that; (a) the quality of ICDS services was very poor; (b) anganwadi workers in charge of the ICDS centres reported that upper caste parents tended to withdraw their children, not wanting their children to sit and eat with Scheduled Caste children; and the trend of high utilisation by SC and ST populations was not seen in outreach services where ICDS workers visited upper caste household more for both maternal and child health services (Pal, 2016).

Maternal and Reproductive Health Care

The disadvantage in maternal and reproductive health status experienced by women from Scheduled Castes and Scheduled Tribes was reported in an early study, which used data for 1992–93. They constructed a Reproductive Health Index (RHI) from a series of reproductive health indicators such as contraceptive use, birth order, birth interval, antenatal care and skilled assistance at delivery, and the higher the value of

---

[4]**Integrated Child Development Services (ICDS)** is a welfare programme of the Government of India. It includes the provision of food, preschool education and primary health care to children under 6 years of age and their mothers.

the index, the better the reproductive health care received by women. This study revealed that 64.4% of upper caste women had a high value for RHI whereas only 36.5% among Scheduled Caste had high RHI (Raj & Raj, 2004).

There was a social gradient by caste in the coverage of pregnant women by antenatal care (ANC). According to Coverage Evaluation Survey of 2009, a smaller proportion of SC (22.7%) and ST (18.9%) women had full ANC coverage as compared to women of other social groups (31.2%) (UNICEF, 2009). Similar findings were reported from studies conducted in Gujarat (Saxena, Vangani, Mavalankar, & Thomsen, 2013) and from Uttar Pradesh (Saroha, Altarac, & Sibley, 2008). Even though all social groups (SC, ST and others) had shown an improvement in ANC coverage between 1992–93 and 2005–06 (NFHS 1 to NFHS-3), improvement was more among women of the *other caste* group (20%) than among SC women (10%) (Pathak, Singh, & Subramanian, 2010).

In addition to inequities in coverage of antenatal care, there may be differences in the quality of ANC services provided to ST women, as reported by a study from Jharkhand. For example only 37% of ST women had their blood pressure checked as compared to 60% of the non-ST women. Non-ST women were 1.5 times more likely to have all required tests and measurements done during antenatal check-ups as compared to ST women (Maiti, Unisa, & Agrawal, 2005). Munuswamy, Nakamura, Seino and Kizuki (2014) similarly reported, based on NFHS data for 2005–2006, that SC/ST status was negatively associated with receiving four or more antenatal visits and receiving the full range of antenatal services.

Inequities in coverage by institutional delivery services by SC/ST status have been consistently reported from 1992–93 through 2005–05 (Baraik & Kulkarni, 2006). In 2005–06, only 18% of Scheduled Tribe women delivered in a health facility compared to 33% of Scheduled Caste women, 38% of women from *Other Backward Castes* and 51% of women from other (forward) castes (International Institute for Population Sciences and Macro International, 2007; Ministry of Tribal Affairs, 2013). In terms of use of contraception, trends show that while the SC/ST groups continued to have the lowest actual usage of contraceptives, they had the highest percentage increase in contraceptive prevalence between 1992–93 and 2005–06, the period covered by the three National Family Health Surveys (Indian Institute of Population Sciences, 1995; International Institute for Population Sciences and ORC Macro, 2000; International Institute for Population Sciences and Macro International, 2007). Despite such improvement, female sterilisation is the most common contraceptive method practiced by SC and ST women, which suggests that they use contraception mainly to limit their family size. The higher acceptance of female sterilisation among these group may be linked to their poor socio-economic conditions and the financial incentives provided by the Government (Ramachandrappa, 2012). The uptake of male sterilisation is highest among the ST group. The reason for this pattern is unexplored (IIPS, 2007; Prusty, 2014).

5.2.1.2 Curative Services

As with preventive health care, national data for 1998–99 showed that children (under age 3) from the Scheduled Tribes and Scheduled Castes were less likely to utilise health care for illnesses than children from Other Backwards Castes and Other Castes (Sadana, 2009). More importantly, within the group of Dalit children, there were significant differences in utilisation of health care between children from poor and better off households. For example, while about 59 and 57% of children from households with low standard of living index (SLI) did not receive medical treatment for Acute Respiratory Infection and diarrhoea respectively, the proportions were 4 and 12% among SC children from high SLI households (Sadana, 2009).

Among the elderly, the probability of utilising healthcare services was significantly affected by social group to which one belonged. The marginal probability of taking treatment was 10.6 points and 9.0 points lower for elderly from ST and SC groups, respectively, as compared to upper caste Hindus. The group least likely to receive medical attention before death were the Adivasis (Borooah, 2010).

A study explored women's participation in Self-Help Groups (SHGs) as a possible pathway to reduce inequities in utilisation of healthcare services in Bihar. It found that when compared to women from *Other Backward Castes*, SC women participating in SHGs reported no change in healthcare knowledge or in the use of Primary Health Centres, antenatal care and post-natal care services. SC women also reported no improvements in health. Participation in SHG did not alter the share of expenditures on food, children's health and preventive healthcare services among SC women. The only tangible change from SHG-participation for SC women was that they were less dependent on money lenders (Kumar, 2007).

5.2.2 Health Outcomes

5.2.2.1 Nutritional Status

Scheduled Tribe and Scheduled Caste adults and children experienced worse nutritional status as compared to their non-SC/ST counterparts. This is seen from data for 2005–06 from NFHS-3. For example, among the social groups, ST men and women had the highest percentage of thin individuals (BMI less than 18.5 kg/m^2) of all social groups and SC men and women also had a prevalence higher than the national average. The scenario was the reverse with regards to overweight or obesity. There had been no change in the prevalence of thin individuals between NFHS-2 (1998–99) and NFHS-3 in all social groups (International Institute for Population Sciences and Macro International, 2000; International Institute for Population Sciences and Macro International, 2007)

Anaemia is a major public health problem in India, with 55% of women and 24% of men suffering from anaemia. ST women (68.5%) and men (39.6%) had the highest prevalence of anaemia among the social groups. SC women and men had a higher prevalence of anaemia than the national average. Among men, SC men had prevalence higher than the national average (International Institute for Population Sciences and Macro International, 2007). At all India level, the gap between SCs and Non-SC/STs is narrower than that between ST and non-SC/ST group (Bansod, 2014).

Low birth weight is an indicator of long-term maternal malnutrition, ill health, hard work and poor health care in pregnancy (World Health Organization, 2010). The overall incidence of low birth weight in India was around 21% in 2005–06. A higher proportion of babies born to SC/ST mothers were low birth weight as compared to babies born to non-SC/ST mothers. Although the incidence of low birth weight births was much lower in the low fertility states of Andhra Pradesh, Kerala and Tamil Nadu when compared with the high fertility states of Bihar, Madhya Pradesh, Rajasthan and Uttar Pradesh, caste-based disparities were comparable: [21% in SC/ST versus 15% in others in low fertility states, and 31% in SC/ST versus 24% in others in high fertility states (Todur, 2010)].

Among children under 5 years of age, children belonging to ST and SC groups had the worst anthropometric indicators of all social groups (International Institute for Population Sciences and Macro International, 2007; Mukhopadhyay, 2015; Bhalotra, Valente, & Soest, 2009). An interesting study by Mukhopadhyay (2015) examined the interplay of inequalities based on caste, economic position or class on the nutritional status of children. Stunting and underweight, and severe stunting and severe underweight were the indicators considered. The study found that caste-based inequities disappeared with increasing wealth and that gender-based inequities were found in poor SC and ST households (Mukhopadhyay, 2015).

Close to 70% of Indian children suffered from any anaemia in 2005–2006, and ST and SC children were at 1.31 times and 1.87 times increased risk of having severe anaemia compared to non-SC/ST children, after adjusting for adult education and household wealth. Stratified analysis indicated that the increased risk of anaemia in SC/SST children was not because of differentials in levels of adult education and household wealth. Caste was an independent determinant of childhood anaemia and appeared to act through mechanisms other than education and wealth (Vart, Jaglan, & Shafique, 2015).

5.2.2.2 Morbidity

Very few studies appear to have engaged with social group-based inequities in adult morbidity. However, a recent systematic review of studies on India observed a social gradient in the prevalence of smoking and alcohol use, with the highest odds for STs followed by SCs. Alcohol use was highly prevalent among ST women (14.1%) compared to the national average of 2.2%. As with smoking and drinking, a strong caste gradient was found for chewing tobacco with the odds lowest for the OBC, SC and being highest for ST (Coelho & Belden, 2016).

There are a small number of studies on infant and child morbidity by SC or ST status. Sadana (2009) reported a higher prevalence of acute respiratory illnesses and diarrhoeal diseases among Dalit children as compared to non-Dalit children, in an analysis based on data from NFHS-2 (1998–99). The reasons attributed for this pattern by the author was unsafe sources of drinking water, and low levels of maternal education (Sadana, 2009). Neonatal morbidity was similarly high among STs and compared to non-STs in a study from Nagpur in Maharashtra. The authors attribute this to the poor childcare practices of mothers and family members, and to the fact that tribal women had less ready-access to healthcare facilities than non-tribal women (Niswade, Zodpey, Ughade, & Bangdiwala, 2011).

5.2.2.3 Mortality

The many disadvantages experienced by those belonging to the Scheduled Castes and Scheduled Tribes culminate in premature mortality. Even after controlling for factors like income, age and residence, the average age at death was 4.9 years lower for Adivasis and 7.1 years lower for Dalits compared to higher caste Hindus (Borooah, 2010). SC and ST women constituted a much higher proportion of maternal deaths than their proportion in the overall population. Of the maternal deaths covered by the MAPEDIR[5] project of UNICEF in 2009, 37% were from the Scheduled Castes (SC) and 24% from the Scheduled Tribes (ST) (Kumar, 2010).

In the case of infant and neonatal mortality we find that unlike for other indicators, it is not Scheduled Tribes but Scheduled Castes who were at a disadvantage. Scheduled Tribes had better infant and neonatal mortality rates than the Scheduled Castes (Joshi, 2014; Niswade et al., 2011). On the other hand, under-five mortality rate which is considerably influenced by exogenous factors was 62% higher among ST and 49% higher among SC as compared to other (forward) castes (Joshi, 2014). Although there has been a decline in infant and child mortality indicators between 1992–93 and 2005–06, the decline was lower for SC and ST, which has meant a widening of the gap. The rate of decline in IMR across the social groups shows relatively less disparity, when compared to under-five mortality rate. Inequities in immunisation, access to health care and in nutritional status are the likely pathways to inequities in under-five mortality (Joshi, 2014).

Two studies showcase, two very different approaches to addressing inequities in neonatal mortality, with quite different outcomes. One is a study of the Integrated Management of Neonatal and Childhood Illnesses (IMNCI) through analysis of secondary data from a cluster randomised controlled trial in Haryana. The study revealed that IMNCI resulted in equitable distribution across castes in terms of early initiation of breast feeding, as it was least demanding in terms of resources. The strategy did not reduce inequities in neonatal and post-neonatal mortality rates by caste (Taneja et al., 2015).

---

[5]Maternal And Perinatal Death Enquiry and Response (MAPEDIR) Project was implemented in 16 districts in six Indian states with high maternal mortality (West Bengal, Rajasthan, Jharkhand, Bihar, Orissa and Madhya Pradesh).

In contrast, an intervention involving mobilising women from marginalised populations into women's groups was effective in achieving a higher reduction in neonatal mortality rates among the SC/ST. Known as the *Ekjut* trial, the intervention was carried out in Orissa and Jharkhand, states with large tribal population. There was a 51% reduction in NMR among SC/ST and a 17% reduction among other population groups. This study provided evidence for how a set of low-cost participatory womens' group activities can contribute to closing the gaps between caste groups (Houweling et al., 2013). The mechanisms which explain this are as follows. The uptake of the intervention was similar among the most and less marginalised groups. Consequently, an effective intervention is likely to have a stronger effect among the high-risk groups.

5.2.3 Geographical Variations in Utilisation of Health Care and in Health Outcomes

Almost all studies made references to variations across states in the extent and nature of health gaps between Dalit, Adivasi and the rest of the population. The differences appear to be mainly between two groups of states: Southern states of Andhra Pradesh, Karnataka, Kerala and Tamil Nadu, and the Empowered Action Group of states which have relatively poorer health and economic indicators. Some contradictory findings emerge. In the case of preventive health care such as child immunisation, Southern states show a much narrower gap between Dalit and Adivasi populations and others. On the other hand, belonging to the SC and ST communities was a significant determinant of child nutritional status in Southern states but not in EAG states (Pradhan & Arokiasamy, 2010). In a similar vein, disparities in nutritional status between SC and ST women and others was more pronounced in the economically better off states including Gujarat, Maharashtra, Tamil Nadu and West Bengal (Baraik & Kulkarni, 2006). The relative significance of caste as compared to class and gender also varied between the Southern states and EAG states (Mukhopadhyay, 2015).

For U5MR, social disparities were high in states which had overall lower mortality rates, as in Tamil Nadu, Maharashtra, Gujarat and Punjab. The gap differential between SC and non-SC/ST was highest in Andhra Pradesh, Gujarat and Punjab. The gap differential between ST and non-SC/ST was highest for Madhya Pradesh followed by Karnataka and Rajasthan (Baraik & Kulkarni, 2006).

There were also variations in gaps in under-five mortality by rural and urban residence. Overall, in urban areas, ST had better childhood mortality indicators than SC, but were performing poor than the other castes. In rural areas, among the social groups ST were performing much worse in terms of childhood mortality indicators followed by SC (Ministry of Tribal Affairs, 2013).

Some studies identify a specific policy or intervention implemented by a state as responsible for the state's better performance in bridging health inequities, but again, these explanations are not based on a rigorous evaluation of the relevant policy or programme. For example, a study compares changing trends in neonatal and under-five mortality rates in the states of Orissa and Madhya Pradesh. The steady decline in neonatal mortality rates among SC and ST group since 2000 in Orissa is attributed to the *Nava Jyoti* scheme which was launched in 2005 to target tribal areas with strategies like community-based safe delivery and new-born care and prompt referrals. In Madhya Pradesh U5MR among SC and ST was at a faster rate compared to other caste group, and this was attributed to the state government's programmes such as *Deenadayal* Mobile Hospital Scheme targeting tribal areas and *Bal Sakthi Yojana* for malnourished children which indirectly targeted Scheduled group as they had a higher proportion of malnutrition (Nguyen, Jimenez-Soto, Dayal, & Hodge, 2013).

Thus, many different post-facto explanations have been offered for these variations. However, there does not appear to be a well-developed argument that knits together these disparate findings to make meaning of it all.

5.2.4 Inequities in Access, Affordability and Availability

5.2.4.1 Discrimination in Healthcare Settings

Despite the vast literature in other countries on the role of discrimination in healthcare settings as a factor underlying inequities in health service utilisation by race and indigenous status, there is a serious dearth of such evidence related to health inequities among the Dalit and Adivasis. Acharya's (2010) study of discrimination in access to health care among Dalit children in Gujarat and Rajasthan makes up for this through its detailed expose' on discrimination from the perspective of those experiencing it as well as those practicing discrimination.

Dalit children experienced discrimination in the form of not being touched by the doctors and informal health providers. Discrimination took the form of less time spent by providers during consultation, and being made to wait for a long time by laboratory technicians and pharmacists. Auxiliary Nurse Midwives discriminated by not entering the house of Dalit children, visiting them last, spending less time with them and not providing information regarding health programmes. The children felt more discriminated by grass root level workers in both private as well as Government health facilities. More discrimination was observed in the public sector compared to private health facilities, but was probably less overt and subtle. Discrimination was most common in the villages which had relatively fewer healthcare centres and in those villages where the healthcare providers were non-Dalit. When there were elected members of local government, teachers, officials and care providers from Dalit caste, less evidence of discrimination was noted. In villages where Dalits were not represented in positions of power, Dalit healthcare providers faced discrimination because non-Dalit populations did not seek their services and visit them and considered their medicines to be ineffective (Acharya, 2010).

Discrimination in healthcare settings is also associated with the caste of the healthcare provider. The 68th Round of the National Sample Survey on employment and unemployment showed that only the middle and upper castes had adequate representation among all health-related occupations ranging from general practitioners, specialist doctors, nurses, technicians and other health staff. Inadequate representation of the discriminated groups further aggravates the existence of discrimination in healthcare setting. States which had lower representation of healthcare providers from SC and ST groups, had a high caste-based disparity in health outcomes irrespective of their overall performance in health, whereas in states which had adequate representation from this social groups, the disparity was negligible (George, 2015).

A study from rural north India identifies the caste of the birth attendant as an important factor in choice of place for delivery by women. The majority of traditional birth attendants *(dais)* belong to the lower caste, and trained birth attendants, such as nurses or doctors belong to the upper caste. Since attending child delivery involved physical contact between the two caste groups, upper caste healthcare providers preferred to cater to upper caste women and lower caste women chose to seek care from traditional birth attendants to avoid the embarrassment of caste discrimination (Saroha et al., 2008).

5.2.4.2 Affordability of Health Care

Health insurance and prepayment schemes are known to be a strategy to improve equitable access of healthcare services by vulnerable groups. As per NFHS-3, only 4.9% of the Indian population are covered by a health scheme or insurance. Caste-based disparity is also observed in coverage by health schemes or insurance. Only 2.6 and 3.3% of ST and SC populations were covered, as compared to 7.8% among other caste groups (Ministry of Tribal Affairs, 2013).

Community-based health insurance schemes are considered as a viable option for ensuring equitable distribution of health care. The Yeshashwini Healthcare programme of Karnataka is one of the largest community-based health insurance scheme in India. A study examined equity in enrolment, renewal of enrolment and utilisation of health services. This study found that the scheme was inequitable in terms of social groups in all aspects. A smaller proportion of SCs enrolled, renewed the enrolment and utilised the health services. Though the scheme was envisioned to reach the disadvantaged, it did not automatically include the poorest and socially excluded people because of their poor ability to pay premium (Aggarwal, 2011). Studies on the Arogyashri of Andhra Pradesh and *Rashtriya Swasthya Bhima Yojana* (RSBY) in Maharashtra, showed that these schemes had a significant impact on male headed household, scheduled caste, rural household, poorest and middle wealth quintile and failed to have a significant impact on female headed household and ST. The schemes were able to cater to vulnerable groups and yet, failed to reach the most vulnerable among them (Rao et al., 2014).

In the absence of large-scale prepayment schemes, affordability of health care and ability to meet Out-of-Pocket (OOP) expenses on health care become the determining factors in ability to utilise healthcare services. An analysis of data from a National Sample Survey reported that OOP expenditure on hospitalisation was lower among households belonging to SC/ST when compared to others. This counter-intuitive finding may be explained as resulting from the inability to afford health care, especially hospitalisation, by those from SC/ST households (Roy & Howard, 2007). A study done in Kottathara Panchayat, Wayanad district of Kerala on healthcare expenditure confirms the existence of a caste gradient in health expenditure. The increase in expenditure in relation to health care need is not uniform across social groups. Paniya households, on average, spent less than 8% of what a need-comparable upper Caste household spent per person. This indicated the inability of Paniyas to spend as much as they should on health care. In absolute terms lower caste household spend the least, but in terms of share of the total expenditure it turns out to be a burden on them for which they had to depend more on loans and donations for meeting total health expenditure than do other caste households (Mukherjee, Haddad, & Narayana, 2011).

5.2.4.3 Availability of Health Services

Poor availability of medical facilities alongside poor availability of other facilities such as water supply and sanitation, *pucca* roads and transportation, schools is the hallmark of districts with a concentration of Adivasi populations (Bhattacharya & Chikwama, 2011). A policy initiative by the Indian state of Odisha, examined by Thomas et al. (2015), suggests that concerted policy action to strengthen the public health system could contribute significantly to bridging health inequities (Thomas et al., 2015).

Odisha's KBK+ region includes the 11 Southern districts of Odisha, is poorer and has a large proportion of ST and SC population than other regions of the State. This region which had poor road connectivity and dense hilly terrains also faced poor health indicators, extreme food insecurity compared to other regions. The state had committed itself to address the inequity issue by developing Health Equity Strategy (2009–12). KBK+ districts were prioritised, targeted investments and many innovations tailored to the needs of these districts to improve the service delivery were made. The innovations that had been introduced in the state include introduction of Mobile health units, which catered to almost 80% of families which reported illness in the past 6 months and also made a reduction in the travel costs incurred by these people. Vulnerability assessment was done by categorising health sub-centres based on composite index, based on flexible funding was provided and prioritisation made. Conditional cash transfer scheme called Mamata, a state initiative and Janani Sishu Suraksha Karyakram a Government of India initiative had made an impact in increasing the institutional deliveries and decrease in OOP expenditure spent on child birth. To tackle the inequity in availability of human resources in Odisha, the state-adopted strategies like posting of newly appointed doctors in KBK+ districts for a minimum of 3 years and provided financial incentives to those working in these districts. The state also provided scholarships for female SC and ST nursing students, with a higher amount for students belonging to KBK+ districts. Other approaches included financial incentives for paramedics and enhanced incentives for ASHA working in difficult areas. These efforts of the state resulted in a dramatic decline in the vacancy rates of healthcare providers from 29.8% in 2008–09 to 6.9% in 2012–13 (Thomas et al., 2015).

5.3 Making Meaning from the Evidence

This section provides an overview of the challenges in the existing literature to address caste-based health inequity. It then attempts to draw out the pathways through which belonging to Dalit or Adivasi communities influences health outcomes, based on the studies included in the synthesis and from the general literature on Dalit and Adivasi populations.

5.3.1 Reflections on the Nature of Evidence

The evidence lends strong credence to the existence of a social gradient in all health status outcomes and in indicators of healthcare utilisation. Adivasi children, women and men have poorer nutritional status, lower utilisation of preventive and curative care and higher rates of mortality and morbidity as compared to non-Adivasi populations, and even as compared to the Dalit. The only exception to this rule is in the case of neonatal mortality, where the Adivasi neonate appears to be doing better than his/her Dalit counterparts. The reasons for this merit further study. It also appears that caste-based differentials become narrower and eventually disappear in the upper wealth quintiles, but this pattern has only been observed in child health. It would be worth examining whether the large mortality disadvantage experienced by Dalit and Adivasi women and men disappear among those from better off households. The nature and extent of inequities appears to vary by geographical location.

While numerous papers were about the same few indicators of maternal and child healthcare utilisation, few looked at other dimensions of health (communicable disease, non-communicable diseases, mental health, injuries); health of women beyond the reproductive age group and of girls above 5 years of age; and the health of men across all ages.

It would be fair to say that most of the studies reviewed used quantitative techniques using large secondary data-sets to examine disparities or gaps between groups in specific health indicators. What was measured was the simple gap between a social group and the reference group, or the ratio of health indicators pertaining to the best or average performing group and a vulnerable group under study. Some papers have used techniques like decomposition analysis to quantitatively explore the associations in terms of what explained the gaps.

Even though it has been well established for several decades that Dalit and Adivasi populations experienced significantly poorer health, there has been a dearth of studies that explore why this is so, and why the gaps have been persistent. The pathways and mechanisms that convert membership in a social group into systematic and pervasive health disadvantages have hardly been examined. The trends of increasing or decreasing gaps, the slopes of the improvement, the lack of ability of certain groups to convert access into benefit all have been mentioned but not probed in great depth.

Based on the perspectives built in the introductory section of the paper and from the review presented above it is clear that all studies have taken the label SC or ST as homogenous groups, completely ignoring the rich literature on within-group complexity referred to in the introductory section. Even the definition of health used for assessing health is at odds with the Adivasi worldview of health. Given such a situation it is questionable as to how representative of the lived reality the mainstream public health literature is with reference to the Dalit's and Adivasi's health and disadvantage.

Given the understanding of the historical nature of the discrimination and oppression of these groups, it is but obvious that there will be regional differences based on historical processes. Thus the significance of the category SC or ST, and what it represents, is likely to differ over both time and place (Guru, 2016). This more nuanced understanding of the categories is completely missing in the literature.

Many studies have put forth hypotheses to explain the gaps observed in the health status of Dalit and Adivasi groups as compared to the general population. We build on these in the next section.

5.3.2 Possible Mechanisms Underlying Health Inequities by Dalit and Adivasi Status

Both Dalit and Adivasi groups form the currently most marginalised social groups in the country. While Dalits have been part of the mainstream social systems for thousands of years, historically the Adivasi groups have remained relatively isolated and free from the caste system till the British rule. In fact in the criteria they set for self-identification evolved in 1994, the Adivasi groups identified the lack of caste hierarchy as one of the characteristic features defining an Adivasi group. Be that as it may, both these groups are presently firmly interlocked into the system of development that characterises the country today.

While the government has recognised the historical processes that have disadvantaged these groups, their recognition and attempts at reversing these disadvantages seem to be largely administrative exercises with little attempt to go to the root of the problem. A study of patterns and trends across studies suggest some possibilities. The inequity-causing mechanisms emerging from the studies may be broadly grouped under three headings:

- Differences due to Intermediary Factors
- Differences due to belonging to the group
- Differences caused by the way institutions behave

5.3.2.1 Differences due to Intermediary Factors

The most common mechanism which had been put forth by many authors to explain caste-based health inequity is through the intermediary pathways like employment, education, income and health. Most of the studies on caste also studied other socio-economic factors like poverty and illiteracy and any difference that was observed between social groups was attributed to these factors.

High rate of illiteracy among this group was also equated to lack of awareness and many a times they were stereotyped as lacking in hygiene. Based on these assumptions, authors suggested creating awareness on hygiene, availability of health services to improve the health status of these population (Shinde, 2013).

The *intermediary factors*-based explanation of health inequities by Dalit and Adivasi status runs as follows. Because of the traditional exclusion faced by Dalits to capital and physical assets, they had to depend on wage income, which also involved underemployment and wage disparity between caste groups. This in turn led to poverty and poor standard of living. Poverty along with illiteracy placed them at an increased risk of illness. Increased risk coupled with their low spending capacity on health determined the inequity in terms of morbidity and mortality. In the case of Adivasis, the starting point was social isolation but the rest of the pathway was the same.

5.3.2.2 Differences Due to Belonging to the Group

From an equity point of view, we need to understand that apart from these socio-economic factors, caste also has a larger and deeper impact on the perceptions and attitudes of the communities. Some studies by applying complex statistical procedures like regression models, decomposition analysis concluded that belonging to a lower caste itself as a significant contributor to poor health outcomes and poor healthcare utilisation. According to Ajay and Anderson, healthcare service use is a function of individual predisposing characteristics, enabling resources and perceived healthcare needs. Caste is considered as an individual predisposing characteristic which has low mutability (Saroha et al., 2008). Being a Dalit or an Adivasi created disadvantages beyond the material. This was also evident from the intervention study which found that increased participation of women in savings and credit activities, or economic attainment did not make a difference to Dalit women's health related knowledge nor healthcare service utilisation (Kumar, 2007).

Discrimination by the larger community emerges as a powerful explanation for why being Dalit or Adivasi became a risk factor for poor health. Studies show that discrimination could be responsible for the social gradient in health outcomes by acting through psycho-social mechanisms resulting from the anxiety and stress caused by everyday experiences of discrimination (Lewis, Cogburn, & Williams, 2015; Borooah, Sadana, & Thorat, 2012). With regard to utilising public services like Mid-day Meal Scheme and ICDS, discriminatory practices by the workers like making the Dalit children to sit separately, offering fewer services to Dalit children, use of abusive words and making caste related remarks has been documented. It is not only the beneficiaries but also Dalit and Adivasi service providers who experienced discrimination. They were not allowed to cook in the ICDS centres, not allowed to enter the house of upper caste people and not allowed to touch upper caste children (Pal, 2016). Acharya (2010)'s detailed documentation of Dalit children's experiences of discrimination suggest many potential routes to health inequities. Apart from vertical discrimination by the non-Dalits on Dalits, this vulnerable population also face horizontal discrimination by the elite Dalits on the vulnerable Dalits (Armstrong et al., 2010).

5.3.2.3 Differences in the Way Institutions Behave

Another other common myth repeatedly used to explain the health disadvantages of Adivasi populations is their physical isolation, which would make it difficult for them to access health care services. This is despite mounting evidence to the effect that mere access to health care services do not translate to benefit in terms of reduction in inequity. Studies have demonstrated that Dalit and Adivasi women receive poorer quality of care, and sometimes experience untouchability and abusive behaviour (Singh, Rai, Alagarajan, & Singh, 2012; Acharya, 2010; Pal, 2016).

Government health services typically fail to reach those who most need them. Diseases like *Kala–azar* go by the famous saying that disease begins where the road ends. These diseases are most often not targeted on a priority basis by the Government because it affects the most vulnerable, who do not have the political clout to demand public investment (Srivatsan, 2015).

At the level of planning and distribution of resources research has shown a negative correlation between ethnic diversity and government spending on public goods. Sengupta and Sarkar (2007) found through a cross-sectional analysis of data on the municipalities in the state of West Bengal found that where the population was fragmented along ethnic lines, there was lower per capita government expenditure on schools and colleges, public works, hospitals, lighting (Sengupta & Sarkar, 2007). The reason for such disparity in per capita government spending was due to the fact that voters supported lower investment on public goods when they believed that a significant fraction of tax revenue collected from the dominant ethnic group may be used to provide public goods to be shared with other ethnic groups. Ethnic diversity tends to increase *interest group* politics, which leads to larger increase in patronage spending relative to spending on non-excludable public goods (Sengupta & Sarkar, 2007).

5.3.3 Moving on from Here

While we have sufficient evidence to establish caste-based inequity, there is only very little insight to understand the mechanisms of such inequity. The mismatch between health policies/programmes, and people's needs and aspirations is an important driver of inequity but is most often not addressed. In case of Adivasis, for instance, there is a mention that they are geographically isolated, but is that all? To what extent does the health system accommodate so that tribals are comfortable accessing it—in terms of language, birthing position during delivery, diet and so on? A one-size-fits-all approach is not equitable. There is a lot of literature on inequities especially in the past 2–3 years, but it often ends up recommending *more of the same* rather than stepping back and looking at the policies themselves. There is also a need for more micro-studies to understand how the communities and the health system interact. Disparity in terms of availability of the health care services and the quality of the services provided has to be studied to have a deeper insight on the level of disparity.

The role of macro-factors on health has not been addressed adequately in any of the studies. Some macro-factors such as the impact of destruction of forests, poor access to traditional sources of food—need to be studied in order to be able to make policy recommendations and take corrective action. It has influence on how equity is shaped. For example, one of the causes of anaemia and morbidity among Adivasis is displacement due to mega projects, deforestation, destruction of sustainable livelihoods, forced migration and so on.

References

Acharya, S. (2010). Access to health care and patterns of discrimination: A study of Dalit children in selected villages of Gujarat and Rajasthan-Children. *Social Exclusion and Development Working Paper Series*, *2*(1), New Delhi: Indian Institute of Dalit Studies and UNICEF.

Aggarwal, A. (2011). Achieving equity in health through community-based health Insurance: India's experience with a large CBHI programme. *Journal of Development Studies*, *47*(11), 1657–1676. Retrieved from https://doi.org/10.1080/00220388.2011.609586.

Armstrong, D., Davenport, C., Klasing, A. M., Macwan, M., Pradeep, M., Vania, S., … Kalra Varma, M. (2010). *Understanding untouchability: A comprehensive study of practices and conditions in 1589 Villages*. Surat and Washington, D.C.: Navsarjan Trust and Robert F. Kennedy Center for Justice & Human Rights.

Bansod, D. W. (2014). Inequality in health and health care utilization among tribes and non-tribes in India. *International Journal of Development Research*. Retrieved from http://www.journalijdr.com/inequality-health-and-health-care-utilization-among-tribes-and-non-tribes-india.

Baraik, V. K., & Kulkarni, P. M. (2006). *Health status and access to health care services—Disparities among social groups in India*. Working Paper Series (Vol. I). New Delhi: Indian Institute of Dalit Studies.

Baru, R., Acharya, A., Acharya, S., Kumar, A. S., & Nagaraj, K. (2010). Inequities in access to health services in India: Caste, class and region. *Economic and Political Weekly*, 49–58.

Bhalotra, S., Valente, C., & van Soest, A. (2009). *The puzzle of Muslim advantage in child survival in India*. Bonn: The Institute for the Study of Labor, Discussion Paper No 4009. Retrieved from http://ftp.iza.org/dp4009.pdf.

Bhattacharya, P. C., & Chikwama, C. (2011). Inequalities in child mortality in India: A district-level analysis. *Asian Population Studies*, *7*(3), 243–261. Retrieved from http://repo.sire.ac.uk/handle/10943/402.

Borooah, V. (2010). *Inequality in health outcomes in India: The role of caste and religion*. Retrieved from https://mpra.ub.uni-muenchen.de/id/eprint/19832.

Borooah, V. K., Sadana, N., & Thorat, S. (2012). Gender and caste-based inequality in health outcomes in India. *Working Paper Series*, 6(3), New Delhi: Indian Institute of Dalit Studies. Retrieved from http://www.dalitstudies.org.in/uploads/publication/1473146220.pdf.

Chatterjee, P. (2010). *Empire and nation: Selected essays*. New York: Columbia University Press.

Coelho, K. R., & Belden, C. (2016). A systematic review of the literature on the relationship between caste membership and health-related risk factors in India. *International Journal of Medicine and Public Health, 6*(2), 61–68.

George, S. (2015). *Caste and care: Is Indian healthcare delivery system favourable for Dalits?* Working Paper 350, Bangalore: Institute for Social and Economic Change. Retrieved from http://www.isec.ac.in/WP%20350%20-%20Sobin%20George.pdf.

Government of India. (2009). *Committee on the welfare of scheduled castes and Schedules tribes (2008–2009)*. New Delhi: Ministry of Tribal Affairs.

Government of India. (2013). *Statistical profile of Scheduled Tribes in India*. New Delhi: Ministry of Tribal Affairs.

Guru, G. (2016). Shifting categories in the discourse on caste and class. *Economic & Political Weekly, 51*(47), 21–25.

Houweling, T. A., Tripathy, P., Nair, N., Rath, S., Rath, S., Gope, R., … Prost, A. (2013). The equity impact of participatory women's groups to reduce neonatal mortality in India: Secondary analysis of a cluster-randomised trial. *International Journal of Epidemiology, 42*(2), 520–532.

Human Rights Watch Report. (1999). *Discrimination and exploitative forms of labor—Broken people: Caste violence against India's "Untouchables" (Human Rights Watch Report, 1999)*. Retrieved from https://www.hrw.org/reports/1999/india/India994-09.htm.

Imdad, A., Herzer, K., Mayo-Wilson, E., Yakoob, M. Y., & Bhutta, Z. A. (2010). Vitamin A supplementation for preventing morbidity and mortality in children from 6 months to 5 years of age. *Cochrane Database of Systematic Reviews*, (12). Retrieved from https://doi.org/10.1002/14651858.CD008524.pub2.www.cochranelibrary.com.

Indian Institute of Population Sciences. (2000). *National Family Health Survey (NFHS-2), 1998–99, Report, India*. Retrieved from http://www.dhsprogram.com/pubs/pdf/FRIND2/FRIND2.pdf.

International Institute for Population Sciences. (1995). *Maternal and child health. National Family Health Survey (MCH and Family Planning), 1992–93, India*.

International Institute for Population Sciences and Macro International. (2007). *National Family Health Survey (NFHS-3), 2005–06, India* (Vol. 1). Retrieved from http://rchiips.org/nfhs/NFHS-3%20Data/VOL 1/India_volume_I_corrected_17oct08.pdf.

International Institute for Population Sciences and ORC Macro. (2000). *National Family Health Survey (NFHS-2), 1998–99, India*.

Joshi, H. P. (2014). *An analysis of levels and trends in infant and child mortality rates in India*. New Delhi: National Institute of Public Cooperation and Child Development. Retrieved from http://nipccd.nic.in/reports/imr.pdf.
Kumar, A. (2007). Health inequity and women's self-help groups in India: The role of caste and class. *Health Sociology Review, 16*(2), 160–168.
Kumar, S. (2010). Reducing maternal mortality in India: Policy, equity, and quality issues. *Indian Journal of Public Health, 54*(2), 57–64.
Lewis, T. T., Cogburn, C. D., & Williams, D. R. (2015). Self-reported experiences of discrimination and health: Scientific advances, ongoing controversies, and emerging issues. *Annual Review of Clinical Psychology, 11*(1), 407–440.
Maiti, S., Unisa, S., & Agrawal, P. K. (2005). Health care and health among tribal women in Jharkhand: A situational analysis. *Studies of Tribes and Tribals, 3*(1), 37–46.
Mukherjee, S., Haddad, S., & Narayana, D. (2011). Social class related inequalities in household health expenditure and economic burden: Evidence from Kerala, south India. *International Journal for Equity in Health, 10*(1), 1.
Mukhopadhyay, S. (2015). The intersection of gender, caste and class inequalities in child nutrition in rural India. *Asian Population Studies, 11*(1), 17–31.
Munuswamy, S., Nakamura, K., Seino, K., & Kizuki, M. (2014). Inequalities in use of antenatal care and its service components in India. *Journal of Rural Medicine, 9*(1), 10–19.
National Commission to Review the Working of the Constitution (NCRWC). (2002). *Issues of social justice: Scheduled Castes, Scheduled Tribes and Other Backward Classes—An unfinished national agenda*. New Delhi. Retrieved from http://www.humanrightsinitiative.org/publications/const/issues_of_social_justice_scst_obc.pdf.
Nguyen, K.-H., Jimenez-Soto, E., Dayal, P., & Hodge, A. (2013). Disparities in child mortality trends: What is the evidence from disadvantaged states in India? The case of Orissa and Madhya Pradesh. *International Journal for Equity in Health, 12*(1), 45.
Niswade, A., Zodpey, S. P., Ughade, S., & Bangdiwala, S. I. (2011). Neonatal morbidity and mortality in tribal and rural communities in central India. *Indian Journal of Community Medicine: Official Publication of Indian Association of Preventive & Social Medicine, 36*(2), 150–158. Retrieved from https://doi.org/10.4103/0970-0218.84137.
Omvedt, G. (1994). *Dalits and the democratic revolution*. SAGE India. Retrieved from https://in.sagepub.com/en-in/sas/dalits-and-the-democratic-revolution/book241336#author-s—editor-s.
Pal, G. C. (2016). Caste and access to public services. *Economic & Political Weekly, 51*(31), 103.
Pandey, P., Sehgal, A. R., Riboud, M., Levine, D., & Goyal, M. (2007). Informing resource-poor populations and the delivery of entitled health and social services in rural India: A cluster randomized controlled trial. *Journal of the American Medical Association, 298*(16), 1867–1875.
Pathak, P. K., Singh, A., & Subramanian, S. V. (2010). Economic inequalities in maternal health care: Prenatal care and skilled birth attendance in India, 1992–2006. *PLoS ONE, 5*(10), e13593. Retrieved from https://doi.org/10.1371/journal.pone.0013593.
Pradhan, J., & Arokiasamy, P. (2010). Socio-economic inequalities in child survival in India: A decomposition analysis. *Health Policy, 98*(2–3), 114–120. Retrieved from https://doi.org/10.1016/j.healthpol.2010.05.010.
Prusty, R. K. (2014). Use of contraceptives and unmet need for family planning among tribal women in India and selected hilly states. *Journal of Health, Population and Nutrition, 32*(2), 342–355.
Raj, P., & Raj, A. (2004). Caste variations in reproductive health status of women: A Study of Three Eastern States. *Sociological Bulletin, 53*(3), 326–346.
Ramachandrappa, S. (2012). Schedule Caste women and family planning in Karnataka—*A critical analysis. International Journal of Humanities and Social Science Invention, 1*(1), 45–49. Retrieved from http://ijhssi.org/papers/v1(1)/Version-2/G114549.pdf.
Rao, M., Katyal, A., Singh, P. V., Samarth, A., Bergkvist, S., Kancharla, M., … Renton, A. (2014). Changes in addressing inequalities in access to hospital care in Andhra Pradesh and Maharashtra states of India: A difference-in-differences study using repeated cross-sectional surveys. *BMJ Open, 4*(6), e004471.

Roy, K., & Howard, D. H. (2007). Equity in out-of-pocket payments for hospital care: Evidence from India. *Health Policy, 80*(2), 297–307. Retrieved from https://doi.org/10.1016/j.healthpol.2006.03.012.

Sadana, N. (2009). *Dalit children in rural India: Issues related to exclusion and deprivation.* Working Paper Series (Vol. III). New Delhi: Indian Institute of Dalit Studies and UNICEF.

Saroha, E., Altarac, M., & Sibley, L. (2008). Caste and maternal health care service use among rural Hindu women in Maitha, Uttar Pradesh, India. *Journal of Midwifery & Women's Health, 53*(5), e41–e47. Retrieved from https://doi.org/10.1016/j.jmwh.2008.05.002.

Saxena, D., Vangani, R., Mavalankar, D., & Thomsen, S. (2013). Inequity in maternal health care service utilization in Gujarat: Analyses of district-level health survey data. *Global Health Action, 6*(1), 19652. Retrieved from https://doi.org/10.3402/gha.v6i0.19652.

Sengupta, J., & Sarkar, D. (2007). Discrimination in ethnically fragmented localities: A study on public good provision in West Bengal. *Economic & Political Weekly, 42*(32), 3313–3321.

Shinde, M. (2013). Scheduled castes: Social and gender inequality. *Sociology, 3*(2), 361–362.

Shrivastwa, N., Gillespie, B. W., Kolenic, G. E., Lepkowski, J. M., & Boulton, M. L. (2015). Predictors of vaccination in India for children aged 12–36 months. *American Journal of Preventive Medicine, 49*(6), S435–S444. Retrieved from https://doi.org/10.1016/j.amepre.2015.05.008.

Singh, P. K., Rai, R. K., Alagarajan, M., & Singh, L. (2012). Determinants of maternity care services utilization among married adolescents in rural India. *PLoS ONE, 7*(2), e31666. Retrieved from https://doi.org/10.1371/journal.pone.0031666.

Srivatsan, R. (2015). Reflections on discrimination and health in India. *Indian Journal of Medical Ethics, 12*(1), 13–17.

Swain, B. K., & Mishra, S. (2006). Immunization coverage among migrant tribal children in slums of Orissa. *Indian Pediatrics, 43*(11), 1011–1013.

Taneja, S., Bahl, S., Mazumder, S., Martines, J., Bhandari, N., & Bhan, M. K. (2015). Impact on inequities in health indicators: Effect of implementing the integrated management of neonatal and childhood illness programme in Haryana, India. *Journal of Global Health, 5*(1). Retrieved from https://doi.org/10.7189/jogh.05.010401.

Teltumbde, A. (2010). *The persistence of caste: India's hidden apartheid and the Khairlanji murders*. London: Zed Books.

Thomas, D., Sarangi, B. L., Garg, A., Ahuja, A., Meherda, P., Karthikeyan, S. R., ... Dembo Rath, A. (2015). Closing the health and nutrition gap in Odisha, India: A case study of how transforming the health system is achieving greater equity. *Social Science & Medicine, 145*, 154–162. Retrieved from https://doi.org/10.1016/j.socscimed.2015.06.010.

Todur, C. (2010). *Trends and correlates of low birth weights in selected states of India: An analysis of NFHS data.* Presented at the Population Association of America 2010 Annual Meeting Program, Dallas, Texas.

United Nations International Children's Fund. (2009). *Coverage evaluation survey*. India: National Fact Sheet. New Delhi: UNICEF. Retrieved from http://www.indiaenvironmentportal.org.in/files/National_Factsheet_30_August_no_logo.pdf.

Vart, P., Jaglan, A., & Shafique, K. (2015). Caste-based social inequalities and childhood anemia in India: Results from the National Family Health Survey (NFHS) 2005–2006. *BMC Public Health, 15*(1). Retrieved from https://doi.org/10.1186/s12889-015-1881-4.

Verma, V. (2011). *Non-discrimination and equality in India: Contesting boundaries of social justice* (Vol. 52). Abingdon Routledge Contemporary South Asia Series, Routledge.

World Health Organisation. (2010). *Nutrition landscape information system (NLIS): Country profile indicators-interpretation guide*. Geneva: WHO.

Chapter 6
Gender-Based Inequities in Health in India

Priyadarshini Chidambaram

Abstract The research synthesised in the present chapter shows that public health research in India has yet to integrate gender as central to the analysis of health inequities. Studies fall into two categories: those that have examined sex as one of the many risk factors for the health outcome being studied; and women-only studies of reproductive health that refer to the gendered nature of the risk factors. Studies show that there was greater mortality and morbidity among girl children as compared to boys, and that women experienced higher prevalence of morbidity and had generally lower utilisation of health care as compared to men. However, for the most part, not all girls or women were disadvantaged, but only those who simultaneously experienced other disadvantages such as lower caste or socio-economic position. Further, gender norms governing women's role in household decision-making, their freedom of movement and freedom to earn and spend money were significant factors affecting the health of women and their children, and especially their utilisation of maternal and child health care services. Very few studies examined the processes through which health inequities have been created and sustained. Further, studies mainly concentrated on proximate and intermediary factors with limited focus on upstream, macro-factors. Overall, the evidence merely confirms what we already know. Crucial areas of study remain unexplored and innovative methodological approaches are rarely adopted that can help generate the evidence necessary for identifying policy entry points or social action.

Keywords Gender inequities in health · Sex differentials in mortality
Women's autonomy · Women's decision-making

6.1 Introduction

Gender as a relatively new entrant in the realm of health equity research emerged in the 1970s, following the second-wave feminist movement's critique of the scanty attention to women in health research except in relation to maternity. Attention to

P. Chidambaram (✉)
M S Ramaiah Medical College, Bengaluru 560054, India
e-mail: cpdarshini@yahoo.com

T.K.S. Ravindran and R. Gaitonde (eds.), *Health Inequities in India*,
https://doi.org/10.1007/978-981-10-5089-3_6

gender in health research originated as women-inclusive and women-centric health research. One of the first steps taken was to produce sex disaggregated data, which made it possible to observe male/female differences in health outcomes. The concepts of gender as introduced by social scientists featured explicitly in health equity research only after the 1990s (Greaves, 2001).

The formation in 1993 of the National Institute of Health's Office of Research on Women's Health led to the investment of substantive resources in women-centric health research and influencing health research not only within the USA but globally. The launching of an Institute of Gender and Health in 2000 as part of the Canadian Institutes of Health Research contributed to the development of conceptual frameworks and methodological approaches to examine how and in what ways both sex and gender influenced the health of women as well as men. The World Health Organization (WHO) brought out a gender policy in 2002, following which substantive work on gender-evidence-building has been carried out by WHO (World Health Organization [WHO], 2001, 2002, 2003).

Over the past decade or so, developments in the conceptualisation of gender have advanced in two major directions. One, the conceptualisation of gender has gone beyond the binary of male and female to acknowledge the existence of a gender continuum, and the many ways in which one's biologically assigned sex at birth may be at variance from the way one identifies oneself. And two, the treatment of women and men as homogenous groups has given way to the consideration of divisions by other axes of stratification within the groups of women and men.

Despite these conceptual developments, there is limited research from low- and middle-income countries which examine how gender, as an axis of social stratification or as a marker of social position, contributes to health inequities.

6.1.1 Sex, Gender and Health

Gender is used to denote the socially constructed norms, behaviours, activities, relationships and attributes that a given society considers appropriate for men and women whereas sex refers to the biological characteristics of a person, usually categorised as male and female based on internal reproductive organs, external genitalia, chromosomal and gonadal differences. Characteristics defining male and female genders vary from culture to culture and are contextual (WHO, 2002, 2015). Gender is also about the power relations between and among women, men, boys and girls (Muralidharan et al., 2015). Gender acts not only at the individual and household level but also at the level of social institutions such as the family, the school and health facilities. Currently, sex and gender are seen as entangled concepts with each acting independently or synergistically to affect health (Springer, Mager Stellman, & Jordan-Young, 2012).

6.1.1.1 Pathways Through Which Sex and Gender Influence Health

Biological differences between women and men result in differences in health risks, conditions and needs. There are conditions specific to women and to men; there are differences by sex in presenting symptoms, severity and prognosis of other health problems and conditions.

In addition to biological differences, there are gender-based differences. Concepts often used to unpack the pathways through which a person's gender may impact his or her health include: gender roles and norms; access to and control over resources and power; status and power; decision-making; agency and autonomy. These are not mutually exclusive concepts and there are considerable overlaps between some of them.

Gender roles are the tasks and activities that are socially assumed to be *men's work* and *women's work*. These gender-specific roles are reflected both in the types of employment available to women and men, and in the roles they play in the household. Gender roles may expose women and men to different sets of risk factors, for example women being more at risk of indoor air pollution from biofuels while men may be at risk of air pollution outdoors or in work-sites.

Gender norms refer to the social and cultural assumptions about the relative value of women and men in society, about what constitutes masculinity and femininity, about women and men's accepted roles and behaviour, their relative power and their rights. Such norms manifest not only in individual and community values and behaviour but in the way that institutions are structured, reflecting the social assumptions about the position and value of men and women in society. Gender norms affect vulnerability of women and men to ill-health and their health-seeking behaviour. Women's restricted mobility or men's reluctance to seek care are examples of gender norms and values that affect health-seeking behaviour.

Access to and control over resources: In most societies, women have lower access to and control over resources as compared to men. Resources are defined broadly to include information, decision-making, power, educational opportunities, time, income and other economic resources (such as land, the capacity to inherit, or credit), as well as internal resources (such as self-esteem and confidence). Access is having a resource at hand, while control is the ability to define and make binding decisions about the use of a resource. Women's lack of access to and control over resources affects their ability to remain healthy and to seek health care when they need it. More important than material resources is perhaps men's power to control key decisions affecting women's lives.

Although conceptually we separate out the health impact of sex differences from those of gender differences, most often the effects of *sex* and *gender* are intertwined and together contribute to avoidable morbidity and mortality on a large scale. For example, women's higher risk of depression is influenced by genetics and hormones, but gender plays a major role in magnifying the relative risk (World Health Organization [WHO], 2000). Similarly, women's longer life expectancy, a biological factor, may underlie the higher burden of chronic and degenerative diseases among women, but women's lack of resources to care for themselves as they grow older contributes to the severity and poorer outcomes.

6.1.2 Recent Conceptual Advances

6.1.2.1 Gender Identity and Gender Expressions

In recent times, the term *gender* is more often used to refer to gender identity than to maleness and femaleness. Gender identity refers to "one's sense of oneself as male, female or transgender" (American Psychological Association [APA], 2011). A person usually identifies oneself as transgender or queer if his/her biological sex and gender identity are at variance. Those with atypical combinations of biological male and female features are identified as *intersex* persons. *Gender Expression* is about how people choose to express their gender identity in terms of what they wear, how they behave and other forms of presentation. Gender identity and gender expression are not the same. A person may identify as female and express herself in what is socially understood as expression of maleness.

Maleness and femaleness and masculinity and femininity are a continuum with individuals in a population located all along the continuum. Further, the congruence between biological sex and gender identity is no longer taken for granted, nor is it considered to remain static during one's life course. The work of Dvorsky on post-genderism takes the concept of gender even further. Gender will soon be seen as a dynamic and fluid characteristic with persons being able to assume different genders at different points in time with the help of technology bypassing biological, psychological and social gendering (Dvorsky & Hughes, 2008).

Individuals whose biological sex, gender identity and gender expression are not aligned encounter stigma and discrimination because they do not fit into the characteristics that they are assigned by society. Discrimination may assume forms which compromise their physical and mental health, and they also face barriers to healthcare services because of discrimination, provider antipathy and insensitivity and strict binary male and female segregation within programmes (Substance Abuse and Mental Health Services Administration [SAMHSA], 2012).

6.1.2.2 Intersectionality

Intersectionality is another direction in which conceptual development in gender has advanced. Although the literature on gender almost always acknowledges that women and men are not homogenous groups and that the diversity among them needs attention, in practice the problems and concerns of marginalised groups of women gets subsumed within those of the dominant groups of women. Passing mentions are made of women from low-income and marginalised groups being especially vulnerable, framing women as victims without agency and without any further attention to groups at a greater disadvantage.

The concept of *intersectionality* addresses this limitation of gender analysis tools. It starts from the premise that people have multiple identities and seeks to understand the ways in which patriarchy, class oppression, racism and other systems of discrimination create inequalities among women and men, placing some at a relative advantage or position of power as compared to the others (Association for Women's Rights in Development [AWID], 2004).

Using the intersectionality approach in health research cautions against assuming within-group homogeneity and failing to examine inequalities among women and men in health research. It also implies not assuming that power relations between men and women always favours men, and recognising that there may be situations where a subgroup of men (e.g. migrant, person with disability) are less privileged and powerless as compared to a different subgroup of women (e.g. local resident, able-bodied).

The next section summarises key findings from articles published during 2000–2014, which have examined sex or gender as a determinant of health.

6.2 Evidence on Sex and Gender-Based Health Inequities

We have organised the summary in terms of evidence on health status and on health-seeking behaviour, in turn categorised into mortality and morbidity; child and adult nutrition; and child and adult utilisation of preventive and curative health services.

6.2.1 Sex/Gender and Health Status

6.2.1.1 Mortality

Mortality in Children

All-India data from the Sample Registration System has consistently reported higher female than male infant mortality rates and child death rates for several years since 2000. In 2013, the total, rural and urban female infant mortality rates were 42, 46 and 28 per 1000 live births respectively, as compared to male infant mortality rates of 39, 43 and 26 per 1000 live births (Registrar General of India [RGI], 2014). Sex differentials in child death rates are much wider in rural areas and disappear in the urban. The total, rural and urban death rates for children age 1–4 years for 2013 were 2.9, 3.5 and 0.6 for females and 1.9, 2.2 and 0.7 for males respectively (Registrar General of India [RGI], 2013).

These patterns from national data were also seen to hold from small-scale studies. A study using data from a Demographic and Health Surveillance System database in Haryana for the years 2002–05 found that death rates for boys (1–59 months) was 50.7 per 1000 as compared to 86.2 for girls. Cause-specific mortality rates of girls for prematurity, diarrhoea and malnutrition carried a relative risk of 1.52, 2.29 and 3.39, respectively compared to boys. Deaths from other infections were also higher among girls though not significantly. A greater proportion of deaths in girl children also tended to be unclassified. Causes of sex differentials in mortality were not studied (Krishnan, Ng, Kapoor, Pandav, & Byass, 2012). The only exception to these generally reported trends is from an analysis of NFHS 2 (1998–1999) data by Subramanian, which found that mortality risk was significantly higher among girl children only in the age group of 2–5 years and that there were no significant differences in the mortality risk among infants and older children (Subramanian et al., 2006).

Mortality in Adults

The study by Subramanian using NFHS 2 data for 1998–99 had also considered age-wise mortality among adults. It showed significantly lower mortality risk among women of all age groups above 19 years as compared to men (Subramanian et al., 2006). Sex differentials in adult mortality were found among the more socially deprived groups and not among other groups, in a study using data from the Sixtieth Round of NSSO (2004). The average age at death was lower for Hindu *Dalit* and *Adivasi* women as compared to men from the same groups, by 4 and 6.5 years respectively. In contrast, the average age at death was higher for women as compared to men from the Muslim community and almost similar to men for women from Hindu OBC and other castes. Gaps in the average age at death within the group of women across caste groups were far wider. The average ages at death of Dalit and Adivasi women, at 39.5 and 40.0 years respectively, were nearly 15 years less than that for forward caste Hindu women (Borooah, Sabharwal, & Thorat, 2012).

Another study illustrates how gender roles may influence risk of mortality from specific causes. A study on deaths due to fire-related causes was based on data for 2001 from death registries—the medical certification of cause of death, survey of causes of death and the sample registration system. It was estimated that there were 1,63,000 fire-related deaths in 2001 of which 65% occurred in women and 57% of female deaths were in women between 15 and 34 years of age. Women in the 15–34 age groups were three times more likely to die of fire-related causes than men of the same age group, suggesting that women in this childbearing age group were particularly susceptible. The authors report that possible causes of fire-related deaths among them maybe kitchen accidents, self-immolation or homicide as a result of domestic violence (Sanghavi, Bhalla, & Das, 2009).

Box 6.1 Summary of Differentials in Mortality

- Female infant and child mortality was higher than male and has been consistently so since 2000.
- Female disadvantage in mortality disappears in older ages where male mortality exceeds that of female.
- This however is not true for all groups of women. The average age at death for Dalit and Adivasi women was lower than for their male counterparts, while the converse was true for other caste groups.
- Inequalities in mortality by caste among women were much wider than that between women and men.
- Young married women in the age group 15–34 years were at a much higher risk of deaths from burns as compared to men of the same age group, which may be the result of the disempowered status within their marital homes, of many young married women.

6.2.1.2 Morbidity

Childhood Morbidity

A study on childhood morbidity has documented sex differentials in prevalence of illnesses in children below 5 years of age. A survey carried out in rural West Bengal in 1998–99 found higher proportion of illness episodes in girls as compared to boys (0–5 years) overall and for several categories of illnesses. The study noted that of the 790 spells of illness recorded in a year, 380 (48.1%) occurred in boys and 410 (51.9%) in girls. Of diarrhoeal episodes, 188 (52.4%) and 171 (47.6%) occurred in boys and girls, respectively. Among these episodes, 52 (27.7%) in boys and 53 (31%) in girls resulted in dehydration. Of ARI episodes, 147 (46.4%) and 170 (53.6%) occurred in boys and girls, respectively. Among these, 14 (9.5%) and 16 (9.4%) episodes, respectively, in boys and girls were of pneumonia. A total of 114 fever episodes were recorded—45 (39.5%) in boys and 69 (60.5%) in girls (Pandey et al., 2002). The paper did not report on why these illnesses were greater among girl children.

Adult Morbidity

As in the case of child morbidity, studies examining sex differentials in adult morbidity are also sparse. A 2014 study compares morbidity data for men and women from the Sixtieth Round of National Sample Survey conducted in 2004. Morbidity is measured as the proportion of ailing persons (PAPs) per 1000 population in the 15 days before the survey. The PAP was higher for women (97 per 1000) than for men (86 per 1000). Higher female than male morbidity had also been reported in the Fifty second Round of NSSO in 1995–96. All states of India except Gujarat, Orissa and Uttaranchal reported higher female than male morbidity in 2004 (Meenakshi, 2014).

A study using WHO Study on Global Ageing and Adult Health in India (SAGE study) of 2007 from six states in India showed that women were at significantly higher risk of reporting poor health as compared to men (RR 1.66, 95% CI 1.430–1.927) after adjusting for socio-economic and demographic characteristics. Prevalence of self-reported disability among women under 60 years of age was twice that among men (Bora & Saikia, 2015). Another study using the SAGE data base found a greater prevalence of hypertension (adults aged 18 and above) among women (26%) compared to men (23%). While urban men had a significantly higher prevalence as compared to rural men, there was no significant rural–urban difference in hypertension among women. For both sexes, hypertension prevalence was higher among the least poor as compared to the poor. About a half of hypertensive women and 70% of hypertensive men were undetected and it was shown that diagnosis was greater among women (Moser, Agrawal, Davey Smith, & Ebrahim, 2014). Higher female than male adult morbidity was also found in a study based on data from the India Human Development Surveys (IIHDS) of 2004–05 and 2011–12 (Saikia, Moradhvaj, & Bora, 2016).

Patterns seen in adult morbidity are also similar for the elderly. Roy and Chaudhury (2008) used NSSO data from 1996 to 1997 to examine sex and gender differences in self-rated health, functional limitations and the presence of disabling or chronic conditions in women and men aged 60 or above. A significantly greater proportion of older women reported worse self-rated health than older men (21.4% vs. 17.1%), functional limitations (11.3% vs. 9.8%), and symptomatic disabling conditions (41% vs. 36.9%). There were no sex differences in the reported presence of chronic conditions. Differentials in health status persisted even after controlling for socio-economic variables such as education and income. However, when other indicators such as property ownership and economic independence were considered, it was found that financially empowered older women may enjoy equal or better health than men in a similar situation (Roy & Chaudhuri, 2008).

Another study based on secondary data from 2006 to 2007 collected from Vadu, rural India, as part of the *INDEPTH-WHO SAGE* study, found that health scores based on self-reported health was better for men age 50 and above than for women of the same age group. Decomposition analysis showed that around 64% of the difference in scores could not be explained by age, education level, marital status, living arrangement and household wealth quintile. According to the authors, gender discrimination may be among factors accounting for the remaining gap (Ng et al., 2010).

The only exception to the consistent pattern of higher female morbidity is from a study (2011–12) among rural elderly (age 60 years and above) in Odisha. This study reported that the odds of prevalence of multi-morbidity were 40–60% higher for males than for females, but the difference was not statistically significant (Banjare & Pradhan, 2014).

6.2.2 *Gender as a Risk Factor for Women's Sexual and Reproductive Health Conditions*

Many studies illustrate the role of gender in rendering women vulnerable to sexual and reproductive health problems. These range from lack of information and a sense of shame over their bodies, to male control over women's sexuality and reproduction, and intimate partner violence against women.

Women's socialisation to be ashamed of their bodies and their lack of information about even its basic functions such as menstruation is demonstrated by a qualitative study among young women from a Delhi slum. There was a veil of silence around discussing menstruation. Young girls were not taught about menstruation and were expected to figure it out for themselves. They were not aware of its significance to fertility thereby making them ill-equipped to handle unwanted pregnancy and predisposing them to infections because of inability to maintain good hygiene. Indian girls showed later sexual maturation but were married off early and were pushed into early sexual activity and fertility. Space constraints and taboos surrounding menstruation also made menstrual hygiene difficult to practice and exposed women to adverse health impacts (Garg, Sharma, & Sahay, 2001).

6.2.2.1 HIV

Several studies have shown that for many women, being married to a man with multiple partners was an important risk factor for HIV (Srikanth et al., 1997; Jacob, John, George, Rao, & Babu, 1995). A Chennai-based study by Thomas et al. (2009) found that more than 50% of 100 women in the study had been married before they were 18 years of age and 65% of them (as compared to only 10% of the men in the study) were tested because their spouses tested positive. Of the women (54%) who had refused to have sex with their husbands, a majority (60%) met with violence from their husbands (Thomas, Chandra, Selvi, Suriyanarayanan, & Swaminathan, 2009).

Sexual violence by spouses as a potential route to HIV infection among women is suggested by the above study. Two other studies reiterate the same possibility. A study analysing a sub-sample of 28,139 women covered by the National Family Health Survey-3 (2005–06) reported that prevalence of HIV was much higher among married Indian women experiencing physical as well as sexual violence (0.73%) as compared to women who did not experience any violence (0.19%) (Silverman, Decker, Saggurti, Balaiah, & Raj, 2008). HIV-positive women in a study from Pune were twice as likely as women who were HIV negative to have ever experienced any violence (OR 2.55, 95% CI 1.25–5.22, $p = 0.05$), and more than five times as likely to have ever experienced sexual violence by their intimate partner (OR = 5.61, 95% CI 1.66–20.85, $p = 0.001$) (Patrikar, Verma, Bhatti, & Shatabdi, 2012).

Sexual violence is also implicated in HIV infection among female sex workers who had been trafficked. In a study of HIV-positive female sex workers, Silverman et al. (2011) found that more than 40% had been trafficked and coerced into sex work. In their first month of initiation into sex work, trafficked female sex workers had experienced much higher levels of sexual violence, higher numbers of clients per day and non-use of condoms (Silverman et al., 2011).

6.2.2.2 Unwanted Pregnancy

Non-consensual sex, ranging from compulsion to outright sexual violence, was found to be one of the main reasons for unwanted pregnancy among women, according two studies from rural Tamil Nadu. Both the studies covered the same geographical area at two points in time over a decade apart, and observed that not much had changed in the role of gender-power inequalities within marriage in causing an unwanted pregnancy. Both studies showed that lack of male responsibility for contraception, husbands' interference with their wives' contraceptive use, and women's routine experience of non-consensual sexual intercourse within marriage underlay many induced abortions. Women undergoing induced abortion were not usually asserting their reproductive rights. They were merely finding a way out of an impossible situation that resulted from their lack of sexual rights within marriage (Sri & Ravindran, 2015).

6.2.2.3 Reproductive/Genito-Urinary Tract Infections

In a study from Kerala using NFHS-2 (1998–99) data, women who had experienced physical or sexual abuse by the partner and women who justified intimate partner violence on any pretext were respectively 1.9 times and 1.2 times more likely to report symptoms of a reproductive tract infection (Sudha, Morrison, & Zhu, 2007).

Lack of health information because of being female was compounded by other axes of deprivation such as belonging to a socially and economically under-developed state and/or to a socially marginalised indigenous community to render women more susceptible to infections of the genito-urinary tract. In Jharkhand, a study based on NFHS-2 data found that prevalence of urinary tract infections was 28% among indigenous or tribal women as compared to only 17% among non-indigenous women. Indigenous as well as non-indigenous women had not heard of HIV/AIDS and also lacked access to any kind of media, cutting them off from information and rendering them more susceptible to sexually transmitted infections (Agrawal & Agrawal, 2010).

A study by Jose and Navaneetham pointed out that not having access to toilet facilities predisposed women to undernutrition (Jose & Navaneetham, 2010). However, it may also be that lack of toilet facilities led women to wait till late in the evening to relieve themselves, and made them prone to many resultant health problems like urinary tract infections, which become a unique problem of women.

A cohort study from Goa illustrates complex interaction between mental health and reproductive morbidity in women, both of which were related to gender-based inequalities. The study showed that 6.6% of women suffered from common mental disorders (CMD). Anxiety-depressive disorder was found to be commonest followed by mild depression and moderate and severe depression. Women who had relatively less education and income or were migrants or in debt or experienced hunger had increased odds of CMD. The risk for CMDs was significantly higher among those who had experienced gender-based disadvantages like relationship issues with husband or in-laws, being married as an adolescent, divorced or separated and having low social support from family and community. Various gynaecological complaints and menstrual complaints were significantly associated with CMDS but reproductive tract infections as diagnosed through laboratory investigations was not significantly associated with CMD. The authors therefore propose that non-specific gynaecological symptoms maybe somatic manifestations of CMD. The hypothesis that CMDs may manifest as non-specific gynaecological symptoms needs to be examined through further studies, though it runs the risk of women's gynaecological symptoms being trivialised as psychosomatic (Patel et al., 2006).

These studies illustrate that limited autonomy and lack of access to resources and to decision-making influences women's sexual and reproductive health. Paradoxically, *empowered* women may also suffer from greater morbidity in some circumstances. A study of women from low-income settlements in Mumbai found that non-pregnant *empowered* women who had greater mobility, control over resources and increased information about services had higher odds of reporting more general health problems. In contrast, empowered women who were pregnant reported lower prevalence of morbidity. The authors explain this paradox as being the consequence of the high value placed on children in Indian society which confers greater power on women in ways that will ensure good birth outcome (Davis et al., 2014).

Box 6.2 Summary of Differentials in Morbidity

- Girl children under 5 years of age suffer from a higher prevalence of morbidity than boys of the same age group.
- Adult and elderly women suffer from higher prevalence of morbidity than men of the same age groups. The reasons for these differentials have not been explored.
- Gender mediates women's health in many ways. Underlying many common sexual and reproductive health problems is women's gender role socialisation to be embarrassed about their bodies and to not seek information about reproduction and sexuality.
- Gender-power inequalities in marriage play a critical role in women's vulnerability to HIV infection and to unwanted pregnancy, and other reproductive health conditions.
- At times, women's feeling of helplessness within their marital homes places them at risk of Common Mental Disorders.

6.2.2.4 Nutrition

Child Nutritional Status

Child nutrition was assessed in terms of anthropometric indicators—weight for age, height for age and weight for height to indicate acute, chronic and combined acute and chronic malnutrition. The intake of nutritious meals by children and duration of breastfeeding were used to assess discrimination, if any, in food intake.

Gender-power equality within the household, manifested as the extent of autonomy enjoyed by the mother, was found to be a significant determinant of infant-feeding practices and nutritional status of children, as per a micro-study carried out in Andhra Pradesh (Shroff et al., 2011). In other words, nutritional status of children of mothers who enjoyed greater autonomy was likely to be better than children of other mothers.

The lower prevalence of exclusive breastfeeding of female infants as compared to male has been reported from all three rounds of the National Family Health Surveys, 1992–93, 1998–99 and 2005–06. Based on a detailed econometric analysis, Jayachandran and Kuziemko (2015) argue that the reason for this observed sex-differential may not be explicit discrimination. A woman who has borne a female child may be keen on getting pregnant again to try for a male off-spring and may discontinue breastfeeding in order to be able to conceive. The study shows that at any birth order, a male child was more likely to be breastfed than a female child and that girl children with female siblings were likely to be breastfed for a much shorter duration than others.

We now turn to gender gaps in child nutritional status. Evidence from national surveys suggests that the gender gap in nutritional status to the disadvantage of the girl child was significant in the 1980s. Between the early 1990s and 2005–06, the gap slightly widened and then narrowed again or even disappeared. Smaller scale studies covering the period before mid 1990s have noted the presence of significant sex differentials disadvantaging the female child. For example, Desai's (1994) extensive review of literature had found a higher prevalence of undernutrition among girls as compared to boys in the under-five age group. Another study based on NCAER data (1993–1994) of 4000 children across all states reported neglect of female children in terms of nutritional value of food intake by children under 5 (Borooah, 2004), while another, based on NFHS-1 in 1992–93 reported a slight advantage in nutritional status in favour of girls. The study also found that during the period of rapid and sustained economic growth in India between NFHS-1 and NFHS-2 (1992–93 and 1997–98), nutritional status of children under 5 improved substantially, but the improvement was faster for boys than for girls (Tarozzi & Mahajan, 2005). In 2005–06, no significant sex differentials in child nutritional status (0–5 years) were found in studies based on the National Family Health Survey-3 data for 2005–06 (Mazumdar, 2010; Tiwari, 2013; Mukherjee, 2014).

Findings from micro-studies in the 2000s are however, equivocal. Some have found significant differences by sex, with underweight, stunting and wasting more common among girls than boys in the age group 0–59 months (Dey & Chaudhuri, 2008), while others have reported a slight advantage for girls in stunting (Biswas, Bose, & Koziel, 2011). Yet another micro-study of school-age children (6–16 years) found a greater proportion of boys than girls to be underweight and stunted (Sen & Mondal 2012).

While the averages may not show sex differentials, many studies confirm that specific sub-groups of girls are significantly more likely to be undernourished as compared to boys. For example, girls of higher birth orders were at a disadvantage as compared to their male counterparts. A higher proportion of 1–5-year girls than boys were underweight when the older sibling was a girl, in a study using NFHS-3 data in eight Indian states that have reached replacement level fertility. In other words, the second girl child in the family was potentially more likely to face discrimination. The second boy child in the family also faced a higher risk of being underweight, but not to the same extent as girls. The author explains that with decline in fertility and sustained son preference, inequity is intensified, and may be called the *intensification effect* (Mukherjee, 2014).

Other studies have reported that not only girls of higher birth order, but those from households with low per capita income; those belonging to disadvantaged caste groups or with parents of low educational status were more likely to be undernourished than boys (Dey & Chaudhuri, 2008).

Substantial regional differences within India in the nature and extent of sex differentials in child nutritional status have been reported from other studies. Borooah (2004) reported based on data for 1993–94 that gender differentials co-existed with regional differences, and children from Central and Eastern parts of India were the most disadvantaged (Borooah, 2004). During the period of rapid and sustained economic growth in India between NFHS-1 and NFHS-2 (1992–93 and 1997–98), improvement in nutritional status was faster for boys than for girls especially in the rural areas of Northern and Eastern states of India. In the Southern states and in urban areas the improvements were more gender equal (Tarozzi and Mahajan, 2005). Regional differences appear to have persisted over time, and while NFHS-3 (2005–06) did not find gender differentials in child nutritional status overall, a significant disadvantage by gender was observed in the states of Uttar Pradesh, Madhya Pradesh, Orissa, Bihar and Andhra Pradesh (Tiwari, 2013).

Gender often acted in conjunction with other disadvantages to influence child nutritional status (Barooah, 2004; Mukhopadhyay, 2015), and the relationship persisted over time. Borooah (2004) showed for 1993–94 that only 2% of the inequalities in child nutrition may be explained by gender-based differences while the remaining 98% was accounted for by differences in maternal literacy, caste/religion and region. This was confirmed by a study using NFHS-3 data for 2005–06, which found that economic advantage had a significantly greater impact on child nutritional status than the combined disadvantages of caste and gender. In other words, non-poor children enjoyed better nutritional status than the poor, irrespective of caste and gender. With increasing poverty, girls began to be disadvantaged (Mukhopadhyay, 2015).

Adult Nutritional Status

Gender differentials in adult nutritional status have been assessed using proportion of women and men below the normal Body Mass Index (BMI), and comparing food consumption patterns of women and men. Most studies have focused exclusively on women, and sought to find associations between women's nutritional status and their autonomy or decision-making power. A few studies have assessed the impact of interventions to address some of the gender-related barriers to adequate food consumption and better nutrition among women.

According to a study based on NFHS-3 data for 2005–06, gender-based differentials in adult nutritional status was found only in a small number of states (Tiwari, 2013). Interestingly, the northern states of Punjab, Rajasthan and UP along with Kerala in the South showed better nutrition among women than men. However, better nutrition was not accompanied by equality in consumption of food of higher nutritional value, and there were significant disparities favouring men in the consumption of milk, pulses, fruits, eggs, fish and meat in the same states (UP, Punjab and Rajasthan).

Inequalities in nutritional status within the group of women based on their access to social infrastructure have been observed by a study based on NFHS-3 data. Women from households with the combined presence of sanitation facilities and use of clean fuel were 53% more likely to be of *normal* nutritional status as compared to those who did not have access to these. The authors' explanations of these findings is that use of biofuels and fetching water from long distances reinforces traditional gender roles and predisposes women to chronic energy deficiency (Jose & Navaneetham, 2010). The type of family in which a woman lived—nuclear, joint with or without in-laws—may make a difference to the autonomy a woman may have for decision-making. However, no association was found between women's BMI and the type of family in which they lived, in a study using NFHS-2 data for 1998–99 (Saikia & Bhat, 2008).

Micro-nutrient deficiencies such as anaemia affected a large proportion of women, and were associated with women's status indicators. UNICEF in 1990 had noted 50–70 and 40–50% anaemia among women in rural and urban India, respectively (Desai, 1994). A study, which examined national data sets from the NSSO, found that the proportion of literate women in a population was negatively associated with the prevalence of anaemia, suggesting a link between women's social position and their nutritional status (Tarique & Samreen, 2014).

A small number of studies have explored the nature of gender biases within households and communities that impact women's food intake and nutritional status. Baseline data collected following community reflection meetings of a nutritional intervention project in Uttar Pradesh showed that in many households, women ate last, ate whatever was left over after the others had eaten and did not eat at all if there was no more food remaining. The take-home rations given to pregnant women from the Integrated Child Development Services (ICDS) centres were shared by all members of the family. Labour force participation of women was not valued and was regarded as light work or as no work at all. This resulted in less allocation of food resources for the woman. On delivering a girl child, women were often deprived of nutritious food. Pregnant women were given limited food also because of cultural beliefs that for an easy delivery, the woman must do hard physical work during pregnancy and eat less (Neogy, 2010).

In an intervention studying the effects of the work of community health workers in Chhattisgarh, three levels of impediment to accessing nutrition by women for themselves and their children was noticed—flaws in the programme, community practices and norms and household level restrictions. The *Mitanins* (community health workers) were able to address these issues through advocacy, monitoring the implementation of programmes and challenging traditional food practices by acquiring adequate information for themselves (Nandi, 2012).

Box 6.3 Summary of Differentials in Nutritional Status

- Sex differentials in childhood (0–5 years) nutritional status were not generalised but restricted to specific groups of children with multiple disadvantages such as being of higher birth order and a second female child in the family, belonging to low-income or the SC/ST communities. Disparities by sex narrowed or disappeared with improved economic status of households. There is some indication that.
- Adult women did not fare worse than their male counterparts in terms of Body Mass Index. Despite the absence of evidence on female disadvantage in nutritional status, qualitative studies have documented overwork and discrimination in allocation of food to women within the household, especially to women who enjoyed a lower level of autonomy.
- Access to social infrastructure (water supply and sanitation, clean fuel) and educational status contributed to within-group inequalities among women in nutritional status.

6.2.3 Sex/Gender and Healthcare Utilisation

6.2.3.1 Utilisation of Preventive Health Care

Immunisation in Children

Studies that have looked into preventive healthcare utilisation and gender disparities have all been in terms of child immunisation alone as this is the major service offered by the health system as a means to reduce childhood mortality.

Lower rates of immunisation for girls as compared to boys are reported from numerous studies analysing data from three National Family Health Surveys carried out in 2005–06, 1998–99 and 1992–93 (Corsi et al., 2009; Mathew, 2012; Mukherjee, 2014; Singh, 2012; Mahapatro, 2012; Pande & Yazbeck, 2003; Gaudin & Yazbeck, 2006). Corsi et al. (2009) trace the trends in immunisation and inequalities from NFHS 1 to 3, i.e. 1992 to 2006. Over the years, although coverage by vaccination had increased for all vaccines for boys and girls, sex differentials to the disadvantage of girls persisted at all three time periods. However, the differentials had not increased over time. The gap was greater for DPT and Measles vaccination than OPV, perhaps because of the intensive programme efforts towards universal coverage with OPV, and especially the active outreach (Corsi et al., 2009). A systematic review, which included other large-scale surveys such as UNICEF (2009–10 and 2005), MoHFW survey in 2001–02 and ICMR survey in 1999, confirm the female disadvantage in immunisation (Mathew, 2012).

A smaller scale study carried out almost 10 years after NFHS-3 showed that the gaps in immunisation still exist. The study conducted in rural UP in 2013–14 found that the percentage of fully immunised children was significantly higher among boys (54.4%) as compared to girls (44.8%), while the percentage of partially immunised was higher among girls (21.3%) than boys (19.5%) (Ahuja, Rajpurohit, & Ahuja, 2014).

Borooah (2004) reported, based on data from a national survey (1993–94), that gender gaps in immunisation were compounded by disadvantages by maternal literacy status, region of residence and caste status of the household. Decomposition analysis revealed that 83% of the gap in immunisation was due to the fact that boys and girls were treated differently (Borooah, 2004). Birth order of the child was also an axis of disadvantage. Girls of higher birth order had the least immunisation coverage in 2005–06 (Corsi et al., 2009). Even in states with replacement level of fertility, second-order girls born after a boy or a girl were more disadvantaged than second-order boys (Mukherjee, 2014).

Policy interventions that are intended to improve the status of the girl child may not in themselves be able to bridge the gaps in immunisation coverage. A study from Haryana reported that schemes such as the *Apni Beti Apna Dhan* (ABAD) and *Ladli* scheme did not result in steeper improvements in the immunisation of girls as compared to boys to bridge the gap (Krishnan, Amarchand, Byass, Pandav, & Ng, 2014). An earlier study based on national data reported that the presence of an *anganwadi* or a midwife in the village only improved immunisation status of boys but not that of girls (Borooah, 2004).

Studies have observed a positive relationship between women's autonomy and their use of preventive and curative care for their children (Mahapatro, 2012; Shroff et al., 2011). Whether daughters of empowered women would be less likely to face disadvantages in receiving immunisation is not explored.

Preventive Healthcare Utilisation in Women

Evidence on utilisation of preventive health care is focused exclusively on women, and pertains to contraceptive services and maternal healthcare services including antenatal, delivery and postnatal care. In this section, we have synthesised studies that illustrate how gender-power relations within the household and community influence women's access to and utilisation of contraceptive and maternal healthcare services.

Contraceptive Services

Utilisation of contraceptive services has been one of the more exhaustively studied domains in preventive healthcare utilisation by women. Although male use of contraception could have been studied as a comparison to contraceptive use by women, the literature focuses exclusively on women. This is probably the result of policies that have combined maternal and child health care with family planning or contraceptive services, and targeting women alone.

All studies confirm the association between women's status and use of contraception. Women who enjoyed a better status within the household and the community were more likely to use a modern method of contraception. The likelihood of contraceptive use increased with age, duration of marriage, years of schooling, remunerated work and exposure to mass media (Kumar, Fuloria, & Taunk, 2012; Chacko, 2001; Dwivedi & Sogarwal, 2008; Saikia & Singh, 2009). In addition to these individual characteristics, caste and ethnicity played a role in contraceptive prevalence, and women belonging to Scheduled Caste and to Scheduled Tribe[1] communities had lower contraceptive prevalence as compared to their non-tribal counterparts (Agrawal & Agrawal, 2010; Kumar, Fuloria, & Taunk, 2012).

Women with greater autonomy as measured by the power they enjoyed for making decisions within the household were also more likely to use a modern method of contraception. The level of autonomy is often assessed based on questions asked in the National Family Health Survey on women's decision-making on everyday household matters; about their own health care; about major expenditures and women's ability to move around as they wished without having to ask for permission from the husband or members of the marital family. A study based on

[1]A note on terminologies is in order here. While we would prefer to use the terms Dalit and Adivasi, and have done so when we are referring to these population groups, where we cite data from published sources, we have maintained the terminologies used by the authors of the study. Thus in almost all places where studies are cited, the terms SC and ST, or as is often the case, SC/ST is used.

national data from NFHS-2 (1998–99) found that financial and physical autonomy was a predictor of modern contraceptive use, but household decision-making autonomy was not (Dwivedi & Sogarwal, 2008). The crucial role of women's autonomy is illustrated by an intervention study in two blocks of Jharkhand. The intervention aimed to increase women's autonomy through, among other things, outreach visits that addressed gender-power dynamics within the household. The intervention led to an increase in women's decision-making regarding use of earning and mobility and also an increase in their met need for contraception (Leon, Lundgren, Sinai, Sinha, & Jennigs, 2014).

Contraceptive use was influenced by whether the settings in which women lived enhanced or restricted autonomy. Saikia and Singh (2009) found, in their analysis of NFHS-2 data that women who lived in nuclear families were more likely to report use of modern contraception as compared to those who lived in joint families, with or without their in-laws. A small-scale study from rural Madhya Pradesh (2005) reveals a slight nuance. While mothers-in-law controlled decisions related to how many children a woman ought to have before she adopted sterilisation and also on the timing of sterilisation, decisions related to use of temporary methods were made by the couples themselves (Char, Saavala, & Kulmala, 2010).

Intimate partner violence is another major gendered determinant of women's use of modern contraception. A study based on data from NFHS 2 and its follow-up survey in 2002–03 in Bihar, Jharkhand, Maharashtra and Tamil Nadu reported that women who had experience of intimate partner violence had restrictions to access contraception and lacked sexual and reproductive health decision-making. Consequently they also reported a higher number of unwanted pregnancies (Stephenson, Koenig, Acharya, Roy, & Koenig, 2011). A qualitative study by Wilson-Williams revealed that women had restricted mobility, autonomy and their sexuality was controlled by husbands and mothers-in-law. When they were perceived to be breaking these roles, domestic violence ensued, which restricted contraceptive use and led to unwanted pregnancies, abortions, miscarriages, STI/HIV and other gynaecological morbidities. At times women resorted to covert use of contraception which triggered domestic violence and led to discontinuation of contraceptive use (Wilson-Williams, Stephenson, Juvekar, & Andes, 2008).

India is among countries known for its pervasive son preference across all sections of society. Studies have found that in India, strong preference for sons drives women's contraceptive practices. In a cross-sectional study in one village of rural West Bengal, women who had two sons opted for permanent sterilisation whereas women with one son tended to use temporary contraception. Women with only one or two daughters tended not to use any method of contraception (Dey Pal & Chaudhuri, 2009). More recent data from NFHS-3 also showed that women with more sons than daughters were more likely to use contraceptives (Dwivedi & Sogarwal, 2008). Son preference was inversely associated with women's educational status: women with greater than primary education had weaker son preference as compared to women with no education or education up to primary level (Pande & Astone, 2007).

Studies that report that use of contraception is associated with specific indicators of autonomy seem to suggest that contraceptive users are necessarily women with agency and decision-making power. However, Pande et al. (2011) point out that contraceptive use may not mean that a woman is empowered or has achieved her desired fertility status. A woman who is restricted from making sexual choices and communicating regarding her sexual needs is deprived of sexual agency and thereby is disempowered. Women without sexual agency may use contraceptives to prevent unwanted pregnancy, but this is not empowering for the woman as she is still at risk of coercive sex and STI/HIV transmission from her partner (Pande, Falle, Rathod, Edmeades, & Krishnan, 2011).

Maternal Healthcare (Antenatal, Delivery and Postnatal) Services

The second most commonly studied aspect of healthcare utilisation by women is maternal health services—antenatal, delivery and postpartum/postnatal health services.

Utilisation of pregnancy-related services is also associated with women's status indicators such as education and wealth (Munuswamy, Nakamura, Seino, & Kizuk, 2014). Women who belonged to SC/ST communities were also less likely to be receiving antenatal care. For example, in Jharkhand, NFHS-2 data (1998–99) showed that no antenatal care was received by 73.7% of women from Scheduled Tribes as compared to 37.3% among non-tribal women. (Agrawal & Agrawal, 2010). From a national survey conducted in 1993–94 it was seen that the proportion of Scheduled Caste women in India who did not receive prenatal care was 26.2% compared to 14.7% in higher caste Hindu women, while women from Scheduled Tribes and *Other Backward Caste* Muslims had even higher proportion of women not receiving prenatal care. The proportion of SC, ST and Muslim women in India who did not receive postnatal care was 36.5, 43.7 and 36.4% respectively, while it was only 26.7% among higher caste Hindu women (Borooah et al., 2012).

Several studies illustrate the effect on utilisation of maternal health care of women's autonomy and decision-making power within a household, or the absence of these as indicated by indices of deprivation, gender-based inequalities or son preference. Mistry et al. (2009) use indicators of women's autonomy from the National Family Health Survey-2 (1998–99) and find that different dimensions of autonomy influenced different dimensions of maternal health care. Postnatal care seeking was most affected by women's autonomy, and was associated with all three dimensions of autonomy i.e. decision-making, mobility and finance. Delivery by trained professionals was solely influenced by financial autonomy and not the other domains of women's autonomy. The relationship between women's autonomy and utilisation of maternal health care was consistent in Southern states of India. Availability of and coverage by healthcare services also significantly enhanced utilisation of maternal health care (Mistry, Galal, & Lu, 2009).

Differential influence of different dimensions of autonomy with use of maternal health care was also found by a study using data from NFHS-3. This study found that mobility of the woman increased the likelihood of receiving prenatal care but had no effect on the probability of having an institutional delivery. Here again, village level factors like its development indicated by income from non-agricultural sources and electrification of the village, increases overall maternal health care (Self & Grabowski, 2012).

Another study using data from NFHS-3 (2005–06) reported that women who have the authority to be sole decision-makers in their households were more likely to use maternal health services (Mahapatro, 2012). Women living in nuclear households were also more likely to utilise antenatal care in the first trimester of pregnancy and seek delivery care from an institution or from trained professionals. Women living in nuclear families are perhaps more able to be the sole decision-making authorities in their households, which may explain this relationship (Saikia & Singh, 2009).

According to a study from Madhya Pradesh, a woman had a higher chance of receiving antenatal care if she had a good quality relationship with in-laws and her husband, and a higher likelihood of institutional deliveries if her relationship with her husband was good. Most of the effect of the quality of marital relationship on use of maternal health care was the result of gains in women's agency or decision-making power. In other words, when a woman has good and amicable relationship with her in-laws and her husband, this enhances her position of power and decision-making within her household and influences positively her use of maternal healthcare services (Allendorf, 2010).

Son preference not only compromised women's reproductive choices and contraceptive use, but may also influence the household's investment on a woman's prenatal care. Self and Grabowski using data from NFHS-3 establish that having sons reduced the probability of a woman receiving antenatal care, while when she had only daughters, she was more likely to receive prenatal care (Self & Grabowski, 2012).

Gender-power inequalities within a household often results in lower educational investment on the girl child, resulting in low educational status of women and their limited capacity and skills for being employed and earning an income. Differential allocation of food within the household and an increased workload may contribute to nutritional deprivation and low BMI in women. Mohanty (2012) used NFHS-3 data to examine the result of economic deprivation, educational deprivation and health deprivation on the use of antenatal, delivery and postnatal services and found that women with multiple deprivations were less likely to receive any of these maternal health services as compared to those with fewer deprivations or none. State-wise analysis showed that the gap between women with multiple deprivations and no deprivation was highest in states where service coverage was low and lowest where service coverage was high. In other words, better availability of healthcare services could compensate for the material deprivations to some extent (Mohanty, 2012).

When faced with external threats like experience of physical violence during their pregnancy, women were less likely to receive any prenatal care, prenatal care from a health worker or receive it only in the third trimester (Koski, Stephenson, & Koenig, 2011). Violence from intimate partners is also associated with abuse from in-laws. Exposure to such abuse increases risk of complications and reduces receipt of maternal health care.

In contrast to observations from most studies, a study using NFHS-3 data found that having reduced education or income than her husband increased receipt of antenatal care by a woman (Namasivayam, Osuorah, Syed, Antai, & Diddy, 2012). The authors suggest that gender inequities within the household may have different manifestations and outcomes in different social settings and that further research is needed to capture these diversities.

Box 6.4 Summary of Differentials in Utilisation of Preventive Health Care

- Girls were less likely to receive complete immunisation as compared to boys and the gender gap in immunisation coverage has persisted at least since the 1990s.
- Women's use of contraceptive services is positively associated with their status and level of autonomy, and negatively associated with less decision-making ability; son preference and experience of intimate partner violence.
- Women's autonomy was most associated with receiving postnatal care and least associated with skilled attendance at delivery. Women's autonomy and their status acted in conjunction with availability of healthcare services and level of economic development of the setting to facilitate use of maternal healthcare services. While autonomy acted positively, son preference acted negatively. Women with a living son(s) were less likely to receive antenatal care than women with a living daughter(s). Women experiencing intimate partner violence were also less likely to use maternal health care, especially prenatal care.

6.2.3.2 Utilisation of Curative Healthcare

Children

Sex differentials in healthcare seeking for childhood illness appear to be driven by son preference, reports an analysis based on NFHS-3 data (2005–06) for eight states of India with replacement level fertility. The study found that the odds of receiving medical treatment were lower for second-born girls as compared to only daughters, and even lower when second-born girls were compared with second-born boys (Mukherjee, 2014). In a survey conducted in rural West Bengal among 530 children under 5 years of age, boys with an illness were 2.6 times more likely than girls to receive qualified medical attention, 4.9 times more likely to be taken to a medical facility or professional within 12 h of onset of symptoms, 4.2 times more likely to have an amount greater than Rs. 30/-spent for medical attention. As the father's income increased this differential treatment between boys and girls tended to decrease (Pandey et al., 2002). The presence of son preference perhaps directed the use of scarce resources towards the male child whereas when resources where plentiful, they were more equitably distributed.

Mothers were less likely to report incidence of illness among their newborn daughters as compared to sons, according to a prospective study of 255 mothers in rural Uttar Pradesh. Health care was sought for both sons and daughters, but newborn girls were taken to cheaper public health facilities while newborn boys were taken to private (including unqualified) healthcare providers who were perceived to provide better quality care. The household spent almost fourfold more on average for the newborn male child (Rs. 243.3 ± 537.2) compared to a newborn female child (Rs. 65.7 ± 100.7) ($p = 0.07$) (Willis et al., 2009).

The consequences of differential investment by sex on health care could be fatal. Girls of age 1 day through 9 years were found to be 1.7% less likely than their male counterparts to die in a hospital. The study based on NSSO data for 1995–96 further showed that infant girls with female siblings were least likely to receive medical help before they died (Asfaw, Klasen, & Lamanna, 2007). Moreover, households were much more likely to use onerous financing strategies such as borrowing, sale of assets and help from friends and relatives for hospitalisation of boys than for hospitalisation of girls. These gender gaps were exacerbated as one moved from the richest to the poorest households (Asfaw, Lamanna, & Klasen, 2010).

Adults

Sex differentials presumably driven by gender-power inequalities were reported in expenditure on health care for adult women and men according to a study based on panel data from two national surveys. While adult women experienced greater morbidity, they had significantly lower average healthcare expenditure than men. The gap in healthcare expenditure between women and men increased between 2004–05 and 2011–12, from INR 1298 to INR 4172. The female disadvantage in healthcare expenditure was found across all socio-economic categories, but was more pronounced in the lower wealth quintiles. Decomposition analysis showed that more than half the difference could not be explained by male–female differences in demographic, socio-economic and healthcare related factors. They existed because female health had not been considered as important as male health (Saikia et al., 2016).

Again, in a study among cancer patients in rural Odisha visiting a tertiary hospital for treatment, the difference in cumulative expenditure for male and female patients was Rs. 32,446 with Rs. 83,626 spent on females and Rs. 116,073 spent on males (Batra, Gupta, & Mukhopadhyay, 2014).

As in the case of children, gender acted alongside other axes of vulnerability. For example, discrimination against women in healthcare expenditure in rural Odisha tended to increase with increase in the age of women. While the difference in cumulative expenditure on health care between males and females was around Rs. 16,185 at the age of 40, the difference at the median age of 50 was Rs. 20,232. Women living in joint families too had less spent on them. Women who came to the tertiary health centre were also more unhealthy than men when they first visited it. It is possible that elderly women had less control over money or savings and younger women were better tended to, since their good health was needed for looking after children (Batra et al., 2014). National data from NSSO 1999–2000 and 2007–08 confirm that healthcare expenditure on older women (age 60 and above) was significantly lower than that for older men. In 1999–2000, out of the total health expenditure on the elderly, 91.2% was spent on men and only 8.8% was spent on women. In 2007–08, women's share had increased by 6%, but the gap remained huge (Maharana & Ladusingh, 2014).

The combined influence of gender with class is illustrated more vividly in an interesting study conducted at Koppal in Karnataka. The study examined the intersections of class and gender in receiving health entitlements like beginning and continuing treatment. Different middle groups like poor men, non-poor women and poorest men were studied to see how different they were from the extreme groups. The study showed that the poorest, poor and non-poor men—all had statistically similar treatment likelihoods, proposing that men have ability to leverage their gender to compensate for poverty. For non-poor women, lack of acknowledgement of their illness prevented them from starting treatment, showing how internalised gender norms trumped economic advantages. For continuation of treatment, it was seen that among poor households, if heads were male they could leverage that to continue treatment but not female heads. If the non-poor woman was an income earner, she was more likely to discontinue treatment than a non-earner. In poorer households, there seemed to be no difference in treatment discontinuation rates among men and women. The amount spent each month on treatment was similar among women of non-poor households and men of poorer households. Women from non-poor households also did not have the means to mobilise resources externally to continue treatment and so ended up bearing other social burdens such as working for longer hours or cutting down on spending for food to be able to pay for treatment (Sen & Iyer, 2012).

6.2.3.3 Gender Factors Influencing Utilisation of Gynaecological Care

Women who justified intimate partner violence on any pretext were less likely than other women to seek treatment for reproductive tract infections (Sudha et al., 2007). A 77% increase in the prevalence of reported intimate partner violence was found between NFHS-2 in 1998–1999 and a follow-up study in 2002–2003. Women who justified violence perpetuated by their intimate partner was 49% (Bourey, Stephenson, & Hindin, 2013). As both studies are based on NFHS 2, it can be inferred that with such a large proportion of women experiencing intimate partner violence, their health care suffers not just by the injuries and trauma inflicted but by restrictions on accessing care for their symptoms of RTI.

Healthcare seeking for gynaecological problems was constrained by women's lack of access to financial resources and decision-making power, and by gender norms which result in socialisation of women to be embarrassed to speak about their reproductive organs. In a study of rural women of Tamil Nadu, it was found that the average time between the first symptom of a prolapse and its reporting was 12.3 years. Most of the women developed the prolapse following early resumption of heavy labour after delivery and trauma caused by physical violence from husbands. This further inhibited them from doing hard work and made difficult sexual intercourse. These women had restrictions to seek healthcare due to reluctance to talk about such a symptom, cost and time associated with surgery and unwillingness of husband to send them for treatment (Ravindran, Savitri, & Bhavani, 1999).

Box 6.5 Summary of Differentials in Utilisation of Curative Health Care

- Gender-based differentials were found in treatment seeking for illness. Treatment was delayed, a closer source of health care was consulted and less money was spent on girls who were ill as compared to boys.
- The cumulative expenditure on medical care for women was found to be lower than that for men. Gender-based disadvantages played an important role in whether or not treatment was sought for gynaecological problems. The disadvantages included experience of intimate partner violence and embarrassment to articulate and seek help for reproductive health problems.
- Although poverty is an important determinant of health, gender may play a more deciding role in a person's ability to start and continue treatment for a health problem, with poor men being able to leverage their gender to compensate for poverty. Not looking at the intersection of class and caste with gender would result in assuming that all belonging to the poor or Dalit/Adivasi groups suffered the same disadvantages and also to ignoring the disadvantages experienced by some non-poor women.

6.3 A Critical Synthesis of Evidence

6.3.1 Pathways to Gender-Based Inequities in Health

The review provides unequivocal evidence on the existence of sex differentials in child mortality, morbidity, nutritional status and utilisation of health care, disadvantaging girls and women across all age groups. Studies also show that gender norms governing women's role in household decision-making, their freedom of movement and freedom to earn and spend money are significant factors affecting the health of women and their children, and especially their utilisation of maternal and child healthcare services. Gender norms prevalent in society restrict young women's access to information on matters related to sexuality and reproduction.

Women internalise the constant social suggestions and reinforcements that they are less important than men. Due to this internalisation many women believe that it is alright for men to hit their wives in some circumstances (Bourey et al., 2013; Wilson-Williams et al., 2008) and everyday violence against women by their intimate partners gets normalised. Women's vulnerability to unwanted pregnancy because of sexual violence or restriction from contraceptive use; to reproductive tract infections and to HIV is rooted in these realities.

These findings are not new. They point to the persistence of long-standing sex differentials in health and the health impact of gender-based oppression of women into the twenty-first century.

What emerges as significant is the understanding that gender operates in conjunction with other forms of oppression or disadvantages. Sex differentials between girls and boys, women and men were found across the entire population only for some health indicators such as mortality and specific morbidities. For the most part, not all girls or women were disadvantaged, but only those who simultaneously experienced other disadvantages. These intersections were indicated in two studies that simultaneously examined more than one axis of disadvantage. For example, not all girls, but girls whose mothers were illiterate and who lived in economically less developed Indian states were more likely to be poorly fed and experience nutritional disadvantages (Borooah, 2004). In another example, although on average older women (above 60 years) had poorer self-rated health, higher prevalence of disabilities and lower utilisation of healthcare services as compared to older men, these disadvantages disappeared and even reversed among older women who owned property and were financially independent (Roy & Chaudhuri, 2008). Neither of these studies were, however, *intersectionality-informed* (vide Chap. 2), in that they did not set out to systematically examine social locations resulting from the intersection of multiple axes of oppression/privilege. Interesting insights are offered by the only two studies in this review which explicitly adopted an intersectionality lens.

In an examination of sex differentials in stunting by wealth status and caste across different states of India, Mukhopadhyay (2015) found that sex differentials in stunting disappeared among wealthier households, and among households of castes other than SC/ST. In other words, wealth and caste/ethnicity are more dominant axes of disadvantage than sex, based on all India data. On the other hand, Sen and Iyer's (2012) study showed gender to dominate over class in terms of access to health care. Their study on access to health care by poorest, poor and non-poor women and men found that gender-based advantages enjoyed by men made up for their class-based disadvantages, so that there was not a significant difference in initiating health care across different classes of men. Non-poor women, although doing better than poor and poorest women, were less likely to initiate treatment as compared to non-poor men, although their health conditions had persisted for a long period. Gender-role socialisation into believing oneself to be less-entitled may have contributed to such behaviour. Mukhopadhyay (2015) also reported variations between North and South Indian states in the case of severe stunting (as compared to any stunting). In the South, Gender < Wealth < Caste, while in the North, Gender < Caste < Wealth for severe stunting in children. What these two studies indicate is the context-specific nature of the interactions across different axes of oppression, resulting in the dominance of a specific axis for a particular group in a particular situation at a given point in time.

From the literature reviewed, we discerned three main themes emerging: son preference, intimate partner violence and women's autonomy as the pathways through which gender-power inequalities impact on the health of women and children. We discuss each of these below.

6.3.1.1 Son Preference

Many studies have identified *son preference* as the pathway to sex differentials in health status and access to health care. Son preference refers to an attitude pervasive in patriarchal societies conferring more value on sons as compared to daughters. In India, sons are important sources of old-age support, and deemed necessary for the continuance of the family line and for performing death-related rituals for parents. Daughters may represent a drain on the family resources because of the dowry-system and social expectations that daughters should be provided for by parents and brothers even after marriage (Clark, 2000). Son preference is usually measured as the ratio of the ideal number of sons desired by women to the ideal number of children desired by them.

Son preference was deemed to be the underlying cause of lower levels of immunisation among girls as compared to boys in studies based on data from three rounds of National Family Health Surveys (Pande & Yazbeck, 2003; Corsi et al., 2009; Mukherjee, 2014). Son preference was also held responsible for the disproportionate improvements in nutritional status in favour of boys, during a period of significant economic growth (1992–93 to 1998–99) in the country (Tarozzi & Mahajan, 2005). While there was no longer an observable sex-differential in stunting by 2005–06, the effort of households in low-fertility states to limit the number of children and yet have at least one son resulted in the neglect of specific groups of girls: girls of higher birth order who had older female siblings were significantly more likely to be stunted than higher order boys with older male or female siblings (Mukherjee, 2014). Son preference also influenced contraceptive use. A woman with no sons or with an only son, was much less likely to use a modern method of contraception (Chacko, 2001; Dey Pal & Chaudhuri, 2009) and women who already had one or more sons were less likely to utilise prenatal care because the household would rather divert the resources to the care of living sons (Self & Grabowski, 2012). Studies have also found that South Indian states tended to have narrower gaps in nutritional and immunisation status as compared to North and East Indian states and have attributed it to weaker son preference in South India (Corsi et al., 2009; Tarozzi & Mahajan, 2005).

With one exception, none of the reviewed studies measured son preference but used proxies such as number of living sons, or sex composition of children, and inferred the presence of son preference based on observed outcomes such as significant gaps in immunisation in girls as compared to boys, or non-use of contraception. Only one study (Mukherjee, 2014) addressed itself to whether son preference intensifies or weakens with fertility transition. The author suggests that the small family norm may be transforming son preference into daughter aversion, because of the need to balance the desire for small families with that for at least one son. It appears that specific categories of girls become *most unwanted* while specific categories of boys become *most wanted*, and this is reflected in their relative nutritional and immunisation status.

What would be the way out of son preference? A study in the early 2000s analysing NFHS data for 1992–93 showed that increasing wealth and economic development did not reduce son preference, but that improvements in women's education at the individual as well as the community and state level significantly reduced son preference. Media exposure was also significantly associated with weaker son preference (Pande & Astone, 2007). Data for 2005–06 showed that son preference had persisted, and contributed to increased vulnerability of specific categories of *unwanted daughters*.

Is son preference one of the drivers of female excess mortality in infancy and childhood, a rare phenomenon observed only in a few countries across the globe? Many studies imply that this may be the case. The evidence we have is from quantitative studies which are at best able to confirm the association of son preference with negative health indicators for girls and women. We are unable to flesh out *son preference* in terms of observed everyday manifestations of preferential treatment severe enough to compromise the health and well-being of girls. Without such knowledge, it would be difficult to identify ways to intervene to prevent the potentially fatal consequences of son preference.

6.3.1.2 Intimate Partner Violence

Intimate partner violence and especially sexual violence emerges as an important mediator for sexual and reproductive health problems in women. Women were prevented from using contraception under threat of violence, experienced unwanted pregnancy, were at a high risk of infections of the urinary-genital tract and HIV (Stephenson et al., 2011; Wilson-Williams et al., 2008; Sri & Ravindran, 2015; Thomas et al., 2009; Silverman et al., 2008, 2011; Patrikar et al., 2012). Several of these were qualitative studies which traced the links between intimate partner violence and the health outcome, rather than quantitative cross-sectional studies showing associations.

6.3.1.3 Women's Autonomy and Empowerment

A recurring theme in a large number of papers is the role of women's autonomy and/or empowerment in determining health and access to health care of women and their children. Autonomy as the control women have over their own lives, in terms equal voice, control over material and other resources, access to knowledge and information, the authority to make independent decisions and freedom from constraints on physical mobility (Jejeebhoy & Sathar, 2001) Autonomy appears to be a state of being, while empowerment is conceived as a process of removing the factors that cause situation of powerlessness. In the words of Kabeer (2001), empowerment is "the expansion in people's ability to make strategic life choices in a context where this ability was previously denied to them." However, in the studies reviewed, the terms autonomy and empowerment were often used interchangeably.

Evidence from the review shows that the absence of autonomy in one or more of the spheres of household decision-making, mobility and finance; or low level of empowerment restricted a woman's access to antenatal care, institutional delivery, professional assistance at birth and postnatal care and could limit her access to contraception. The converse was true for women with autonomy or for empowered women (Mistry et al., 2009; Namasivayam et al., 2012; Mahapatro, 2012; Davis et al., 2014; Self & Grabowski, 2012; Chacko, 2001; Dey Pal & Chaudhuri, 2009; Leon et al., 2014; Dwivedi & Sogarwal, 2008). The positive influence of women's autonomy extended to their off-spring. Women with greater autonomy were found to adopt better infant-feeding practices as compared to less autonomous women, and were also more likely to ensure immunisation of their children (Shroff et al., 2011; Mahapatro, 2012). Women living in nuclear households, and by implication, with greater decision-making power, had higher levels of utilisation of antenatal care and institutional delivery, and even enjoyed better nutritional status (Saikia & Singh, 2009).

The meaning of this body of evidence and its implications for effecting change on the ground is unclear for many reasons, some related to the measurement of autonomy and others, to its conceptualisation.

In terms of measurement of autonomy, almost all studies use one or more of three key dimensions taken in various combinations—(i) Decision-making within the household including economic decisions, (ii) Physical mobility, (iii) Economic independence. Within each dimension, there are different variables, and there are variations across studies in the set of variables chosen under each dimension. For example, decision-making autonomy is usually about buying everyday items for the household and decisions related to children including taking a sick child to a health centre, but some studies also include purchases for self and making decisions related to one's own health. Economic or financial autonomy includes having cash on hand and being able to retain one's own earnings, while some studies also enquire into decision-making regarding one's own employment. So even when two studies arrive at the same conclusion about the influence of physical mobility or economic independence on a given health outcome, they may not mean the same things.

Second, each dimension of autonomy is measured as a simple sum of a series of dichotomous variables scored as 1 if the response is positive and 0 if negative. All variables within a dimension are given the same weightage, which may or may not be valid. None of the studies have accounted for the measurement errors within the variables used to measure different dimensions of autonomy (Agarwala & Lynch, 2006). These limitations can affect the strength of association between a health outcome and a dimension of autonomy, and in effect, lead to erroneous conclusions on the role of financial or mobility autonomy on health.

In addition to these definitional and measurement issues, there are some conceptual issues as well. A major gap in the conceptualization of autonomy is that none of the studies included sexual and reproductive decision-making as a dimension of women's autonomy, even though it is well accepted that control over women's sexual and reproductive decision-making is at the heart of gender-based power inequalities. Sexual and reproductive autonomy is a separate and crucial dimension of women's autonomy, and women with financial autonomy may still not enjoy sexual or reproductive autonomy (Pande et al., 2011).

The use of a uniform set of indicators within each dimension of autonomy is problematic, because what represents autonomy may vary by social location of women even within the same community. For example, while freedom of movement may be the result of empowerment for middle class or middle caste women who are expected to be in *purdah* (veil), this may not be so for poorer women from Dalit and Adivasi communities who are compelled to work for other communities because of their caste and/or economic status.

It is assumed that increased autonomy and empowerment always predict positive health outcomes. This may not be so. In the words of Davis, et al. (2014), "where choice, voice, agency and income conflict with social and cultural norms of patriarchal societies" (p. 11), empowered and autonomous women may experience considerable stress, resulting in poor health outcomes. Contextual factors and policy measures that affect and influence women's autonomy are important to factor-in, but have not been explored in these studies. For example, gender-transformative policies could facilitate the process of leveraging resources and power by empowered women, through reservation of seats in local government, providing land and house deeds in women's names and so on. Although some studies identified regional differences in women's autonomy between the North and the South of India, they did not unpack the reasons for these differences in terms of differences across states in positive policy measures, economic development and differences in cultural and social norms.

6.3.2 What We Still Do Not Know

Public health research in India has yet to integrate gender as central to the analysis of health inequities. *Most of the studies reviewed have examined sex and not gender*, as one of the many *risk factors* for the health outcome being studied. None go beyond the male/female binary to examine other gender identities and expressions, or even look at the spectrum of traditionally male or female roles adopted by individual women and men across the life cycle and under varying circumstances. Only a handful of studies adopt an intersectionality lens. Barring a few studies comparing women's vulnerability to HIV with that of men, studies that refer to the gendered nature of the risk factors, are women-only studies of women's reproductive health. Reproductive health including contraception appears to have been conceived by researchers exclusively as a woman's issue, and men are conspicuous by their absence as study participants.

Studies reporting sex differentials in health status or health-seeking behaviour have seldom addressed the reasons for the observed differences. The lack of evidence on reasons underlying sex differentials in health is in some part related to the fact that most studies have used quantitative data, and have measured the extent of the gaps, the relative odds of illness, poor nutrition or healthcare seeking by sex and factors associated with the observed patterns in health status and healthcare seeking.

As a consequence, we do not yet have explanations for higher female than male adult morbidity; and higher female than male mortality in infancy and childhood. There is no specific policy focus on addressing these gaps, either. While there are many policy interventions to improve the health and well-being of the girl child, these do not seem to have reached girl children from economically and socially disadvantaged groups. We need more evidence on whether the reason is faulty design arising from an inadequate understanding of the root causes; or poor implementation of a well-designed policy; or a combination of the two.

There exist conceptual tools such as the gender analysis matrix (WHO, 2011) to examine the pathways through which female or male status translates into positive or negative health outcomes. For example, gender roles and norms; gender-based division of labour; lower access to and control over resources and decision-making; and lower power and voice—are some of the mechanisms which individually or in some combination influence women's health outcomes. The literature reviewed has not used these tools. It has focused on only one aspect—autonomy or decision-making, and used it in a rather mechanistic manner, through quantitative studies focused on measuring and establishing associations. There were only a handful of qualitative or mixed method studies documenting the processes through which health inequities are created. There is urgent need for studying the role of *power inequalities* in shaping the health experiences of boys and girls, men and women in various social locations (by gender, class, caste, age, geographic location, etc.).

Various factors at proximate, intermediate and distal levels are associated with gender-based differentials in health. However, the evidence mainly concentrates on proximate and intermediary factors with limited focus on upstream, macro-factors. For example, the presence of a robust health system would facilitate women's utilisation of health services. A small number of studies that have examined the gendered consequences of poorly designed, poorly functioning and poorly governed health systems are discussed in Chap. 8. Our observation is that literature on gendered aspects of health systems looks only at maternal health services, rendering invisible other healthcare needs through the life cycle. Studies on whether and how policies impact differentially on health by gender are also limited. State provisions for child care, food subsidies and maternity leave for employed women are all impacting factors on women's healthcare choices. The aggressive push for the two-child norm to achieve the national goal of Total Fertility Rate (TFR) of 2.1 may be resulting in intensified neglect of a higher birth-order girl child.

Macro-economic changes in India have resulted in spiralling food prices, insecure jobs, withdrawal from the labour market of women from the upper and middle economic groups and increase in the labour market participation of their poorer counterparts (vide Chap. 1). It is worth exploring whether the increased risk of domestic violence among employed women (Audinarayana, 1997; Chacko, 2001; Char, Saavala, & Kulmala, 2010; Dwiivedi & Sogarwal, 2008; Mistry et al., 2009; Wilson-Williams et al., 2008) is related to these larger changes. What is the net result of the contradictory effects of remunerated employment (autonomy on the one hand and increased IPV on the other) on women's health?

To conclude, the evidence base merely confirms what we already know. Crucial areas of study remain unexplored and innovative methodological approaches are rarely adopted that can help generate the evidence necessary for identifying policy entry points or social action. It is time to break out of this impasse.

References

Agarwala, R., & Lynch, S. M. (2006). Refining the measurement of women's autonomy: An international application of a multi-dimensional construct. *Social Forces, 84*(4). Retrieved from http://krieger.jhu.edu/sociology/wp-content/uploads/sites/28/2012/02/Refining-the-Measurement-of-Womens-Autonomy-An-International-Application-of-a-Multi-dimensional-Construct.pdf.

Agrawal, P. K., & Agrawal, S. (2010). To what extent are the indigenous women of Jharkhand, India living in disadvantageous conditions: Findings from India's national family health survey. *Asian Ethnicity, 11*(1), 61–80.

Ahuja, R., Rajpurohit, A. C., & Ahuja, R. (2014). Gender inequalities in immunization of children in a rural population of Barabanki, Uttar Pradesh. *Indian Journal of Community Health, 26*(4), 26–29.

Allendorf, K. (2010). The quality of maternal of family relationships services and use in India. *Studies in Family Planning, 41*(4), 263–276.

American Psychological Association. (2011). *The guidelines for psychological practice with Lesbian, Gay, and Bisexual clients*. Adopted by the APA Council of Representatives. Retrieved from http://www.apa.org/pi/lgbt/resources/guidelines.aspx.

Asfaw, A., Klasen, S., & Lamanna, F. (2007). *Intra-household gender disparities in children's medical care before death in India.* Bonn: Institute for the Study of Labor (IZA). Discussion Paper 2007 (2586). Retrieved from http://ftp.iza.org/dp2586.pdf.

Asfaw, A., Lamanna, F., & Klasen, S. (2010). Gender gap in parents' financing strategy for hospitalization of their children: Evidence from India. *Health Economics, 19*(3), 265–79. doi:10.1002/hec.1468 pmid:19267357.

Association for Women's Rights in Development. (2004). *Intersectionality: A tool for gender and social justice*. Ontario: AWID.

Audinarayana, N. (1997). The effect of status of women on fertility in an Urban setting in Tamil Nadu. *The Indian Journal of Social Work, 58*(4), 542–556.

Banjare, P., & Pradhan, J. (2014). Socio-economic inequalities in the prevalence of multi-morbidity among the rural elderly in Bargarh district of Odisha (India). *PLoS One 9* (6), e97832. doi:10.1371/journal.pone.0097832.

Batra, A., Gupta, I., & Mukhopadhyay, A. (2014). *Does discrimination drive gender differences in health expenditure on adults: Evidence from Cancer patients in rural India Does discrimination drive gender differences in health expenditure on adults.* Discussion Paper 14-03, Delhi: Indian Statistical Institute.

Biswas, S., Bose, K., & Koziel, S. (2011). Effect of some social factors on nutritional status among rural Bengalee preschool children from Eastern India. *International Journal of Human Sciences, 8*(1), 289–300.

Bora, J. K., & Saikia, N. (2015). Gender differentials in self-rated health and self-reported disability among adults in India. *PLoS One, 10*(11), e0141953. doi:10.1371/journal.pone.0141953.

Borooah, V. K. (2004). Gender bias among children in India in their diet and immunisation against disease. *Social Science and Medicine, 58*(9), 1719–1731.

Borooah, V., Sabharwal, N. S., & Thorat, S. (2012). Gender and caste-based inequality in health outcomes in India. *Working Paper Indian Institute of Dalit Studies New Delhi, VI*(3). Retrieved from http://www.dalitstudies.org.in/uploads/publication/1473146220.pdf.

Bourey, C., Stephenson, R., & Hindin, M. J. (2013). Reproduction, functional autonomy and changing experiences of intimate partner violence within marriage in rural India. *International Perspectives on Sexual and Reproductive Health, 39*(4), 215–226. Retrieved from https://doi.org/10.1363/3921513.

Chacko, E. (2001). Women's use of contraception in rural India: A village-level study. *Health & Place, 7*(3), 197–208.

Char, A., Saavala, M., & Kulmala, T. (2010). Influence of mothers-in-law on young couples' family planning decisions in rural India. *Reproductive Health Matters, 18*(35), 154–162. Retrieved from https://doi.org/10.1016/S0968-8080(10)35497-8.

Clark, S. (2000). Son preference and sex composition of children: Evidence from India. *Demography, 37*(1), 10–95.

Corsi, D. J., Bassani, D. G., Kumar, R., Awasthi, S., Jotkar, R., Kaur, N., & Jha, P. (2009). Gender inequity and age-appropriate immunisation coverage in India from 1992 to 2006. *BMC International Health & Human Rights, 9* (Suppl 1), S3. doi:10.1186/1472-698X-9-S1-S3.

Davis, L. M., Schensulb, S. L., Schensulc, J. J., Vermad, R. K., Nastasie, B. K., & Singh, R. (2014). Women's empowerment and its differential impact on health in low-income communities in Mumbai, India. *Global Public Health*, (1). Retrieved from https://doi.org/10.1080/17441692.2014.904919.

Desai, S. (1994). *Geographic inequalities and demographic behaviour—India*. New York, USA: The Population Council.

Dey, I., & Chaudhuri, R. N. (2008). Gender inequality in nutritional status among under five children in a village in Hooghly district, West Bengal. *Indian Journal of Public Health, 52*(4), 20–218.

Dey Pal, I., & Chaudhuri, R. N. (2009). Gender preference and its implications on reproductive behavior of mothers in a rural area of West Bengal. *Indian Journal of Community Medicine: Official Publication of Indian Association of Preventive & Social Medicine, 34*(1), 65–67. Retrieved from https://doi.org/10.4103/0970-0218.45377.

Dvorsky, G., & Hughes, J. (2008). Postgenderism : Beyond the gender binary. *Institute for Ethics and Emerging Technologies*, IEET Monograph Series. March 1–18. Retrieved from https://ieet.org/archive/IEET-03-PostGender.pdf.

Dwiivedi, L. K., & Sogarwal, R. (2008). Understanding contraceptive adoption in India: Does women's autonomy matter? *The Journal of Family Welfare, 54*(1), 24–34.

Garg, S., Sharma, N., & Sahay, R. (2001). Socio-cultural aspects of menstruation in an urban slum in Delhi, India. *Reproductive Health Matters, 9*(17), 16–25. Retrieved from https://doi.org/10.1016/S0968-8080(01)90004-7.

Gaudin, S., & Yazbeck, A. S. (2006). Immunisation in India 1993–1999: Wealth, gender, and regional inequalities revisited. *Social Science and Medicine, 62*(3), 694–706.

Greaves, L. (2001). Why put gender and sex into health research? *Health (San Francisco)*, 3–14.

Jacob, M., John, T. J., George, S., Rao, P. S., & Babu, P. G. (1995). Increasing prevalence of human immunodeficiency virus infection among patients attending a clinic for sexually transmitted disease. *Indian Journal of Medical Research, 101*, 6–9.

Jayachandran, S., & Kuziemko, I. (2015). Why do mothers breastfeed girls less than boys? Evidence and implications for child health in India. *Quarterly Journal of Economics, 126*(3), 1485–538. doi:10.2307/23015706.

Jejeebhoy, S. J., & Sathar, Z. (2001). A women's autonomy in India and Pakistan: The influence of religion and region. *Population Development Review, 27*(4), 687–712.

Jose, S., & Navaneetham, K. (2010). Social infrastructure and women's undernutrition. *Economic & Political Weekly, 45*(13), 83–89.

Kabeer, N. (2001). Reflections on the measurement of empowerment. *In Discussing Women's Empowerment–Theory and Practice.* SIDA Studies No. 3, SIDA.

Koski, A. D., Stephenson, R., & Koenig, M. R. (2011). Physical violence by partner during pregnancy and use of prenatal care in rural India. *Journal of Health, Population and Nutrition, 29*(3), 245–254. Retrieved from https://doi.org/10.3329/jhpn.v29i3.7872.

Krishnan, A., Ng, N., Kapoor, S. K., Pandav, C. S., & Byass, P. (2012). Temporal trends and gender differentials in causes of childhood deaths at Ballabgarh, India—Need for revisiting child survival strategies. *BMC Public Health, 12*(1), 555. Retrieved from https://doi.org/10.1186/1471-2458-12-555.

Krishnan, A., Amarchand, R., Byass, P., Pandav, C. S., & Ng, N. (2014). "No one says 'No' to money" a mixed methods approach for evaluating conditional cash transfer schemes to improve girl children's status in Haryana, India. *International Journal of Equity in Health, 13* (11), 1–10.

Kumar, A., Fuloria, K., & Taunk, A. (2012). A comparative study of tribal and non tribal women in the state of Uttarakhand (India) in the field of women's autonomy, contraceptive used and family planning. *Journal of Research in Peace, Gender and Development, 2*(7), 156–161.

León, F. R., Lundqren, R., Sinai, I., Sinha, R., & Jennings, V. (2014). Increasing literate and illiterate women's met need for contraception via empowerment : A quasi-experiment in rural India. *Reproductive Health, 11*(1), 74. doi:10.1186/1742-4755-11-74.

Mahapatro, S. R. (2012). Utilization of maternal and child health care services in India: Does women's autonomy matter? *Journal of Family Welfare, 58*(1), 22–33.

Maharana, B., & Ladusingh, L. (2014). Gender disparity in health and food expenditure in India among elderly. *International Journal of Population Research,* Retrieved from http://dx.doi.org/10.1155/2014/150105.

Mathew, J. L. (2012). Inequity in childhood immunisation in India: A systematic review. *Indian Pediatrics, 49*(3), 23–203.

Mazumdar, S. (2010). Determinants of inequality in child malnutrition in India. *Asian Population Studies, 6*(3), 307–333.

Meenakshi. (2014). Gender differentials of morbidity in India. *International Research Journal of Commerce Arts and Science,* 5(11), 52–62.

Mistry, R., Galal, O., & Lu, M. (2009). Women's autonomy and pregnancy care in rural India: A contextual analysis. *Social Science and Medicine, 69*(6), 926–933. Retrieved from https://doi.org/10.1016/j.socscimed.2009.07.008.

Mohanty, S. K. (2012). Multiple deprivations and maternal care in India. *International Perspectives on Sexual and Reproductive Health, 38*(1), 6–14. Retrieved from https://doi.org/10.1363/3800612.

Moser, K. A., Agrawal, S., Davey Smith, G., & Ebrahim, S. (2014). Socio-demographic inequalities in the prevalence, diagnosis and management of hypertension in India: Analysis of nationally-representative survey data. *PLoS One, 9*(1). https://doi.org/10.1371/journal.pone.0086043.

Mukherjee, R. (2014). *Selective gender differences in child health among small families in eight Replacement Fertility States of India.* Paper presented for the 2014 Meeting of the Population Association of America, Boston.

Mukhopadhyay, S. (2015). The Intersection of gender, caste and class inequalities in child nutrition in Rural India. *Asian Population Studies, 11*(1), 17–31. doi:10.1080/17441730.2015.995150.

Munuswamy, S., Nakamura, K., Seino, K., & Kizuk, M. (2014). Inequalities in use of antenatal care and its service components in India. *Journal of Rural Medicine, 9*(1), 10–19.

Muralidharan, A., Fehringer, J., Sara, P., Rottach, E., Das, M., & Mandal, M. (2015). *Transforming gender norms, roles, and power dynamics for better health evidence from a systematic review of gender-integrated health programs in low-and middle-Income countries.* Washington, D.C.: Health Policy Project, Futures Group.

Namasivayam, A., Osuorah, D. C., Syed, R., Antai, D., & Diddy, A. (2012). The role of gender inequities in women's access to reproductive health care : A population-level Study of Namibia, Kenya, Nepal and India. *International Journal of Women's Health, 4*, 351–364. Retrieved from https://doi.org/10.2147/IJWH.S32569.

Nandi, S. (2012). *The role of Community Health Workers (CHWs) in addressing social determinants of health in Chhattisgarh, India.* Dissertation, University of the Western Cape.

National Sample Survey Organization. (2004). *Morbidity and Healthcare*, 60th round. New Delhi: National Sample Survey Organisation, Ministry of Statistics and Programme Implementation.

Neogy, S. (2010). Gender inequality, mothers' health, and unequal distribution of food: experience from a CARE project in India. *Gender & Development, 18*(3), 479–489. Retrieved from https://doi.org/10.1080/13552074.2010.522027.

Ng, N., Kowal, P., Kahn, K., Naidoo, N., Abdullah, S., Bawah, A., … Chatterji, S. (2010). Health inequalities among older men and women in Africa and Asia: Evidence from eight health and demographic surveillance system sites in the INDEPTH WHO-SAGE Study. *Global Health Action*, (2), 96–107. Retrieved from https://doi.org/10.3402/gha.v3i0.5420.

Pande, R. P., & Astone, N. M. (2007). Explaining son preference in rural India: The independent role of structural versus individual factors. *Population Research and Policy Review, 26*(1), 1–29. Retrieved from https://doi.org/10.1007/s11113-006-9017-2.

Pande, R. P., & Yazbeck, A. S. (2003). What's in a country average? Wealth, gender, and regional inequalities in immunisation in India. *Social Science and Medicine, 57*(11), 2075–2088.

Pande, R. P., Falle, T., Rathod, S., Edmeades, J., & Krishnan, S. (2011). "If your husband call, you have to go": Understanding sexual agency among young married women in urban South India. *Sexual Health, 8*, 102–109.

Pandey, A., Sengupta, P. G., Mondal, S. K., Gupta, D. N., Manna, B., Ghosh, S., … Bhattacharya, S. K. (2002). Gender differences in healthcare-seeking during common illnesses in a rural community of West Bengal, India. *Journal of Health Population and Nutrition, 20*(4), 306–311.

Patel, V., Kirkwood, B. R., Pednekar, S., Pereira, B., Barros, P., Fernandes, J., … Mabey, D. (2006). Gender disadvantage and reproductive health risk factors for common mental disorders in women: a community survey in India. *Archives of General Psychiatry, 63*(4), 404–413. Retrieved from https://doi.org/10.1001/archpsyc.63.4.404.

Patrikar, S., Verma, A. K., Bhatti, V. K., & Shatabdi, S. (2012). Measuring domestic violence in human immunodeficiency virus-positive women. *Medical Journal, Armed Forces India, 68*(2), 136–141.

Ravindran, T. K. S., Savitri, R., & Bhavani, A. (1999). *Women's experiences of utero-vaginal prolapse: A qualitative study from Tamil Nadu* (pp. 166–172). In Safe Motherhood Initiatives: Critical Issues; Reproductive Health Matters.

Registrar General of India. (2013). *Sample registration system (SRS).* New Delhi: Office of the Registrar General and Census Commissioner.

Registrar General of India. (2014). *Sample registration system (SRS).* New Delhi: Office of the Registrar General and Census Commissioner.

Roy, K., & Chaudhuri, A. (2008). Influence of socioeconomic status, wealth and financial empowerment on gender differences in health and healthcare utilization in later life: evidence from India. *Social Science and Medicine, 66*(9), 1951–1962. Retrieved from https://doi.org/10.1016/j.socscimed.2008.01.015.

Saikia, N., & Bhat, P. N. M. (2008). Factors affecting adult mortality in India: An analysis of national family health surveys of 1992–1993 & 1998–1999. *Demography, 37*(2), 291–302.

Saikia, N., & Singh, A. (2009). Does type of household affect maternal health? Evidence from India. *Journal of Biosocial Science, 41*(3), 329–353. Retrieved from https://doi.org/10.1017/S0021932008003209.

Saikia, N., Moradhvaj, & Bora, J. K. (2016). Gender difference in health-care expenditure: Evidence from India human development survey. *PLoS ONE, 11*(7), e0158332. doi:10.1371/journal. pone.0158332.

Sanghavi, P., Bhalla, K., & Das, V. (2009). Fire-related deaths in India in 2001: A retrospective analysis of data. *The Lancet, 373*, 1282–1288. Retrieved from https://doi.org/10.1016/S0140-6736(09)60235-X.

Self, S., & Grabowski, R. (2012). Son preference, autonomy and maternal health in rural India. *Oxford Development Studies, 40*(3), 305–323.

Sen, G., & Iyer, A. (2012). Who gains, who loses and how: Leveraging gender and class intersections to secure health entitlements. *Social Science and Medicine, 74*(11), 1802–1811. https://doi.org/10.1016/j.socscimed.2011.05.035.

Sen, J., & Mondal, N. (2012). Socio-economic and demographic factors affecting the composite index of anthropometric failure (CIAF). *Annals of Human Biology, 39*(2), 129–136.

Shroff, M. R., Grif, P. L., Suchindran, C., Nagalla, B., Vazir, S., & Bentley, M. E. (2011). Does maternal autonomy influence feeding practices and infant growth in rural India? *Social Science and Medicine, 73*, 447–455. Retrieved from https://doi.org/10.1016/j.socscimed.2011.05.040.

Silverman, J. G., Decker, M. R., Saggurti, N., Balaiah, D., & Raj, A. (2008). Intimate partner violence and HIV infection among married Indian women. *Journal of the American Medical Association, 300*(6), 703–710.

Silverman, J. G., Raj, A., Cheng, D. M., Decker, M. R., Coleman, S., Bridden, C., ... Samet, J. H. (2011). Sex trafficking and initiation-related violence, alcohol use, and HIV risk among HIV-infected female sex workers in Mumbai, India. *Journal of Infectious Diseases, 204*(5), S1229–S1234.

Singh, A. (2012). *Gender based within-household inequality in immunisation status of children: Some Evidence from South Asian countries*. Retrieved from https://editorialexpress.com/cgi-bin/conference/download.cgi?db_name=res2012&paper_id=913.

Springer, K. W., Mager Stellman, J., & Jordan-Young, R. M. (2012). Beyond a catalogue of differences: A theoretical frame and good practice guidelines for researching sex/gender in human health. *Social Science and Medicine, 74*(11), 1817–1824. Retrieved from https://doi.org/10.1016/j.socscimed.2011.05.033.

Srikanth, P., John, T. J., Jeyakumari, H., Babu, P. G., Mathai, D., Jacob, M., ... Zachariah, A. (1997). Epidemiological features of acquired immunodeficiency syndrome in southern India. *Indian Journal of Medical Research, 105*, 191–197.

Stephenson, R., Koenig, M. A., Acharya, R., Roy, T. K., & Koenig, A. (2011). Domestic violence, contraceptive in rural Use, India and unwanted pregnancy. *Studies in Family Planning, 39*(3), 177–186.

Sri, B. S. & Ravindran, T. S. (2015). Safe, accessible medical abortion in a rural Tamil Nadu clinic, India, but what about sexual and reproductive rights? *Reproductive Health Matters, 22* (44), 134–143. Retrieved from https://doi.org/10.1016/S0968-8080(14)43789-3.

Sudha, S., Morrison, S., & Zhu, L. (2007). Violence against women, symptom reporting, and treatment for reproductive tract infections in Kerala state, Southern India. *Health Care for Women International, 28*(3), 268–284. Retrieved from https://doi.org/10.1080/07399330601180164.

Subramanian, S. V., Nandy, S., Irving, M., Gordon, D., Lambert, H., & Davey Smith, G. (2006). The mortality divide in India: the differential contributions of gender, caste, and standard of living across the life course. *American Journal of Public Health, 96*(5), 818–825. Retrieved from https://doi.org/10.2105/AJPH.2004.060103.

Substance Abuse and Mental Health Services Administration. (2012). *Top health issues for LGBT populations information & resource kit. HHS Publication No 12–4684.*

Tarique, M., & Samreen, S. (2014). Gender inequalities in education and its effect on health of women and child. *International Journal of Research, 1*(4), 673–690.

Tarozzi, A., & Mahajan, A. (2005). Child nutrition in India in the Nineties: A story of increased gender inequality? *SIEPR Discussion Paper No. 04–29, 94305*(4).

Tiwari, A. K. (2013). Gender inequality in terms of health and nutrition in India: Evidence from national family health survey -3. *Pacific Business Review International, 5*(1), 24–34.

Thomas, B. E., Chandra, S., Selvi, K, J., Suriyanarayanan, D., & Swaminathan, S. (2009). Gender differences in sexual behaviour among people living with HIV in Chennai, India. *Indian Journal of Medical Research, 129*(6), 690–694.

Willis, J. R., Kumar, V., Mohanty, S., Singh, P., Singh, V., Baqui, A. H., … Darmstadt, G. L. (2009). Gender differences in perception and care-seeking for illness of newborns in rural Uttar Pradesh, India. *Journal of Health, Population and Nutrition, 27*(1), 62. Retrieved from http://www.ncbi.nlm.nih.gov/pmc/articles/PMC2761808/pdf/jhpn0027-0062.pdf.

Wilson-Williams, L., Stephenson, R., Juvekar, S., & Andes, K. (2008). Domestic violence and contraceptive use in a rural Indian village. *Violence Against Women, 14*(10), 1181–1198.

World Health Organization. (2000). *Women's mental health: An evidence based review*. Geneva: WHO.

World Health Organization. (2001). *Gender disparities in mental health*. Geneva: WHO, Department of Mental Health and Substance Dependence, (vol. 48).

World Health Organization. (2002). *Integrating gender perspectives in the work of WHO: WHO Gender Policy*. Geneva: WHO, Department of Gender and Women's Health.

World Health Organization. (2003). *Gender, health and tobacco*. Geneva: WHO, Department of Gender and Women's Health.

World Health Organization (2011). *Gender mainstreaming for health managers: a practical approach*. Geneva: WHO, Department of Gender and Women's Health.

World Health Organization. (2015). WHO-gender factsheet. Retrieved from http://www.who.int/mediacentre/factsheets/fs403/en/.

Chapter 7
Other Socially Constructed Vulnerabilities: Focus on People Living with HIV/AIDS and Internal Migrants

Grace A. Chitra

As long as poverty, injustice and gross inequality persist in our world, none of us can truly rest.

—Nelson Mandela

Abstract This chapter focuses on the other socially constructed vulnerabilities with a special focus on People Living with HIV/AIDS (PLHAs) and internal migrants. The systematic denial of equal rights to a specific group of individuals through social sanction, programmes and policies would be *social construction of vulnerability*. PLHAs face stigma and discrimination which have negative social consequences (particularly among women PLHAs), decreased quality of life and systematic denial to access health and healthcare services. The large population of internal migrants also faces stigma and discrimination leading to lower access to general healthcare and maternal and child health services. Migration is a major contributor to ill health among adults and children. These vulnerabilities collude against the health and well-being of migrant PLHAs. The diagnosis and treatment of HIV among migrants is convoluted and often delayed. Their women partners face layered inequalities in accessing health care and social justice. Lower socio-economic status and being a woman often contributes to the social construction of vulnerability among PLHAs and internal migrants. Migration itself should be considered as an axis of health inequity, in this context. The neo-liberal policies prevailing in the current consumerist society, compounded by public programmes and policies insensitive to the specific needs of PLHAs and internal migrants; layered by the stigma and discrimination and compounded by layered vulnerabilities due to gender, class and caste leads to systemic denial of access to health and health care resulting in health inequities among PLHAs and internal migrants.

Keywords Socially constructed vulnerabilities · PLHA · Internal migrants Migrant PLHA · Stigma and discrimination

---

G.A. Chitra (✉)
Global Institute of Public Health, Ananthapuri Hospitals and Research Institute, Chacka, Trivandrum 695024, Kerala, India
e-mail: achitragrace@gmail.com

T.K.S. Ravindran and R. Gaitonde (eds.), *Health Inequities in India*,
https://doi.org/10.1007/978-981-10-5089-3_7

7.1 Introduction

Webster's Dictionary defines vulnerability as "the state of being vulnerable or exposed" or "the susceptibility to injury or attack." The term is most often used in the context of response to disasters, where *vulnerability* is the degree to which a population, individual or organisation are unable to anticipate, cope with, resist and recover from the impacts of disasters (Adams & Wisner, 2002).

Vulnerability in health is often defined as greater risk for poor health status and healthcare access (Shi & Stevens, 2005). Vulnerabilities may be physical, psychological or social, and often a combination of these. Those vulnerable in terms of physical needs include, for example, persons living with physical disabilities, pregnant women and children at high risk of morbidity or mortality, those suffering from chronic physical health conditions, and persons living with HIV/acquired immunodeficiency syndrome. Those living with serious or common mental disorders, having a history of alcohol or substance use or are suicidal may be considered as psychologically vulnerable. Socially vulnerable populations include those living in abusive or dysfunctional families, and those who for any reason, may experience social exclusion, as in the case of migrants or refugees (Aday, 1991).

Studies use the concepts of both *vulnerable individuals* and of *vulnerable categories or groups*. Conceptual approaches likewise differ in their characterisation of vulnerability as innately located within an individual or as the result of a social process. Mechanic and Tanner (2007) view vulnerability as the interaction between an individual's capacity and actions and the social stressors such as socio-economic deficits, exclusion, illness and disability that s/he is exposed to. The likelihood that the person becomes *vulnerable* depends on the intensity of the stressors experienced and the resources (education, income and wealth, cognitive ability, the support from families, social networks and community resources) available to manage the situation. The process is mediated by individual coping mechanisms, which is an individual process but shaped by the social environment such as social support networks (Mechanic & Tanner, 2007).

According to the *social construction of vulnerability* approach, vulnerabilities are often the result of systematic denial of equal rights to a group through social sanctions, programmes and policies. Gill (2006) writes about the social construction of vulnerability in the context of people with disabilities. She quotes a person with disability who observed "All my life I've been told that I can't get into my neighbourhood restaurant because my legs won't take me upstairs. Now I know it's because the restaurant owner won't build a ramp." Thus, people are rendered vulnerable by the social and policy environment that does not accommodate and address their physical and psychological needs and differences (Gill, 2006, p. 183).

Literature on gender and health amply illustrates how biological factors interact with socially constructed disadvantages experienced by women in terms of social devaluation, lack of power and disadvantaged access to and control over resources to make women a vulnerable group in terms of health (vide Chap. 6). In the Indian context, those who are in the lowest rungs of the caste hierarchy and those from Scheduled Tribe communities, among others, constitute a socially constructed vulnerable group denied equal access to social determinants of health and health care.

Being vulnerable is a matter of lack of power. Disadvantaged groups struggle with narrowed choices and barriers in access to resources, and when state-provided health and social care services are weak or non-existent, this results in them becoming a vulnerable group and forms the basis of the health inequities they face (Gill, 2006).

Individuals face multiple vulnerabilities in many cases. Some vulnerable groups experience stigma and discrimination which compound their disadvantages and powerlessness. One example is people living with severe mental illnesses, who, in addition to their psychological vulnerability, face economic vulnerability because of social attitudes to employing persons with mental illness, as well as social exclusion and isolation because of stigma and discrimination making them socially vulnerable.

In this chapter, we have focused on two specific groups not covered in the previous chapters, who experience health inequities because of their socially constructed vulnerability. These are Persons Living with HIV and AIDS (PLHA) and internal migrants, and the intersection of the two, migrant PLHA. The disease (in the first case) and the displacement (in the second case) lead to stigma and discrimination, restricted resources and inequitable access to health care. We have restricted the studies synthesised in this chapter to those which show how PLHAs and internal migrants are socially vulnerable owing to various processes and how this results in inequities in health and well-being and in access to and quality of health care. The chapter first gives a summary of evidence of health inequalities faced by the PLHAs and internal migrants and explores how the coexistence of these vulnerabilities deepens the health inequalities. This is followed by a critical interpretation based on the studies, of the mechanisms underlying the creation and sustenance of health inequities based on these socially constructed vulnerabilities.

7.2 Health Inequities—Summary of Evidence

7.2.1 People Living with HIV/AIDS (PLHAs) as a Vulnerable Group

India had about 2.2 million people living with HIV/AIDS (PLHA) in 2015 (National AIDS Control Society [NACO], 2015). The adult prevalence of HIV has come down to 0.26% in 2015 from 0.34% in 2007 and 0.28% in 2012 (0.3% among males and 0.2% among females). Around 64.4% of PLHAs are concentrated in seven high prevalence states of India; Undivided Andhra Pradesh and Telangana had the highest number, followed by Maharashtra, Karnataka, Gujarat, Bihar and

Uttar Pradesh. A large number of PLHAs are already socially marginalised and from socially excluded groups such as sex workers and Men having Sex with Men (MSM), and injecting drug users. Poverty is also a significant risk factor. Stigma and discrimination of PLHAs then compounds these issues, which leads to problems in accessing care; in seeking care, getting diagnosed, starting and sustaining the treatment. In the case of HIV/AIDS the disease itself jeopardises livelihoods, makes it difficult to lead a *normal* and active life because of many opportunistic infections. In addition, other social consequences related to widowhood, having to care for an HIV-positive child and other family members compound the burden.

Despite knowledge of the viral aetiology, HIV-positive people face social stigma. Most of the studies related to PLHAs looked at stigma and discrimination as the driver of the health inequities they experience. Many of the studies used primary data, with several studies using qualitative research approaches. The qualitative studies have provided scope to understand the many ways in which stigma and discrimination affect the health status of PLHAs and their ability to seek timely health care.

In the following sections, we summarise evidence from studies published from 2000 to 2014, on PLHAs and stigma and discrimination with a focus on health status and healthcare seeking. We start with how stigma is conceptualised in HIV studies, and then describe the prevalence, sites and sources of stigma, followed by the health consequences of stigma and discrimination for PLHA.

7.2.1.1 HIV Stigma and Discrimination: Concepts

Stigma is the devaluation of an individual or group based on the socially constructed meanings associated with a specific attribute or condition. The devaluation results in lower power and access to valued resources of society. Three types of stigma have been commonly mentioned by studies. The first, *enacted* stigma is related to interpersonal actions, and refers to actions of discrimination or hostility. The second and third are intrapersonal. *Perceived* or *felt-normative* stigma is an individual's subjective perception of being treated differently or unfairly. *Internalised* stigma is the acceptance of stigma by individuals or groups who are being stigmatised (Steward et al., 2008). Discrimination is conceptualised as enacted stigma, the manifestation of stigma.

HIV stigma is the shared knowledge in and acceptance by society of the devaluation of PLHA. PLHA experience stigma within their households and neighbourhoods, in schools, public spaces and in health facilities. All over the world, stigma and discrimination related to HIV status has been shown to cause pain and suffering with unequal access to health care to the PLHAs. In most cases, the behavioural manifestations of HIV stigma are driven either by the fear of transmission of HIV through casual contact, HIV-related misconceptions and/or pre-existing prejudices, shame, blame and moral judgment towards PLHA (Ekstrand, Ramakrishna, Bharat, & Heylen, 2013).

Chakrapani and Bharat (2014) categorise HIV stigma as having four dimensions. In addition to two of three dimensions of stigma mentioned above, viz. enacted stigma and internalised stigma, they also identify instrumental stigma (fear of transmission of HIV through casual contact, HIV-related misconceptions) and symbolic stigma (shame, blame and moral judgment towards PLHA).

Parker and Aggleton (2003) have challenged the conceptualisation of stigma as an interpersonal phenomenon related to attitudes and behaviours of individuals, without reference to the context. They postulate that *stigmatisation* is a social process inherently linked to the production and reproduction of structural inequalities. Stigma results in the exclusion from access to resources and social and political participation of those who are stigmatised, resulting in their powerlessness as a group. Moreover, HIV-related stigma is often layered over other forms of social disadvantages based on class, gender, race and sexualities (Bharat, 2011).

7.2.1.2 Extent of Stigma and Discrimination

Evidence suggests the persistence of significant levels of stigmatisation and discrimination against PLHA into the current decade as well. There are two strands of studies about the extent of stigma and discrimination: those interviewing the general population or specific population groups about their perceptions and attitudes, and those speaking to PLHA and capturing their experiences. The variety of tools and instruments used make it somewhat difficult to compare across studies, but we may discern overall patterns.

The general population appears to have negative and judgemental attitudes towards PLHA, often fuelled by misconceptions on modes of transmission. A national survey in 2009–10 covering urban populations from 18 states reported that about one-third of the people feared that HIV could be transmitted through casual contact, for example in situations where children played with HIV-infected children. More than 60% of the general population blamed PLHA for their condition and believed this was a punishment. However, the majority (72%) disapproved of discriminatory acts against PLHA (Chakrapani & Bharat, 2014). In an earlier study among the general population in Hyderabad, more than 80% had said that they would not take care of any family member other than their spouse or children living with HIV or AIDS, and more than half had wanted a public list of PLHA to be prepared and circulated so that contact with them, and hence infection, may be prevented (Sudha, Vijay, & Lakshmi, 2005).

Misconceptions about how HIV is transmitted and discriminatory attitudes towards PLHA were present also among educated young people. In a 2011 study, 18, 22 and 32% of college-going youth respectively believed that PLHA should be isolated; that they would be reluctant to live in the same building; or share food with them (Shetty & Kowli, 2011). One-fifth of rural youth covered by a study in Gujarat thought that transmission of HIV was possible through casual contact, sharing food and mosquito bite (Yadav, Makwana, Vadera, Dhaduk, & Gandha, 2011).

Unmindful of the possibility that they may themselves be affected, two-fifths of pregnant women respondents in a study conducted in antenatal clinics opined that all pregnant women and couples awaiting marriage should be compulsorily tested. About a third said that PLHA should not have children and that they should not marry (Rahbar, Garg, Tripathi, Gupta, & Singh, 2007).

Studies with PLHA as respondents confirm the pervasiveness of stigma and discrimination. Social exclusion and isolation were the commonest forms of stigma experienced by up to one-third of PLHA followed by loss of social status and role (Chakrapani & Bharat, 2014). A community-based cross-sectional study carried out in seven districts of Tamil Nadu, India, among 400 PLHA reported that 27% of PLHA had experienced severe forms of stigma. Overt acts of discrimination were experienced by 29, 18% perceived negative public attitudes and 26% were afraid of disclosure owing to fear of stigma (Charles et al., 2012). While almost all PLHA (above 90% in more than one study) experienced perceived stigma, less than a third of them experienced discriminatory behaviour (Thomas et al., 2005; Subramanian, Gupte, Dorairaj, Periannan, & Mathai, 2009). A study of PLHA in Kolkata found that about 41% of 105 had experienced any type of discrimination. About a third reported discrimination within the family, 18.4 and 17.5%, respectively reported experiencing discrimination in healthcare settings and the community at large. Discrimination in the workplace was far less common, with only 6.8% reporting this (Deb, Sun, & Strodl, 2013).

PLHA internalise the stigma they experience and significant proportions report feelings of shame, guilt and self-blame associated with their HIV-positive status (Chakrapani & Bharat, 2014; Charles et al., 2012). Experience of both external and internalised stigma appears to be especially pronounced for some populations as compared to others. For example, PLHA who had no schooling and those who were on antiretroviral treatment were more likely to experience severe stigma as compared to those with high school education or above and those not on ART, respectively (Charles et al., 2012); and children were reported to experience a low level of stigma (Bharathi, Pai, & Nayak, 2014).

Groups facing layered stigma and double discrimination include PLHA who are from groups already experiencing stigma because of their social identity. Some examples are Female Sex Workers (FSW), Men who have Sex with Men (MSMs) and Injecting Drug Users (IDU). HIV-positive FSW were often faced with denial from their owners/*gharwalis* who would continue to force them to work till they were too sick to work, and faced dual stigma as *dhandewalis* and as PLHA (Bharat, 2011).

MSM individuals also face double discrimination if their sexual identity is disclosed along with their HIV-positive status. MSM risk ridicule and ostracism and fear rejection from family and even fear loss of secure livelihood (Bharat et al., 2001). Another group where individuals are faced with multiple vulnerabilities are the IDUs. IDU-related problems are reported largely in the north-east regions of India, very unlike the rest of India (where the main route of HIV transmission is through heterosexual contact). The highly addictive nature of drug use makes them vulnerable for transmission of the virus (Chakrapani, Newman, Shunmugam, & Dubrow, 2011).

Gender differences in experience of HIV stigma have been reported from many studies. However, their findings vary. Malave, Ramakrishna, Heylen, Bharat, and Ekstrand (2014) found that among men the knowledge that they became HIV positive due to extramarital relationships resulted in self-blame and guilt, leading to higher internalised stigma than women. Women on the other hand, experienced higher enacted stigma—i.e. actions of discrimination than men (Malave et al., 2014). An earlier (2005) study reported no differences between women and men in internalised stigma, but a significant difference in experience of discrimination (Thomas et al., 2005). Other studies using stigma assessment scales have reported gender differences in discrimination experienced, but these were not statistically significant (Deb et al., 2013; Charles et al., 2012). The 2009–10 survey of urban populations in 18 states unequivocally stated that more women reported all forms of self-stigma, especially self-blame and felt they deserved to be punished for having HIV. Women PLHA had experienced more forms and higher levels of discrimination than men with HIV, and widows were especially vulnerable (Chakrapani & Bharat, 2014).

Many factors seem to contribute to higher levels of discrimination experienced by women. Women are routinely tested for HIV during pregnancy and this results in many of them being diagnosed earlier than their husbands (from whom they often contract the disease). They are therefore blamed for bringing the infection to the family. Even when the husband is diagnosed first, wives may be blamed for failing to control their husbands' extramarital relations (Bharat, 2011). Because gender norms restrict women's presence in the public space, their frequent hospital visits following diagnosis as HIV positive make it more difficult for them to keep the diagnosis private and not known outside the family (Thomas, Nyamathi, & Swaminathan, 2008).

van Hollen (2010) researched heterosexual HIV-positive women's own perspectives on the gendering of stigma. Her research revealed that some women faced disproportionate stigma (in private sphere especially with their in-laws they face blame, while in public sphere they receive sympathy and pity than men). The women thought that they were blamed for transmitting HIV to husbands due to their gendered bodies (a double standard of sexual morality). Many of them admitted that they were blamed as being promiscuous after the husband's death as a ploy to exempt the in-laws from taking responsibility of the widow and children (van Hollen, 2010).

> Society is more unkind to HIV-positive women. The women are condemned and blamed more. My parents-in- law never scold their son. But they often ask me: "*in which inauspicious time did our son marry you?*" [i.e., astrologically speaking] and say that I have brought HIV and all these problems into the family. Gossip is also much more focused on HIV-positive women than on positive men. People always say: "*she was so good and so well once upon a time. But now look what has become of her* – Women PLHA (van Hollen, 2010, p. 7).

7.2.1.3 Stigma and Discrimination in Healthcare Facilities

Healthcare settings are a major site of many forms of stigma and discrimination of PLHA. Studies report that discrimination started at the time of admission and then continued through all points of care. Nurses, ward boys, attenders and doctors exhibited discriminatory attitudes (Deb et al., 2013). Healthcare providers often blamed PLHA for having contracted the disease.

> High risk population means lower class people—they live in slums in unhygienic conditions. One sleeps with anybody and everybody; extramarital affairs are common and also drug users and sex workers come in this category – Doctor (Mahendra et al., 2006, p. 18).

In the study by Chakrapani and Bharat (2014) in urban areas of eight states, more than 40% of healthcare providers believed that HIV was punishment for bad behaviour while more than 60% thought that female sex workers and promiscuous men were to be blamed for spreading the infection. About half of them agreed that work-related exposure to HIV infection was the most common mode of transmission of HIV to healthcare providers. Discriminatory practices included providing less care and attention to those suspected to be HIV positive than other patients; taking extra care in sterilising instruments; requiring patients to undergo mandatory HIV testing before any invasive procedure; and using latex even to touch the patient (Chakrapani & Bharat, 2014). This study confirms the persistence of very high levels of stigma and discrimination reported by many earlier studies (Kermode, Holmes, Langkham, Thomas, & Gifford, 2005; Mahendra et al., 2006; Thomas, Nyamathi, & Swaminathan, 2009; Deb et al., 2013).

Exaggerated perception of the threat posed by HIV-positive persons could result in health provider behaviour that violates PLHA's human rights. For example, more than 90% of the doctors, nurses and ward staff in a study conducted in Mumbai and Bengaluru endorsed mandatory testing for surgery patients and female sex workers, and more than 50% believed that PLHA should be prevented from having children and 50–83% thought that PLHA deserved what they got (Ekstand et al., 2013). The right to informed consent for testing and right to confidentiality with respect to the result are often denied, although this may not be specific to PLHA. However, the consequences are especially damaging for PLHA.

> I went to this Pallahalli doctor, got the test done. Then I knew that I have HIV. Then I thought: What if my mother-in-law gets to know this? She will scold me, criticize me, thinking I knew this and did not tell. Later the doctor called her and then she started to look at me as her enemy – Pregnant woman PLHA (Madhivanan et al., 2014, p. 5 of 9).

Reluctance to deal with HIV-positive patients may also result in *referral games* enacted by health facilities. Providers unwilling to admit critically ill PLHA may refer them from one department to another and from facility to facility till the patient gives up and quits or dies (Palanisamy & Subramanian, 2011). Another study describes the *referral game* experienced by one woman which had a more fortunate outcome. Despite not being an obstetric emergency, she was transferred four times when in labour from a taluk hospital, to a district hospital, a teaching hospital, a private hospital, only to return to the first facility where she had a normal delivery (Subramaniyan, Sarkar, Roy, & Lakshminarayanan, 2013).

Routine HIV testing at the time of antenatal care without pre-test counselling is discriminatory practice by the health system, which fails to consider the potentially serious social consequences for women diagnosed to be positive. Women usually get diagnosed as HIV positive during their antenatal check-up. The government policy demands that if the pregnant woman is found to be HIV positive she should be immediately referred for ART care. HIV-positive women seeking delivery care seem to be particularly vulnerable to abuse and discrimination (Thomas et al., 2009; Subramanian et al., 2013; Madhivanan et al., 2014). In a study of 60 mothers living with HIV/AIDS, more than 97% reported facing discrimination in healthcare settings. Untouchability was widely practised by healthcare providers who would be loath to touch the mother or newborn during and after delivery. Health workers often failed to keep confidential the women's HIV status (Thomas et al., 2009).

> In the maternity hospital, when I went for delivery, the ward boy sent me last to the theatre. I was put in a corner, in the last bed where [there were] no facilities; not even a fan was there. The doctors and nurses were aware of what had happened to me but did not bother. I never went back to that hospital (Thomas et al., 2009, p. 995).

> I was given a place adjacent to the toilet before and after the delivery of my twin babies. Both the infants died within 2 days of birth. Because of these incidents and discrimination in care by the health care providers, I preferred—(hospital) for my two subsequent deliveries, without disclosing my HIV status (Subramaniyan et al., 2013, p. 3).

In a healthcare setting, both the individual and institutional factors contribute to stigma and discrimination against PLHA. Healthcare providers come with prejudices and misconceptions about HIV. This along with lack of adequate training from the institution lead to differential treatment of PLHA. Using a pre/post-test evaluation design Mahendra et al. (2006) demonstrated that with proper training to create awareness about the transmission pathways of HIV and ensuring work safety, healthcare providers' stigma and discriminatory attitude against the PLHAs reduced to a great extent (Mahendra et al., 2006).

Negative Consequences of Stigma and Discrimination

Evidence from the studies shows that due to stigma and discrimination PLHAs faced severe setbacks in securing sustainable livelihoods, have poor quality of life and mental well-being; and hampered access to health care.

Social Consequences

Social consequences of HIV stigma included being rejected, facing hostility and humiliation in many settings, threat of divorce, instigation for committing suicide and having to change one's residence either because of ill treatment by family members or because of being forced to vacate a rented premise (Deb et al., 2013).

There were gender differences in the social consequences of stigma and disclosure, as per a review of 30 studies on stigma and discrimination in India

(Bharat, 2011). Not only do women living with HIV shoulder disproportionate blame, they are more likely to be expelled from their marital homes following the death of their husbands, and at times, even when their husbands are alive (Bharat, 2011; Malave et al., 2014). They may be denied access to their children and to a share in their deceased husband's property. The review noted that in contrast, men received greater support and acceptance at least from their immediate families (Bharat, 2011).

Quality of Life and Mental Well-being

Stigma and discrimination significantly affected the quality of life and mental well-being of PLHA. Two studies carried out in Tamil Nadu during 2000–2010 sought to examine the association between various forms of stigma experienced by PLHA and their reported quality of life. Quality of life was measured using the WHO BREF scale which has four domains of quality of life: physical, psychological, social and environmental. Both studies found a significant association between severe internalised stigma and poor quality of life in the environmental domain (Charles et al., 2012; Thomas et al., 2005). Environmental domain includes aspects such as freedom, quality of home environment, physical safety and security, financial status and access to and quality of health and social care. It is possible that a person who internalises stigma and feels low self-esteem would isolate oneself and be loath to seek social and financial support from others, which in turn could seriously lower his/her quality of life. Fear of disclosure leading to hiding one's status may also contribute negatively to progression of the disease in HIV-positive individuals (Thomas et al., 2005).

Charles et al. (2012) also assessed the mental well-being of respondents using a screening tool for depression. They found that PLHA who experienced severe personalised stigma were three times more likely to have severe depression ($p < 0.05$). A Kolkata-based study also found that more than half the PLHA ($n = 105$) interviewed experienced symptoms of severe depression and around 20% had suicidal thoughts due to the stigma and discrimination they faced (Deb et al., 2013). Children orphaned by HIV/AIDS were twice as likely to experience bullying or ill treatment by friends or relatives, and more likely to suffer from depressive symptoms as compared to children orphaned because of reasons other than HIV/AIDS, in a 2014 study from Hyderabad. Age and gender of the children also played a part. A higher percentage of orphaned girls of a higher age had depressive symptoms (Kumar, 2014).

Stigma and discrimination meted out in healthcare settings may contribute to a high level of stress compromising the mental well-being of PLHA. For example, being referred from facility to facility because of providers' reluctance to admit PLHA adds stress to the already stressed, and could result in rapid disease progression following deprived immunological status (Palanisamy & Subramanian, 2011).

Testimonies of women seeking antenatal care and institutional delivery highlight the negative impact on mental well-being of pregnant PLHA:

Participant: She said… you must know about HIV already. You were given information yesterday. And then she said… that you have it. They ask me whether I had any affair anywhere. Then they ask all kind of information about me and my husband. I felt very bad. It was a blemish on me.

Interviewer: What do you mean by blemish?

Participant: I mean that they don't talk to you properly. And people scorned at you a lot. I felt very bad that I have landed in such a scenario.

Interviewer: And what were you thinking about at that time?

Participant: I felt a lot of pain. Why is it that everyone looks at me this way? So I wanted to commit suicide. I thought I should not live anymore."

– Woman PLHA after an interview with an ICTC HIV post-test counsellor (Madhivanan et al., 2014, p. 7 of 9).

Consequences for Healthcare Seeking

Stigma and discrimination affect both care-seeking and care received in health facilities in numerous ways, ranging from avoidance of or delayed care-seeking all the way through being compelled to undergo unsought services.

Individuals who were unaware of having been exposed to HIV infection such as those who had acquired it through occupational exposure and transfusion of blood tended to present for HIV treatment at a later stage, as did those who had acquired the infection through homosexual transmission and individuals unwilling to disclose probable route of HIV acquisition (Mojumdar, Vajpayee, Chauhan, & Mendiratta, 2010).

In many instances, HIV-positive ANC clinic attendees of private clinics were sent to public providers for further care. One of the reasons was that the private clinics feared that the presence of HIV-positive patients in their facilities may affect attendance by other clients. The few practitioners who were willing to provide pregnancy and delivery care charged very high fees, leaving low income with no option but to move to the public sector health facilities (Dandona, Lakshmi, Kumar, & Dandona, 2006).

Non-disclosure of their HIV-positive status was a strategy used by PLHA to gain care without stigma and discrimination (Mahendra et al., 2006).

"Actually we [HIV-positive patients] do not disclose our status straight away. What is the use in revealing your status if you will not get treatment? So generally we don't reveal our status in the hospital." – PLHA (Mahendra et al., 2006, p. 22).

Those who faced discrimination in one health facility would decide to avoid disclosure in the next, so that they are assured of care:

"The ANM and staff nurse threw the records on my face and asked me to go to JIPMER for delivery. During that time my membranes ruptured. So I went to JIPMER, throwing my records (in frustration) and delivered there without disclosing my HIV status." — HIV positive mother with twin pregnancy (Subramaniyan et al., 2013, p. 3).

Non-disclosure of HIV status when seeking health care is an important consequence of stigma and discrimination in healthcare settings. In the example, the woman who did not disclose her HIV-positive status would miss out on receiving ART, at significant jeopardy to her health. Non-disclosure by PLHA also places healthcare providers and other patients at risk of HIV infection.

Studies indicate that seeking ART may be stressful. For example, Charles et al. (2012) found a significant association between availing ART services and poor QOL, with those availing ART facing twice the risk of experiencing poor quality of life as compared to those who did not (Charles et al., 2012). While many PLHA delayed care-seeking fearing stigma and discrimination, for many others, fear was outweighed by the need for medicines and better health and therefore, PLHA opted to face stigma and discrimination to access ART regularly (Nyamathi et al., 2011).

Studies on health provider attitudes have indicated that some of them believed that PLHA should not have children. Very few studies have examined whether these attitudes translate into non-consensual care and infringement of reproductive rights by health providers. In the Indian sample of Paxton's study, about 10% of HIV-positive women were reported to have been forced into abortion or sterilisation (Paxton, Gonzales, & Uppakaew, 2005).

In summary, stigma and discrimination is the process through which PLHA are denied their right to citizenship and equal participation in society. This is compounded by their physical vulnerability due to the infection and their socially disadvantaged status by class, gender, gender identity, sexual orientation and engagement in socially disapproved behaviour. Unequal access to appropriate and good quality health care is one of the immediate consequences, as is poor quality of life and high levels of stress. The result is highly compromised physical and psychological health, for the most part from avoidable causes.

In the next section, we examine the specific vulnerabilities faced by internal migrants in India in their place of destination and their consequences for health inequities by migration status.

7.2.2 Internal Migrants as a Vulnerable Population

7.2.2.1 Internal Migration in India

The term *migrants* usually suggest individuals who have shifted permanently or for long term from one administrative unit to another, inclusive of the shift in the physical and sociocultural milieu of those individuals. The Census of India defines two types of migrants; A person who is enumerated at a place other than his/her place of birth is a migrant by place of birth, while a person who is enumerated at a place other than his/her place of last residence is a migrant by place of last residence. The National Sample Survey Organisation's (NSSO) definition of migrant is of a person whose place of enumeration is different from his/her last "usual place of residence" (National Sample Survey Organization [NSSO], 2001)—almost similar to the Census definition of migrant by place of last residence.

According to NSSO (2007–2008), there were 326 million internal migrants in India, constituting 28.5% of the population. Projections for 2011 put the numbers at 400 million, or roughly a third of the total population of India (Rajan, 2013). Marriage was the most important reason for migration of women, while employment was the most important reason in men. NSSO figures for 2007–2008 reveal that rural-to-rural migration was the most dominant form of migration (62%), followed by rural-to-urban (20%), urban-to-urban (13%) and urban-to-rural (6%). However, for male migrants rural-to-urban and urban-to-urban migration in search of employment was most dominant, accounting respectively for 39 and 25% of all male internal migrants respectively (NSSO, 2007–2008).

The major *source* states for migration were Uttar Pradesh, Bihar, Rajasthan, Madhya Pradesh, Chhattisgarh, Jharkhand, Orissa, Uttarakhand, Tamil Nadu and Andhra Pradesh. The first eight states form the Empowered Action Group (EAG) states, which lag behind in key development indicators like education and health. The key destination states for the internal migrants were Delhi, Maharashtra, Gujarat, Haryana, Punjab and Karnataka. In the destination sites, the migrants would be generally employed in semi-skilled or unskilled work areas like construction, domestic work, textile, brick kilns, transportation, mines, quarries and agriculture (The United Nations Educational, Scientific and Cultural Organization [UNESCO] & The United Nations International Children's Emergency Fund [UNICEF], 2012).

Migration could be long term or short term. Long-term migrants are those who relocate as individuals or along with their households to another place either permanently or for several years, whereas short-term migrants are those who have migrated from their usual place of residence for more than 30 days but less than 180 days. Estimates of the numbers of short-term migrants vary, from 15 million according to NSSO (2007–2008) to as high as 100 million (Deshingkar & Akter, 2009). This wide variation in estimates of numbers of "short-term migrants" may be the result of varying definitions as to which group counts as migrants and which does not. There are many types of short-term migration, including circulatory or seasonal migration (back and forth movement from the source to a destination); irregular short-term migration (mainly due to unexpected contingencies), medium-term migration (migrating for a fixed period of up to a few years in a particular occupation), long distance commuting (travel across distances outside the perimeter of normal movement, mainly for work) and migration for family care (for unpaid care work other than marriage migration) (Mazumdar, Neetha, & Agnihotri, 2013).

In a comprehensive overview of migration and human development in India, Deshingkar and Akter (2009) use small-scale studies to show that short-term migration accounts for the bulk of migration in India, and that the Census and NSSO have tended to grossly underestimate the extent of short-term migration. Contrary to findings from large data sets, their analysis shows that the bulk of short-term migration happened among poorer households, and among Scheduled Caste and Scheduled Tribe households[1] (Deshingkar & Akter, 2009).

One example of short-term migration is found in a study of rural-to-urban short-term migrants in the National Capital Territory Area around Delhi. Migrant families reported being forced to migrate to *earn and eat*. Limited family income, family indebtedness, limited land ownership and inability to practice agriculture in native land due to poor soil fertility, the poor from rural areas had been pushed to urban areas in search of work and better living conditions (Betancourt, Shaahinfar, Kellner, Dhavan, & Williams, 2013).

Short-term migration to earn a livelihood appears to be the consequence of decades of jobless growth in the Indian economy following neo-liberal economic reforms since the 1990s. Although the share of agriculture in GDP has been declining, not enough jobs have been generated in other sectors to accommodate those who can no longer find jobs in agriculture. Short-term migration and commuting in search of work become an important part of the survival strategy of households with low resource base, whose members have low levels of education and skills (Chandrasekhar & Sharma, 2014; Agrawal & Chandrasekhar, 2015).

Migration renders individuals and households vulnerable on many fronts, and this is especially true for short-term migrants and short-term or long-term rural–to-urban migrants. They often live in poor housing, are engaged in dirty, dangerous and degrading work, are exposed to the vagaries of the labour market, paid low wages, and may lack social support and feel socially and culturally alienated in their new surroundings. They lack the right to political participation and representation, and without residency rights, do not enjoy access to many government services (The United Nations Educational, Scientific and Cultural Organization [UNESCO], 2013). While few Indian studies have explored it, studies from countries like China which have a huge movement of people from rural to urban areas have found that migrants are stigmatised as outsiders and face discrimination (Li, Staton, Fang, & Lin, 2006; Wang, Li, Stanton, & Fang, 2010)

Unequal access to the social determinants of health (described above) on the one hand and poor access to appropriate health care on the other make migrants vulnerable to ill health. Besides unequal access to the resources necessary for good health, migrants may, in their destinations, be exposed to infectious diseases that they have not developed immunity for. Stigma and discrimination affect their mental well-being. Difficulties in accessing health care include lack of information about location of health services; lack of time to visit public facilities and unaffordability of private services; language barriers; and fear of discrimination by health providers. To add to these, migrants are excluded from many government schemes meant for households living below poverty level, and other programmes

[1]A note on terminologies is in order here. While we would prefer to use the terms Dalit and Adivasi, and have done so when we are referring to these population groups, where we cite data from published sources, we have maintained the terminologies used by the authors of the study. Thus in almost all places where studies are cited, the terms SC and ST, or as is often the case, SC/ST is used.

meant for local residents. Some examples include the social protection health scheme such as the *Rashtriya Swasthya Bhima Yojana* (RSBY), the *Janani Suraksha Yojana* (JSY) Conditional Cash Transfer for mothers delivering in health facilities and the Tuberculosis Programme in the Public Health Sector providing treatment free at the point of delivery, and the Integrated Child Development Scheme (ICDS) providing nutritional supplementation and preschool education. Migrants rarely feature in the lists of programme beneficiaries maintained by community health workers.

In the next sections, we synthesise evidence from studies that have focused on health inequities experienced by migrant communities. We begin with a consolidation of evidence on migration as a contributor to ill health, followed by evidence on their inequitable access to healthcare services.

7.2.2.2 Migration as a Contributor to Ill Health

Adult Health

High levels of prevalence of food-, water- and vector-borne diseases among rural-to-urban migrants were reported from a study of 150 migrant households, 50 each from the cities of Kochi, Mumbai and Surat. More than 50% of the migrant households lived in Kutcha households with access only to public toilets. Leaking roofs, damp walls and floors and unstable structures were commonly reported. Fifteen percent of the migrant households reported having experienced severe food and water-borne diseases in the past year, which required 1–3 weeks of treatment. A third (32%) of the migrants from Surat had suffered from typhoid, while 4% each in Kochi and Mumbai had suffered from acute diarrhoea. Vector-borne diseases had affected 44 and 60% of migrant households in Surat and Mumbai respectively. While all the cases in Surat were of malaria, in Mumbai the cases included malaria, dengue and chikungunya (Santha et al., 2015).

Two studies suggest a higher prevalence of psychosocial distress and compromised mental well-being among migrants. A study in Jammu among internally displaced migrants who were compared with residents found that major depressive episodes (21.5% vs. 13%), general anxiety disorders (13.8% vs. 7.5%) and post-traumatic stress disorders (6.8% vs. 2.5%) were significantly higher among migrants as compared to non-migrants. Among migrants, women (37.3%) had a significantly higher prevalence of psychiatric disorders as compared to men (32%) (Banal et al., 2010). An analysis of data from the Indian Migration Study carried out during 2005–07 in four cities–Lucknow, Nagpur, Hyderabad and Bengaluru—found that 7.3% reported suffering from mental distress soon after migration and 4.7%, even after resettlement. A greater proportion of women (10.5%) than men (6.5%) reported mental distress soon after migration and after resettlement (4.5% in women and 3.2% in men respectively). Men and women who had migrated due to *push* factors such as economic necessity and impoverishment were six times more likely than other migrants. Inability to adjust to the new surroundings and a feeling of not being accepted at the workplace even after one year of migration were both factors that increased the odds of mental distress many fold (Agrawal & Chandrasekhar, 2015).

Obesity and overweight was higher among rural-to-urban migrants, especially among women, as per a study using the NFHS-3 data set. The study suggests that as women who migrated from rural to urban area had a 50% increased odds of being overweight or obese. In the sample, 80% of the migrants were women, who had presumably migrated following marriage (Varadharajan, Thomas, Rajaraman, Kurpad, & Vaz, 2013). In another study, a rapid rise in adiposity on first moving to the urban environment and higher and sustained insulin resistance forming the major cardiovascular risk factors were found to be increased among the rural-to-urban migrants when compared to their non-migrant sibling living in the rural area. The change was particularly marked in persons of lower socio-economic status. This study, based on data from the Indian Migration study brings to focus that the stress and acculturation associated with the process of migration and the changes in food habits and lifestyle in the new urban environment could be contributing to the problem (Kinra et al., 2011).

Maternal and Child Health and Nutrition

Maternal and child health is an important indicator of the health status of any population. Two studies analysing data from National Family Health Survey-3 (2005–06) found children of parents who were rural-to-urban migrants were disadvantaged in health status. The first study reported that children of rural-to-urban migrant mothers were 1.4 times more likely to have below normal BMI, 1.2 times more likely to be anaemic, 1.2 times more likely to have had a diarrhoeal episode in the past 15 days, and 1.3 times more likely to have been breastfed after 1 h of birth (Kumar, Reshmi, & Hemalatha, 2016). The second study by Prusty and Keshri (2015) focused on nutritional indicators and showed that children of rural-to-urban migrants were more likely to be stunted, wasted or underweight as compared to children of urban non-migrants and children of urban-to-urban migrants. Among the rural-to-urban migrant population, those from the poorest sections of the population and belonging to the SC or ST populations were significantly more likely to be stunted, wasted or underweight (Prusty & Keshri, 2015). These studies confirm findings from an earlier study based on NFHS-2 data for 1998–99 by Choudhary and Parthasarathy (2009), on the higher probability of stunting of children from migrant households in Mumbai. Choudhary and Parthasarathy also found that children from households of recent rural-to-urban migrants (0–4 years) were more disadvantaged as compared to households of all migrants. Further, rural migrant mothers were more likely to have a below normal BMI than urban migrant or non-migrant mothers, and mothers who were recent migrants were more likely to be undernourished than all migrant mothers (Choudhary & Parthasarathy, 2009).

Observations from a study based in low-income migrant settlements of Delhi portray the multiple vulnerabilities experienced by children of migrant workers. They were often left unsupervised by their parents who were both at work, but sometimes the contractors provided crèche services for the children. Many older children worked as child labourers to contribute to the meagre family income. Some migrant children who went to school faced stigma and discrimination from the school staff. They were unable to study as they did not have a proper study environment at home (Betancourt et al., 2013).

7.2.2.3 Access to Health Care

General Health Care

A small number of studies have looked at access to general health services among urban migrants. In general, migrants had little access to government health services and relied on private health providers (Babu, Swain, Mishra, & Kar, 2010; Mishra, Kusuma, & Babu, 2015; Surabhi & Kumar, 2007; Santha et al., 2015). Language barriers made them hesitant to approach the crowded government health facilities (Narayan, 2013). For medical emergencies, they often returned to their native places (Surabhi & Kumar, 2007; Santha et al., 2015). For example, in a study on access to health services among Santali migrants to Bhubaneshwar, it was found that 60% were not aware of any health personnel visiting the community. Three quarters (73%) went to a private health provider close to home and 11% to a pharmacist for minor ailments. For serious ailments, they went to government facilities at the secondary or the tertiary level or other large private hospitals. However, these facilities were not preferred as they were *expensive*. Services were usually available in the morning hours and the migrant workers could not avail services and get back to work, resulting in loss of wages. In comparison to the lack of access to health and healthcare services in the urban area, the migrants were satisfied with the services available in their place of origin. In the native place (the place of origin for the migrants), they had access to primary health centres and their health workers. They also utilised their traditional institutions of healing (Babu et al., 2010).

For construction workers in Delhi, medical aid was available on-site the construction area only during working hours. For any health issue during the non-working hours, they had to seek health care off-site and pay out of pocket. The lack of government health facility near their place of work pushed them to approach private practitioners. The cost of paying for health care, medications and other expenses like transport became a burden to the migrant workers. They could not access state-sponsored social protection health schemes due to lack of proof of their residence. In case of any health emergency, the migrant construction workers were forced to take loans from loan sharks or contractors, the need to replay which prolonged their migration status (Betancourt et al., 2013).

When migrants are seen to bring with them new diseases, they may face discrimination from local health administrators and residents, as this news report from Kochi illustrates:

> We need them, but we don't want them. That in essence is the sorry state of migrant labourers in the city. Following protests and pressure from local leaders and residents of

> Palluruthy, a migrant worker, who was detected with malaria, was sent home by the contractor. He was also forced to shut his labour camp and shift all 98 workers housed in the building…The labourer, who developed fever, was first detected as having malaria by a private hospital. Following an alert, the health department immediately tested 98 workers, including the person who contracted malaria, living in the labour camp on Wednesday… But despite assurance given by the health department, the residents' association in the locality,… wanted the owner of the building housing labourers to shift them out immediately… (Times of India, 2014) (Santha et al., 2015, p. 37).

Maternal and Child Health Care

Evidence consistently points to lower levels of utilisation of antenatal and delivery care among migrant pregnant women as compared to their non-migrant counterparts. For example, the proportion of non-migrant women receiving three or more antenatal visits (44%) was more than twice as that for migrant women (18%) in a Chandigarh-based study (Kaur, Singh, Gupta, Bahuguna, & Rani, 2015). A study in a low-income settlement of the National Capital Territory of Delhi found that even among migrants, there were gradations in the extent of vulnerability, with a lower proportion of recent (less than 5 years) migrants receiving adequate[2] antenatal care (Kusuma, Kumari, & Kaushal, 2013). In Mumbai, only 21.4% of migrant women in a low-income settlement received basic[3] antenatal care and almost a quarter of them (23.5%) delivered at home, figures that are vastly different from the averages for Mumbai as per NFHS-3 (Gawde, Sivakami, & Babu, 2016).

Poverty and migrant status combine to make poor migrant women most disadvantaged with respect to access to safe delivery care. However, even non-poor migrant women face some disadvantages when compared to their non-migrant counterparts. These were the findings from a study using data from the three National Family Health Surveys. The study further found that between 1992–93 and 2005–06, utilisation of safe delivery care registered a marginal decline for poor migrant women, from 49.7 to 49.5%. Poor non-migrant women did much better than their migrant counterparts, but did not register much improvement during the same period, the utilisation rates being 65.8 and 66.8%, respectively. Safe delivery care utilisation rates for non-poor migrant and non-migrant women rose respectively from 74.4 to 84.5% and 85.5 to 91.8% (Singh, Rai, & Singh, 2012).

Child immunisation rates and especially full immunisation rates are significantly lower among children of migrant than among children of non-migrant parents according to several studies. Prusty & Keshri (2015) explored how migration leads to disparities in child immunisation in urban India using NFHS-3 all-India data. The rate of full immunisation among rural–urban migrant children was significantly lower (54%) as compared to children of non-migrants (60%) and urban–urban migrants

---

[2]Adequate antenatal care was defined as at least four antenatal visits, the first of which would be in the first trimester, and receiving 100 Iron and Folic Acid tablets.

[3]Basic antenatal care was defined as at least 3 antenatal visits, one tetanus toxoid injection and 100 Iron and Folic Acid tablets.

(66%) (Prusty & Keshri, 2015). Full immunisation rates were much lower among children of seasonal migrant sugarcane harvesting labourers of Beed District of Maharashtra (Pakhare et al., 2014) and children of migrant parents in Hardwar, Uttarakhand (Nath, Kaur, & Tripathi, 2015) when compared to children of non-migrants. Kusuma, Kumari, Pandav, and Gupta (2010) reported children of recent migrants to be more disadvantaged in terms of full immunisation when compared to children of settled migrants. At first, the migrants' use of vaccination was comparable to that of the general population. However, by the time the child was 10–14 weeks old the differences between *recent* migrants and the *settled* migrants showed up. Full immunisation against six vaccine-preventable diseases fell to around 81% among the *settled* migrants and to around even lower 64% among the *recent* migrants, as compared to 83.2% among the general population (Kusuma et al., 2010).

Inadequate outreach efforts by government health workers and other health system barriers resulting from blindness to the specific needs of migrant communities appear to be important factors contributing to low utilisation of maternal and child health services by migrants. For example, in the Chandigarh study only 29% of the migrant women had interacted with local health workers as compared to 67% of non-migrants (Kaur et al., 2015). Among migrant women in Delhi slums, there were wide disparities in the quality of advice that settled migrants received as compared to recent migrants. For example, 40% of the new migrants received no advice at all on family planning, breastfeeding or immunisation and only 27% received advice on all these, while for settled migrants the comparable figures were 27.5 and 40%, respectively (Kusuma et al., 2010). Among migrant women in Mumbai slums, fear of verbal and physical abuse in government health facilities especially because of their high parity was yet another barrier to accessing maternal health care (Gawde et al., 2016).

In the case of child immunisation, migrant parents reported not knowing the time and place of vaccination, the time of sessions being inconvenient, ASHA/ANM seldom visiting their homes and giving information or counselling on vaccines and number of doses (Pakhare et al., 2014). Outreach staff of the government health system did not include short-term migrants in their plans as they often lacked clarity about the number of migrant labourers, their arrival and departure and the location of their place of work (especially brick kilns). They thus remain invisible to the government healthcare policies and healthcare delivery net (Silan & Kant, 2014).

Although access to care may be better in urban settings, weak social networks compel migrant women to return to their hometowns for pregnancy and delivery, as in the case of the Mumbai slums where around 63% of migrant women did so.

> There is no one here to do work [household work or taking care of women during pregnancy and after delivery], in village [home town] there are many who support, elder sister-in-law is there – Migrant woman from an EAG state (Gawde et al., 2016, p. 10).

Recent migrants tended to have weaker social networks and were more likely to return to their native place for delivery and related services. The proportion of hospital deliveries among women who returned to their hometowns (69.9%) was significantly lower than among migrant women who delivered in Mumbai (87.5%).

Another advantage of returning to their hometowns was that women were more likely to receive benefits from the conditional cash transfer programme (*Janani Suraksha Yojana*) because in Mumbai they did not have address proof; and also because in Mumbai (and Maharashtra) the cash transfer programme was restricted to the first two births whereas it was available to all women irrespective of parity in EAG states (Gawde et al., 2016).

Religion and caste of the migrants significantly influence the utilisation pattern of maternal health care (Singh et al., 2012). A smaller proportion of poor migrant Muslim women utilised maternal health care when compared to poor migrant Hindu women, and the same is true for Dalit women as compared to women of other castes. Social group inequality endures the process of migration and travels with the migrants. This is further compounded by the existing social inequality present in the host community.

7.2.3 *When Vulnerabilities Collude: HIV/AIDS Among Internal Migrants*

Compared to a substantive number of studies documenting that migrant men engage in risky sexual behaviour, few studies document how the vulnerabilities of being HIV positive and being a migrant collude in the lived experience of migrant persons living with HIV or AIDS. The following section summarises this limited evidence.

7.2.3.1 The Links Between HIV/AIDS and Internal Migration

Internal migrants in India were estimated to have an HIV prevalence rate of 0.9% (2011), almost four times the national prevalence of 0.27% (NACO, 2012). There are many hypotheses, only a few of which have been substantiated through research, about the reasons for elevated risk of HIV infection among internal migrants, especially circular migrants and commuters.

Migrants are believed to engage in risky sexual behaviours and alcohol and drug use owing to their sense of alienation and social exclusion; stressful working conditions; separation from regular sexual partners for long durations and a sense of anonymity (Institute of Medicine [IOM], 2003). However, some recent studies provide a more nuanced picture. One study showed that rather than migration inducing risky sexual behaviour, the reverse was true. Migrant men initiated risky sexual behaviour in their place of origin and continued this in their place of destination. Return migrants (men who have returned from migration and not migrated in the past one year) continued the risky behaviour in their native place (Saggurti, Mahapatra, Swain, & Jain, 2011). Another study explains the differences in HIV risk among migrants to be related to HIV among non-migrating partners who live in the place of the migrant's origin (Deering, Vickerman, Moses, Ramesh, & Blanchard, 2008).

Another pathway to higher HIV risk among migrants may be the limited or no access to preventive HIV care such as condom distribution and education on safe sex; and HIV information, counselling and testing. Migrants may not be aware of their risk of HIV infection, or may perceive themselves to be at low risk. A 2011 survey showed that the proportion of migrants with comprehensive knowledge on HIV ranged from 20% among migrants from Northern Bihar to 50% in Orissa and 60% in Thane in Maharashtra (HIV and AIDS Data Hub for Asia Pacific (www.aidsdatahub.org)).

The difficulties faced by seasonal migrants in accessing preventive HIV care is illustrated by the case of seasonal migrant fishermen from Karnataka who came to Goa for engaging in fishing activities. They usually lived away from their wives. During the time they docked, around 13% of them had sexual relations with *lovers* or non-spousal partners. However, many of them did not perceive that they could be at risk of contracting HIV infection. They had been sourcing condoms from an NGO, but with a change in funding policy, this group of migrants were no longer a priority for HIV prevention activities. They reported facing difficulties in accessing HIV testing facilities, and said that they usually sought health care from quacks rather than accessing public healthcare facilities (Bailey, 2011).

In addition to compromising safe sexual behaviour among migrants, limited access to HIV prevention services would also cause delay in HIV testing and diagnosis when they experience repeated bouts of illness due to HIV infection (IOM, 2003).

7.2.3.2 Diagnosis and Treatment of HIV Among Migrant PLHAs

Migrant men with HIV reached the point of diagnosis through a convoluted pathway. Following diagnosis, their status as migrants imposed many difficulties in accessing ART, available free of cost in government hospitals. Two studies by Rai, Lambert, and Ward, (2015, 2016) among 33 HIV-positive persons attending an ART clinic in Allahabad provide insights into these difficulties.

Many of the migrant PLHAs were from resource poor households and were unskilled or semi-skilled labourers who migrated from rural to urban areas in search of a livelihood. They did not perceive themselves to be at risk of HIV, and when they fell ill frequently with diarrhoea or fever, they sought treatment from formal or informal private healthcare providers. Their weakening physical health made working in physically demanding dangerous jobs increasingly difficult. They were faced with significant financial debts which had accumulated over the course of prolonged unexplained illness at the destination site.

Inability to work and the mounting debt burden motivated the migrant worker to return to his home and family. Testing and diagnosis usually occurred when the worker developed a medical emergency and had to be hospitalised. Following the diagnosis, ART was initiated. While ART was seen as godsend, the migrant workers also faced pressure to resume work once their health improved following start of ART. The workers, whose physical health was extremely weak, felt insecure to return to work in the urban area. Not being able to migrate and not being able to take up certain jobs in their native village (due to caste affiliations and household status) led to unemployment and financial impoverishment. Migrants, who were supporting the family financially over a period, became dependent on other family members like fathers, brothers or sons. Family members' immediate concern in the early stages of ill health changed to *grudging charity* as time progressed (Rai, Lambert, & Ward, 2016).

The organisation of ART services appears to be blind to the specific needs of migrant workers. Migrant PLHA were required to return once a month to collect their medications at the hospital near their native place where they started the treatment. Being short term, seasonal and circular migrants without a fixed place of work, transferring the ART to another health facility closer to their place of work was not feasible, either. The demanding treatment regimen with rich diet and access to clean drinking water and sanitation facilities to avoid infections was not possible in the destination work sites of the migrant workers. Treatment seeking resulted in loss of wages or disruption in employment, and eventually made migration for income generation a distant reality for them (Rai et al., 2016).

7.2.3.3 Women Partners of Migrant PLHA

Rai et al. (2015) describe the multiple vulnerabilities of women partners of migrant PLHA. When the migrant PLHA moved back to their native place because they were too debilitated to work, their HIV status was not always known. Women partners of migrant PLHA often sought HIV testing after they discovered the positive status of their husbands. A few also came to know about their HIV status through routine provider-initiated screening. However, some were unaware of their personal risk to HIV, or could not go to a health facility for testing and further treatment (if needed) without the help of male relatives. While the sick men were safe-guarded in the household, the wife's situation was precarious. Once diagnosed, they did not usually enjoy the support of their marital family to seek treatment. Widowed women either had to return to their natal homes or continue in the marital home if they had children, especially sons. They had to battle the disease with minimal or no emotional and financial support from their martial families, which acted as barriers to access health care (Rai et al., 2016).

7.3 A Critical Synthesis of Evidence

7.3.1 *Pathways to Health Inequities Among PLHAs and Internal Migrants*

The evidence reviewed shows that PLHAs and internal migrants face much vulnerability which is socially constructed. Stigma and discrimination, and in the case of migrants, also *social exclusion* or *othering* are the mechanisms through which vulnerability is created. The drivers of stigma and discrimination against PLHAs are fear of HIV transmission from casual contact, and prejudiced moral values and attitudes regarding sexuality (Bharat, 2011), while discrimination against migrants may be rooted in their different appearance, language and culture, or because they belong to what are considered to be backward states and rural locations[4] (Surabhi & Kumar, 2007; Majumdar & Dasgupta, 2015; UNESCO, 2013; Babu et al., 2010). Migrant PLHAs may face double stigma based on their migrant and HIV-positive status (United Nations Development Programme [UNDP], 2004).

Vulnerability based on HIV or migrant status is overlaid on other socially constructed vulnerabilities such class, caste, ethnicity and gender. For example, pregnant HIV women in India often bear the burdens of being HIV infected, mothering potentially infected infants and being caregivers for infected husbands or other family members. Migrant health especially among women is mainly linked to residential segregation and detached social networks (Singh et al., 2012). Migration is also found to increase risk of exposure to HIV infection among men, especially those who migrate alone in search of livelihoods and feel socially excluded and alienated from their working and living environments (Chaudhuri & Prince, n.d.) Once infected, lower financial status and wage insecurity pushes the migrant men to choose quick, inexpensive symptom management from private providers, which hamper their chances of knowing their HIV-positive status. The insecure conditions of work hamper migrant men's access to preventive and diagnostic services (Rai et al., 2015).

Discrimination of PLHAs by healthcare providers appears to be widespread at all levels of health care. For example, it has been noted that there is "disturbingly high rates of stigma attitudes and an intent to discriminate" PLHAs among the doctors and other healthcare staff in healthcare delivery settings (Ekstrand et al., 2013; Mahendra et al., 2006), while migrant families appear to be outside the radar of the public health system (Santha et al., 2015; Gawde et al., 2016; Singh et al., 2012; Babu et al., 2010; Kusuma et al., 2013; Kaur et al., 2015).

Few studies have located the experiences of PLHAs and migrants within the macro economic and political factors which constitute the context which facilitates exposure to risk of HIV infection and risk of migration. Such an exercise is essential if we are to intervene to alter the upstream determinants of health inequities suffered by PLHAs, migrants and migrant PLHAs and by specific sub-groups among them. We have relied on our understanding of the structural drivers of health inequities laid out in Chap. 1 to do so (Fig. 7.1).

The growth of a small group of ultra-rich and the neo-liberal ideology that celebrates their success has made conspicuous consumption acceptable amidst stark poverty. The sex industry has developed as an integral part of such a model of economic development. On the other, impoverishment and insecurity of households makes women susceptible to sexual exploitation through trafficking, or seeking transactional sex as a means of livelihood (Barry, 1995; Sanders, n.d). These factors

[4]Most studies reviewed by us were about rural-to-urban migrants.

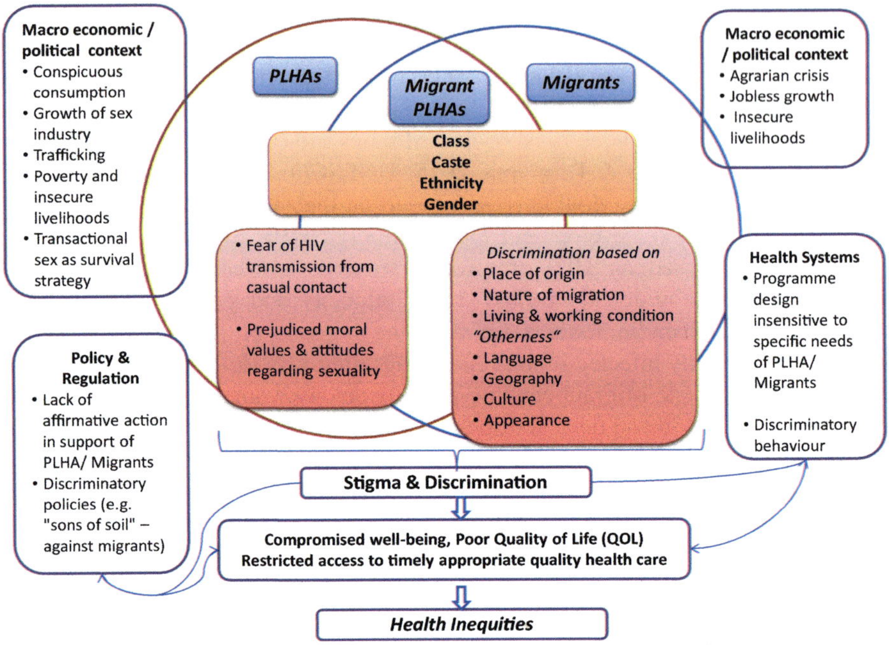

Fig. 7.1 Socially constructed vulnerabilities leading to health inequities for PLHAs, internal migrants and migrant PLHAs

contribute to the HIV/AIDS epidemic in India, contributing to increasing PLHA population. Agrarian crises have also contributed to internal migration from rural to urban areas, and to the growth of short-term and circular migration in search of jobs, from rural to urban as well as rural areas. Poor migrants often end up in dirty, dangerous and difficult jobs which are in the lower segments of the labour market and live and work in hazardous conditions.

Policies and regulations can play a major role in mitigating the vulnerabilities faced by PLHAs and migrants. However, in the present context, there has been dilution of pro-labour legislations, increasing the vulnerability of the poor migrants in a new destination without major social and financial support systems (Human Rights Law Network [HRLN], 2016). There are no laws and regulations promoting affirmative action in favour of PLHAs and migrants, or at the least, preventing discrimination against them. There have been several judgements of the Indian Supreme Court upholding non-discrimination of PLHA (Helpline Law, n.d.) but recourse to courts for justice is beyond the reach especially of those who may need it most. Unfortunately, many states have *sons of the soil* policies, which actively discriminate against migrants from outside the state (Weiner, 2015; Singh, 2000).

A responsive Public Health System has the potential to both, prevent the unequal exposure to health risks faced by vulnerable groups, and provide services that improve their quality of life. Besides overt discrimination, evidence points to blindness and insensitivity on the part of the Public Health system in the design of programmes to meet the needs of PLHAs and migrants. For example, pregnant women are tested for HIV status as a routine part of antenatal care, often without their informed consent (Madhivanan et al., 2014). ART services are not made available at the primary care level, and PLHAs travel long distances and brave waiting lines in their compromised state of health for treatment (Nyamathi et al., 2011). Migrant households are often left out of maternal and child health services and migrants with tuberculosis may not be eligible for free care at their destination (Kumar, 2011).

Stigma and discrimination faced by the PLHAs and migrants compound other layers of vulnerability by class, caste, gender and so on, and lead to stress. More importantly, they restrict the access of PLHA and migrants to timely, appropriate, quality health care, resulting in poor quality of life and compromised well-being, and potentially avoidable morbidity and mortality among PLHAs, migrants and migrant PLHAs.

It appears to us that gender is not merely one of the layers of vulnerabilities experienced by PLHA and internal migrants but a key axis of disadvantage. Gender plays a major role in the growth of sex industry, in trafficking and in women's use of sex as a survival strategy. The literature presented is replete with accounts of overt discrimination specifically against women. The role of gender norms restricting women's access to health care (delaying early diagnosis and ART) and having to bear disproportionate stigma due to gendered bodies have been highlighted with an impact on both the plight of women and children. The experiences of other gender identities living with HIV/AIDS also indicate the central role of gender.

7.3.2 Reflections on the Nature of the Evidence-Base on Health Inequities Among PLHA, Migrants and Migrant PLHAs

We have reviewed more than 34 papers about PLHA as a group experiencing health inequities because of their health condition. Many of the papers looked at stigma and discrimination as a contributor to poor quality of life, compromised mental health and restricted access to health care. The prevalence of various types of stigma has been quantified using scales. A complex phenomenon such as stigma, with potentially diverse interactions across multiple context-specific factors, has been reduced to mere percentages. The papers have also not looked at contexts and groups of people who do not perpetuate stigma and why they tend to be different. The intricate pathways which lead to stigma and discrimination and further health inequities among marginalised groups are rarely explored. The interaction of various layers of vulnerability has been studied as *correlates* and not as *pathways*. For example, variations in stigma scores are examined across sex, caste and ethnicity and socio-economic status, and while we learn that one group has a higher prevalence of a specific outcome as compared to another, we do not know why and whether the results are time and location specific. An exception to this pattern is found in qualitative studies on how gender-based inequalities accentuate stigma and discrimination of women PLHA. Studies evaluating interventions to address and mitigate vulnerabilities are also very few. While several studies have documented pervasive discrimination and intent to discriminate among healthcare providers at all levels, the solutions offered are rather simplistic, and are related to addressing misconceptions and improving information base. The inherently elitist character of the health system and how this impacts on health provider behaviour has not been unpacked in any study. Overall, the macro and micro social determinants of the specific vulnerabilities of PLHA has not been explored. It may be fair to say that the studies do not provide enough *knobs to turn* for making effective policy or programmatic interventions.

Many issues have barely been explored. Concerns of entire population groups of PLHA have not been covered such as young people; children who were born HIV positive; and older persons. Intersections of layered vulnerabilities and their health impact have rarely been examined, for example across persons in varying stages of the infection, and across age, caste, class or gender. Inequities in health issues of PLHA other than HIV, access to ART as well as other health care; inequities in costs of HIV-related care and in coping strategies, among others, are areas about which little is known.

In contrast to studies on PLHA, almost no study among migrants sought to examine stigma, discrimination or stereotyping, although negative experiences tantamount to these were reported in several studies. Variation within the group of migrants was captured to some extent, by distinguishing between rural-to-urban and urban-to-urban migrants and between short-term and long-term migrants. Studies on migrants share with the PLHA studies the tendency to remain limited to associations and risk assessments rather than on processes and lived experiences. A couple of studies by Rai et al. (2015, 2016) are good examples of how a careful documentation of the lived experiences of a small number of persons has the potential to yield rich insights on drivers of vulnerability and potential entry points for interventions.

The tendency to classify the study population across characteristics in a rather mechanical manner obfuscates within-group variations, which in some cases may be significant. One example is the classification of migrants into two broad groups by caste: SC/ST/OBC versus the *General caste*, which masks the complex social stratification by caste and ethnicity in India and their intersections with other axes of vulnerability such as migrant status. As pointed out by Kaur et al. (2015), if the education status of the migrant women are higher, the nuance would be that there are less number of individuals from the *lower caste* in the sample (Kaur et al., 2015). Specific subgroups of migrants who are at greater risks of developing disease are getting missed out in many ways.

Researcher *positionality* and researcher attitudes towards marginalised groups like PLHAs, internal migrants and migrant PLHAs are other areas of concern. We have remarked earlier that most studies end with the identification of socio-economic and demographic characteristics associated with higher risk of a negative behaviour or health outcome. When authors then make the leap towards policy recommendations, the result is further stereotyping of some population groups. In the following example, the authors have studied self-reported risky sexual behaviour among a sample of migrant workers:

> Within .... migrants, those who are single, earning more, youths, the less educated and daily wage labourers (only for STI) are particularly vulnerable to RSB*, low HIV knowledge, and STI. New migrants who are likely to be younger are curious about sex workers and greatly influenced by their new peers ....Those earning higher also appear to be more vulnerable which indicates they may be spending their money to indulge in RSB (Risky Sexual Behaviour) (Seedat, 2011, p. 18).

Some authors had resorted to use crude and exclusionary words to describe PLHA and migrant behaviour:

> The worse status of rural migrants can be explained through the high prevalence of women's illiteracy, negligence towards women's health, ignorance, low skill and gender discrimination in rural areas (Choudhury & Parthasarathy, 2009).

The undertone of the text is reflective of the biases of the researcher, which would influence the nature of research questions pursued and the interpretation of research results. This may be one of the first areas that need to change if the purpose of public health research is to promote health equity or at the least, do no further harm.

References

Adams, J., & Wisner, B. (2002). *Environmental health in emergencies and disasters. A practical guide* (Vol. WHO Librar). Geneva: World Health Organization (WHO). Retrieved from https://doi.org/10.1136/emj.2003.011981.

Aday, L. A. (1991). Who are the vulnerable? *At risk in America: The health and health care needs of vulnerable populations in the United States* (2nd ed., pp. 1–15). San Francisco, California: Jossey-Bass.

Agrawal, T., & Chandrasekhar, S. (2015). *Short term migrants in India: Characteristics, wages and work transition*. Mumbai: Indira Gandhi Institute for Development Research. Retrieved from http://www.igidr.ac.in/pdf/publication/WP-2015-07.pdf.

Babu, B. V., Swain, B. K., Mishra, S., & Kar, S. K. (2010). Primary healthcare services among a migrant indigenous population living in an eastern Indian city. *Journal of Immigrant and Minority Health, 12*, 53–59. Retrieved from https://doi.org/10.1007/s10903-008-9181-z.

Bailey, A. (2011). Left at sea: HIV vulnerability among migrant fishermen in Goa, India. *International Maritime Health, 62*(2), 116–122.

Banal, R., Thappa, J., Shah, H. U., Hussain, A., Chowhan, A., Kaur, H., ... Thappa, S. (2010). Psychiatric morbidity in adult Kashmiri migrants living in a migrant camp at Jammu. *Indian Journal of Psychiatry, 52*(2), 154–158. Retrieved from https://doi.org/10.4103/0019-5545.64597.

Barry, K. (1995). *The prostitution of sexuality*. New York: New York University Press.

Betancourt, T. S., Shaahinfar, A., Kellner, S. E., Dhavan, N., & Williams, T. P. (2013). A qualitative case study of child protection issues in the Indian construction industry: Investigating the security, health, and interrelated rights of migrant families. *BMC Public Health, 13*(1), 858. Retrieved from https://doi.org/10.1186/1471-2458-13-858.

Bharat, S. (2011). A systematic review of HIV/AIDS-related stigma and discrimination in India: Current understanding and future needs standing and future needs. *Journal of Social Aspects of HIV/AIDS Research Alliance, 8*(3), 138–149.

Bharat, S., Aggleton, P., & Tyrer, P. (2001). *India: HIV and AIDS-related discrimination, Stigmatization*. Geneva: Joint United Nations Programme on HIV/AIDS (UNAIDS).

Bharathi, Pai, M. S., & Nayak, B. S. (2014). Stigma and discrimination among children living with HIV (CLHIV) in South India. *Asia Pacific Journal of Research, I*(XVIV), 75–81.

Chakrapani, V., & Bharat, S. (2014). *Getting to Zero? A national survey on HIV-related stigma and discrimination in urban India*. New Delhi: UNDP India.

Chakrapani, V., Newman, P. A, Shunmugam, M., & Dubrow, R. (2011). Social-structural contexts of needle and syringe sharing behaviours of HIV-positive injecting drug users in Manipur, India: A mixed methods investigation. *Harm Reduction Journal, 8*, 9. Retrieved from https://doi.org/10.1186/1477-7517-8-9. (May 2008).

Chandrasekhar, S., & Sharma, A. (2014). *Urbanization and spatial patterns of internal migration in India*. Mumbai: Indira Gandhi Institute for Development Research. Retrieved from http://www.igidr.ac.in/pdf/publication/WP-2014-016.pdf.

Charles, B., Jeyaseelan, L., Pandian, A. K., Sam, A. E., Thenmozhi, M., & Jayaseelan, V. (2012). Association between stigma, depression and quality of life of people living with HIV/AIDS (PLHA) in South India—A community based cross sectional study. *BMC Public Health, 12*(1), 463. Retrieved from https://doi.org/10.1186/1471-2458-12-463.

Chaudhuri, A., & Prince, M. (n.d.). *HIV and migration*. Asia Pacific Region Thematic Analysis Paper—4. Bangalore: Swasti Health Resource Centre. Retrieved from http://www.swasti.org/images/projects/research/Migrants_And_HIV.pdf.

Choudhary, N., & Parthasarathy, D. (2009). Is migration status a determinant of urban nutrition insecurity? Empirical evidence from Mumbai city, India. *Journal of Biosocial Science, 41*(5), 583–605.

Dandona, L., Lakshmi, V., Kumar, G. A., & Dandona, R. (2006). Is the HIV burden in India being overestimated? *BMC Public Health, 6*, 308. Retrieved from https://doi.org/10.1186/1471-2458-6-308.

Deb, S., Sun, J., & Esben, S. (2013). Discrimination experienced by HIV/AIDS infected persons and its associations with mental health in an Indian sample. *Stigma Research and Action [Ceased]*. Retrieved from http://eprints.qut.edu.au/56672/1/stigma2012002.pdf.

Deering, K. N., Vickerman, P., Moses, S., Ramesh, B. M., & Blanchard, J. F. (2008). The impact of out-migrants and out-migration on the HIV/AIDS epidemic: A case study from south-west India. *AIDS, Suppl, 5*, 165–181. doi:10.1097/01.aids.0000343774.59776.95.

Deshingkar, P., & Akter, S. (2009). *Migration and human development in India*. New York: United Nations Development Programme. Retrieved from http://hdr.undp.org/en/content/migration-and-human-development-india.

Ekstrand, M. L., Ramakrishna, J., Bharat, S., & Heylen, E. (2013). Prevalence and drivers of HIV stigma among health providers in urban India : Implications for interventions, *Journal of the International AIDS Society, 13*(16(Suppl 2)), 1–12. doi:10.7448/IAS.16.3.18717.

Gawde, N. C., Sivakami, M., & Babu, B. V. (2016). Utilization of maternal health services among internal migrants in Mumbai, India. *Journal of Biosocial Science*, 1–30. Retrieved from https://doi.org/10.1017/S0021932016000195.

Gill, C. J. (2006). Disability, constructed vulnerability, and socially conscious palliative care. *Journal of Palliative Care, 22*(3), 183–189.

Helpline Law. (n.d). *Rights of HIV/AIDS patients in India*. Retrieved from http://www.helplinelaw.com/civil-litigation-and-others/RHPI/rights-of-hivaids-patients-in-india.html.

Human Rights Law Network. (2016). *Labour law amendment proposals show government's anti-labour direction: Colin Gonsalves*. Retrieved from http://www.hrln.org/hrln/labour-rights/reports/1541-labour-law-amendment-proposals-show-governments-anti-labour-direction-colin-gonsalves.html#ixzz4aj1iOK6C.

Institute of Medicine. (2003). *Population mobility and HIV/AIDS*. Geneva: International Organization for Migration.

Kaur, M., Singh, S., Gupta, M., Bahuguna, P., & Rani, S. (2015). Inequity in access to health services between migrants and natives of Chandigarh, India. *International Journal of Migration, Health and Social Care, 11*(2), 147–155. Retrieved from https://doi.org/10.1108/IJMHSC-03-2014-0010.

Kermode, M., Holmes, W., Langkham, B., Thomas, M. S., & Gifford, S. (2005). HIV-related knowledge, attitudes & risk perception amongst nurses, doctors & other healthcare workers in rural India. *Indian Journal of Medical Research, 122*(3), 258–264.

Kinra, S., Andersen, E., Ben-Shlomo, Y., Bowen, L., Lyngdoh, T., Prabhakaran, D., ... Ebrahim, S. (2011). Association between urban life-years and cardiometabolic risk. *American Journal of Epidemiology, 174*(2), 154–164. Retrieved from https://doi.org/10.1093/aje/kwr053.

Kumar, A. (2014). Does male out-migration and household structure matter in maternal health services does male out-migration and household structure matter in maternal health services utilization in India? *International Journal of Science and Research, 3*(8), 626–633.

Kumar K, A., Reshmi S, R., & Hemalatha, N. (2016). Effect of women's migration on urban children's health in India. *International Journal of Migration, Health and Social Care, 12*(2), 133–145. Retrieved from https://doi.org/10.1108/IJMHSC-04-2014-0015.

Kusuma, Y. S., Kumari, R, Pandav, C. S., & Gupta, S. K. (2010) Migration and immunization: Determinants of childhood immunization uptake among socioeconomically disadvantaged migrants in Delhi, India. *Tropical Medicine & International Health, 15*(11), 1326–1332.

Kusuma, Y. S., Kumari, R., & Kaushal, S. (2013). Migration and access to maternal healthcare: Determinants of adequate antenatal care and institutional delivery among socio-economically disadvantaged migrants in Delhi, India. *Tropical Medicine & International Health, 18*(10), 1202–1210.

Li, X., Stanton, B., Fang, X., & Lin, D. (2006). Social stigma and maternal health among rural-to-urban migrants in China: A conceptual framework and future research needs. *World Health Population, 8*(3), 14–31.

Madhivanan, P., Krupp, K., Kulkarni, V., Kulkarni, S., Vaidya, N., Shaheen, R., ... Fisher, C. (2014). HIV testing among pregnant women living with HIV in India: Are private healthcare providers routinely violating women's human rights? *BMC International Health and Human Rights, 14*(1), 7. Retrieved from http://doi.org/10.1186/1472-698X-14-7.

Mahendra, V. S., Gilborn, L., George, B., Samson, L., Mudoi, R., Jadav, S., ... Daly, C. (2006). Reducing AIDS-related stigma and discrimination in Indian hospitals. *Horizons Final Report*. New Delhi.

Majumdar, K. S., & Dasgupta, P. (2015). Migration in India: Questions of social exclusion. *International Research Journal of Social Sciences, 4*(4), 87–91.

Malave, S., Ramakrishna, J., Heylen, E., Bharat, S., & Ekstrand, M. L. (2014). Differences in testing, stigma, and perceived consequences of stigmatization among heterosexual men and women living with HIV in Bengaluru, India. *AIDS Care, 26*(3), 396–403. Retrieved from http://doi.org/10.1080/09540121.2013.819409.

Mazumdar, I., Neetha, N., & Agnihotri, I. (2013). Migration and gender in India. *Economic & Political Weekly, 48*(10), 54–64.

Mechanic, D., & Tanner, J. (2007). Vulnerable people, groups, and populations: Societal view. *Health Affairs, 2626*(105), 1220–1230.

Mishra, S., Kusuma, Y. S., & Babu, B. V. (2015). Migration and health-care access: Barriers to access government health services by migrant tribal community living in an eastern Indian city. *International Journal of Medical Science and Public Health, 4*(1), 101–108.

Mojumdar, K., Vajpayee, M., Chauhan, N. K., & Mendiratta, S. (2010). Late presenters to HIV care and treatment, identification of associated risk factors in HIV-1 infected Indian population. *BMC Public Health, 10*, 416. Retrieved from https://doi.org/10.1186/1471-2458-10-416.

Nath, L., Kaur, P., & Tripathi, S. (2015). Evaluation of the universal immunization program and challenges in coverage of migrant children in Haridwar, Uttarakhand, India. *Indian Journal of Community Medicine, 40*(4), 239–245.

Narayan, L. (2013). Addressing language barriers to healthcare in India. *The Nationl Medical Journal of India, 26*(4), 236–238.
National AIDS Control Organization. (2012). *Annual report 2011–12*. New Delhi: Department of AIDS Control. Ministry of Health and Family Welfare.
National AIDS Control Organization. (2015). *Annual report 2015–16*. New Delhi: Department of AIDS Control. Ministry of Health and Family Welfare.
National Sample Survey Organization. (2001). *Migration in India 1999–2000*. Government of India: Ministry of Statistics and Programme Implementation, Government of India.
National Sample Survey Organization. (2007–2008). *India—Employment and unemployment and migration survey: NSS 64th Round: July 2007–June 2008*. Ministry of Statistics and Programme Implementation, Government of India.
Nyamathi, A. M., Sinha, S., Ganguly, K. K., William, R. R., Heravian, A., Ramakrishnan, P., … Rao, P. V. R. (2011). Challenges experienced by rural women in India living with AIDS and implications for the delivery of HIV/AIDS care. *Health Care Women International, 4*(164). Retrieved from https://doi.org/10.1126/scisignal.2001449.Engineering.
Pakhare, A. P., Pawar, R., Lokhande, G. S., Datta, S. S., Pawar, R., … Datta, S. S. (2014). Does seasonal migration for sugarcane harvesting influence routine immunization coverage? A cross-sectional study from rural Maharashtra. *Indian Journal of Public Health, 58*(2), 116–120. Retrieved from https://doi.org/10.4103/0019-557X.132288.
Palanisamy, J., & Subramanian, S. (2011). Health care discrimination in HIV care. *World Journal of AIDS, 1,* 100–103. doi:10.4236/wja.2011.13015.
Parker, R., & Aggleton, P. (2003). HIV and AIDS-related stigma and discrimination: A conceptual framework and implications for action. *Social Science and Medicine, 57,* 13–24.
Paxton, S., Gonzales, G., & Uppakaew, K. (2005). AIDS-related discrimination in Asia. *AIDS Care, 17*(4), 413–424.
Prusty, R. K., & Keshri, K. (2015). Differentials in child nutrition and immunization among migrants and non-migrants in Urban India. *International Journal of Migration, Health and Social Care, 11*(3), 194–205. Retrieved from https://doi.org/http://dx.doi.org/10.1108/IJMHSC-02-2014-0006.
Rai, T., Lambert, H. S., & Ward, H. (2015) Complex routes into HIV care for migrant workers: A qualitative study from north India. *AIDS Care, 27*(11), 1418–1423.
Rai, T., Lambert, H. S., & Ward, H. (2016). Migration as a risk and a livelihood strategy: HIV across the life course of migrant families in India. *Global Public Health*, 1–15. Retrieved from https://doi.org/10.1080/17441692.2016.1155635.
Rajan, S. I. (2013). *Internal migration and youth in India: Main features, trends and emerging challenges*. New Delhi: UNESCO. Retrieved from http://unesdoc.unesco.org/images/0022/002214/221487e.pdf.
Rahbar, T., Garg, S., Tripathi, R., Gupta, V. K., & Singh, M. M. (2007). Knowledge, attitude, behaviour and practice (KABP) regarding HIV/AIDS among pregnant women attending PPTCT programme in New Delhi. *The Journal of Communcable Diseases, 39*(3), 179–184.
Saggurti, N., Mahapatra, B., Swain, S. N., & Jain, A. K. (2011). Male migration and risky sexual behavior in rural India: Is the place of origin critical for HIV prevention programs? *BMC Public Health, 11*(Suppl 6), S6. Retrieved from https://doi.org/10.1186/1471-2458-11-S6-S6.
Sanders, A. (n.d.). *Sex trafficking in Southeast Asia how neo-liberalism has bolstered the global sex trade*. Not dated. Retrieved from http://web.uvic.ca/~onpol/spring2012/One%20-%20Adrienne.pdf.
Santha, S. D., Jaswal, S., Sasidevan, D., Datta, K., Khan, A., & Kuruvilla, A. (2015). Climate change, livelihoods and health inequities: The vulnerability of migrant workers in India cities. Mumbai: Tata Institute of Social Sciences, *Asian Cities Climate Resilience*, Working paper series 16. Retrieved from http://pubs.iied.org/10728IIED/.

Seedat, F. (2011). *Determinants of HIV risk among male migrant workers in Mumbai.* London: London School of Economics, Working paper, Migration Studies Unit. Retrieved from http://www.lse.ac.uk/government/research/resgroups/MSU/documents/workingPapers/WP_2011_03.pdf.

Shetty, P., & Kowli, S. (2011). Knowledge and attitude of youth in Mumbai towards people living with HIV-AIDS. *Indian Journal of Maternal and Child Health, 13*(2).

Shi, L., & Stevens, G. D. (2005). Vulnerability and unmet health care needs. The influence of multiple risk factors. *Journal of General Internal Medicine, 20*(2), 148–54. Retrieved from https://doi.org/10.1111/j.1525-1497.2005.40136.x.

Silan, V., & Kant, S. (2014). Maternal healthcare and perinatal mortality among brick kiln migrant workers: A case study. *National Medical Journal of India, 27*(5), 280–282.

Singh, G. (2000). *Ethnic conflict in India: A case study of Punjab.* London: Palgrave Macmillan.

Singh, P. K., Rai, R. K., & Singh, L. (2012). Examining the effect of household wealth and migration status on safe delivery care in urban India, 1992–2006. *PLoS One, 7*(9), e44901. Retrieved from http://doi.org/10.1371/journal.pone.0044901.

Steward, W. T., Herek, G. M., Ramakrishna, J., Bharat, S., Chandy, S., Wrubel, J., & Ekstrand, M. L. (2008). HIV-related stigma: Adapting a theoretical framework for use in India. *Social Science and Medicine, 68*(8). Retrieved from http://doi.org/10.1016/j.socscimed.2008.05.032.

Subramanian, T., Gupte, M. D., Dorairaj, V. S., Periannan, V., & Mathai, A. K. (2009). Psycho-social impact and quality of life of people living with HIV/AIDS in South India. *AIDS Care, 21*(4), 473–481.

Subramaniyan, A., Sarkar, S., Roy, G., & Lakshminarayanan, S. (2013). Experiences of HIV positive mothers from rural South India during intra-natal period. *Journal of Clinical and Diagnostic Research*, 2203–2206. Retrieved from http://doi.org/10.7860/JCDR/2013/5782.3471.

Sudha, R. T., Vijay, D. T., & Lakshmi, V. (2005). Awareness, attitudes, and beliefs of the general public towards HIV/AIDS in Hyderabad, a capital city from South India. *Indian Journal of Medical Sciences, 59*(7), 307–16. Retrieved from http://doi.org/10.4103/0019-5359.16506.

Surabhi, K. S., & Kumar, N. A. (2007). *Labour migration to Kerala: A study of Tamil Nadu migrant laboures in Kochi.* Kochi: Centre for Socio-economic & environmental studies. Working Paper No. 16. Retrieved from http://www.csesindia.org/admin/modules/cms/docs/publication/16.pdf.

Thomas, B. E., Rehman, F., Suryanarayanan, D., Josephine, K., Dilip, M., Dorairaj, V. S., & Swaminathan, S. (2005). How Stigmatizing is Stigma in the life of people living with HIV: A study on HIV positive individuals from Chennai, South India. AIDS Care, *17*(7), 795–801.

Thomas, B. E., Nyamathi, A., & Swaminathan, S. (2009). Impact of HIV/AIDS on mothers in southern India: A Qualitative study. *AIDS Behaviour, 13*(5), 989–996. doi:10.1007/s10461-008-9478-x.

Times of India. (2014). *Migrant workers forced to flee over malaria scare.* Retrieved from http://timesofindia.indiatimes.com/city/kochi/Migrant-workers-forced-to-flee-over-malaria-scare/articleshow/45486036.cms.

United Nations Development Programme. (2004). *No safety signs here: Research study on migration and HIV vulnerability from seven South and North East Asian Countries.* New York: UNDP. Retrieved from https://www.unodc.org/documents/hiv-aids/publications/Migration_HIV_South_East_Asia_undp_safety_here_0408.pdf.

United Nations Educational, Scientific and Cultural Organization, & United Nations International Children's Fund. (2012). *Internal migration in India initiative for a better inclusion of internal migrants in India policy briefs.* New Delhi: UNESCO and UNICEF.

United Nations Educational, Scientific and Cultural Organization. (2013). *Social inclusion of internal migrants in India.* New Delhi: UNESCO.

van Hollen, C. (2010). HIV/AIDS and the gendering of stigma in Tamil Nadu, South India. *Culture, Medicine and Psychiatry, 34*(4), 633–657. Retrieved from https://doi.org/10.1007/s11013-010-9192-9.

Varadharajan, K. S., Thomas, T., Rajaraman, D., Kurpad, A. V., & Vaz, M. (2013). Overweight and obesity among internal migrants in India. *Asia Pacific Journal of Clinical Nutrition, 22*(3), 416–425. Retrieved from https://doi.org/10.6133/apjcn.2013.22.3.14.

Wang, B., Li, X., Stanton, B., & Fang, X. (2010). The influence of social stigma and discriminatory experience on psychological distress and quality of life among rural-to-urban migrants in China. *Social Science and Medicine, 71*(1), 84–92.

Weiner, M. (2015). *Sons of the soil: Migration and ethnic conflict in India*. Princeton, USA: Princeton University Press.

Yadav, S. B., Makwana, N. R., Vadera, B. N., Dhaduk, K. M., & Gandha, K. M. (2011). Awareness of HIV/AIDS among rural youth in India: A community based cross-sectional study. *Journal of Infection in Developing Countries, 5*(10), 711–716.

Chapter 8
The Role of the Health System

Rakhal Gaitonde

Abstract Health systems are developed and invested in with the express goal of ensuring a basic minimum of health care for all. This chapter points out that health systems are emergent from the sociopolitical and cultural power distribution in a given society and thus reflect these in its structure, design and functioning. As the Health System Knowledge Network (of the Commission on Social Determinants of Health) pointed out, health systems can contribute to the reduction of health inequities or indeed to their sustenance or even worsen. It is also pointed out that apart from the material effects of the health system, any such system also sends out messages to the users (and indeed those who cannot use it) regarding the way they are seen by those in power. The health system, by the way it functions, can support or challenge the larger sociopolitical arrangements. Given this perspective and the evidence of inequity presented in the previous four chapters it is clear that the health system in India is not playing the role it is expected to. It is from this perspective that the chapter reviews and engages with the literature on out-of-pocket expenditure, and health systems utilisation, structure, design and financing. The chapter identifies a few mechanisms from the literature reviewed and recommends the need for a multi-level framework to adequately understand the role played by health systems in health inequity.

Keywords India · Health inequities · Health systems · Multi-level framework
Health systems knowledge network

8.1 The Health System and Health Inequities

According to the World Health Organization, the health system "includes all actions whose primary purpose is to promote, restore, or maintain health (World Health Organization [WHO], 2000, p. xi)". The Commission on the Social Determinants of

R. Gaitonde (✉)
Centre for Technology and Policy (CTaP) IIT-M, Chennai, India
e-mail: rakhal.gaitonde@gmail.com

T.K.S. Ravindran and R. Gaitonde (eds.), *Health Inequities in India*,
https://doi.org/10.1007/978-981-10-5089-3_8

Health notes that health systems are *intermediate determinants* of health and are in a crucial position of mediating between the structural determinants of health and the actual health outcomes and the distribution of these outcomes (Commission for Social Determinants of Health [CSDH], 2008).

More importantly the CSDH report points out that the health systems can play an important (and lead) role in the reduction of inequity, but that in certain circumstances poorly functioning health systems may perpetuate the effects of larger structural injustice and social stratification (Gilson, Doherty, Loewenson, & Francis, 2007). However, the CSDH report also notes that health systems, especially through the practices that they institutionalise, do have more *upstream* effects as well, with the possibility of affecting the broader socio-economic reality in turn. The direction of interaction is thus two way, and this underlines the importance of focusing on the health systems as a crucial point of analysis while studying health inequities.

This first section of the chapter sets out our perspective on health systems. In Sect. 8.2 we summarise the key findings from the literature reviewed. In Sect. 8.3 we first critique the underlying assumptions of the studies, and the frameworks used and offer likely aspects of an overarching framework that would engage with this critique.

8.1.1 Conceptual Framework for Viewing Health Systems

The design and functioning of health systems reflect the balance of power at the societal level (Freedman, 2005; Gaitonde, 2015).

The Health system by definition includes both the public sector as well as the private sectors. In the post-World War II period with the rise of the welfare state, public systems were sought to be developed and strengthened. Post-Independence India too initially developed the public health system as the critical provider of health care. However, within decades policy changed (reflected also by global shifts discussed in Chap. 1) with the private sector being expected to play an increasing role in the provision of health care (Saxena, 2010). The motivation and vision of each of these sectors is quite different and will be discussed in sequence.

Health systems in the public sector, as with public systems in general, are designed based on the premise that provision of a universal basic package of social services to people regardless of ability to pay would ensure a basic minimum amount of welfare. Public systems were developed with the explicit aim of protecting the poor and marginalised from inequities induced by the market mechanism (Jayal, 1994).

In the private sector, unlike the public sector, healthcare provision is considered a legitimate means of income generation, and indeed surplus extraction (Loeppky, 2010). It is often characterised by lax regulation, the blurred boundaries between personnel's who worked in the public sector as well as the private sector (especially in developing countries), and the huge influence of the pharma sector, with the market logic ruling the development of services rather than *Rights* or *Need* of the community. In India too private sector has similar characteristics and has developed into a highly extractive system providing the best of care for those who can afford it, but being out of reach or indeed impoverishing for those who could not afford it. Better quality is the false premise on which it promotes itself. In addition a range of unethical practices has been documented (Gadre & Shukla, 2016).

Thus while the public sector was ridden with issues of governance and corruption (rent seeking), the private sector became an extension of the pharma and medical equipment industry, not only leading to an increasing commodification and medicalisation of health, but also becoming willy-nilly the benchmark against which the public sector sought to model itself.

Any discussion on the role of the health system and health inequities has to encompass the effects of this diversity of subsystems each with its motivation and factors sustaining and driving it.

The view that the health system plays a key role in the production and maintenance of inequity is also developed in Freese and Lutfee's (2011) extension of the Fundamental Cause theory (Phelan, Link, & Tehranifar, 2010). In this, one of the mechanisms they suggest as underlying the *fundamental* nature of the socio-economic conditions is the role of institutions in society. Freese and Lutfey start by challenging the underlying assumption that mere access to institutions will ensure welfare for individuals, thus agency lying purely with individuals. They showed that there was variation in care provided to patients based on their socio-economic status (Freese & Lutfey, 2011). "The medical system is not a neutral conduit through which resources are exercised ... Rather, it is a dynamic institution that may respond directly to a patient's efforts to mobilise resources for health, but may also either amplify or mitigate those same efforts". They conclude by saying that according to this insight, "Access, utilisation and adherence are moot if one's SES potential for purposive health improvement is undermined by the action of the institutions and its agents (Freese & Lutfey, 2011, p. 74)".

The Health Systems Knowledge Network (HSKN) of the Commission on the Social Determinants of Health has evolved a framework to study health systems (Fig. 8.1).

As per this framework the health system is intimately linked to both the national-level sociopolitical context as well as the global context in which the national context is embedded and intimately inter-connected.

Reviewing the literature with a special focus on drawing lessons for low- and middle-income countries, the Health systems Knowledge Network pointed out four broad ways by which the health system contributes to health inequity. These are (a) when there is a generally weak health equity orientation in the leadership and vision, neglecting comprehensive primary health care; (b) healthcare access issues, high opportunity costs for accessing health care; (c) demeaning experiences while accessing the healthcare system; and (d) impoverishment (Gilson et al., 2007).

This is further underlined by thinking in the field of economics for example that recognises the importance of the role of public systems. One of the key aspects of Amartya Sen's capability approach is his critique of the Rawlsian conclusion of the

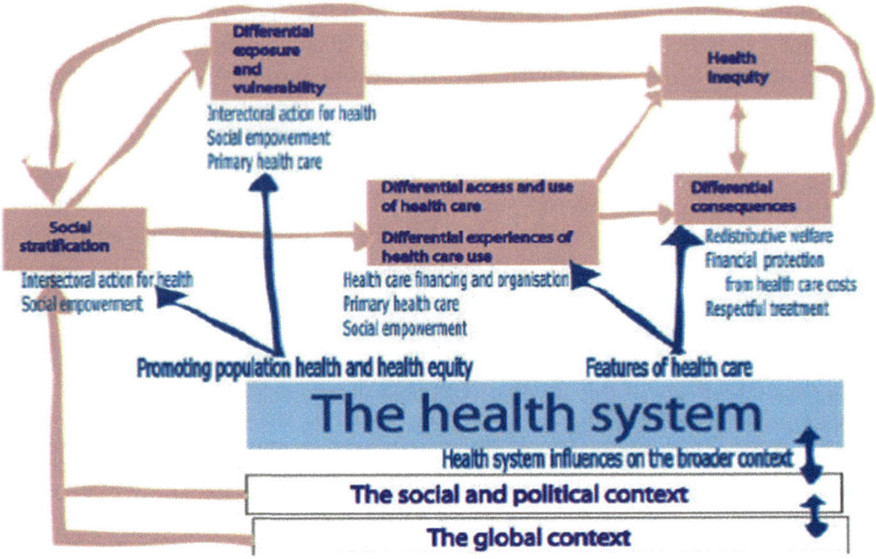

Fig. 8.1 The pathways of positive potential for health systems: points of intervention. World Health Organization Commission on the Social Determinants of Health (WHO-CSFDH) (2007). *Final Report Knowledge Network on Health Systems*. p. 6. Retrieved from http://www.who.int/social_determinants/resources/csdh_media/hskn_final_2007_en.pdf

sufficiency of equality of primary resources to ensure fairness and equality (Sen, 1992). Sen rightly points out that what is missed in this analysis is the fact that individuals and indeed communities can vary in their ability to *convert* this basket of primary resources into *welfare* for themselves. The key underlying issue is that the reasons for the inability to convert these resources into valued well-being may not necessarily be within the control of either individuals or indeed communities, or sections of society. This is very similar to the concept that Culyers uses, which he terms as the *health production function* of a community for a given input or intervention by the health system (Culyer, 2016). Thus, Culyer is also asking us to focus on the capacity of an individual, as well as a community to *convert* an input/intervention of the health system to improve health into actual benefit (Culyer, 2016).

One of the key insights on the role of the health system comes from the eco-social theory of Nancy Krieger. Among the key tenets of this theory are those of *agency and responsibility*. This basically asks the question whether those in positions of power and with resources to make changes are actually doing so in the best interests of communities (Krieger, 2011). The eco-social theory also explicitly demands the unravelling of mechanisms by which the socio-economic arrangements in a society are embodied in individuals and groups. Given the critical role played by the health system in protecting individual and societal health, the experience of marginalised groups when they attempt to access the healthcare systems is a crucial pathway for such embodiment (Krieger, 2011). In his critique of

Tamil Nadu's *successful* health system, Gaitonde points to the extremely narrow set of parameters around which this *success* is built. He further proposes a classification of health systems drawing from the contention of the CSDH, into those that accept the status quo and are shaped by it, those functioning well and mitigating any ill effects (at least along a narrow set of parameters) but in effect not questioning the structures as they are, and finally those systems that actually challenge these structures, by empowering the communities they serve (Gaitonde, 2015). This draws on the social construction framework of policy implementation which notes that "Policy designs have both material and symbolic (reputational or interpretive) effects on target populations that impact their attitudes and political participation. These effects occur through the structuring of opportunities that shape life experiences and subtle messages about how government works and how they are likely to be treated (Schneider, Ingram, & Deleon, 2014, p. 116)".

Thus regardless of the role public systems are meant to play *in theory*, they evolve as core social institutions that reflect the power distribution as well as the hierarchies in any given society. The current structure and functioning of a public system need to be seen thus as a dynamic resultant of the compact in any given society between the various groups and the ruling/dominant elite who wield power. From an institutional perspective these institutions may be seen as mechanisms put in place by the government (and ruling classes) to ensure some amount of redistribution of resources. However, such institutions by virtue of reflecting the hierarchies in any society also have to serve the interests of the power elite, and this dialectic of redistribution and the resulting legitimacy in the eyes of the larger public and extraction and the resulting support of the dominant elite is an abiding theme in studying the evolution and functioning of public systems and especially public health systems. While public systems are premised on the reduction of inequity, the actual design and functioning may perpetuate inequities in a given society, or at most they work within the frameworks of inequity not questioning them or challenging them.

8.1.2 Effect of the Larger Global and National Turn to Neo-Liberal Governance on Health Systems

Health systems are intimately dependent on the larger national and global balance of power for their evolution and functioning. Studies like the *Dying for Growth* collection and others have from the 90s been using a range of methods to document and link the rise of neo-liberal economic thinking and the weakening of publicly funded health systems all over the world (Kim, Millen, Irwin, & Gershman, 2000).

Ever since the early experiments of privatisation of public systems in Latin America in the 70s and 80s, this form of thinking has crystallised into its more recognisable form called neo-liberalism described in detail in the opening chapter of the book. In this section I will only briefly present the now mounting evidence of the impact of this thinking on publicly funded health systems.

The impact of these trends may be seen in several dimensions:

- One of the key dimensions of the impact of neo-liberal thinking is on the way health systems are designed and developed. While immediately after independence the public sector was developed as the main provider of health care regardless of ability to pay, the move towards neo-liberal governance calls for all provision and allocation of resources to be market mediated, with the role of the public sector reduced to a facilitator of the market and provider of services that are defined as public goods (basically on which there is no profit to be made). Within the system too, governance moves from a right-based approach to one of the managerialisms (Lister, 2013; Sivaramakrishnan, 2011).
- The other is related to fiscal thinking at national level where public services are defined as *non-priority* expenditure and governments are coerced into shifting payments into servicing loans or to develop infrastructure that essentially is meant to stimulate the functioning of the markets. Thus we find trends of privatisation of education, health and other social sectors in countries all over the world (Pal & Ghosh, 2007).
- In parallel there has been a weakening of global structures of the United Nations bodies—the World Health Organization and UNICEF for example—both directly by severely restricting the funding they receive from governments, but also substantially increasing funds from private philanthropies and bringing in people from the private sector to head these organisations (Lister, 2013).
- Financial organisations like the World Bank and private philanthropies such as the Bill & Melinda Gates foundations (for example) have taken over the mantle of leadership in terms of health policy all over the world. This has led to a narrow and unimodal sort of thinking about health problems, with an emphasis on technology-based solutions that can be produced and bought in a market setting, thus fuelling private profit (Lister, 2013).

These trends have resulted in the weakening of public systems in general and health systems in particular all over the world including in India. The particular case of the Indian health system is discussed in more detail in subsequent sections of the chapter. In this Chapter, I will explore the role the health system in India plays in the reduction or indeed production of inequity in health. The chapter focuses on issues of design and financing that impact on access, utilisation and out-of-pocket expenditure, as well as the actual interaction of people with the health system personnel. The study of "health systems" refers specifically to the aspects of access, utilisation, financing and programme design along the axes of gender, caste, class and geography, and how they contribute to or mitigate health-related inequity in health. In India a number of studies have pointed out that significant disparity between outcomes in a variety of dimensions of health is underpinned by inequities in availability, access and quality of health services. Similarly, a number of studies have shown that one of the main drivers of poverty in India today is expenditure on medical care. Similarly, studies have shown that medical conditions and the expenses related to these are one of the key precipitating factors of suicides by farmers in India. National Sample Surveys (NSS) over the years have shown that while the percentage of people not approaching any formal system for care is constant over nearly three decades, the reasons for not approaching are changing with a significant increase in the number saying that "facilities were not available" or "financial reasons" were on the increase (Selvaraj & Karan, 2009). Thus the health system needs to be seen as key determinant not only for the overall health of a society, but also equally for the level of inequity in it.

In sum therefore we see the health system and the interaction with it by different groups of people as having at least three distinct effects. One is the material effect of accessibility or lack of it, relief obtained and the impact of that experience on both the individual and the community from which that individual comes. The experience of efficacy of contact with the health system plays a crucial role in the evolution of health-seeking behaviour, especially among marginal communities who draw on indigenous forms/alternative world views, etc. The second impact is the subliminal messages conveyed to various users of the health system. This is the "feed forward" mechanism referred to above (Schneider et al., 2014). In this, the way the health system *treats* individuals and groups reflects way the health system *thinks* about them. The third impact of the health system functioning as mentioned in the HSKN report (Gilson et al., 2007) and in the framework suggested by Gaitonde (Gaitonde, 2015) is the possible role of the way it treats marginal communities in contributing to its becoming the facilitator of an alternative consciousness and thus playing a role in questioning and challenging the hierarchical arrangement in a given society.

What would a health system that is actively engaging in reduction of inequity look like? As a start, the system will be actively working on the social determinants of health, not only through action through the department, but more importantly through leadership in inter-sectoral action. By its actions and attitude towards the marginalised sections, the health system would facilitate empowerment. The system would strive to minimise barriers of all kinds (taking into account the specific sociopolitical–cultural and environmental context) to access services that are of the highest quality and based on the best available evidence. Would be sensitive to the cultural and social uniqueness of the community it serves, and ensure that the benefits of its services reach the poor and other marginalised sections.

8.2 The Role of the Health System: A Summary of the Literature

8.2.1 Key Terms Used in the Literature

8.2.1.1 Access

While some studies like Levesque (Levesque, Haddad, Narayana, & Fournier, 2006) defined utilisation in a nuanced way as "the opportunity to reach and obtain appropriate healthcare services. Access results from the interface between the characteristics of persons, households, social and physical environments and the characteristics of health systems and organizations (Penchansky & Thomas, 1981, p. 290)". Factors to consider in the assessment of access could thus pertain to "supply-side features of health systems and organizations, to demand- side features of populations, and to process factors describing the ways in which access is realized (Daniels, 1982, p. 290)". Most other studies merely looked at utilisation as a simple proxy to access and failed to discuss the nuances referred to above. However, following the capabilities approach, and invoking the "health production function" (Culyer, 2016), one sees the inadequacy of the concept as a stand-alone, except as a not-so-reliable proxy for health system development and functioning. This is also brought about in the literature where it has been shown that efforts purely aimed at increasing access that do not necessarily reduce inequity in terms of actual health benefits/outcomes (Jain, 2010; Randive, San Sebastian, De Costa, & Lindholm, 2014).

8.2.1.2 Utilisation

Like the concept of access, one finds highly nuanced definitions of utilisation which, "measure utilisation (the actual quantity of healthcare services and procedures used) (Shengelia, Murray, & Adams, 2003, p. 290) and non- utilisation in the face of perceived need for services and severity of illness enables inferences about potential access to care (Waters, 2000)". The care that individuals consume thus being a function of their demographic, social and economic characteristics as well as those of the health systems. The interaction between these factors and household and individual characteristics would generate ability to reach facilities and opportunity to choose (Levesque et al., 2006, p. 290). Despite the above and the description of multi-layered and multiple vulnerabilities (Mohindra, Narayana, & Haddad, 2010)—by and large—the concept is reduced to the question of utilisation of OP or IP services in a given time period, which is the only available indicator in the large-scale surveys like the NSSO. Apart from this the insights presented above that mere use of services does not automatically translate to benefit holds for utilisation too.

8.2.1.3 Coverage of Services

While this is essentially similar to the utilisation of services, the difference is in the fact that in studies of utilisation or access, persons utilising the services have to make the effort to go to the medical institutions. On the other hand services researched under "coverage" measures services that the government mandates to reach all people (who require it) as an entitlement. Such services include ANC, PNC, immunisation, etc.

One of the key assumptions is that by tackling the extra effort to reach the people in their villages and provide these services free of cost, the extra indirect costs of accessing these services otherwise would be reduced and thus reducing inequity (Oster, 2009). However, as discussed in the earlier section on access, while the inequity in coverage of assured entitlements reflects the structural barriers operating, mere filling the gap may not necessarily result in equitable outcomes (Phelan et al., 2010).

This discussion with regards to access, utilisation and coverage further underline the importance of a theoretical approach to inequity that goes beyond the dominant "risk-factor" approach to invoke research methods that uncover mechanisms.

8.2.2 Key Findings from the Literature Review

The examination of the literature on the health system is based on the literature on inequity in outcomes reviewed and presented in the earlier four chapters. I will focus on two broad areas. One is what the literature has to say on the experience of individuals, groups who have tried to reach or actually accessed the health system. The second broad aspect is that of issues of policy, programme, institutional design and their determinants. In the first part I will discuss issues relating to utilisation of the public healthcare system in terms of general medical and surgical care and of inpatient and outpatient care. I will then present the literature on the aspect of affordability of the present health system (covering both the public and private where available) to highlight the impact of health care seeking on the financial status of families/communities. I will also briefly refer to the inequity in access/utilisation of preventive services from the perspective of the role of the health system and reduction of inequity. The main indicator here is the study of out-of-pocket expenditure. In the next part I will focus on health system development, programme and institutional design and financing and issues broadly under the topic of health system governance.

The earlier four chapters (Chaps. 4–7) have reviewed and consolidated the available evidence of inequity in a range of crucial health outcomes along various axes like socio-economic position, gender, Dalit and Adivasi status and other socially constructed vulnerabilities. This chapter does not repeat those same findings, but focuses on the specific question as to what we can learn about the contribution of the health system in inequity. While the earlier Chaps. 4–7 have demonstrated a range of inequities in various health-related outcomes, it is important to note that the groups of people who are negatively affected are the very same group who are affected by the broader macro-forces and suffer other forms of socio-economic inequities. The fact that the very same groups who bear the brunt of the socio-economic models of development are also those who have the worst health outcomes—while not surprising—is an indictment of health system design and functioning.

8.2.2.1 Inequities in Health System Utilisation

People engage with or approach health systems in two ways. The first is when people seek out the health system in response to an illness or problem faced, and the second is when the health system (usually the public health system) reaches out to individuals and communities (many of them healthy in many instances) for the provision of health care, preventive and promotive services deemed essential for the health and welfare of that community by the state. In this part we focus on the former and draw on the previous four chapters.

Those who are poorer off, and those from more marginalised and vulnerable sections are likely to have a higher need for health services. Their poor living conditions, lack of food and livelihood security, poor and sometimes dangerous working conditions, etc., lead to a higher need for healthcare services. In such a situation, a measure of equity in healthcare provisioning/utilisation would be (as per the definitions of horizontal and vertical equity) equal utilisation for equal need, and conversely increased utilisation for increased need. Equally importantly the services utilised must be of the same quality, be effective and not lead to further impoverishment. However, in reality the utilisation of an individual or a group is more than just a simple function of availability of services or accessibility alone (Levesque et al., 2006). Utilisation at a minimum includes perception of need, exercise of choice and an ability to act on that choice.

Socio-economic Position

The literature on inequity of healthcare utilisation shows two broad trends. One is that regardless of the way the data is disaggregated, perceived or self-reported morbidity (a proxy for need) is less among the poor and marginalised groups (Levesque et al., 2006; Mukherjee & Levesque, 2010), while objectively measured morbidity showed higher incidence among the poor (Garg, 1998; Mondal, 2013). Similarly, the indicators of actual utilisation of services show lower utilisation by the poor of both inpatient services (IP) (Garg, 1998; Mukherjee & Levesque, 2010; Prinja, Kanavos, & Kumar, 2012; Prinja, Kumar, Pinto, Jan, & Kumar, 2013) and outpatient services (OP) (Levesque et al., 2006; Mukherjee & Levesque, 2010) services.

Studies reviewed found that hospitalisation in the public sector was pro-poor (in terms of a larger proportion of poor using these services) while the private sector hospitals were pro-rich (Prinja et al., 2012). Studies showed that between the period of the 52nd (1994–95) and the 60th round of the NSSO (2004) the overall economic status related inequity in inpatient care utilisation reduced (Mukherjee & Levesque, 2010). Alongside this narrowing of the gap in utilisation, there was an accompanying rise in out-of-pocket expenditure for each admission thus effectively reducing any benefits of such a decrease in inequity (Mukherjee & Levesque, 2010).

Dalit and Adivasi Status

Just one paper was retrieved that looked at the axis of social marginalisation and utilisation. This study was the outcome of an action research project done in one panchayat area in Kerala, and studied in-depth the vulnerability of a particular Adivasi group called Paniyas. While a number of issues have been discussed in this study, one of the findings pertinent to caste and health sector utilisation was that Paniyas (like other marginalised groups described above) reported levels of health that were comparable to the highest ranked groups, although they had the worst measures of objective health (Haddad, Narayana, & Mohindra, 2011).

In another interesting correlation it was shown that women with low caste affiliations but were members of SHGs—they were less likely to be excluded from the health system (Haddad et al., 2011).

Gender

In terms of utilisation of both inpatient and outpatient services (George, 2005; Roy & Chaudhuri, 2008), studies demonstrate the disadvantages faced by women. Sen and colleagues have shown that, more than caste, class modulates the effect of gender in terms of access to and the continuation of treatment in rural Karnataka (Sen & Iyer, 2012; Sen, Iyer, & George, 2007). Exploring the mechanisms the authors noted that one of the key mechanisms was the lack of acknowledgement of the fact that the woman was suffering from something that needed treatment. The researchers felt that this was due to deeply ingrained gender norms that reduce self-worth and result in a lack of confidence, and hence underplaying their own illness (Sen et al., 2007). In a study focusing on health seeking among the elderly in India, while elderly women showed a disadvantage in terms of lower healthcare utilisation, this disadvantage disappeared among women who had greater control on finances (Roy & Chaudhuri, 2008), again reiterating the modulation of gender by financial autonomy.

A study of the characteristics and outcomes of patients approaching Arvind Eye Hospital (located in Madurai, Tamil Nadu) aimed specifically at the exploration of gender differentials at various stages of diagnosis, treatment and outcomes, noted that women came later in the natural history of a given disease than men, though they attend screening camps at the same rate. The outcomes (in terms of magnitude of improvement) were no different. This shows that there was the difference in access but not in delivery of services (Jayaraman, Ray, & Wang, 2014).

Urban–Rural

In general urban areas are considered to be more favourable in terms of healthcare services given the concentration of services there compared to rural areas. Moreover, in general incomes are higher. This is borne out by the evidence, which showed that IP and OP differentials favoured urban populations despite there being greater perceived morbidity in rural areas (Ghosh, 2014). While studies regarding IP differentials were generally pro-rich when studied in rural and urban settings separately, in general inequity in utilisation seemed to be lower in urban areas, but catastrophic expenditure was higher (Ghosh, 2014). In a study focusing on rural issues relating to utilisation, one study demonstrated that there were higher expenditures related to issues peculiar to rural agricultural practices like pesticide use (Meeta & Lochan, 2010).

Using the indicator of "mean length of stay in hospital" one study found a significant pro-poor distribution and especially so in the urban areas. The authors opine that this could be more due to the health need and inability to access good quality care (for quick cure) than anything else (Ghosh, 2014).

In terms of changes over time, a comparison of the 52nd and 60th rounds of the NSSO showed that overall inpatient hospitalisation had increased in rural areas with more substantial increase among the poor (167%) than among the rich (18%) (Mukherjee & Levesque, 2010). Studies also showed that in the nearly two decades between the 42nd and 60th rounds of the NSSO, while the proportion of persons reporting "no treatment" in rural and urban areas remained constant, the reasons had changed significantly. The proportion reporting "no treatment" due to "lack of availability or institution" and "financial problems" went up from 18 to 40% in rural areas as compared to the rise from 10 to 21% in the urban areas (Meeta & Lochan, 2010).

Some other associations with greater rural inequity are lower per-capita expenditure on rural populations (Ghosh, 2014) and more difficult terrain needing to be traversed for the same given distance (Sabde, De Costa, & Diwan, 2014).

Inter-state

State-level trends in inequity of utilisation by socio-economic position showed very disparate trends. The lack of any a priori theorisation on the factors acting at the state level, or the way that these would impact on healthcare utilisation means that most analysis of inequity was retrospective and speculative. All that one can conclude is that there is extremely high variation of various indicators of utilisation when studied at a state level, trends vary significantly over time, but states show very different trends when different indicators are used.

The overall picture of rural dependence on government institutions for hospitalisation showed a decline of a quite varying degree. Some interesting patterns were described. Thus states like Andhra Pradesh, Assam, Madhya Pradesh and Tamil Nadu did not decline, while Uttar Pradesh, Haryana and Punjab showed prominent declines (Ghosh, 2014). Similarly, both Kerala and Tamil Nadu with very well-developed private sectors continued to show very high rates of public sector utilisation, while Andhra Pradesh (well-developed private sector) and Bihar (not developed private sector) had very low utilisation of public sector. The set of well-performing states in terms of those who made the most gains in inequity either had good network of private hospitals or were more developed industrially or in the field of agriculture (Ghosh, 2014).

Two significant correlations of healthcare utilisation highlighted are the association of per-capita government spending (Ghosh, 2014), and the presence of a robust private sector and well-developed industrial and agricultural sector (Mukherjee & Levesque, 2010).

8.2.3 Differential Health Service Impacts on Consumers—in Terms of Out-of-Pocket Expenditure (OOPE)

While the public health services as noted in the introduction were put in place particularly to right historical wrongs to weaker and vulnerable groups, poorly functioning public health systems can instead contribute further to worsening of individual- and community-level health and socio-economic status. A number of studies in the retrieved articles refer to this aspect of the health systems, but a few studies particularly examine this problem.

Socio-economic Position

Studies, however, showed that despite less gap in utilisation during this period (NSSO 60th round), the poor paid a higher proportion of their annual income as out-of-pocket expenditure for health care compared to the rich and was thus termed as "regressive" for both IP and OP utilisations. This potentially worsened the overall impact on those who could least afford the services (Prinja et al., 2012).

At the national level Baru et al. note that in rural areas close to a fifth of health expenses for OP care is financed through borrowing, while the corresponding percentage for hospitalisation is 40% (Baru, Acharya, Acharya, Kumar, & Nagaraj, 2010). The poor on an average spend 7–8% of their annual expenditure on health, as compared to the 2–3% that rich people pay (Garg, 1998). Another study showed that poor in rural areas paid 33% of their consumption expenditure (including wages lost etc.) on routine day-to-day health needs compared to 17% in urban areas. A number of studies show that significant amounts of the cost of accessing and availing healthcare services are financed through debt (Garg, 1998; Selvaraj & Karan, 2009).

There has been a consistent increase in the cost of health care both in public sector and the private sector. When combined with a decrease utilisation of government hospitals and an increase in the cost of care in both the public and private sectors (more so in the private than in the public), the combined effect is actually one of poorer welfare (Mukherjee & Levesque, 2010).

An all India level study showed counter-intuitively that catastrophic expenditure occurred most commonly for common illnesses and routine services like women and child care issues, and not only rare illnesses (Selvaraj & Karan, 2009). Garg (1998) noted that the poor spend on an average 7–8% of their Annual Expenditure on health compared to the 2–3% spent by the rich. The poor pay more on transportation, second only to what they pay for practitioner's fees and medicines, compared to the rich who pay more for hospital charges and surgery after practitioner fees and medicines (Garg, 1998). Another study of three states reported that the concentration index for catastrophic expenditure was negative, meaning that there was an over-representation of the poor, while in two of the three states both admission in public sector institutions and in the free ward were significantly negative—again showing an over-representation of the poor (Prinja et al., 2012). Thus, despite the seemingly pro-poor nature of the public health system, the poor do not enjoy adequate financial protection.

Studying the effect on OOPE of the large-scale tertiary care health insurance schemes a research study looking at Andhra (Arogyashri) and Maharashtra (RSBY and Rajiv Gandhi Jeevandayee) found that in general the slightly less vulnerable rather than the most vulnerable groups tended to benefit more from these schemes, with so-called non-financial issues acting as critical barriers from the most vulnerable groups (Rao et al., 2014).

In another study on OOPE it was noted that "Our findings indicate that out-of-pocket payments, both absolute and as a share of consumption, increase with ability to pay. The relationship between ATP and both payments and payments share is retained across different subgroups that differ by gender, social code, provider type, region or state of residence (Roy & Howard, 2007, p. 297)".

Dalit or Adivasi Status

In an in-depth study, Mukherjee, Haddad, and Narayana (2011) reported the findings of the action research project done in one panchayat of Kerala. In this study the authors showed that although the Adivasi Paniya households had amongst the lowest per-capita health expenditure, a quarter of this had to be financed by loans and donation (Mukherjee et al., 2011).

Rural–Urban

Meeta points out that in rural areas the average medical expenditure per episode of illness is just slightly lower than urban, and at Rs. 5695 is thrice the monthly income of average farmers (Meeta & Lochan, 2010). Studies also showed a higher rate of irrationality and unnecessary drug prescriptions in rural areas—potentially increasing the expenditure per illness episode in rural areas unnecessarily (Bhatia & Cleland, 2004; Bhatnagar, Mishra, & Mishra, 2003).

Cost of Care

A number of studies have pointed out that the increasing cost of care both in the public as well as the private sectors means that people are avoiding care due to these costs. Studies have documented the rapid rise in costs of both therapeutics and diagnostics (Balarajan, Selvaraj, & Subramanian, 2011). Another study showed that the poor tended to use simpler services and thus the actual benefit accruing to the poor reduces as we move up the therapeutic hierarchy from primary to tertiary services (Prinja et al., 2012).

8.2.4 Health System Design, Performance and Governance Issues

One of the key aspects of studying the health system is to discern mechanisms that result in the health system either contributing to the reduction, sustenance or the worsening of health inequities. As discussed in the introductory sections a number of theories and frameworks have been suggested for this. Before we summarise the literature from India on how health system design, performance and governance issues impact on health equity, we first explore the literature that pertains to the macroeconomic factors that underlie these.

8.2.4.1 Structural Determinants of Health System Design, Performance and Governance—Macro-trends

The European welfare state was inspired by the need to provide corrective measures for the socio-economic inequalities of market economies. In the Indian case, despite rhetoric, the model is that of a mixed economy, with the state playing a relatively weak role compared to commercial interests. The health sector is characterised by a weak and struggling public health sector and a large unregulated private sector (Jayal, 1999). Further given that the idea of the welfare state was the result of ruling elite who took over the reins of power from the British and not a social movement or demand by the national bourgeoise, its deficiency and erosion has gone unchallenged (Jayal, 1999). This forms a crucial political setting for understanding the development of and therefore the role of the health system, especially the public sector in health in India.

In a paper that has lucidly charted out the broad macroeconomic trends in India post the 1991 crisis and the formal adoption of economic reforms as part of the neo-liberal agenda, Pal and Ghosh deal with the fiscal pressures, the financial sector reforms and other general trends. They start by highlighting the broad trends of this period. The shift towards neo-liberal policies meant the erosion of the governmental commitment as a provider and creator of equity, in line with the move towards liberalisation, privatisation and globalisation (Pal & Ghosh, 2007).

Two broad aspects of reform were undertaken during this period—fiscal reform and financial sector reform. To reduce the fiscal deficit the government needed to raise additional resources, however, as this was being done in the neo-liberal paradigm, it was accompanied with a cut in both indirect taxes and domestic duty. With these potential tax-based resources unavailable to the government, the only way balance could be achieved was through expenditure cuts. This led to massive cuts in capital expenditure as current expenditure could not be meddled with. Thus public investment in crucial areas like agriculture, rural development and infrastructure was scaled down leading to a collapse of public systems. There were also cuts in food subsidy. A reorganisation of the tax system with a reduction of central sales tax and increase in VAT and non-shareable parts of the direct taxes meant a reduction in the financial transfers to the states as well as drop in the ability of the states themselves to raise resources. This will obviously have a very serious implication on the health system which is almost completely funded by the state governments (Pal & Ghosh, 2007). The authors also note that during this period rural inequality increased, the disparity between the poorest and the richest states shot up during the 90s and the trends in Gini coefficients of states showed that inter- and intra-state inequality grew in India (Pal & Ghosh, 2007).

During a similar time period there was a decline in Central government grants to the state. This essentially meant a freezing of capital expenditure and almost all the money being used for salaries and supplies. This resulted in a literal stop to health sector expansion and maintenance (Garg, 1998). Over the periods 74–82, 82–89 and 92–93 the grant from central government declined from 19.9 to 5.8% and further to 3.3%. Even in the disease control programmes and public health expenditure where the Central government had a relatively larger fraction, there was a decline in Central government expenditure—from 41.47 to 18.5% in disease control programmes during 84–85 and 92–93, and from 27.92 to 17.7% in public health over the same period (Purohit, 2001).

And as Selvaraj points out, the neo-liberal growth means extreme vulnerability in general and health insecurity in particular and these leading to abysmal poverty levels. In addition "public health infrastructure was left to decay while private sector was wooed with a plethora of incentives, in keeping with pro-market agenda of the ruling regime (Selvaraj & Karan, 2009, p. 55)".

The above trends in the reduction of public spending on the expansion and development of the public health sector builds on the already great inter- and intra-state maldistribution of healthcare infrastructure. Two studies refer to the differing patterns of investment by different states as a key determinant to inequities at that level (Baru et al., 2010; Ghosh, 2014).

8.2.4.2 Health System Design and Other Structural Factors

Design

How does health system design affect inequities in health? In her paper on gender in design of UHC systems, Ravindran notes that there are a number of points at which gender should influence policy/programme design. For example she notes that since a significant proportion of women do not participate in wage employment and if they do it is informal, thus social insurance schemes are likely to miss them. While programmes tend to target subsidies and waivers based on wealth differentials (for example), the author pointed to studies that showed that due to gender dynamics within the family women from non-poor household also faced financial obstacles (Ravindran, 2012). In another study looking at schemes that gave cash benefits for institutional deliveries, Ravindran noted that "the poorest and most marginalised women were excluded in a larger proportion than their share in the population, from such schemes (Balasubramanian & Ravindran, 2012)". Finances were not the only issue that led to lack of access. Citing data from NFHS-3, Ravindran (2012) noted that about 20% women cited "lack of permission" and between 30 and 66% reported not willing to go alone (Ravindran, 2012). Another study looking at the way in which gender needs to be taken into account at the stage of policy formulation/programme design notes that "passive case finding may miss potential diagnoses particularly among women who have lower access to health system" and further that gender differences in healthcare access may influence gender differences in HIV testing, case detection and clinical needs (Sinha, Peters, & Bollinger, 2009). Thus in order to overcome gender disadvantage one has to look beyond merely unidimensional solutions like expanding infrastructure or making the system more physically accessible

Similarly Mohindra discussing the findings of the in-depth action research project involving Paniya groups in Kerala notes "The provision of culturally sensitive health services among indigenous populations require understanding indigenous views on health and illness, their health needs, cultural beliefs and practices and ideally services should be under control of indigenous communities" (Mohindra et al., 2010, p. 492).

The state of Odisha has explicitly adopted health equity into its health policy agenda. A study on the roll out of this policy found that the concept of equity appeared to evaporate at the level of implementation. Studying subsequent policymaking and attempts at actualisation of health equity the author notes that "While equity was prominent in the agenda-setting stage the subsequent stages faced desertion of equity, as comprehensive issues of vulnerable groups are omitted" (Gopalan, Mohanty, & Das, 2011, p. 10). The author further notes that "'actors and contexts' limited the equity approach in the policy process and outcomes on account of (a) information asymmetry among departments, (b) non-willingness or lack of awareness of collective approaches to health, (c) limited experience with decentralisation and involvement of civil society organisations, and (d) multidimensional relationships between mandate of funding agencies and federal and state governments" (Gopalan et al., 2011, p. 8). Path dependence[1] made the translation of innovative approaches into practice difficult. "Context-specific planning was hindered by adherence to overarching national and state agendas, lack of confidence in unconventional approaches, lack of techno-managerial competencies" (Gopalan et al., 2011, p. 6).

System Functioning

A number of studies highlight problems such as poor perceived quality of care, staff absenteeism, lack of reliable supply of drugs and diagnostics. This discourages the more vulnerable groups who are more dependent on the public sector from using public sector health services. They are forced to use the more extractive and costly private sector (Baru et al., 2010; Haddad et al., 2011; Meeta & Lochan, 2010; Pande & Yazbeck, 2003). Other studies also pointed to the fact that after accessing public sector services despite all odds, a lack of integration and poor referral systems meant that the poor died despite reaching a health centre (George, 2007). In addition to these issues the staff present may not be fully trained to respond to people with a variety of special needs (Sinha et al., 2009). However, there are also

---

[1]**Path dependence** means that the way decisions are made at a given point in time is dependent on past decisions made and knowledge trajectory, which in turn influences the competence and knowledge-base of decision-makers. In other words, history matters for current decision-making situations and has a strong influence on strategic planning.

studies, which showed that given political will and committed officers significant reductions can indeed be made through state intervention at scale (Thomas et al., 2015).

Studies also showed that an increased per-capita government expenditure was related to a reduction in inequity (Prinja et al., 2012). The only other clear association of potential determinants was with quality of services. "The results show that the quality is a more significant predictor of utilisation (clinical quality of index $P < 0.001$ and interpersonal quality index $P < 0.001$) of utilisation of antenatal care than access (proximity to public or private facility, which was statistically insignificant) (Rani, Bonu, & Harvey, 2008)".

Meeta also points out that given the dependence of poorer and rural communities on a diverse range of private practitioners, the latter's practices can have a significant effect on those who seek their services (Meeta & Lochan, 2010). Thus in one study it was shown that overall in rural areas 66% prescriptions were irrational. Eighty percent of unlicensed practitioners, 60% of private practitioners and 40% of doctors in the public health system showed irrationality (Bhatnagar et al., 2003). Another study on women's OP visits in Karnataka showed that while private practitioners were more comprehensive in their diagnosis and had a better doctor–patient relationship, they prescribed significantly more unnecessary drugs (Bhatia & Cleland, 2004).

Accountability

Many have pointed out the complete lack of accountability of systems to the people they serve as a key aspect of functioning that contributes to the perpetuating of inequity. Lack of accountability was found in the both the private as well as the public sectors but in quite different ways (Baru et al., 2010). Further, "Bad roads means that the ANM cannot come regularly to the far off villages, that and the fact that she is not formally accountable to the Panchayati Raj institutions means that her work is guided more by the national and state priorities and disease control missions that what the community wants" (Meeta & Lochan, 2010, p. 45).

In a study from Karnataka the author notes that "As observed through multiple review meetings and other kinds of supervision activities, accountability efforts routinely sought scapegoats to allocate blame, rather than attempt to resolve local problems constructively (George, 2007, p. 99)". As observed by the same authors based on another study from the same area, "The end result of the combination of an unaccountable government health system and an unregulated private health system is that women have few qualified providers who can handle obstetric complications. In an emergency, women and their families are forced to run from one provider to the next, often back and forth between government and private providers, all too often without being assured of the services they desperately need (Sen et al., 2007, p. 19)".

The Practitioners in the Health System

While there has been discussion of system—design and functioning highlighting the many issues with the public systems and the unregulated and extractive nature of the private sector—very little research has been done on the practitioners who run the healthcare system, and the determinants of their functioning in situations of health inequity. Little attention has been paid to the inherent inequities of resources, motivations, drivers and policy attention in the public and private sectors. Most articulations of quality for instance lay the blame on frontline health workers, often not factoring in the structures into which frontline workers are embedded. In understanding the ways in which the macro-trends and the policy are translated into systems, one of the crucial dimensions to understand is the way the practitioners respond.

In some early studies, Sen quoted in Dreze notes that the caste composition of practitioners in Southern states is more similar to the groups of people they serve due to the robustness of the caste-based reservations. This was hypothesised to be one of the reasons why there was less perceived alienation of people from the public health system (Visaria, 2000).

Exploring practitioners' responses to national guidelines and especially their deviation from them, a study suggests that the "systems of meaning" (Yanow, 1999) that doctors inhabit, and the gap between these and the logic of public systems and programmes, as a cause for divergent courses of action (Rein & Schon, 1993).

Inadequate Infrastructure

A key aspect of the realities within which practitioners of all levels function is structural inadequacies. It has been noted that "Government health workers in rural areas cope with poor housing conditions, unreliable transport systems, unpredictable drug supplies and inadequate schooling for their children. Notwithstanding the importance of these tangible factors in terms of infrastructure and logistics, less attention is paid by policymakers to the less visible, social experiences of providing primary health services within a government context" (George, 2012, p. 15).

A study looking at the inter-state and intra-state distribution of health workforce compared found that southern and eastern states of India had a significantly higher level of health workforce relative to their share of healthcare infrastructure than other regions. The study also showed that factors such as the presence of all-weather roads connecting the villages and presence of a primary school explained higher presence of health workforce at the district level (Pallikadavath, Singh, Ogollah, Dean, & Stones, 2013). This clearly points to the determinants of health workforce being both within and outside the health system.

Research on the maldistribution of physicians suggests that the Western system of medicine imparted by medical education in our country gives rise to prestige-based hierarchy (Kumar, Jaiswal, Tripathi, Kumar, & Idris, 2007). This would make serving in rural and poorer settings unattractive to medical graduates, contributing to workforce inadequacies in rural and economically disadvantaged areas.

One study reported that in conversations with frontline workers, what was striking was a sense of *exposed vulnerability*. The authors of this study note that "They (frontline workers) make individual adjustments that act as strained safety nets for services that are under-funded and mismanaged at higher levels. Despite having secure government jobs with concomitant bureaucratic entitlements, many health assistants reported being engaged in a losing battle of delivering services with few resources (George, 2012, p. 34)".

Unpredictable Changes in Policy Directions

Tracing the history of the development of policy around the frontline workers category of Auxiliary Nurse Midwives (ANMs) in India, Mavalankar and colleagues note the twists and turns in policy and understanding of the role of the ANM in rural public health services. From the initial focus on safe delivery at home to the primary providers in the family planning programme, to the shift to multi-purpose workers and then the reintroduction as it were of their skilled birth attendance skills, the role of the ANM has undergone numerous changes. The authors have noted that "the programme created a conceptual conflict through its fixed day schedule by giving more priority to routine primary preventive services such as immunisation and family planning, as compared to emergency services such as delivery care and diarrhoea management (which were community priorities) (Mavalankar, Vora, & Sharma, 2010, p. 49)".

The authors conclude by saying "we have shown that despite increases in infrastructure and human resources, shortcuts taken with regards to training, lack of policies supporting career pathways, skewed vertical programming and lack of attention to crucial human resources management issues specific to ANMs have undermined their role in midwifery (Mavalankar et al., 2010, p. 53)". It is safe to say that this sort of policy conflict and lack of understanding can be a crucial determinant of the constraints any frontline worker (and not only the ANM) faces to fulfil his/her tasks.

"Deep Factors" Shaping Health Services

In a study that explores the impact of changes in the health system on doctors working in the public health system, it has been shown that the structural changes in society get reflected at the institutional and individual levels, and plays a crucial role in shaping attitudes, beliefs and values over a period of time. The responses of doctors reveal "the complex interaction between class background, institutional and socio-economic factors that produce changes in values and aspirations" (Baru et al., 2010, p. 94).

The literature on the role of the health system in health inequity in India thus provides a picture of a health system that is actually contributing to the production of inequity, while there are obvious exceptions, there seems to be overall support for this contention. The literature also provides a range of associations/correlations of the axes along which these inequities occur. A few studies also explore in-depth the actual mechanisms at play both at the macro-, institutional and the individual levels that play a role in the creation of this inequity.

In the next section I will offer a critique to some of the key assumption and concepts used in the literature, and before going on to presenting mechanisms that were suggested by the literature in the concluding section, I summarise what this research means overall for the study and tackling of health inequity.

8.3 Critical Synthesis of the Evidence

8.3.1 Methodologies Used by Papers

While the studies documenting the inequities in inpatient, outpatient utilisation and out-of-pocket expenditure, etc. were largely quantitative in nature, the studies looking at the functioning of the health system and at programme design and the macro-factors used a variety of methods including qualitative and case study methods.

The studies used a variety of quantitative methods with the use of regressions including multivariate regression being very common. Overall of the studies using quantitative methods about two-third used regression of some kind, while the remaining one-third constructed concentration indices, and used additional methods like calculating Kakwani Index, Lorenz curves, decomposition analysis, etc.

Most of the quantitative studies reported on utilisation and horizontal inequity—defined as equal care for equal need. There were two broad approaches: one was the exploration of the phenomenon of inequity through the measurement of correlates and identifying various variables that were statistically related to the outcome measure of interest. These studies are really exploring the correlates to the disparities found in a particular phenomenon. The other approach was to use the concentration index to measure the extent of inequity, and then perform other methods like decomposition analysis to explore the determinants of the inequity. In such studies what is studied is the distribution of the outcome of interest and gives a better representation of inequity than does the earlier approach.

A number of approaches were used in the qualitative studies including case study, policy analysis, participatory methods and in-depth ethnography and mixed methods. In the qualitative studies we were able to see authors going beyond statistical associations and engaging with and suggesting mechanisms underlying this inequity. This is probably a direct reflection of the importance of choice of methods used to study health inequities for the type of questions answered.

8.3.2 A Critique of Underlying Concepts and Assumptions Used in the Literature

- Only a small number of papers define access keeping in mind the multi-factorial nature of the concept. Its measurement has been limited to that of utilisation, especially given the limited nature of the variables in large national-level data sets. With very few qualitative studies the multidimensionality of the term could not be explored. In the literature, the nature of the doctor–patient relationship is one of principal agents. Given the enormous differential in information and power between them, any consumption of services is not going to be purely a function of what the agent (the patient) wants. Thus given the large amount of irrational practices documented, the treatment of utilisation as a true reflection of the extent of need (in some papers) and as a reflection of access is problematic.
- Similarly, using the variable "mean length of stay" to show severity of illness is problematic—given the common practice of refusing to discharge unless the full bill is paid, and of hospital delays in completing various investigations, for example.
- One of the underlying assumptions that come across is the uncritical reporting of the pro-poor nature of utilisation of public sector health facilities. While authors have indeed noted that even the poor are moving more and more away from the public health system, the continuing characterisation of the public sector as pro-poor may actually reflect the compulsion of the extremely marginalised to use the only (or cheapest) service available. Another important aspect of this assumption is the need to relate utilisation with health outcomes among the marginalised groups who use these services. Here we find that despite some "pro-poor" tendencies in utilisation data, this is not reflected in inequity gaps in health outcomes. Thus as in the discussion on the terms above there is an almost one-dimensional discussion around these terms. The key aspect of this is that merely increasing access and utilisation of health services—as being indicated by pro-poor trends in services—is not enough to ensure reduction in inequity.
- Another assumption that comes across repeatedly is treating the reduction of inequity along one dimension as the key required outcome. This goes against the assumptions of the Fundamental Cause Theory for example which talks about the fact that unless the fundamental causes (or root causes) like the socio-economic inequity is removed, tinkering with the more superficial mechanisms will only reduce that particular form of inequity, while opening other avenues or dimensions where inequities will be apparent (Phelan et al., 2010).
- In one paper we find the following: "In a context where health insurance is almost non-existent and the population depends on private health care providers to a large extent, households' out-of-pocket health expenditure can be a good reflection of their health care consumption and their effective access to quality health care". As mentioned in points above this completely neglects the principal–agent relationship in the doctor–patient relationship and the extreme

power differential. This ultimately questions the simple assumption that expenditure is a reflection of consumption. Thus one MRI scan (Rs. 8000) for a simple headache will give a very different picture than 15–20 OP visits. Similarly, the literature talks not about the cost of the health care—but the maximum potential expenditure as a better indicator—as many may be able to have one or two OP visits, but much fewer may be able to afford the investigations, and still fewer will be able to afford the investigations and then go back for follow up.

- One of the key assumptions seems to be the acceptance of the inverted U-shaped model of the relationship between access and equity. This basically posits that inequity is inevitable in the face of improvement or expansion of services. This is problematic to say the least. This merely buys into the dominant thinking of inequity merely being a result of the "consumption" of services, and fails to ask the question of what needs to be done by the system to avoid such a situation/pattern.
- There is a tendency to treat a statistical association of measured variables with outcomes as equivalent to causes or mechanisms. This is particularly acutely visible with concentration indices and decomposition analysis as well as in multivariate regression analysis. This is quite different from the school of social mechanisms which draw on the work of Mario Bunge for example. We think that there is a need to focus on and study mechanisms rather than only look at statistical associations.

8.3.3 Mechanisms

In this section I attempt to read across the literature and summarise some of the key processes that seem to explain the trends and patterns that emerge. Some of these were hinted to by the authors, while some of them are being lifted up by a perspective of healthcare services that I presented in the first section. This list is more in terms of suggested mechanisms and obviously, more research is needed to establish these. These mechanisms are being presented as a way of looking forward to the type of research that we feel in key to not merely explain health inequities, but contribute to actually changing them in the real world.

Listing the mechanisms reveals that the mechanisms in fact are playing out at different hierarchical levels in a systems perspective. While some are relevant to the individual level, some are playing out at the collective action or community level, while some are playing out at the constitutive level (Ostrom, Cox, Schlager, & Schlager, 2014).

Among the mechanisms that emerge from looking at the literature as a whole, some stand out:

- *Systematic starvation of the public health system while encouraging an unregulated private sector.* A number of studies have pointed out that the public systems are being systematically starved of funds and that the private sector is being encouraged to fill in the gaps; however, this growth is happening in a completely unregulated and haphazard manner (Jayal, 1994). This is leading to a situation in which the institutional mechanism that is meant to protect the poor is in fact being systematically destroyed. This is linked to the twin goals of fiscal management and privatisation of the neo-liberal paradigm of development (Pal & Ghosh, 2007). Thus it is clear that macro- policies not only lead to a restriction of expenditure on the social sector, but do so in such a way that the poor and marginalised who are most dependent on it (and which is the only service they can afford) are the most affected. On the flip side, it has been shown that there is an association between higher government per-capita expenditure and lower inequity (Prinja et al., 2012). *It is obvious from these two points that the decreased investment in the public health sector in the face of increasing insecurity in livelihoods and precariousness in incomes, could have had a direct role in the fuelling of inequity to a significant extent.*
- *The fragmentation of the market.* The emergence of a fragmented market in health care with a clear division into a systematically weakened public sector and a haphazardly developed and unregulated private sector, a direct outcome of the path of development of healthcare services that the Indian state has chosen to follow. This fragmentation means that the public sector is no longer able to effectively play the safety net role it was originally supposed to. Fragmentation has numerous potential implications for equity, through the following scenarios. The middle class moves from patronising the public health system to the private sector and this entails that those with a voice in society today had moved away from the public sector. Further it is well known that if a dominant ethnic group does not perceive a benefit from the system they would not agree to allot resources to it (Sengupta & Sarkar, 2007). Further by allowing the private sector to become the dominant sector (by allowing unregulated growth) it lays down the benchmarks rather than the public sector and this entails the aping of the irrationalities and the commodification of medicine that mark the private sector. Also the private sector by virtue of access to resources is able to lure away human resources from the public sector—thus in way getting subsidised by it. This also means that the private sector is in fact feeding off the public sector. *The mechanism here refers to the way in which the fragmentation of the healthcare delivery services into a weak public sector and a strong private sector contributes to the production of inequity in health.*
- *Political commitment/path dependence/historical development.* This mechanism is essentially about "path dependence" that notes that system that worked better in the past work better in the future (Mukherjee & Levesque, 2010). This is not a fatalistic or cynical perspective but borrows from systems thinking. The key

lesson is that one cannot hope to understand the present functioning of the system without understanding its history. The key relevance to understanding mechanisms of inequity is that while most studies look at cross-sectional snapshots to understand the particular balance of forces, *there is the need for a historical perspective in order to truly understand the emergence of inequity over time and as it is in the present moment.* The study of Odisha is the most revealing in this context, documenting how a commitment to reducing inequity and the translation of this commitment into a number of approaches actually led to the decrease in inequity among the Adivasis in Odisha (Thomas et al., 2015).

- *The impact of macro-changes on the health system personnel.* Studies that have looked at the healthcare personnel and their responses to the various macro-forces have shown that the infrastructural erosion has negatively impacted upon health workers' ability to provide services (George, 2012), and the fragmentation may also have significant impact on their motivation and commitment to serve the underprivileged (Baru et al., 2010). Thus is it safe to suggest that *these macro-level forces not only have a negative impact on the infrastructure of the public sector but also on the ability of those working within the private sector to provide quality services to those from the poorest and most marginalised backgrounds who are the prime users of the public sector and for whom there are few other choices.*
- *Design issues*—A number of studies point to how the policies and programmes evolved and implemented are invariably not sensitive to the special needs of the groups that it aims to protect in the first place. This is highlighted in the examples of the paniyas (Mohindra et al., 2010), and the example of HIV testing (Sinha et al., 2009). While the exact reasons for these design issues are not fully expounded their presence along the axes of caste, class, gender (Sen et al., 2007) and the suffering from particular stigmatising diseases like HIV (Sinha et al., 2009) *suggest that the health system is not sensitive to the needs of the most marginalised and is not designed keeping their special needs in mind.*
- A number of studies point out to the *non-financial barriers* as key to explaining inequity in access and utilisation. In an interesting insight two studies identify the slightly less vulnerable groups as being the most able to take advantage of newly introduced programmes (Rao et al., 2014; Sen & Iyer, 2012). *The hypothesis is that while those who are not the most vulnerable or broadly the middle groups have some resources to tap into either in terms of material, social or cultural that in some way minimise or neutralises their disadvantage*, those who are the most vulnerable have little resources to fall back on. This is supported by the research documented here where girls/women are less likely to begin treatment, to continue treatment and are more likely to drop out of treatment and of immunisation compared to men/boys (Pande & Yazbeck, 2003), the research on the way access to economic resources modifies the effects of belonging to a particular social group (Roy & Chaudhuri, 2008; Sen et al., 2007). One study at least documents this by showing that when there are no services there is relative equity (with neither the poor or the rich benefiting), but that the moment there is an expansion in the services the rich benefit the first,

thus leading to an increase in inequity. The study suggests that only when the services expand to such an extent that it is well spread out and that not too many resources are needed to access them does the inequity start decreasing (Oster, 2009). However, this was disputed by another study (Gaudin & Yazbeck, 2006). In summary *while there is enough evidence that non-financial barriers are crucial to access among the poorest, the mere expansion of public services has not been shown to have a uniform effect in reducing these inequities.*

- At the health system level (and in public systems in general) research has suggested that those services that required a one off and clearly objective and measurable output (like the construction of water tank), etc., or that have high political commitment behind them are likely to be provided in a more equitable fashion (Mohan, 2005).
- Studies have also shown that at the health system level, the usual accountability measures may not have very much effect given that the social hierarchies continue to play within the health system settings. This has been studied extensively and in-depth in the field of gender, where based on extensive work in rural Northern Karnataka, George, Iyer and Sen have described the way gender plays out in health system through two broad mechanisms—failures of acknowledgement (discussed in the next point) and failures of accountability. It is only if healthcare personnel go out of their ways to be sensitive to these social disadvantages, or alternatively the system allows for the more marginalised to have a voice and indeed encourages it, *traditional accountability mechanisms are unlikely to benefit the more marginalised groups* (George, Iyer, & Sen, 2005; Sen et al., 2007).
- *Failures of acknowledgment*, this plays out by the systemic and indeed social underplaying of women's needs. But the authors point out that this socially existent bias is institutionalised, "into indifference in health systems through the design of budget lines, suspension systems, staffing patterns, drug allocations, training curricula etc." Within this broad mechanism the authors describe two other mechanisms which are named as "Bias through illegitimacy" and "Bias through institutional indifference". While bias through illegitimacy is basically the undervaluing of women's perceptions, priorities and expectations and meanings by those within the health system, bias through institutional indifference includes such issues as the relative neglect of preventive services in the health programme, as the authors note, "thus providers are held accountable for the distribution of iron tablets but not for the outcomes". Apart from this the persistent mismatch between the funds needed for a programme to actually work and cover all those intended to be covered and what is actually allocated, and the persistent danger of corruption at all levels in the healthcare system and its neglect by higher officials are all seen as reflections of this indifference (George et al., 2005).
- Another general mechanism links the reduced perception or expressed perception of illness as a possible cause of accessing healthcare services and utilising them to a lesser extent. Thus studies of the Paniya showed lesser perceived morbidity (though showing worse health in terms of objective measures) (Haddad et al., 2011). Similarly, Gita Sen and colleagues showed that women tended to seek care much later in the illness (Sen et al., 2007); this was reiterated

by the study of the Arvind Eye Hospital too (Jayaraman et al., 2014). Thus various pathways leading to the decreased perception/expressed perception seem to be playing a role. Towards this there are two explanations—one is the cognitive or perception bias as described by Amartya Sen, and the other is that the lack of resources, or the lack of control over resources leads to the more marginalised groups to underplay their illnesses and health needs.

- *The perception bias of Amartya Sen.* Some have suggested that increasing costs of care could push the poor not to consider themselves sick. This under-reporting tendency, also found in various developing countries, could result in the underestimation of disparities in access. While this basically talks about costs of care, there are a number of possibilities that come to mind. Thus the Paniyas under-reporting need for health care can be linked not only to costs of care (huge and impoverishing as they are) but equally to the fact that the Paniyas as a group have accessed a very poor quality healthcare system and generations of being excluded may well have contributed to this "perception bias (Haddad et al., 2011; Mohindra et al., 2010)". Similarly when Jayaraman talks about the fact that the women have worse diagnosis on presentation, but that this is not so for men, she is essentially pointing to gendered mechanism where resources are available (going for a check-up), but once an illness is detected, the women's issues are prioritised less than other competing priorities in the house and the women try to push accessing health care to the last possible moment (Jayaraman et al., 2014). It is thus clear that *a number of factors including perceived cost of treatment, and other socially ingrained perspectives contribute to the poor and marginalised underestimating or underplaying their need for health care.*

The above set of suggested mechanisms was derived from reading across the literature as mentioned above. It is easy to discern that each of the mechanisms is actually playing out at a different systemic level—while mechanisms 1–3 refer to macro-level factors that impinge on the health systems, mechanisms 4 through 10 refer to processes acting within health systems, that impact their functioning and thus their ability to respond to the needs of the most marginalised, the mechanism discussed in point 11 focuses on processes at the individual level. While there is obviously need to further research, confirm and further delineate these mechanisms, it is important to point out some gaps too. Thus the reasons for the persistence of decrease in funding despite evidence of harm to the population—this points to the influence of the larger neo-liberal forces, and in spite of the evidence of increasing inequity are not researched. Similarly, the other gap is the lack of work on the way these political commitments are translated into the actual institutional and programme design. Another key issue not explored in these studies is the question of capabilities/health production functions of marginalised groups, and what determines these and what are the roles of various institutions to compensate for these. In other words most studies stop at identifying barriers to access and utilise health services, while no studies (except the work of the Koppal group and other work on gender) actually explored the ability to benefit from these institutional arrangements.

8.3.4 What Emerges from the Above Reading of the Literature

- Inequity is being studied as individual components at different levels, with trends being studied of that particular component rather than across components. Thus while there is a study of inequity in utilisation over time, and geography, there is no linking of this with larger trends in mortality, in general. Inequity in a particular indicator being the focus rather than the larger level driving factors. Inequity as being not static, but dynamic across time and space.
- Given the nature of the data sets available inequity is reduced to the consumption of a set of services/interventions, rather than being seen as the complex multidimensional concept it is. Thus many of the studies point to factors such as lack of awareness, illiteracy, etc., which ultimately leads to victim blaming. There is no attempt at actually revealing the underlying design of these systems and thus seeing inequity as a designed outcome rather than a mistake. Thus the fact that the public sector is poorly functioning or has poor quality cannot be separated from the fact that it is being systematically starved of funds.
- Given the largely quantitative nature of studies the most authors seem to do is hypothesise on correlations or suggest mechanisms, with little empiric work on the establishing of mechanisms themselves. Despite this I have been able to collect an impressive set of mechanisms that were both implicitly and explicitly present in the literature. The lack of empiric work of this kind may reflect not only the limitations of the data sets, but also probably reflects the way in which inequity is being conceptualised and discussed.
- There is an overall lack of theory-driven research that draws on the rich diversity of frameworks that have been used in the study of inequity. Some of these are referred to in Chap. 2 of this book. This needs to be overcome urgently if the research is to contribute to possible strategies for change.
- There is need to study the intersectional reality—which is not even alluded to in most papers. Despite the advances in the discourse on intersectionality—the simultaneous study of many axes in one person—there is little reflection of this trend in the studies reviewed. All studies (barring a few exceptions) seem to study and conceptualise inequity in a unidimensional way. This leads to a false fragmentation of reality and possibly missing key aspects of inequity that could help us get a deeper understanding.
- While most studies derive explanatory variables there is little attempt to go beyond this to see what sustains the health system and justifies the continuation of such an iniquitous system. Thus one of the important questions that need to be explained is how and why inequity is being tolerated even as it is present and growing. What are the mechanisms through such an inequity creating system is being propped up? Given the lack of larger level conceptualisation of inequity, these questions are hardly discussed by the literature.

References

Balarajan, Y., Selvaraj, S., & Subramanian, S. V. (2011). Health care and equity in India. *The Lancet, 377*(9764), 505–515.

Balasubramanian, P., & Ravindran, T. K. S. (2012). Pro-poor maternity benefit schemes and rural women findings from Tamil Nadu. *Economic & Political Weekly, 47*(25), 19–22.

Baru, R., Acharya, A., Acharya, S., Kumar, A. S., & Nagaraj, K. (2010). Inequities in access to health services in India: Caste, class and region. *Economic & Political Weekly*, 49–58.

Bhatia, J., & Cleland, J. (2004). Health care of female outpatients in South-central India: Comparing public and private sector provision. *Health Policy and Planning, 19*(6), 402–409.

Bhatnagar, T., Mishra, C. P., & Mishra, R. N. (2003). Drug prescription practices: A household study in rural Varanasi. *Indian Journal of Preventive and Social Medicine, 34*(1), 33–39.

Commission on Social Determinants of Health. (2008). *Closing the gap in a generation: Health equity through action on the social determinants of health: Final report of the Commission on Social Determinants of Health*. Geneva: World Health Organization. Retrieved from http://apps.who.int/iris/handle/10665/43943.

Culyer, A. J. (2016). Equality and Equity. *The encyclopaedia of global bioethics* (pp. 1–11). New York: Springer.

Daniels, N. (1982). Equity of access to health care: Some conceptual and ethical issues. *The Milbank Memorial Fund Quarterly Health and Society*, 51–81.

Freedman, L. P. (2005). Achieving the MDGs: Health systems as core social institutions. *Development, 48*(1), 19–24.

Freese, J., & Lutfey, K. (2011). Fundamental causality: Challenges of an animating concept for medical sociology. In B. A. Pescosolido, J. K. Martin, J. D. McLeod, & A. Rogers (Eds.), *Handbook of the sociology of health, illness, and healing* (pp. 67–81). New York: Springer. Retrieved from http://link.springer.com/10.1007/978-1-4419-7261-3_4.

Gadre, A., & Shukla, A. (2016). *Dissenting diagnosis* (Latest edition). Gurgaon (India): Penguin Random House.

Gaitonde, R. (2015). Tamil Nadu a critical engagement. In I. Qadeer (Ed.), *India: Social development report 2014: Challenges of public health* (pp. 113–123). New Delhi: Oxford University Press.

Garg, C. C. (1998). *Equity of health sector financing and delivery in India* (pp. 1–47). Mimeo: Cambridge (USA): Harvard School of Public Health.

Gaudin, S., & Yazbeck, A. S. (2006). Immunisation in India 1993–1999: Wealth, gender, and regional inequalities revisited. *Social Science and Medicine, 62*(3), 694–706.

George, A. (2007). Persistence of high maternal mortality in Koppal district, Karnataka, India: Observed service delivery constraints. *Reproductive Health Matters, 15*(30), 91–102.

George, A. (2012). Government rural health assistants as social beings. In K. Sheikh & A. George (Eds.), *Health providers in India: On the frontlines of change* (pp. 15–37). Retrieved from https://books.google.co.in/books?hl=en&lr=&id=6uHfCgAAQBAJ&oi=fnd&pg=PA15&dq=Government+Rural+Health+Assistants+as+Social+Beings&ots=hY31_fXMkR&sig=SwMwLHqHPvtrY2I06tgEXq7illY.

George, A., Iyer, A., & Sen, G. (2005). *Gendered health systems biased against maternal survival: Preliminary findings from Koppal, Karnataka, India*. Retrieved from https://opendocs.ids.ac.uk/opendocs/handle/123456789/4046.

Ghosh, S. (2014). Equity in the utilisation of healthcare services in India: Evidence from National Sample Survey. *International Journal of Health Policy and Management, 2*(1), 29–38.

Gilson, L., Doherty, J., Loewenson, R., & Francis, V. (2007). *Challenging inequity through health systems*. Final report of the knowledge network on health systems. Retrieved from http://cdrwww.who.int/entity/social_determinants/resources/csdh_media/hskn_final_2007_en.pdf.

Gopalan, S. S., Mohanty, S., & Das, A. (2011). Challenges and opportunities for policy decisions to address health equity in developing health systems: Case study of the policy processes in the Indian state of Orissa. *International Journal for Equity in Health, 10*(1), 55.

Haddad, S., Narayana, D., & Mohindra, K. S. (2011). Reducing inequalities in health and access to health care in a rural Indian community: An India-Canada collaborative action research project. *BMC International Health and Human Rights, 11*(2), S3.
Jain, A. K. (2010). Janani Suraksha Yojana and the maternal mortality ratio. *Economic & Political Weekly, 45*(11), 15–16.
Jayal, N. G. (1994). The gentle leviathan: Welfare and the Indian state. *Social Scientist*, 18–26.
Jayal, N. G. (1999). The Gentle Leviathan: Welfare and the Indian state. In M. Rao (Ed.), Disinvesting in India: World Bank's prescriptions for health. New Delhi: Sage Publications.
Jayaraman, R., Ray, D., & Wang, S.-Y. (2014). Engendered access Or engendered care? Evidence from a major Indian hospital1. *Economic & Political Weekly, 49*(25), 47–53.
Kim, J. Y., Millen, J. V., Irwin, A., & Gershman, J. (2000). *Dying for growth: Global inequalities and the health of the poor*. Retrieved from https://repository.library.georgetown.edu/handle/10822/930075.
Krieger, N. (2011). Ecosocial theory of disease distribution: Embodying societal & ecologic context. *Epidemiology and the People's Health: Theory and Context*. New York: Oxford University Press, Chapter 7.
Kumar, R., Jaiswal, V., Tripathi, S., Kumar, A., & Idris, M. Z. (2007). Inequity in health care delivery in India: The problem of rural medical practitioners. *Health Care Analysis, 15*(3), 223–233.
Levesque, J.-F., Haddad, S., Narayana, D., & Fournier, P. (2006). Outpatient care utilisation in urban Kerala, India. *Health Policy and Planning, 21*(4), 289–301.
Lister, J. (2013). *Health policy reform: Global health versus private profit*. Libri Publishing.
Loeppky, R. (2010). Certain wealth: Accumulation in the health industry. In L. Panitch & C. Leys (Eds.), *Morbid symptoms: Hesalth under capitalism* (pp. 59–83). Retrieved from http://socialistregister.com/index.php/srv/article/view/6764.
Mavalankar, D., Vora, K., & Sharma, B. (2010). The midwifery role of the auxiliary nurse midwife. In K. Sheikh & A. George (Eds.), *Health providers in India: On the frontlines of change* (pp. 38–56). Retrieved from https://books.google.co.in/books?hl=en&lr=&id=aAFzJWe8aH8C&oi=fnd&pg=PA38&dq=The+Midwifery+role+of+the+Auxiliary+Nurse+Midwife.&ots=keYFfqPGz-&sig=zCZJYiq6zqMfm6jA_2LAnBjojDY.
Meeta, & Lochan, R. (2010). Inequities in health, agrarian distress and a policy of avoidance. *Economic & Political Weekly*, 41–47.
Mohan, P. (2005). Inequities in coverage of preventive child health interventions: the rural drinking water supply programme and the universal immunisation programme in Rajasthan, India. *American Journal of Public Health, 95*(2), 241–244.
Mohindra, K. S., Narayana, D., & Haddad, S. (2010). 'My story is like a goat tied to a hook'. Views from a marginalised tribal group in Kerala (India) on the consequences of falling ill: A participatory poverty and health assessment. *Journal of Epidemiology and Community Health, 64*(6), 488–494.
Mukherjee, S., Haddad, S., & Narayana, D. (2011). Social class related inequalities in household health expenditure and economic burden: Evidence from Kerala, South India. *International Journal for Equity in Health, 10*(1), 1.
Mukherjee, S., & Levesque, J.-F. (2010). Changing inequalities in utilisation of inpatient care in rural India: Evidence from the NSS. *Economic & Political Weekly*, 84–91.
Mondal, S. (2013). *Health care services in India: A few questions on equity*. Retrieved from http://file.scirp.org/Html/8-8201834_26520.htm.
Oster, E. (2009). Does increased access increase equality? Gender and child health investments in India. *Journal of Development Economics, 89*(1), 62–76.
Ostrom, E., Cox, M., Schlager, E., & Schlager, E. (2014). An assessment of the institutional analysis and development framework and introduction of the social-ecological systems framework. In P. A. Sabatier & C. M. Weible (Eds.), *Theories of the policy process*. Philadelphia: Westview Press.
Pal, P., & Ghosh, J. (2007). Inequality in India: A survey of recent trends. New York: United Nations, Department of Economic and Social Affairs, Working paper no. 45. Retrieved from http://www.chereum.umontreal.ca/activites_pdf/Session%201/Inequality%20in%20India%20(1).pdf.

Pallikadavath, S., Singh, A., Ogollah, R., Dean, T., & Stones, W. (2013). Human resource inequalities at the base of India's public health care system. *Health & Place, 23,* 26–32.
Pande, R. P., & Yazbeck, A. S. (2003). What's in a country average? Wealth, gender, and regional inequalities in immunisation in India. *Social Science and Medicine, 57*(11), 2075–2088.
Penchansky, R., & Thomas, J. W. (1981). The concept of access: Definition and relationship to consumer satisfaction. *Medical Care, 19*(2), 127–140.
Phelan, J. C., Link, B. G., & Tehranifar, P. (2010). Social conditions as fundamental causes of health inequalities theory, evidence, and policy implications. *Journal of Health and Social Behavior, 51*(1 suppl), S28–S40.
Prinja, S., Kanavos, P., & Kumar, R. (2012). Health care inequities in north India: Role of public sector in universalizing health care. *Indian Journal of Medical Research, 136*(3), 421.
Prinja, S., Kumar, M. I., Pinto, A. D., Jan, S., & Kumar, R. (2013). Equity in hospital services utilisation in India. *Economic & Political Weekly, 48*(12), 52–58.
Purohit, B. C. (2001). Private initiatives and policy options: Recent health system experience in India. *Health Policy and Planning, 16*(1), 87–97.
Randive, B., San Sebastian, M., De Costa, A., & Lindholm, L. (2014). Inequalities in institutional delivery uptake and maternal mortality reduction in the context of cash incentive programme, Janani Suraksha Yojana: Results from nine states in India. *Social Science and Medicine, 123,* 1–6.
Rani, M., Bonu, S., & Harvey, S. (2008). Differentials in the quality of antenatal care in India. *International Journal for Quality in Health Care, 20*(1), 62–71.
Rao, M., Katyal, A., Singh, P. V., Samarth, A., Bergkvist, S., Kancharla, M., ... Renton, A. (2014). Changes in addressing inequalities in access to hospital care in Andhra Pradesh and Maharashtra states of India: A difference-in-differences study using repeated cross-sectional surveys. *BMJ Open, 4*(6), e004471.
Ravindran, T. K. S. (2012). Universal access: Making health systems work for women. *BMC Public Health, 12*(1), S4.
Rein, M., & Schon, D. (1993). Reframing policy discourse. In F. Fischer & J. Forester (Eds.) *The argumentative turn in policy analysis and planning* (pp. 145–166). London: Duke University Press. Retrieved from http://www.citeulike.org/group/14168/article/8040014.
Roy, K., & Chaudhuri, A. (2008). Influence of socioeconomic status, wealth and financial empowerment on gender differences in health and healthcare utilisation in later life: Evidence from India. *Social Science and Medicine, 66*(9), 1951–1962.
Roy, K., & Howard, D. H. (2007). Equity in out-of-pocket payments for hospital care: Evidence from India. *Health Policy, 80*(2), 297–307.
Sabde, Y., De Costa A., & Diwan, V. A. (2014). Spatial analysis to study access to emergency obstetric transport services under the public private "Janani Express Yojana" program in two districts of Madhya Pradesh, India. *Reprod Health [Internet], 11,* 57. Available from http://www.ncbi.nlm.nih.gov/pubmed/25048795.
Saxena, K. B. (2010). *Health policy and reforms: Governance in primary healthcare* (1st ed.). Delhi: Aakar Books.
Schneider, A. L., Ingram, H., & Deleon, P. (2014). Democratic policy design: Social construction of target populations. In P. A. Sabatier & C. M. Weible (Eds.), *Theories of the policy process* 3, 105–149.
Selvaraj, S., & Karan, A. K. (2009). Deepening health insecurity in India: Evidence from national sample surveys since 1980s. *Economic & Political Weekly, 44*(40), 55–60.
Sen, A. (1992). *Inequality reexamined.* Clarendon Press. Retrieved from https://books.google.com/books?hl=en&lr=&id=D6_eCtTK6-oC&oi=fnd&pg=PA1&dq=A+Sen+1992&ots=GL_SrFAGIG&sig=j7mXW-L_hWLFzDYhcACRcCcIPjs.
Sen, G., & Iyer, A. (2012). Who gains, who loses and how: Leveraging gender and class intersections to secure health entitlements. *Social Science and Medicine, 74*(11), 1802–1811.
Sen, G., Iyer, A., & George, A. (2007). Systematic Hierarchies and systemic failures: Gender and health inequities in Koppal District. *Economic & Political Weekly*, 682–690.
Sengupta, J., & Sarkar, D. (2007). Discrimination in ethnically fragmented localities: A study on public good provision in West Bengal. *Economic & Political Weekly*, 3313–3321.

Shengelia, B., Murray, C. J., & Adams, O. B. (2003). Beyond access and utilisation: Defining and measuring health system coverage. In C. J. L. Murray & D. B. Evans (Eds.), *Health systems performance assessment: Debates, methods and empiricism*. Geneva: World Health Organization (pp. 221–34). Retrieved from https://books.google.co.in/books?hl=en&lr=&id=Ut_xcxWHobYC&oi=fnd&pg=PA221&dq=Beyond+access+and+utilisation:+defining+and+measuring+health+system+coverage.&ots=jh4Cb8XUPn&sig=E0EGhmilNJVGYU6IgGWjOmSA0eY.

Sinha, G., Peters, D. H., & Bollinger, R. C. (2009). Strategies for gender-equitable HIV services in rural India. *Health Policy and Planning, 24*(3), 197–208.

Sivaramakrishnan, A. (2011). *Public policy and citizenship: Battling managerialism in India*. SAGE India.

Thomas, D., Sarangi, B. L., Garg, A., Ahuja, A., Meherda, P., Karthikeyan, S. R., … others. (2015). Closing the health and nutrition gap in Odisha, India: A case study of how transforming the health system is achieving greater equity. *Social Science and Medicine, 145*, 154–162.

Visaria, L. (2000). "Innovations in Tamil Nadu." Unhealthy Trends: A Symposium on the State of our Public Health System. Retrieved from http://www.indiaseminar.com/2000.489.htm.2000.

Waters, H. R. (2000). Measuring equity in access to health care. *Social Science and Medicine, 51*(4), 599–612.

World Health Organization. (2000). *The world health report 2000: Health systems: Improving performance*. Geneva: WHO. Retrieved from https://books.google.co.in/books?hl=en&lr=&id=luqgKK2euxoC&oi=fnd&pg=PR7&dq=The+World+Health+Report+2000+Health+ystems:+Improving+Performance&ots=sLq3657DYb&sig=RARHCatzUrxiamdCcNXmbqK1rts.

Yanow, D. (1999). *Conducting interpretive policy analysis* (*Vol. 47*). Thousand Oaks (USA): Sage Publications. Retrieved from https://books.google.co.in/books?hl=en&lr=&id=WWHWCQAAQBAJ&oi=fnd&pg=PR5&dq=Conducting+interpretive+policy+analysis&ots=PhsNmWKwpF&sig=pH1tzA_Ek9fUbpgYOJBVMccOq4w.

Chapter 9
Health Equity Research: A Political Project

T.K. Sundari Ravindran, Rakhal Gaitonde, Prashanth Nuggehalli Srinivas, Sudharshini Subramaniam, Priyadarshini Chidambaram and Grace A. Chitra

Abstract In the first section of this concluding chapter we present highlights from the syntheses of research on health inequities in India and a critique of the limitations of this evidence. Health equity research in India is clearly at an early and formative stage. There is a large body of literature around the patterns of health inequities along several axes, but for this literature to mature into actionable knowledge, and result in the implementation of meaningful policies, programmes and interventions, there is still a long way to go. Section 9.2 seeks to make meaning of the evidence through an attempt to weave the various strands of explanations presented in the literature together into a coherent approach for researching health inequities. It identifies the *Coleman's boat* that helps organise various social mechanisms; the institutional focus and the intersectional lens as critical components to any approach that attempts to engage with the complex phenomena of health inequities in a meaningful fashion. The concept of embodiment, which

T.K.S. Ravindran (✉)
Achutha Menon Centre for Health Science Studies, Sree Chitra Tirunal Institute for Medical Sciences and Technology, Thiruvananthapuram 695011, India
e-mail: ravindransundari@gmail.com

R. Gaitonde
Centre for Technology and Policy (CTaP) IIT-M, Chennai, India
e-mail: rakhal.gaitonde@gmail.com

P.N. Srinivas
Faculty at the Institute of Public Health, Bangalore, India
e-mail: prashanth.ns@gmail.com

S. Subramaniam
Institute of Community Medicine, Madras Medical College, Chennai, India
e-mail: sudharshini.subramaniam90@gmail.com

P. Chidambaram
M S Ramaiah Medical College, Bengaluru 560054, India
e-mail: cpdarshini@yahoo.com

G.A. Chitra
Global Institute of Public Health, Ananthapuri Hospitals and Research Institute, Chacka, Thiruvananthapuram 695024, Kerala, India
e-mail: achitragrace@gmail.com

T.K.S. Ravindran and R. Gaitonde (eds.), *Health Inequities in India*,
https://doi.org/10.1007/978-981-10-5089-3_9

makes the link between institutions and individual bodies, is an integral part of such an approach. Section 9.3 draws on this to suggest our thoughts on what needs to be done differently in health equity research, to make a tangible impact, especially on those affected the most.

Keywords Health inequities · Research gaps · Coleman's boat Embodiment · Intersectionality · Institutions · Mechanisms

9.1 Introduction

This book was motivated by a desire to engage with and draw attention to critical gaps in public health research on health inequities in India; and to highlight the urgent need for sustained engagement by the public health research community in generating knowledge that can inform policy change and social action. We have done this through synthesising recent public health literature on this subject. We have also examined the extent to which the current evidence base provides an understanding of the underlying mechanisms and pathways, so that entry points may be identified for mitigating or addressing health inequities.

The first section of this concluding chapter presents highlights from the syntheses of research on health inequities in India and a critique of the limitations of this evidence. Section 9.2 seeks to make meaning of the evidence through an attempt to weave the various strands together into a coherent approach for researching health inequities. Section 9.3 draws on this to suggest our thoughts on what needs to be done differently in health equity research, in order to make a tangible impact, especially on those affected the most.

9.1.1 What Does the Evidence Tell Us About Inequities in Health in India and Its Drivers?

The evidence confirms that there are significant inequities in health in India by socio-economic position, among the Dalit and Adivasi communities compared to other social groups, by gender and among other socially constructed vulnerable groups such as Persons Living with HIV and AIDS and internal migrants. Inequities were found across a wide range of health indicators such as child and adult survival, morbidity, nutritional status and preventive and curative healthcare services. In addition to inequitable coverage and access, there were also inequities in the quality of services provided and in the coverage of populations by social protection schemes for health. Health inequities have persisted during the period of rapid economic growth since the 1990s, and in some instances and for some health indicators, the gap has in fact widened.

Many hypotheses have been put forth by authors to explain the existence of health inequities. Son preference, restrictions on women's autonomy and intimate partner violence emerge as key explanations for health inequities by sex and gender. It may be noted that such an approach identifies the reason for the health gap as located within the household. We did not find any studies on the role of gender discrimination in healthcare settings, gender-role stereotyping or of gender-blindness in health programmes and policies in creating and maintaining health inequities.

Inequities by Dalit or Adivasi status are often attributed to the concentration of poverty and poor educational status among these groups. While this is true to some extent, it is inadequate as the sole explanation. Being a Dalit or an Adivasi is found to be an independent determinant of health inequities even after controlling for other socio-demographic and economic variables. The evidence suggests two possible reasons. One is capability poverty among Dalit and Adivasi households arising from their historical disadvantages, which constrains their ability to translate an adequate income into significantly improved health. The second is overt discrimination in service delivery settings and by health and social service providers, which results either in reluctance to access services, or in poorer quality of services accessed.

Stigma and discrimination not only in service delivery settings but in the society at large is the main route to compromised well-being and poorer access to services among Persons Living with HIV and AIDS, while for internal migrants it is one of many factors contributing to their vulnerability, alongside displacement, insecure livelihoods and cultural and language barriers.

The role of multiple and simultaneous disadvantages in health inequities is a recurrent finding across many studies. Thus, not all girls or women, and not all Dalit and Adivasi persons experience the same kind of disadvantages: Dalit and Adivasi women have much poorer survival chances than other women, and poorer Dalit children have a many-fold higher prevalence of morbidity than their well-off counterparts. This is all the more true in the case of PLHA and internal migrants, among whom vulnerability based on HIV or migrant status is overlaid on other socially constructed vulnerabilities such class, Dalit or Adivasi status and gender.

The public health system has failed to fulfil its expected role of protecting the poor and marginalised from inequities induced by the market mechanism. In fact, it seems that the public health system is a major contributor to reproducing rather than mitigating health inequities in India. Decades of under-investment in the public sector has rendered it weak and dysfunctional, while the increasingly explicit policy support combined with lack of regulation has led to the emergence of a powerful private sector with considerable policy clout. There was maldistribution of public healthcare services in the country disadvantaging poorer regions and localities. In addition, there were major structural inadequacies such as poor infrastructure, equipments and inadequate human resources. The design of health programmes seemed to be determined by administrative convenience and not by the needs of the user. This is best illustrated by the location of ART services in district hospitals and not at the Primary Health Centre, requiring ailing patients to undertake long journeys to receive free treatment. Descriptions of extreme callousness and abuse of women PLHA in heath facilities in study after study calls to question the core values of the public health system and its accountability to the community it is meant to serve. When the public health system, aimed at providing affordable healthcare malfunctions, it would hurt the most disadvantaged in society more than others. Rather than expand availability, access to and affordability of health care through sustained public investment in health, the country has witnessed stagnant or declining public investment in health.

Although not stated explicitly, the influence of neo-liberal economic policies on health inequities may be deduced from this body of evidence. Widening economic inequalities in India have had an influence on health inequities. Inequities in health across various axes have persisted since the 1990s, the era of economic liberalisation. For some health indicators and in some states of India, the health gaps between urban and rural areas and between the non-poor and the poor, and Dalits/Adivasis versus others have widened. In other words, economic progress and the health benefits that have accrued from it have disproportionately benefited those who were already privileged. Caste and gender-based discrimination have not abated with increasing prosperity, and continue to determine a person's chances of survival and well-being. Jobless growth in the Indian economy in the past decades has had a wide impact, including on internal migration and trafficking, increasing vulnerability to poverty and poor health.

Equity-oriented state policies can make a significant difference to bridging the gap in health status. It has been observed that individuals of the same socio-economic position were less likely to be undernourished or over-nourished if they lived in a more egalitarian area as compared to a less egalitarian one (Subramanian, Kawachi, & Smith, 2007), through state policies that supported food security. Barring a few exceptions, there is lack of political support for public funding and provisioning of health care, education and social protection, and for legislations supporting affirmative action in favour of vulnerable populations (e.g. PLHAs and internal migrants). Even where a policy commitment to equity was made, it tended to evaporate as it proceeded from the drawing board to the ground (Gopalan, Mohanty, & Das, 2011). Elite capture of policy space could be an important explanation for the persistence of health inequities at a time of economic growth and prosperity.

There is much that we do not know anything about. The lack of research on entire population groups and health issues is itself a significant contributor to the perpetuation of health inequities. To give just a few examples, health equity research on Dalit and Adivasi populations is especially sparse; other under-represented groups include children 6–10 years of age, men of all ages and the elderly. Public health research on communicable and non-communicable diseases and mental health and injury in India has not engaged adequately with issues of equity. Other socially constructed vulnerabilities such as disabilities, stigmatising diseases, non-conforming gender identities and sexual orientation are all neglected areas of research. Appendix to this chapter presents a more detailed picture on the content gaps in health equity research in India.

The next section presents a critical overview of the nature of research on health inequities in India.

9.1.2 Limitations of the Current Evidence on Health Inequities in India

Health equity research in India is clearly at an early and formative stage. There is a large body of literature around the patterns of health inequities along several axes, but for this literature to mature into actionable knowledge, and result in the implementation of meaningful policies, programmes and interventions, there is still a long way to go. A critical appraisal of the literature in terms of its potential translation into actionable knowledge leading to long-term change, reveals several gaps. These need to be addressed in setting the future research agenda for health inequity research in India.

9.1.2.1 Predominant Reliance on Large-Scale Data Sets Collected for Purposes Other Than the Study of Disparity

Most of the quantitative studies are based on secondary data from NFHS and NSSO. These data are not collected with a view to examining disparities in health, and therefore limit what can be researched and what cannot, related to health inequities. This limitation is seen, for example, in the health conditions and caste and economic categories that data permit us to study. Second, that which does not lend itself to measurement, e.g. alienation, power dynamics are seldom studied.

9.1.2.2 Association Fatigue

A corollary to the reliance on national data sets is that there is more research exploring the existence of gaps or statistical associations across socio-demographic or economic categories of population. This is an important first step in exploring possible underlying factors, but has its limitations since it does not seek to ask the "why" and "how" questions. Pathways and mechanisms through which health inequities are created and sustained (discrimination, prejudice, stigma, humiliation, social exclusion) are rare to find.

9.1.2.3 Deficit Finding and Blaming the Victim

In several instances, courageous policy recommendations are made based on statistical associations. Often, the language used belies an implicit (or even explicit) *blaming the victim* such as when mothers or the poor are spoken of as having to *catch up* with the rest, as if they are falling behind merely because of their own reasons.

9.1.2.4 Lack of Theorising and/or Post-facto Theorising

There is scant application of current theoretical knowledge, both from within the public health and epidemiological literature and research in other disciplines on health inequities to frame research questions or conduct analysis. Although human societies have distinct differences in the way they manifest particular phenomena, wider commonalities across societies allows for application of theories on health inequities in our context, either to test or refine them. For instance, Nancy Kreiger's critique of the use of race as a label rather than as a social construction could be used to critique the way caste, tribal- or poverty-related identities manifest in our settings (Krieger, 2000). What is sometimes seen is a *post-facto* theorising without an actual effort to apply these theories at the time of data collection or analysis. In other instances, literature shows no effort at all in adding to or borrowing from existing theory.

9.1.2.5 Inadequate Engagement with Intersections of Multiple Axes of Disadvantages

Barring about three or four studies, intersections of multiple axes of disadvantages have largely been ignored. Not taking cognisance of intersections results in a false assumption of heterogeneity within a population category. This may render invisible those with extreme disadvantages.

9.1.2.6 The Dynamic and Context Specific Nature of Health Inequities is Not Visible in the Research

The nature and patterns of health inequities and the population groups most affected is not static over time and space. But there are few studies that have sought to understand how, for example, poverty affects health across different contexts and how the nature of this relationship has changed over time.

9.1.2.7 Thin on Action/Evaluation

Literature is very scarce on possible interventions or actions to mitigate or address inequities. This is possibly a reflection of there being very little active effort at developing, funding or promoting such interventions. At the same time, critical evaluations of large-scale policies or programmes either related to health equity, or examining reforms with a health equity lens are lacking.

9.1.2.8 The Current Evidence Base Offers Limited Scope for Meaningful Action to Change Health Inequities

For the many reasons discussed above, the current evidence base on health inequities in India does not provide the kind of nuanced information that is needed for policy action to bridge health inequities. While there is nothing wrong with identifying only correlates of an outcome, the problem arises when such research becomes the basis on which policy decisions are made. Given the lack of understanding of mechanisms, strategies are driven by preconceived and invariably expert-driven notions about the reasons for the associations. The resulting intervention may be a poor fit and not succeed in achieving its objectives.

According to the Fundamental cause theory, targeting these superficial or specific associations while leaving undisturbed the underlying causes will only reduce (if at all) the specific association (Link & Phelan, 1996). Other mechanisms and pathways will form to express the continued inequity-generating forces. To give one example, there may be an increase in the institutional delivery rates because of providing cash incentives, but the maternal mortality ratio may not decline significantly. Women may not die of direct obstetric causes which may now be adequately dealt with in the health facilities, but because the underlying poverty, social exclusion and gender inequalities have not been addressed, deaths from severe anaemia, malaria and other indirect causes may become more prominent.

In the next section we draw on the various conceptual approaches discussed in chapter two to understand the mechanisms underlying health inequities in India.

9.2 Multiple Interacting Mechanisms of Health Inequity

Reading across the literature that we have synthesised in the previous five chapters, we have attempted in this section to draw on broader literature and theoretical frameworks to better understand the mechanisms that create, sustain and promote inequities in health. These frameworks may not have been explicitly part of the authors' intentions, but do add explanatory value to the findings they have presented. In this section we thus start with a theoretical understanding that could help discover mechanisms across the pathways and patterns, contributing to building a theory: "a framework of interconnected concepts that gives meaning and explanation" to patterns and empirical observations (Lipsey & Pollard, 1989).

To explain or understand the drivers or reasons for health inequity, it is important to begin with a theoretical understanding of why or how inequity exists in the first place. For this we require engaging empiric reality with previous theoretical contributions. Such undertakings lead to the development of new theory that takes into account the recorded reality, which in turn sets off further iterations of theorisation. Research aiming for change perforce is critical of *dominant* paradigms that invariably tend to sustain the status quo. Indeed, research that is not explicitly theory-driven tends to by default fall back on such status quo-sustaining belief structures.

Hedstrom and Swedberg (1998), based on Jon Elster's work, state that "the search for mechanisms means that we are not satisfied with merely establishing systematic covariation between variables or events; a satisfactory explanation requires that we are also able to specify the *social cogs and wheels* that have brought the relationship into existence" (Elster, 1989, p. 3 as quoted in Hedstrom & Swedberg, 1998, p. 7).

While explaining the mechanisms driving social exclusion in social health protection schemes in India and in a few African countries, Vermeiren and Soors (2014) posit that "to explain tangible social events we must rely on a number of elementary mechanisms, as one is not enough. Often the mechanisms counteract one another, sometimes they work together" (p. 3 of 12). Such insights into the mechanisms of social exclusion are also found in a range of other approaches to inequity like the eco-social theory with its emphasis on uncovering the way in which injustice is literally embodied in biology, or in the work using the intersectionality lens for example that forces us to engage with the reality that multiple axes of oppression are invariably converging on individuals and each such axis may have varying effects in different times and places.

There is often an assumption that mechanisms and their interactions too are at the level of these variables. Such an assumption may be due to the large number of research approaches that aggregate variables obtained through surveys, and then examine the interaction between these variables. Social action however, is brought about through human action; variables capture an empirical level of observations of these actors. Mechanisms on the other hand rest within the interplay between social structures, institutions and configurations of these in association with the agency exercised by actors within these structures. Thus unveiling mechanisms entails a completely different order of research and analysis.

While the earlier chapters have summarised the knowledge on drivers of health inequity in India, it is important to acknowledge the complexity of *isolating* mechanisms within a given context. The complex nature of inquiry into social systems requires that we understand that (one or more) mechanisms do not work in isolation, but in active interaction within a given context. Consequently, the mechanism(s) of social change is(are) likely to be a combination of mechanisms of various kinds working in tandem, either reinforcing, countering or even insulated from each other's effects. For example, macroeconomic reforms of the 1990s could have driven changes in the configuration of private hospital networks, pharmaceutical innovation and private practitioner behaviour in a certain way. And these macroeconomic configurations are in constant interaction with local social norms and over time could influence solidarity within or across social groups in each setting, further triggering inter-individual competition in a previously cohesive community. In Bunge's words, all uni-factorial (in particular uni-causal) explanations of social change are at best partial. Various mechanisms are constantly interacting, across various societal levels (ranging from individuals to households, neighbourhoods, communities, geographies and administrative hierarchies) to result in the patterns that researchers seek to describe and explain.

In this book, as is the case with literature on health inequity as well, we have considered health inequities along major axes such as caste, socio-economic position, gender and other vulnerabilities. Such distinctions are useful in describing or understanding the phenomenon. For individuals, families, neighbourhoods and larger geographies and times that experience inequity, these distinctions between axes of inequity are a mirage, hiding away or stereotyping an experience that is a unique admixture of what researchers see as multiple and distinct drivers of these inequities. Moreover, given that many of the research methods that researchers use are more suited for describing or understanding population level phenomena, research on health inequities tends to be shorn of the dynamic range of interactions at various levels (across individuals, organisations and within and across micro–macro institutions). Hence, it is useful to organise mechanisms operating across macro (institutional) levels and micro (individual) levels allowing for a comprehensive assessment of the interplay across these levels.

A synthesis of the literature as done in the five preceding chapters and the emerging mechanisms collected at the end of each chapter suggests that any attempt to arrange these mechanisms into a coherent framework that can be used to engage with the issue of health inequity requires to be multilevel, interactive and dynamic. Such a framework needs to engage with the fact that, "…social change is likely to be biological, psychological, demographic, economic, political, and cultural-either simultaneously or in succession" (Bunge, 1997).

We would like to reiterate that such frameworks need to be clearly recognised as epistemological or pedagogical tools rather than ontological statements. The idea is not to describe the truth, but to evolve ways of arranging empiric facts in order to unveil the complex mechanisms underlying their relationships over time and space, and through this process attempting at building usable and actionable knowledge, that in its turn is subject to empiric findings and further iterations of praxis.

In our analysis the essential features of such an emergent framework needs to adequately conceptualise multilevel and multidirectional pathways, needs to engage with intermediary structures that modulate and translate a number of forces in different dimensions into their ultimate biological expression with which we are ultimately interested, as well as engage at the individual level with the complexity of identity in a situation of multiple interacting or interlocking axes of oppression.

One of the typologies that helps organise various social mechanisms is Hedstrom and Swedberg's (1998) typology that begins with macro–micro–macro model, commonly adapted from *Coleman's boat* (or bathtub in European literature), referring to its origins in the work of the American educational sociologist and theorist, James Samuel Coleman (Fig. 9.1).

Social mechanisms operating at macro-level could influence behaviour of individual actors thus shaping certain forms of mechanismic interaction driving macro–micro changes. This is characterised as type 1 (situational) mechanism. The various household or individual level effects in a given context due to larger institutional drivers is one way of viewing situational mechanisms. The effects of neo-liberal

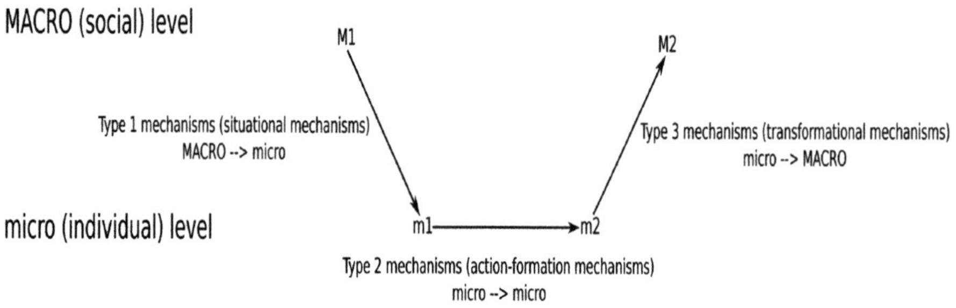

Fig. 9.1 Coleman's boat. Redrawn from Vermeiren and Soors (2014) based on their adaptation from Coleman (1986) and Hedstrom and Swedberg (1998)

macroeconomic policies on within-household or across household interactions and behaviours are other examples. Typically, situational mechanisms require an active application of theory in framing research questions and studying them. They also require larger time-frames to be able to study changes across decades. Very few studies explicitly sought to investigate situational mechanisms or macro–micro interactions by defining this as the problem a priori. A few studies however did acknowledge and frame arguments implicating neo-liberal economic policies at the macro-level as possible explanations for patterns seen in NSSO data (Selvaraj & Karan, 2009). However, disentangling variable and intersectional micro-effects within or across households of such macroeconomic policies were not found among the studies we reviewed. In the gender axis, son preference and intimate partner violence were both seen as an internalisation of oppression and hence wider societal/institutional mechanisms reinforcing discrimination based on caste or gender could be seen as a macro–micro driver of such inequity. Among the other socially constructed vulnerabilities (PLHA and internal migration) the macro–micro and micro–micro processes are clearly visible although not explicitly studied or explained. For example, the role of economic policies that facilitate *markets* around sale and trafficking of women (the sex industry); their role in destabilising livelihood security; the pressures of urbanisation and geographic inter-state and inter-district inequity and its role in fuelling internal migration; all clearly illustrate the hidden part of the iceberg which is often missed out while investigating these vulnerabilities.

While social structures reinforced over generations and centuries may not be easily countered by simple interventions, acknowledging and mitigating the ill-effects of health inequity is a foundational element of a health system. Evidence however shows that the health system either reproduces or reinforces health inequities. Again, the health system's mitigatory (or reinforcing role) in health inequity could be seen as a macro (institutional) interaction having effects at the individual level.

The second type of mechanisms is the action-formation mechanisms, which operate across individuals (micro–micro). These are mechanisms that typically operate within communities or households and draw upon individual agency.

Intra-household interactions typically fall in this domain and are driven by individual desires, beliefs and opportunities. Intra-household healthcare decision-making, resource allocation and prioritisation of problems within health or between health and competing interests such as child's education or elderly care for example are driven by such mechanisms. Individual psycho-social practices shaped by cultural norms are also typically situated in this mechanism. The individualisation and breakdown of solidarity within or across households due to entrepreneurial pressures, is another example. A positive example could be state-led efforts encouraging communitisation or participatory platforms. Action-formation mechanisms have been postulated and studied in the literature we reviewed. Some of the studies investigated the role of social cohesion in promoting equity or protecting neighbourhoods or groups from inequity (Houweling et al., 2013; Story & Carpiano, 2015; Subramanian et al., 2007).

These inter-individual or micro–micro interactions are possibly better developed in gender and caste. Discrimination by gender and caste, albeit reinforced by social structures that span generations and timescales, ultimately manifest in interactions between individuals at the micro-level. Among the literature on health inequity by caste, three prominent mechanisms stand out as being the underlying driver of caste inequity, but clearly also interacting with other axes: Identity/discrimination/internalisation of oppression and differential opportunities and unequal access to resources and power based on a particular caste. In studies on gender, the role of women's autonomy in shaping access to women's access to household power, decision-making and resources has been explored but the wider institutional mechanisms reinforcing these have not been explored. Although maternal autonomy manifests at an individual or household level, the role of wider social structures in shaping and facilitating such individual- or household-level autonomy across generations cannot be ignored.

In the case of research on health systems, there is a huge gap in any research on human resources and precious little on human behaviours: the culture and ethos of service delivery that govern relationships between patients and different levels of providers; also little understanding of everyday functioning of and encounters within health systems. Many processes related to health service provider interaction with each other or with patients are likely to be pathways at the micro-level (micro–micro). Apart from some research on unequal maternal health advice given and a few papers on discrimination at the point of service delivery, very little research exists on inter-individual or micro-drivers of health inequities within the Indian health system.

And finally, in type 3 (transformational) mechanism, we see how individual action within and between people could be transformed into an intended or unintended collective outcome (micro–macro). These are typically scenarios when emancipatory action occurs through inter-individual interaction resulting in a transformative action at a higher level, typically at organisational or societal levels. Questioning and/or striving to change well-established social structures, norms and practices through people coming together is an example. Well-designed interventions that lead to impact could be situated here. Participatory action research for example is an example of a methodology that could trigger or align with such transformative mechanisms. Typically, among the studies we reviewed, there have been a few papers exploring social cohesion and its effects either through measuring cohesiveness, or through exploring theoretical frameworks on cohesion as possible explanation for patterns of inequities seen. Other papers have explored possible transformative mechanisms through studying civil society or community based organisation's engagement in participatory platforms or through action rising upwards from the grassroots level, either in the form of locally managed community health insurance programmes or self-help groups coming together (Houweling et al., 2013; Story & Carpiano, 2015; Subramanian et al., 2007).

In addition to these three processes (M → m, m → m and m → M), interactions across macro-processes (M → M) may also be envisioned. Indeed, this is often the case where various macro-institutional or policy processes often interact. The linkages between macroeconomic processes with those related to health professional education and market forces within health for example are crucial in explaining various downstream effects at individual and household levels, as well as in explaining deficiencies in public health systems.

The model's ability to serve as an abstract and a *meta* framework within which to map and understand any of the several mechanisms operating within individuals or the collective and its ability to embrace both structure and agency with equal importance makes it ideal to explain and understand mechanisms underlying a range of interacting axes of inequity. It is important to reiterate that "macro" and "micro" do not necessarily indicate particular levels in a hierarchy, but merely serve as place holders in order to delineate multiple interacting levels. Thus it is possible to use Coleman's boat at different levels from the global to the household, with each level in turn being linked to a higher or lower level as the case may be.

For the authors of this chapter, the Coleman's boat offers two more important reasons to be an important component of any explanatory attempt. One is its conceptualisation of *feedback* in terms of the micro–macro pathways, and the other is the presence of micro–micro pathways.[1] The fact that these are in addition to macro–micro pathways, and that all three are given equal prominence and validity is crucial to what we would like to call its liberatory potential. That the micro can impact on the macro shows that actions at the lower level in a hierarchical situation can affect the higher level, meaning that individual action can impact on the institutional level and indeed institutional action can impact on the larger systems level. Thus there is a clear pathway for research and institutional and programme design to have transformative potential even as they are influenced by the level above them. Equally importantly the positing of micro–micro interactions does two things. The first is that it allows for many micros, thus allowing for the heterogeneity of effect of the influence of the macro on the micro. Second, it allows for

[1]Of course both types of interactions are well described in systems thinking and other multilevel theories of system change like the transitions theory.

such influence to potentially feedback to the macro-level too. This is in contrast to the overbearing nature of the macro–micro pathway in most research.

We turn now to the institutional level. A number of conceptual frameworks highlight the importance of this level. Probably one of the most prominent is that of Ostrom (2009). In this framework, institutions are seen as mechanisms for problem solving or redistribution of resources. What is important from our point of view is that the "rules" by which an institution functions are evolved from the society in which these institutions are embedded, or indeed from whence these institutions evolved.

A number of thinkers talk about the way in which institutions mediate between the larger macro-level systems of oppression to the actual pathways that translate these socially structured relationships into health outcomes. In our opinion one of the most comprehensive theories in this regard is the eco-social theory by Nancy Krieger and its concept of embodiment (Krieger, 2005). Another sociologist/philosopher whose approach has been used in the study of inequity and intersectionality is Pierre Bourdieu, especially in his use of the concept of "habitus" and "field" (Anna, Callahan, & Kang, 2013; McNay, 1999).

While both Krieger and Bourdieu (among many others) talk about embodiment, Krieger's approach arises from the dialectical and epidemiological traditions (Krieger, 2000). According to her the core concept of embodiment is that we literally embody biologically, our lived experience in the societal and ecological context, thereby creating population patterns of health and disease. The idea of embodiment posits that the determinants of current and changing societal patterns of disease distribution are exogenous to people's bodies and cannot be reduced to allegedly *innate* characteristics, even as individual biological characteristics and variability do matter. This also includes the following three tenets:

- Bodies tell stories about—and cannot be studied divorced from—he conditions of our existence;
- Bodies tell stories and often—but not always—match people's stated accounts; and
- Bodies tell stories that people cannot or will not tell, either because they are unable, forbidden, or choose not to tell.

Reading these various theories together, and looking at the patterns and trends that are emergent in the literature describing health inequity, it is easy to see the way in which advantage and disadvantage are further consolidated through institutional functioning, manifested in the design and the implicit and explicit set of rules governing such institutions. Thus the way in which gender plays out in the health system through the mechanisms of *lack of acknowledgement* as explicated by Sen, Iyer and George (2007), is a great example of the way in which mechanisms may be dissected out.

The institutional focus then allows us to interrogate health systems as crucial intermediaries between the larger macro forces and individual effects. In such a situation health systems, "can choose to either maintain status quo, mitigate the impact of power imbalances on individual and collective health, or contribute to the empowerment of communities. … Where along the continuum the system is, probably depends on the balance of forces between internal and external determinants, and to some extent, on path dependence (Gaitonde, 2015, p. 115)."

At the individual level, the concept of intersectionality provides a crucial lens through which to understand social inequalities and health inequities. It draws attention to the fact that axes of oppression or vulnerability act simultaneously on individuals. The intersectionality lens draws attention to vulnerable subgroups within a broad category, which may be hidden by averages, and helps reveal the true extent of health gaps that may be missed when single identities are considered. Viewed through this lens, individuals do not draw on social resources in silos and in isolation from others that constitute them. Thus class, caste, gender and other attributes intersect, and individuals draw on privileges in terms of some attributes and disadvantages in terms of others (e.g. Adivasi, college-educated, man) to occupy a position of advantage or disadvantage, in a given context at a particular point in time. In fact, the intersectionality lens is about not viewing caste or gender as labels but as outcomes of systems of privilege and oppression, such as patriarchy, racism, heterosexism. *Power* is central to an intersectional view of inequalities, and the key question with which to query an observed gap is "*what are the power dynamics and systems of privilege and oppression causing the gaps"?* Intersectionality thus offers a more nuanced lens through which to understand the forces underlying pervasive inequities in health.

To us these three—Coleman's boat, the institutional focus and the intersectional lens are critical components to any approach that attempts to engage with the complex phenomena of health inequities in a meaningful fashion. The concept of embodiment, which makes the link between institutions and individual bodies, is an integral part of such an approach.

9.3 Moving Towards a Coherent Body of Knowledge on Health Equity

The critical gaps we find in health inequity literature highlights the need to bring together very fragmented bits of evidence that are separately too weak, but hold a potential to build up together into a coherent and actionable body of knowledge on health inequities. In this section, we first outline how health equity researchers may be guided by a self-critical and conscious choice of analytical approaches, research questions and methodologies. This is followed by a reflection on the changes needed in research funding and architecture to foster research that can produce coherent and actionable evidence on inequities in health.

9.3.1 Theory-Driven Research

More theory-driven research that begins with stating current theoretical understanding of health inequity, and builds upon it drawing from empirical data from the field on one hand, and borrowing from wider body of knowledge (theory) on the other, while critically examining and refining these theories, is the need of the hour in health inequity research. As outlined in the previous section, we think that an approach that draws on a range of theories and frameworks: the Coleman's boat; the institutional focus and the concept of embodiment; and the intersectional lens is well-aligned with the purpose of identifying mechanisms and pathways underlying health inequities. The reasons why have been discussed in detail in the previous section.

9.3.2 Asking the Right Questions

There is clearly a need to relook at the research questions comprising the health inequity research agenda. Rather than remain limited to asking questions such as "why is group x worse than group y", it may be useful to shift our focus to "what are the structures, processes and mechanisms that make group x worse than group y?". Questions about power relationships, resource allocations, everyday managerial decisions that leave people out because they do not *fit* the average picture are needed. At the same time, questions around transformational mechanisms (see earlier sections) as well as research on what kind of policies, structures, governance promotes health equity are much needed.

Many a times the right questions emerge from one's own observations of everyday life. To pursue such questions may require the courage to venture beyond the beaten path and to risk being challenged on the validity of the research.

9.3.3 Methodological Innovations Drawing on Multiple Disciplines

Public health researchers studying health inequities may have to venture beyond the comfort zone of survey research, in-depth interviews and focus group discussions to seek-out methods that allow for voices from the ground to be heard, and learning from people's lived experiences. The research questions that we pose may require us to cobble together unconventional approaches to the collection and interpretation of data, such as photo-voices, Forum Theatre and other participatory and bottom-up approaches to knowledge construction. These would also be ways of minimising power differentials between the researcher and the researched.

Researcher reflexivity is another key requirement especially in the study of issues related to equity and social justice. This is important for understanding how the researchers' social location may have influenced the nature of information collected as well as its interpretation. Sharing the preliminary results of the study with the participants in the study to allow for their inputs into its interpretation would not only establish a more equal relationship between the researcher and the researched. It would also be a way of validating the interpretation and improving the quality of data analysis,

9.3.4 Fundamental Changes in Research Funding and Governance

Moving towards building a coherent and actionable body of knowledge will not happen without a conscious steering and alignments among various actors, at various levels. The lack of such coherence calls for a questioning of the current model of research funding and agenda-setting within and across the global, national and local research community. Innovative and hierarchy questioning approaches like participatory action research and lay epidemiology for example also point the way to altering the dominant research governance structures.

Research on health inequities suffers from a serious lack of funding. Globally, international funding for health research is skewed heavily towards biomedical research. In a paper published in the WHO Bulletin, Pratt and Loff (2012) assert that the current research models are unlikely to be interested in funding research promoting global health equity, because bilateral donors are interested in disease-focused product development research, which would bring economic benefits to the donor country. While this is the case for all health research that is not of a biomedical nature, health equity research faces some specific challenges. As suggested by Navarro (2008), sponsors of research both governmental and private, are institutions that are a part of the status quo, and may have serious conflicts of interests with supporting research on health inequities.

Funding for public health research in India is particularly abysmal. The annual per capita health research funding in India during 2007–08 to 2011–12 including international and national sources was estimated to be less than US$ 1 of which 3% was spent on public health research (Dandona, 2015).

The limited funding that does come in, usually takes the form of research collaborations with universities in the Global North, or bidding on calls for research from donor agencies. There is little scope in such modes of funding for consultative agenda-setting with partner organisations, and none at all for involving research participants or potential beneficiaries in defining their priorities.

An increasing tendency towards trivialising research to a management model is seen in recent years, with every step along the research cycle being tightly controlled in the name of accountability. However, the severe resource crunch in public health research funding does not leave researchers with many options. Zafrullah Chowdhury's critique of research as a method of colonisation (1981) is even more relevant now. In his essay, Chowdhury had described how Northern-expert led, funded and controlled research in health and family planning in Bangladesh did little by way of finding tangible solutions to local problems. The villages of Bangladesh essentially served as training ground for early career researchers from high-income countries who may eventually return some years later as expert advisors to the local governments and institutions (Chowdhury, 1981). The limited money allocated for international health research, thus may not be available for in-country researchers, especially those not located in premier institutions in metropolitan cities.

Our vision for health equity research, on the other hand, calls for flexible funding, decentralised and participatory agenda-setting, being aware of the power inequalities that underlie health inequities and having the courage to challenge accepted wisdom that upholds the status quo. Thus, the nature of current research funding and governance is incompatible with the kind of research needed for action to bridge the health equity gap.

There are major changes required at every level, from the allocation of resources for research on inequities in health; the people involved in the agenda-setting and in the formulation of the research question; to what theories and assumptions are drawn upon to design the study; the transparency of the analysis; the extent and nature of participation of the affected communities at all stages of the research; in how research results are fed back not only to the policy level, but also to the affected communities; and so on.

We see research as one vital component of the battle against health inequity, as it has the capacity to uncover key mechanisms and effects of the various determinant of health inequity. More importantly given the present context, scientific research has the legitimacy required to be heard in elite spaces where decisions regarding policies and the distribution of resources are taken. Thus there is a critical responsibility of research to play this supportive and facilitatory role in the larger struggle against social injustice and inequity. It is because of this that we reiterate in conclusion, that unless such work is seen as being political at heart, it will remain superficial and impotent before the true task before it, that of enabling a more just and equitable world.

We believe, that the coming together of committed public health researchers who find unacceptable and unjust the avoidable suffering and loss of lives that health inequities represent, can create a bottom-up pressure towards shifting the health research architecture, governance and funding. This book is a call to all like-minded researchers to join this political project.

Appendix

Content gaps in health equity research in India identified through mapping and syntheses exercises

Categories	Content gaps
Population groups	• Dalit and Adivasi populations • Children above 5 years of age; adolescents; elderly; persons living with disabilities (physical and mental); persons living with specific stigmatised health conditions; migrant workers; sex workers; people of non-conforming gender identity and sexual orientation
Health conditions	• Non-communicable and communicable diseases • Mental health • Injuries • Reproductive health issues beyond maternal health • Well-being
Geographic locations	• Urban poor areas • North-Eastern States, Goa

References

Anna, M., Callahan, J. L., & Kang, H. (2013). Gender and caste intersectionality in the Indian context. *Human Resource Management, 6*(95), 31–48.

Bunge, M. (1997). Mechanism and explanation. *Philosophy of the Social Sciences, 27*(4), 410–465.

Chowdhury, Z. (1981). Research: A method of colonization. *Medico Friend Circle Bulletin, 62,* 1–3.

Coleman, J. S. (1986). Social theory, social research, and a theory of action. *American Journal of Sociology, 91*(6), 1309–1335.

Dandona, L. (2015). Analysis of health research funding in India over five years. *British Medical Journal Open, 5*(Suppl 1), A1–A53.

Gaitonde, R. (2015). Tamil Nadu: A critical engagement. In I. Qadeer (Ed.), *India social development report 2014: Challenges of public health* (pp. 113–123). New Delhi: Oxford University Press.

Gopalan, S. S., Mohanty, S., & Das, A. (2011). Challenges and opportunities for policy decisions to address health equity in developing health systems: Case study of the policy processes in the Indian state of Orissa. *International Journal for Equity in Health, 10*(1), 55. Retrieved from https://www.ncbi.nlm.nih.gov/pmc/articles/PMC3239384/pdf/1475-9276-10-55.pdf.

Hedström, P., & Swedberg, R. (1998). *Social mechanisms: An analytical approach to social theory.* Cambridge (UK): Cambridge University Press. Retrieved from https://books.google.co.in/books?id=-iUmQRcYSIEC&printsec=frontcover&dq=Social+Mechanisms:+An+Analytical+Approach+to+Social+Theory&hl=en&sa=X&ved=0ahUKEwjpy7zbmYDTAhWCu7wKHS6sB5cQ6AEIGzAA#v=onepage&q=Social%20Mechanisms%3A%20An%20Analytical%20Approach%20to%20Social%20Theory&f=false.

Houweling, T. A., Tripathy, P., Nair, N., Rath, S., Rath, S., Gope, R., … Prost, A. (2013). The equity impact of participatory women's groups to reduce neonatal mortality in India: Secondary analysis of a cluster-randomised trial. *International Journal of Epidemiology, 42*(2), 520–532.

Iyer, A., Sen, G., & George, A. (2007). The dynamics of gender and class in access to health care: Evidence from rural Karnataka, India. *International Journal of Health Services, 37*(3), 537–554.
Krieger, N. (2000). Refiguring "race": Epidemiology, racialized biology, and biological expressions of race relations. *International Journal of Health Services, 30*(1), 211–216.
Krieger, N. (2005). Embodiment: A conceptual glossary for epidemiology. *Journal of Epidemiology and Community Health, 59*(5), 350–355. doi:10.1136/jech.2004.024562.
Link, B. G., & Phelan, J. C. (1996). Understanding sociodemographic differences in health—The role of fundamental social causes. *American Journal of Public Health, 86*(4), 471–473.
Lipsey, M., & Pollard, J. A. (1989). Driving toward theory in program evaluation: More models to choose from. *Evaluation and Program Planning, 12*(4), 317–328.
McNay, L. (1999). Gender, habitus and the field: Pierre bourdieu and the limits of reflexivity. *Theory, Culture and Society, 16*(1), 95–117.
Navarro V. (2008). Politics and health: A neglected area of research. *European Journal of Public Health, 18*(4), 354–355.
Ostrom, E. (2009). A general framework for analyzing sustainability of social-ecological systems. *Science, 325,* 419–422. Retrieved from http://www.era-mx.org/biblio/Ostrom,%202009.pdf.
Pratt, B., & Loff, B. (2012). Health research systems: Promoting health equity or economic competitiveness? *Bulletin of the World Health Organization, 90*(1), 55–62.
Selvaraj, S., & Karan, A. K. (2009). Deepening health insecurity in India: Evidence from national sample surveys since 1980s. *Economic & Political Weekly, 44*(40), 55–60.
Story, W. T., & Carpiano, R. (2015). Household social capital and socioeconomic inequalities in child undernutrition in rural India: Exploring institutional and organizational ties. *Annals of Global Health, 81*, 119–120. Retrieved from http://dx.doi.org/10.1016/j.aogh.2015.02.775.
Subramanian, S. V., Kawachi, I., & Smith, G. D. (2007). Income inequality and the double burden of under-and overnutrition in India. *Journal of Epidemiology and Community Health, 61*(9), 802–809.
Vermeiren, P. P., & Soors, W. (2014). Mechanisms of social exclusion in social health protection schemes. In Health Inc Consortium (Ed.), *Towards equitable coverage and more inclusive social protection in health* (p. 208). Antwerp: ITGPress.